Cardinal Richelieu

and the Making of France

Cardinal Richelieu

and the Making of France

Anthony Levi

CARROLL & GRAF PUBLISHERS, INC.
New York

Carroll & Graf Publishers, Inc.
19 West 21st Street
New York
NY 10010-6805

First published in the UK by Constable 2000,
an imprint of Constable & Robinson Ltd.

First Carroll & Graf edition 2000

ISBN 0–7867–0778-X

Printed and bound in the EU

For Christopher and Ian

Contents

List of Illustrations

Foreword

T his biography was originally conceived not only on account of the
fascination of its enigmatic subject's complex personality, but also
as an appropriate way of probing both the strong resurgence and the
incipient collapse of the euphoric moral and religious values of early
seventeenth-century France. Richelieu's career itself reciprocally
illuminated and was illuminated by the new values which were at
first embraced, and then began to be rejected by French society.

Richelieu had a prodigious capacity for mastering detail, and for
combining the widest vision of strategic political objectives with
detailed attention to the minutiae not only of military organisation
and political tactics, but also of ecclesiastical proprieties and
relatively trivial personal and domestic concerns. Immensely intelligent, he was given to meticulous observance of the formalities,
and was obsessively fastidious in his personal arrangements. He
had great charm, delicate sensibilities, and came to care even
for the choice of patterns into which the starched napkins were
folded for his table. He was a sharp pastoral theologian, a devout
bishop, a pragmatic, cunning and devious constitutional innovator,
a dedicated patriot, a skilled military strategist, and a chief minister
of immense vision. He inaugurated the unifying domestic reforms
which created for France its own cultural identity.

Main-line biographers and historians, while reflecting the individual preoccupations of their own periods, have invariably concentrated on Richelieu's political activity, and on the creation of
his centralising political machinery. The need for a new biography

arises firstly out of an understandable earlier neglect of the specific literary evidence for the values informing the mixture of aristocracy, educated bourgeois and creative minds at the apex of French social life. Secondly, it derives from a failure among most secular historians to be sensitive to the spiritual and theological realities behind the different branches of the counter-reformatory movement known as the 'Catholic revival' in the early seventeenth century.

On the first count it must be remembered that Voltaire invented the 'grand siècle' to coincide with the reign of Louis XIV. Literary historians have only in the past decade or so begun to include early seventeenth-century French literature on university syllabuses at all, having with Voltaire missed the point of the period's imaginative production. Intent on making aesthetic judgements, they dismissed it as an immature prelude to the introduction of 'classicism' instead of noticing the massively important testimony to the nature of cultural history it actually provides.

On the second count, it is true that the religious history of the Catholic revival was treated sensitively and copiously by Henri Bremond in his *Histoire littéraire du sentiment religieux en France,* (12 volumes, Paris 1921–36), but he was writing in the wake of the 'modernist' crisis in the Catholic church. Suspect of sympathising with the modernists, he avoided doctrinal controversy, preferring to authenticate the faith of his subjects by reference to its spiritual fruits. It had been easy in the French academic establishment's period of embattled secularising around the turn of the twentieth century to neglect what seemed at worst the bothersome fact that Richelieu was a sincerely devout reforming bishop.

This biography naturally draws on all its predecessors, as also on historians of literature and of the Catholic revival. Since important sources also include works of philosophy, theology, spirituality and law, and since all important direct sources are mentioned in the notes, it has not seemed necessary to add a separate bibliography which would necessarily have ranged too widely and in too many different directions. Special acknowledgement, however, is due to the painstaking recent work of Professor J. Bergin on the archival sources, and to Louis Batiffol, whose numerous books on Richelieu and his period, mostly published before World War II, are always vivid, accurate and helpful. I have drawn copiously on the work of both.

It remains only for me to express my personal thanks to those who have been particularly helpful to me. First of these is my late wife. Academically, her interests converged with my own when she started to work on Richelieu's artistic patronage and unearthed the notaried inventory of Richelieu's possessions at death. She subsequently published it (*Archives de l'art français,* nouvelle période, vol. xxvii, Nogent-le-Roi 1985, pp. 9–83) and I have been able to draw on her collection of books and her private notes and papers.

I also owe thanks notably to the members of the Oxford graduate seminar who subjected themselves to a paper from which this book grew, and whose audible gasps of astonishment at some of what it contained contributed much to my subsequent reflections. The staffs especially of the Bodleian, Taylorian and Christ Church libraries at Oxford were always helpful much beyond the call of duty. I have particularly benefited from discussions with Professor Richard Parish who, while stimulating me to thought, is certainly not responsible for any errors or infelicities in which that tiresome and time-consuming process may have resulted.

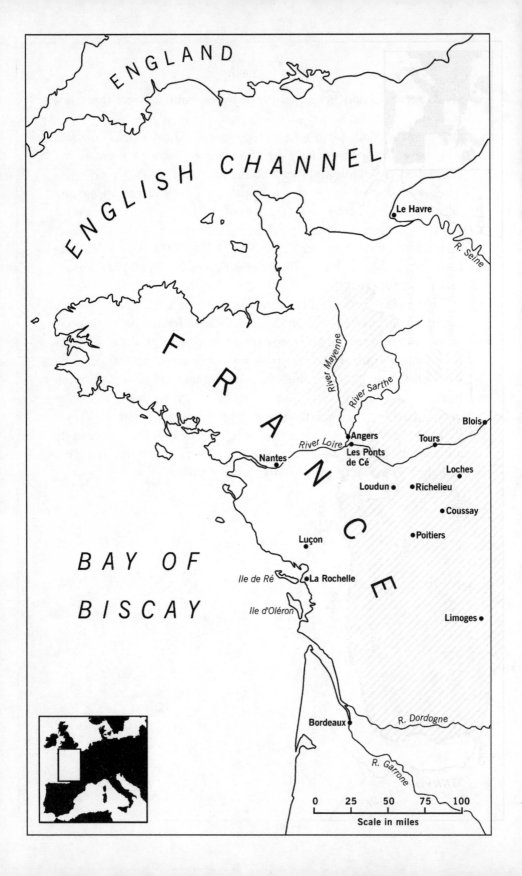

ENGLAND

ENGLISH CHANNEL

Le Havre

R. Seine

FRANCE

River Mayenne

River Sarthe

Blois

River Loire

Angers

Tours

Nantes

Les Ponts
de Cé

Loches

Loudun

Richelieu

Coussay

Poitiers

Luçon

BAY OF

BISCAY

Ile de Ré

La Rochelle

Ile d'Oléron

Limoges

Bordeaux

R. Dordogne

R. Garrone

0   25   50   75   100

Scale in miles

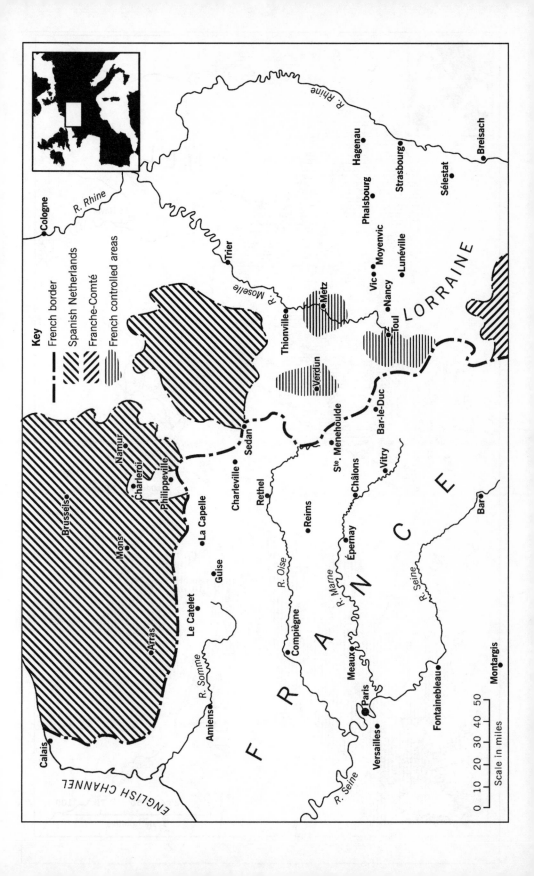

Key

- French border
- Spanish Netherlands
- Franche-Comté
- French controlled areas

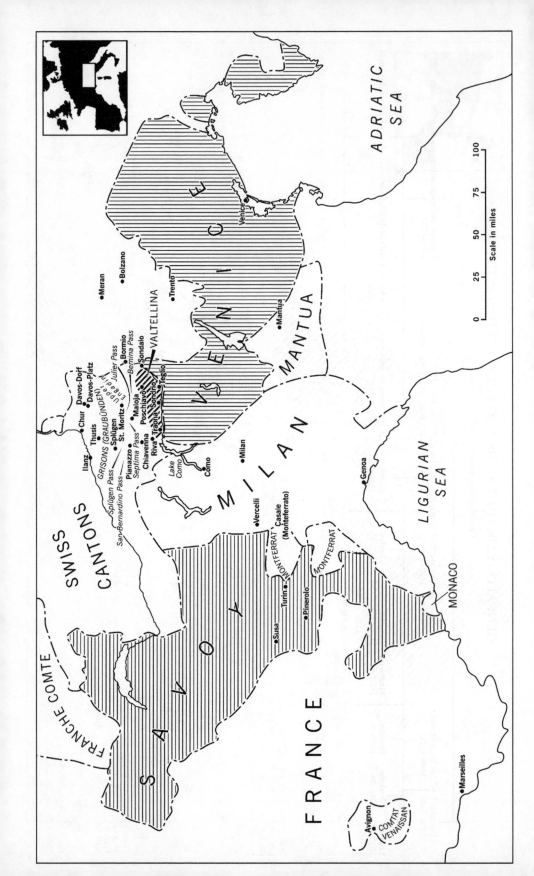

ADRIATIC SEA

LIGURIAN SEA

100
75
50
25
0
Scale in miles

Venice

Meran
Bolzano
Trento
Mantua

VALTELLINA

Bormio
Bernina Pass
Sondalo
Julier Pass
Teglio
Sondrio
Traona
Riva
Chiavenna
Poschiavo
Maloja
St. Moritz
Septima Pass
Pianazzo
Splügen
Splügen Pass
Davos-Dorf
Davos-Platz
Chur
Thusis
Ilanz

Upper Engadine

GRISONS (GRAUBÜNDEN)

San-Bernardino Pass

SWISS CANTONS

FRANCHE COMTE

Lake Como
Como
Milan

M I L A N

V E N I C E

MANTUA

Genoa

Vercelli
Casale (Monteferrato)
MONTFERRAT
MONTFERRAT
Turin
Susa
Pinerolo

S A V O Y

F R A N C E

Marseilles

MONACO

Avignon
COMTAT VENAISSAN

GENEALOGY OF THE VALOIS AND BOURBON DYNASTIES

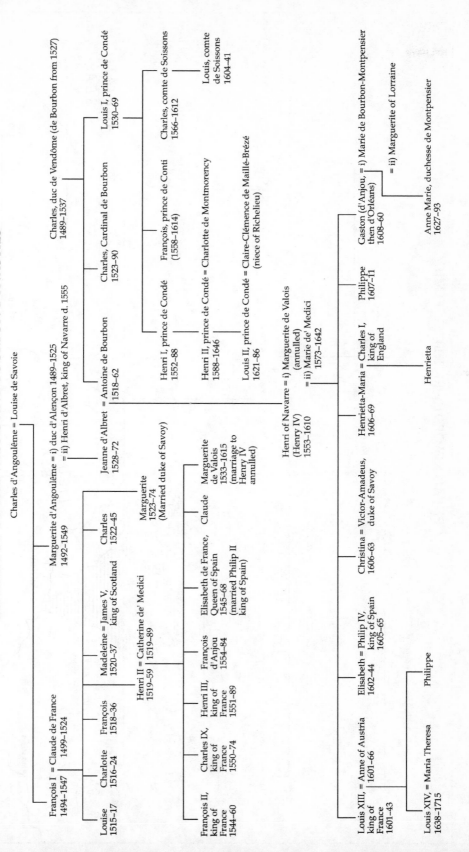

GENEALOGY OF THE RICHELIEU FAMILY

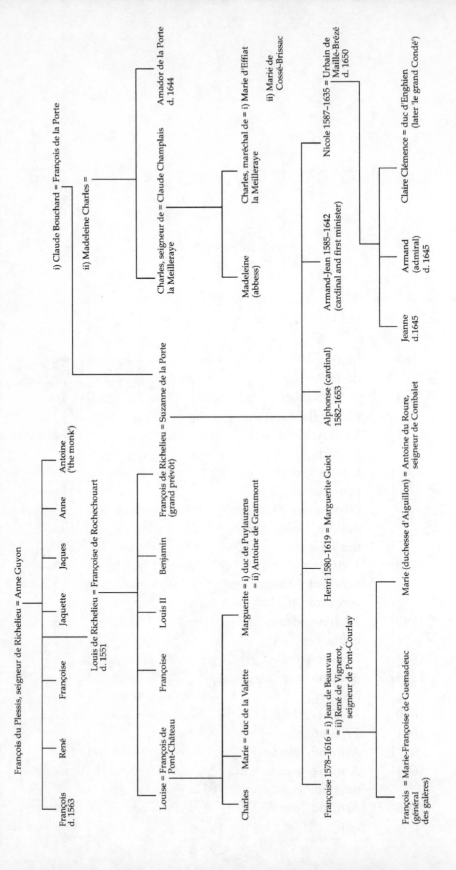

Chronology

1569	Marriage of François de Richelieu to Suzanne de la Porte.
1585	9 September: Birth of fourth child Armand-Jean du Plessis de Richelieu at Paris on 9 September.
1588	13 May: Henri III flees Paris. Mother and children retreat to Richelieu in Poitou.
	Estates-General convoked at Blois, solidly in support of pro-Spanish Holy League.
	December: Murder at Blois on orders of Henri III of duc de Guise and his brother the cardinal, leaders of the League.
1589	1 August: Henri III murdered. François de Richelieu, father of Armand-Jean, present as *grand prévôt*, supports accession of Huguenot Henri de Navarre.
1590	10 June: death of François de Richelieu, leaving huge debts.
1594	Consecration of Henri de Navarre as Henri IV.
1594/5	Armand-Jean returns to Paris and enters Collège de Navarre.
1600	17 December: Henri IV marries Marie de' Medici.
1601	27 September: birth of future Louis XIII.
	Armand-Jean at Pluvinel's military academy.
1603	Armand-Jean agrees to replace his brother Alphonse as nominee to family see of Luçon.
1606–7	Armand-Jean receives in Rome age dispensation for

bishopric, and is ordained priest and consecrated bishop (17 April).

1607 2 June: takes oath of loyalty to Henry IV at Fontainebleau. 29 October: receives doctorate of theology; made member and fellow of the Sorbonne.

1608 15 December: enters diocese.

1610 14 May: assassination of Henri IV, regency of Marie de' Medici.

1612 Franco-Spanish marriages agreed: Louis to marry Anne of Austria, Spanish infanta, and his sister Elisabeth of France to marry future Philip IV of Spain.

1613 Concino Concini made maréchal d'Ancre.

1614 7 June: Estates-General convoked.
2 October: majority of Louis XIII, now 13 years old, proclaimed.
27 October: Estates-General opens.

1615 23 February: bishop of Luçon's address to regent on behalf of the clergy.
November: marriage of Louis XIII and Anne of Austria. Armand-Jean Du Plessis made grand almoner to the new queen.

1616 14 November: death of Suzanne de la Porte.
November: du Plessis enters royal council as minister.

1617 24 April: assassination of Concini. Luynes takes power. Du Plessis follows queen mother to exile at Blois, and is then exiled to Luçon.
8 July: execution of Léonora Galigaï.

1618 Du Plessis exiled to Avignon.

1619 22 February: escape of Marie de' Medici to Angoulême. March: recall of du Plessis from Avignon and mission to court of Marie de' Medici.
8 July: Henri de Richelieu killed in duel. Armand-Jean du Plessis assumes Richelieu name.

1620–22 October 1620–October 1622: anti-Huguenot campaigns of Louis XIII.

1621 Death of Paul V and election of Gregory XV.
14 December: death of Luynes.

1622 2 September: Richelieu elected *proviseur* of Sorbonne.
5 September: Richelieu's cardinalate announced. Red

	hat conferred 22 December at Lyons.
1623	Death of Gregory XV and election of Urban VIII.
1624	29 April: Richelieu member of king's council.
	13 August: Richelieu principal minister.
1625	11 May: marriage of Henrietta-Maria, king's sister, to Charles I of England.
1626–27	5 August: marriage of Gaston d'Orléans to Marie de Bourbon-Montpensier.
	Assemblée des notables 2 December 1626–24 February 1627.
1627–28	Hostilities with Huguenots lead to siege and capitulation of La Rochelle.
1629	Promulgation of Code Michad.
1630	Italian campaign. Life-threatening illness of Louis XIII. 'Day of Dupes' confirms Richelieu in power and defeat of queen mother's party. Michel de Marillac exiled, and Louis de Marillac arrested (executed 10 May 1632).
1632	Imprisonment and flight of Marie de' Medici.
	3 January: marriage of Gaston d'Orléans to sister of duke of Lorraine, Marguerite de Vaudémont. Gaston's planned invasion of France to coincide with rising of Montmorency. Execution of Montmorency (30 October) after defeat at Castelnaudary.
1635	France formally declares war on Spain, so entering the Thirty Years War (1618–48).
1636	Uprising of 'Croquants'
1637	9 January: first night of *Le Cid*. Ensuing debate exploited by Richelieu to lead to registration of letters patent by *Parlement de Paris* which brings Académie into existence.
	Royal confessor fails to persuade Louis XIII to dismiss Richelieu.
	Louis XIII consecrates France to Blessed Virgin (10 December, renewed 10 February 1638).
1638	5 September: birth of future Louis XIV to Anne of Austria.
	18 December: death of Père Joseph
1639	Uprising of 'Nu-pieds'.
1640	September: birth of second son, Philippe d'Anjou, to Anne of Austria.

1642   Treaty between Cinq-Mars and Spain.
            3 July: death of Marie de' Medici at Cologne.
            12 September: execution of Cinq-Mars and de Thou.
            4 December: death of Richelieu.
1643   14 May: death of Louis XIII.

Author's Note

Most books about Armand-Jean du Plessis de Richelieu, at periods of his life a bishop, a cardinal, and a duke and peer, normally refer to him simply as 'Richelieu'. But the title 'Richelieu', when used alone, referred to Armand-Jean's elder brother, Henri, until 1619, when Henri was killed in a duel. We cannot always without ambiguity call our subject 'the future cardinal' either, because his other brother, Alphonse, also became Cardinal Richelieu. We cannot even refer to him by the name of his diocese, 'Luçon', because his contemporaries used that as a term of derision, Luçon being poor, remote and rural. On the whole, therefore, particularly because Richelieu was not born great, but was among those who had to achieve greatness, it seemed better to adhere to the usage of the documents of his time in referring to him as 'du Plessis', between his boyhood, when he is here called Armand-Jean, and 1619, when he became Richelieu. At that date he was still a bishop, but not yet a cardinal.

Other French names can cause confusion. Females, according to the custom with which we are still familiar, normally changed names on marriage, but male names changed, too, with succession or elevation to titles, or because brothers sharing a name used subordinated titles, or even because there are alternative legitimate ways of referring to the same person at any given time. The brother of Louis XIII, Gaston, was born duc d'Anjou, was known from babyhood simply as 'Monsieur', but was later elevated to the duchy of Orléans. Whenever it is not incongruous, he is here referred to throughout as Gaston. Efforts have been made to avoid possible confusions, as among the Valette, Sourdis, Ganzague/Gonzaga and Marillac families, but if any arise, reference to the index will make it clear which member is being referred to. The text has been written in the hope that it is fully intelligible without reference either to the index or to the notes, although students may wish to consult either or both.

One inevitable difficulty lies in making even the roughest estimate of the value of money. At the rural retail level, France scarcely operated a monetary economy at all. Payments in kind or in labour were the norm. Where money was involved, as at the numerous fairs, often specific to a single commodity, it had two values, nominal, normally based on the *livre tournois,* and real, according to the amount of silver or gold a coin actually contained. The coinage was frequently debased, whether by royal decree or by private paring away of metal, and the value of silver and gold constantly changed both absolutely and relative to one another. Furthermore, the value of a sheep, for instance, was unstable, since most stock had to be killed off over the winter. The price of luxury goods, always high, was also volatile, depending on political and mercantile relations and the equally variable, if invariably high, cost of transport, which could double or triple the price.

The purchasing power of the *livre tournois* differed therefore with time, place and the nature of the goods for sale. Taking the extremes of all three together, that is the worst date, the worst town, and the most valuable luxury commodities, but confined within France and between the dates of Richelieu's birth and death, the purchasing power of the *livre tournois* could easily differ by a multiple of ten or more.

In decrees of 1425 and 1455, the church had allowed the lending of money against security at interest not exceeding 10 per cent, and in the sixteenth century royal and municipal borrowing in France was paying interest on bonds as low as 8 per cent and as high as 16 per cent. On the other hand, a ship returning safely from the east might make as little as 20 per cent or as much as 150 per cent of the outlay for a single voyage. Small business ventures based on a trade or craft were beginning to flourish, and speculative builders putting up town houses for rent, like bankers and administrative officials charged with tax collection, were all making and sometimes losing fortunes, but money was an insecure store of value. It was normally turned into income as quickly as possible, most often by using it to purchase a revenue-bearing office.

1

Churchman and Statesman: Aims and Ambitions

Armand-Jean du Plessis de Richelieu first emerged into French
national life when, as the twenty-nine-year old bishop of
Luçon, he was chosen by the representatives of the clergy to
address Louis XIII on their behalf at the end of the Estates-General.[1]
He was not well known, but had negotiated on behalf of the clergy
during the Estates, had not compromised himself by adhering to
any faction, had a powerful patron in Cardinal François de Sourdis,
archbishop of Bordeaux, and was acceptable for family reasons
in the entourage of the thirteen-year-old king. He delivered his
address on 23 February 1615.

At that date France existed only as a geographical entity with
an unstable eastern boundary. It was rather smaller than it is
today, unified chiefly by theoretical acknowledgement of an only
sporadically enforced supremacy of royal over regional, local, and
feudal jurisdictions. Its border to the north-east at first followed
the Somme upstream, just including Amiens, but leaving Arras and
Mons to the north. It turned south well before reaching the Rhine.
Dijon and Lyons were included within the French boundaries by no
very generous margin, even after Henri IV had recovered the nearby
provinces of Bresse and Bugey in 1600. In the south-west Roussillon
was a Catalonian dependency north of the Pyrenees. Beyond the
smooth line of the north-east border, France owned the much-
disputed territories of the bishoprics of Toul, Metz, and Verdun.

Until the mid-fifteenth century, the kings of France had commanded allegiance virtually nowhere north of the Loire, and in only

half the territory south of it. Then the English were driven out of Normandy and Gascony in the 1440s, and the lands of the dukes of Burgundy, Anjou and Brittany were annexed by the king before the end of the century. Since they included Provence, that left only Avignon and the nearby papal state, the Comtat Venaissin, within French boundaries in the south-east, but not subject to the French king.[2] On the Meuse, Sedan remained an independent principality. In the southwest the independent kingdom of Navarre extended across what is now the Spanish border at the extreme west of the Pyrenees.

The real political difficulty for France was caused by the inheritance of Charles V (1500–58). He had bribed his way to the imperial throne ahead of France's François I, whose rival and enemy he remained, and had inherited from each of four grandparents. He acquired most of the Iberian peninsula, Sicily, Naples and Sardinia from Ferdinand of Aragon and his wife, Isabella of Castile, adding to that inheritance Milan and Tunis. From Mary of Burgundy he inherited most of the Netherlands, himself acquiring the northern provinces, and from Maximilian of Habsburg he received Austria, the Tyrol and Alsace, adding Bohemia, Moravia, Silesia and parts of Hungary.

By 1618 only Savoy, stretching from the Lake of Geneva to the Mediterranean, Lorraine, which included the duchy of Bar, and the Swiss confederation formed independent buffer zones between France's eastern border and Habsburg territory. True Habsburg mastery of Europe depended on communication across the Alps between the Spanish Habsburg territories in Milan and those on the Rhine and the Danube, reached through the Swiss cantons and down the upper Rhine, navigable from Chur. In the way were the Grisons (Graubünden), three Protestant leagues forming a small federation ('Bund') of alpine territory. The Grisons contained the only passes outside Venetian control leading north over the Alps from the Catholic valley known as the Valtelline which ran east from the northern tip of Lake Como. France needed to be able to control those passes.

France's population was about fifteen million, less than the largely forested land might have sustained, but exploited by a tiered structure of local overlords, and subject to the general debilities brought about by a diet too heavily dependent on cereals and vulnerable to regional starvation in times of famine. A mechanism for upward social mobility near the apex of the urban social structure had been institutionalised in 1604 when the *de facto* hereditary transmission of legal and administrative offices was regularised. Legal offices conferred noble status with consequent social distinction and the financial privilege of tax exemptions, and office-holders were now charged an annual tax known as the *paulette* in exchange for which they could, subject to some restrictions, bequeath or sell their offices.[3] These salaried offices, which also conferred noble status, were thereby virtually turned into perpetual annuities which were heritable or saleable. They much increased in value and, since their creation also enriched the treasury, their numbers exponentially increased.

The standing of these newly ennobled office-holders, invariably drawn from among the law graduates or 'magistracy', was midway between that of the old military *noblesse d'épée,* from whom the provincial governors were still drawn, and a newly enriched and educated bourgeois merchant class which was increasingly encroaching on what had once been a clergy monopoly of administrative competence.

Loyalties, primarily feudal, regional or religious, were not yet national. Regional dialects spoken by the people from Brittany to Provence and from Gascony to Alsace largely precluded unification of the nation through a common language. Customs, crop cultivations, life-styles and the exploitation of mineral and other natural resources differed within the country, particularly with proximity to the sea, differences of climate and the quality of the land. The customary law of the north differed from the system of Roman or imperial law obtaining in the south, and the religious allegiances of Catholics and Huguenots continued to clash between the promulgation of the Edict of Nantes, giving limited 'toleration' to Huguenots in 1598, and its revocation in 1685. France, being impelled forward by economic forces to match the prosperity attained by the rest of western Europe during its own damaging religious wars in the second half of the sixteenth century, still lacked any national cultural identity. Richelieu's life's work was to centre on creating one.

Much of the available archival material relevant to Richelieu's career has still never been published, but enough has recently been trawled to chronicle the steps by which Richelieu rose to status, power and wealth. We know much about his highly strung and hypersensitive personality, his huge energy, nervous intensity and remarkable abilities, disguised by the cold, austere imperiousness projected in the haughty portraits by Philippe de Champaigne. Biographical attention has more recently, if still controversially, been drawn to the introverted uncertainties, the sickliness, insomnia, ulceration and migraines against which Richelieu constantly had to struggle, and which also made him subject to a sometimes debilitating hypochondria.[4] A great deal none the less still remains to be taken into account.

Richelieu was pious, for more than a decade a reforming bishop, pastorally concerned, and a dedicated religious controversialist. Any new biography must now include an account of Richelieu's relationship to those branches of *dévot* Catholicism with the political and spiritual tendencies developed by Bérulle and his like-minded associates. Richelieu's genuine attempts to forge a single national culture in which, once their political ambitions had been crushed, the Huguenots would play their full part, need re-assessing against the backdrop of a Europe in which philosophies of 'toleration' struggled against the principle of a single state religion embodied in the axiom, 'cuius regio eius religio'. Richelieu needs to be seen against the background of the whole history of the Catholic revival, and of his personal divergence from the Oratorian devotional attitudes which developed into what has become known as the *école française* of spirituality,[5] as well as from the political overtones generated by Bérulle's mystical theology.

In particular, Richelieu has never been seen against the background of the immensely powerful surge of cultural optimism which swept through France in the first decades of the century, when the personal grandeur and social virtues explored by painters and poets, novelists and playwrights, philosophers and architects, manifested a hitherto unconceived trust in the innocence of what is natural and instinctive and in the moral and even physical might of human individuals.[6]

It was against this background that Richelieu discovered the power of cultural propaganda. He systematically set about achieving control of the country's literary and artistic activities, which in turn meant setting in motion the tide which led to the state's control of France's principal cultural institutions. When they have noticed them at all, Richelieu's biographers have tended to see the creation of an academy, the official protectorship of the Sorbonne flowing from Richelieu's appointment as its *proviseur,* the promotion of the theatre, the erection of buildings of extravagant magnificence, the policy of promoting everywhere both Jesuit and independent educational establishments, the assiduous collecting of works of art, and the interest in gardens, as so many cultural add-ons to a more important political, social or military history. They were in fact part of an increasingly meticulous plan to mould France into a cultural unity with its own national identity.

It was from the wave of imaginative euphoria which immediately followed the formal end of the religious wars in 1594 that were born both Louis XIII's visions of military conquest and Richelieu's dream of moulding France into a cultural unity. Very little seemed impossible in an environment in which kings and princes were commonly portrayed and promoted as mythological figures with super-human powers, in which Philippe de Champaigne could paint Louis XIII being crowned by Victory herself,[7] or Rubens could portray Marie de' Medici magnificent on horseback accompanied by angels bearing all manner of accoutrements denoting victory after her defeat at the skirmish at Ponts-de-Cé, in which marriage as much as chastity could be seen as the foundation for Christian sanctity,[8] and in which Descartes believed he could provide a guaranteed path to the universal acquisition of the ultimate in both happiness and virtue. We need not only to understand the buoyancy of Richelieu's vastly ambitious dream of a culturally controlled France, but also to realise how systematically he exploited the mythologisation of the anointed monarch to strengthen the French throne.

In what concerned the arts, and especially their value as instruments of propaganda, Richelieu was more personally committed than any previous French prince or prelate. He used them all, painting, literature, architecture, drama, dancing, music, sculpture and decoration, as instruments to manipulate educated opinion into a consciousness of national glory. Only his training and experience as priest, bishop and senior ecclesiastic did not allow him to be totally uncritical of those aspects of the cultural euphoria inspiring his contemporaries which appeared to him to be incompatible with properly understood Christian attitudes.

As early as 1626, before Richelieu had consolidated any real power, drama had itself become a political propaganda tool. In 1626 it was proposed that Gaston, the king's younger brother and heir to the throne, should marry the immensely rich Marie de Bourbon-Montpensier. Any male issue of that marriage would make more remote the possibility that succession to the throne would ever revert to the Prince de Condé, currently second after Gaston in line for the throne.[9] The Condé family, based at Chantilly, were naturally opposed to a marriage threatening to increase their distance from the succession, and sought to spread their opposition by commissioning from France's greatest dramatist, Jean Mairet, the pastoral *tragi-comédie La Sylvie* in which to great acclaim but no effect it was attacked. Gaston, who was only eighteen, duly married, and was in 1626 raised to the duchy of Orléans, the traditional honour conferred on the heir to the throne. Richelieu, who was on balance in favour of the marriage, quickly saw the value in a largely illiterate society of serious drama as a propaganda tool. He became its patron, practitioner and practically its creator as a respected literary genre in France.

Richelieu himself composed, or inspired the composition of accounts of much of what happened during his career. The *Mémoires,* the *Testament politique,* the correspondence, and the numerous accounts from other pens in the official *Le Mercure français,* and the less formal *Gazette,* sought to project the particular light in which Richelieu wished his own thoughts and activities to be understood.[10] It is none the less possible to piece together with reasonable accuracy the political plots, strategems and alliances which form the background of the public life, to analyse the constraints to which Richelieu was at various times subject, and to assess how much he learned from experience.

Fearsome mental powers gave him an astonishing grasp of detail as well as a wider vision of what might be achieved. He notably perceived both the necessity and the practical possibility of making France into a great maritime power, the pre-condition of the mercantile enrichment which was currently being enjoyed by Spain, England and Venice. He combined to spectacular effect in the service of his country his sharp intelligence and grandiose imagination, while at the same time opening up for himself a vast potential for personal enrichment. The story of his public life is dominated by the intrigues, conspiracies, betrayals and silences in which his personal qualities as much as his political position involved him.

The enigma of the personality, which perplexed or antagonised contemporaries, is not insolvable, and the personality which finally emerges from beneath the layers of embattled historical accounts turns out to differ from what has been supposed. Diplomatic correspondence attests that a genuine charm concealed the brisk understanding, and Richelieu certainly had to steel himself to pursue the policies which his intellect led him to persuade the king to follow.

His loyalty was not so much to Louis XIII personally as to the God-given sovereign of France. Richelieu worked for the grandeur of a king who was happiest as a military leader but who was inclined to be authoritarian, even petulant, rigorist, excessively touchy, gnawed by scruples, without intellectual gifts, and who was very little suited to the non-military aspects of his role as sovereign. Of determining importance, especially after 1630, were the king's lack of a son to succeed to the throne, and his relationships with his mother, his wife, his brother, and the nobility headed by the princes of the blood, descended from his father's cousins.

To build a powerful and united France, Richelieu needed his famous spider's web of private informants. They extended throughout Europe and, while not as numerous or as organised as the skilled use made by Richelieu of the information he received from them has led subsequent generations to assume, they were strategically placed. In fact much important information came to him as the result of fortuitous circumstances. He was certainly devious, ruthless in exploiting the detailed information he compiled, just as he was relentless in covering his own tracks. He prided himself in always putting as little as possible that was diplomatically sensitive into writing.

He was indeed to become a master of dissimulation, and made no secret of the importance he attached to the silence which has too often reduced posterity to conjectural speculation. He was shrewd enough to realise that the achievement of his strategic ambitions sometimes depended on the concealment of his aims, and he was cunning enough to protect them by the powerful weapon of impenetrable silence. He became increasingly concerned to gather and destroy evidence about his actions and intentions, and enough documents were burnt for it to be clear that we shall never know just what risks Richelieu took in promoting the interests of France and its sovereign. They were certainly considerable, and an assessment of them imposes on us new views of Louis XIII and of France under Richelieu's administration.

The power he required and achieved was inextricably both political and personal. He needed political success in order to establish his personal position, but he needed personal power in order to achieve the integration and independence of France by a strategy which he knew himself to be uniquely capable of implementing. One result of this intertwining of duty and ambition was the compatibility or even congruence of his political and religious loyalties. His religious duty to God did not preclude political alliances with schismatic powers in furtherance of France's political strength because divine authority, vested in the pope only as spiritual sovereign, was wholly bestowed on the king in secular matters. We shall find Richelieu mustering forces against the pope's armies, while humbly seeking a papal dispensation from his time-consuming religious obligation daily to recite the breviary. His view of the separation of sacred and secular sovereignties was for his day extreme.

His habits and tastes were austere. The public rooms of the Palais-Cardinal exuded wealth and grandeur, but the furnishings of Richelieu's private apartments were simple.[11] He would entertain lavishly but himself eat frugally. He sought and acquired the wealth unavailable to his family in his youth, but, in accordance with the aristocratic values he cultivated, his ambition was not for luxury, but for power and its display. The centralisation of financial, military and administrative control were all integral to the attainment of his vision of a powerful France loyal to its God-given sovereign. He could be cruel, and was at times and places the object of jealousy and even loathing, but at heart, Richelieu was an idealist. From his assumption of the family bishopric of Luçon in 1607 until his death, Richelieu's loyalty to his own vision for France did not waver even if, like so many intelligent and effective idealists, he acted in ways which made him feared.

Even late in life Richelieu took care always to act on the

authority of the king, and never to usurp it for himself. He was a person of steely self-discipline, outstanding courage, penetrating intelligence and deep commitment, but also of warmth and charm. The story of how these qualities allowed him to discover openings, and then to avail himself of opportunities and create strategies, is itself fascinating, but it also has a wider context. An understanding of Richelieu's aims and methods is essential to an appreciation of how far, during the reign of Louis XIII, France was welded into a single nation. It is the contention of these pages that Richelieu's achievements depended on a surge of new cultural values in France, and that his most enduring legacy to the king and country in whose service he spent his life was the forging of a sense of French national identity.

2

Family Background and Family Bishop

The Richelieu estate was situated in richly wooded country sixty kilometres south-west of Tours. It lay on the river Mable, whose waters eventually flow into the Loire, then broader and more navigable than it is now. The estate's modest origins can be traced back to the twelfth century. In 1420 it had passed by marriage to a family whose daughter, Perrine, had married a du Plessis, and it was Perrine's son, François, who became the first du Plessis to be *seigneur* of Richelieu. By the late sixteenth century the land, used for grazing, cereals, and vines as well as woods, was largely let to tenants who paid in kind. Its seigneurial owners, like those of its neighbouring estates, provided major household officers as well as military captains for the great French aristocratic families of the Loire valley.

The du Plessis family traditionally served the Montpensiers, and in 1506 the marriage of Richelieu's great-grandfather, François III du Plessis, brought into the family the nearby Le Chillou estate, feudally dependent on the Montpensiers. Of the eight or more children of François III, we know only of Antoine, a cleric who had himself dispensed from the obligations of his ecclesiastical state to fight in the Italian wars as a captain of *arquebusiers* commanded by the first duc de Guise, head of the younger branch of the ruling house of independent and firmly Catholic Lorraine. The Guise family owed its recent ascendancy to the favour of Diane de Poitiers, the twenty-seven–year-old beauty who was mistress of Henri II on his accession in 1547, and the first duke obtained the government of

Champagne and Burgundy. His lands were the first not belonging to a prince of the blood to be erected into a *duché-pairie*.[1]

Antoine du Plessis became captain of the garrison at Chinon, was made a *gentilhomme ordinaire de la chambre du roi,* and led a party which murdered a hundred unarmed Huguenots in a church at Tours in 1562. He died in a Paris street brawl involving prostitutes on 19 January 1576.[2] The only one of Antoine's siblings known to have had children was his eldest brother, Louis de Richelieu, Richelieu's grandfather. He served the Montpensiers as a lieutenant and in 1542 married the daughter of the colonel of his regiment, Françoise de Rochechouart.

The Rochechouart family was ancient and noble, and Françoise had spent much of her time at court. Her marriage to Louis de Richelieu therefore conferred social elevation on him. The eldest of their five children, also Louis, served in the regiment of Montpensier's son and duly succeeded to the Richelieu estates and titles as well as to his uncle's position as lieutenant of his regiment. He was, however, assassinated by a neighbour in 1565 after a squabble over precedence in the parish church, and avenged by his younger brother François, Richelieu's father, who ambushed and murdered the assassin by rolling a cartwheel to unhorse him at a ford before murdering him in the water.

We do not know whether François faced trial or flight. The avenging murder was too high in profile to be submerged in the routine outbreaks of banditry which characterised the early years of the religious wars,[3] and it would be surprising if François escaped at least the need to seek royal pardon, likely to have been granted almost automatically.[4] His marriage contract with Richelieu's mother, Suzanne de la Porte, is dated August 1566 and was signed before a Parisian notary. Since she was the only daughter by his first wife of François de la Porte, an influential lawyer enriched in the service of Charles IX and a prominent member of the Paris *parlement,* Richelieu's father cannot still have been in legal disgrace in 1566.

The *parlements,* of which Paris, with jurisdiction over a third of the country, was by far the most important, were essentially the regionally grouped courts of criminal and civil justice, not political bodies, but with administrative responsibilities and without whose registration no laws or other promulgations were valid. Their principal offices entailed ennoblement. Although sovereign, the *parlements* theoretically held their jurisdiction by delegation from the king, and were occasionally overruled by him. If the king wished to remove jurisdiction from a *parlement* for some particular case, or to resolve some intractable situation to his satisfaction, he held a *lit de justice,* reclaiming the sovereignty he had delegated.

Although Suzanne's father had risen in the service of the Guise family to become a member, perhaps president, of the Paris council of Mary Stuart, dowager queen of France from the death of her husband, François II, in 1560, Françoise de Rochechouart is said to have disapproved of her la Porte daughter-in-law, since her family's nobility came only from legal rather than military offices.[5] François de Richelieu is described as a *gentilhomme de la chambre du roi.* Suzanne, however, brought to the marriage the considerable dowry of 10,000 livres, the maximum at that date allowed by law, together with a number of seigneurial estates near Paris which she had already inherited from her mother.

The contract suggests that some of these lands would have to be sold to restore the Richelieu family to solvency, several dowries owing under earlier family marriage contracts having remained unpaid. In return, François was to make over to his wife in 1572 a half-share of the seigneurie of Le Chillou. Suzanne also inherited the equivalent of 15,000 livres on her father's death in April 1572. Most of it went to pay off creditors, although 3,000 livres was spent on adding to the Richelieu lands.[6] Since in 1566 François was only eighteen and Suzanne fifteen, their marriage itself was postponed until 1569.

It is unclear what happened to François de Richelieu between avenging his brother's murder and his marriage, or between 1569 and his appointment as *grand prévôt de France* on 28 February 1578 and his subsequent nomination as *conseiller d'état* in May.[7] Aubery,[8] the cardinal's first biographer, thinks that François belonged to the retinue of the future Henri III of France, who had accepted the Polish throne in May 1573. But François was certainly in Paris during the early months of 1574, and it is more likely that his appointment as *grand prévôt* was a reward for military services rendered during the third of the religious wars under the overall generalship of the future Henri III, perhaps in the victorious army commanded by Montpensier at Moncontour, where François distinguished himself in the field. We know that on the death of his uncle Antoine in 1576, he was promoted to the regiment's captaincy.[9]

By 1577 François was involved in delicate high-level diplomatic negotiations on behalf of Henri III. Henri, brother of the king, Charles IX, and at the time duc d'Anjou, had in 1573 accepted the throne of Poland, but clandestinely fled that country when, in 1574, his brother died and he received news of his accession to the throne of France. He almost immediately instigated fruitless negotiations with the leadership of both the Huguenots and the new moderate liberal Catholic party with a view to re-establishing peace in France. François was clearly a good military officer and a competent negotiator, and early in 1577, Henri III began systematically to promote and rely on trustworthy members of the lesser nobility, like François, who were unembroiled in the political feuding of the grander aristocracy.

Within a year, François de Richelieu, now *grand prévôt,* was a member of the Paris *parlement,* and, although not himself a lawyer, held jurisdiction over both civil and criminal cases involving the king's household. He was entitled to attend the king's *grand conseil,* and was also made a member of one of the chivalric orders, although not yet of the new order of the Holy Spirit, founded by the king late in 1578 in the hope of instituting a fresh chivalric elite in France. François was appointed to it only in 1585.

In 1585 the *grand prévôt* had a staff of ninety-nine, and his judicial functions extended beyond trials for crimes committed at court, or by its members.[10] He condemned for unlicensed brigandage a roving band purporting to belong to Montpensier's men. The skirmishes of the wars often provided cover for such groups, but the members of this one were executed and their severed heads displayed to deter unauthorized freelance marauding.

The *grand prévôt* was charged with enforcing payments by the great nobles for food and lodging at court for themselves and their households, and supervised matters ranging from the prices charged by court merchants, or by others in places where the court lodged, to the conduct of the 'filles de joie' who ordinarily followed the court. His combination of managerial, administrative and judicial responsibilities gave François considerable but unostentatious power, and naturally afforded him a wide range of lucrative opportunities which he would have been expected to seize. His salary as *grand prévôt* of 8,000 livres was plainly inadequate for the holder of the post to sustain the style of life which he was expected to maintain.

Without recourse to anything that might in the circumstances have been regarded as bribery, he could virtually sell licences to make merchants into court purveyors, and he could fix the prices at which they, and often others, might supply the court's needs. He could reasonably expect a fee for facilitating access to the king, or for furthering a cause or a request. No false accounting was required in distributing petty favours of all sorts for cash, or even in managing the *'filles de joie'*, but much more profit is likely to have been made through association with the financiers who raised the large amounts of money required by the king.[11]

It looks as if François may have participated in loans to Henri III, and have been alerted by his contact with the financiers to opportunities for investment in commercial trading ventures, whether or not opened up by political decisions. We know that, in association with others, he bought, sold, and traded with ships, no doubt borrowing money, and sometimes acted as a member of, or a front figure for, a consortium. It appears certain that his position enabled him to reduce the family debt, and to finance soon after his appointment the purchase of the hôtel de Losse, an ample town house near the Louvre. A series of accounts suggest that he was financing an extravagant style of living to go with it.[12] He could rely on his patron, Henri III, to protect him from the consequences of any commercial disaster.

Henri III's position declined throughout the 1580s, and in 1587 the fifty-odd deputies, known as 'les Seize' from the sixteen quarters of Paris which had appointed them, formed a revolutionary government which delivered the city over to the Guise family. By 1588 the remarkable ascent of the three Guise brothers, and the popularity of the third duke, allowed them to hope to take over power in France.[13] Their instrument was the Catholic League, ostensibly founded to defend Catholicism against Calvinism in 1576, but by 1586 dominated by the Guise family and the political tool by which they hoped to seize power, perhaps subjecting France to Spanish dominion, and certainly imposing state Catholicism.

Henri III's mother, Catherine de' Medici, tried to mediate

between her son and the duc de Guise, but Henri, reacting against Guise's calculated insolence, ordered the murder of the duke at Blois on 23 December 1588, followed the next day, Christmas eve, by the murder of his brother, the cardinal de Guise. The duties of the *grand prévôt* included the arrest of the powerful supporters of the League, many of whom were assembled at Blois and who were now led by the third Guise brother, the duc de Mayenne. When Catherine de' Medici died in January 1589, the Sorbonne, which had no jurisdiction of any kind, gave as its opinion that Henri III had forfeited all right to the crown. Only Bordeaux, Caen, Blois, Tours, Saumur, and some towns of the lower Loire remained faithful to him.

Henri III had come to regard Henri de Navarre, in spite of his relapse into the Calvinism he had once been made to abjure, as his legitimate successor. When Henri III was himself assassinated on 2 August 1589 while at Saint-Cloud preparing the assault to take back from the League the city of Paris, François de Richelieu was among the first to recognise the Huguenot Navarre as the new king, as soon as he had promised 'to take instruction' prior to reconversion to Catholicism. François, as *grand prévôt,* had been in Henri III's camp at the moment of the assassination, and was obliged to hold trial over the body of the instantly murdered assassin of Henri III, Jacques Clément.

François was to become close to Henri de Navarre, whose military position at first seemed virtually hopeless. Navarre held his own, however, with 7,000 men at Arques against Mayenne's army of 30,000 on 21 September, and began to win over important towns like Le Mans, Bayeux and Lisieux. By the end of 1589 his situation had become stronger, although he still badly needed to retain the loyalty of his Huguenot supporters. François fought the campaigns of 1589 and 1590 with Navarre, and continued to carry out for him the secret diplomatic missions which an escalation in recorded payments show him to have begun under Henri III.

The popularity of the Guise family and the League cannot be explained in terms alone of the defence of Catholicism, although France was certainly not ready to accept a Calvinist king. The League also purveyed a liberal constitutional theory implying a pact between king and people, dissolved if dishonoured by tyranny, which sundered any obligations of allegiance. However, the death in

1590 of the aged uncle of Henri de Navarre, put up by the League as 'Charles X', meant that by the end of 1592 Navarre only needed to abjure Calvinism again to secure the throne.[14]

He abjured at Saint-Denis in July 1593 and, since the traditional place of coronation, Reims, was still in League hands, was crowned and anointed as Henri IV at Chartres in 1594 in a ceremony still half sacerdotal in character. In March that year he made his entry into Paris, and in 1595 he received from the pope formal absolution from his relapse into Calvinism. Paris had broken with the League, and the claim to the French throne of the Spanish infanta, daughter of the eldest child of Henri II to leave issue, although strong on grounds of heredity, was being treated with derision. Navarre had married the sister of Henri III, Marguerite de Valois, in 1572 in the hope of generating a generally acceptable successor to the throne, but because that marriage proved childless it was to be annulled, whatever the canonical pretext, and on 5 October 1600, as Henri IV, Navarre was to marry Marie de' Medici, daughter of the grand duke of Tuscany.

Meanwhile, François's own sudden death at Gonesse on 10 July 1590 unhappily cut off the income from which his debts were being serviced, and suddenly left his family close to ruin. His wife and family instantaneously became vulnerable to his creditors, and his widow was left on her own to bring up five children, of which the oldest, Françoise, was just twelve. The fourth child was the subject of this biography, Armand-Jean.

Armand-Jean du Plessis de Richelieu was born in Paris on 9 September 1585 and publicly baptised in the parish church of Saint-Eustache on 1 May of the following year. Armand-Jean's godfathers were two marshals of France, Armand de Biron, governor of Poitou, and Jean d'Aumont, who together account for the full name Armand-Jean. The godmother was his grandmother, Françoise de Rochechouart.

Armand-Jean was the fourth child probably of five, three boys and two girls. There may have been a sixth child, Isabelle, whose existence appeared to have been established only in 1936, but that now seems improbable.[15] All his siblings and their offspring were to impinge substantially on his career, and the early choices about how their lives should be spent were interdependent. They were all largely determined, like his own, by the family's calamitous indebtedness.

The eldest child of François de Richelieu, Françoise, was born in 1578 and was briefly married in 1597 to Jean de Beauvau, whose family interests the cardinal subsequently advanced.[16] In 1603 Françoise married René de Vignerot, seigneur de Pont-Courlay, a member of the court of Henri IV. Françoise lived until 1616, and Vignerot until 1625. They had two children, the elder of whom, François, Richelieu was to make *Général des galères* in 1635, although he disapproved of his expenditure. Richelieu paid his debts twice, but left him out of his will. The younger child of Vignerot and Françoise was Marie, the cardinal's favourite niece. She was to be made duchesse d'Aiguillon in 1638, nursed Richelieu as he was dying, and was the cardinal's residual heir.

Henri, the second child of the *grand prévôt*, was born in 1580. Impetuous, and certainly not risk-averse, he resourcefully, courageously and successfully, if with the help of his father's connections and a little luck, devoted himself to restoring the family fortunes and buying back the properties which had belonged to his father's bankrupt estate. He was strong-willed, independent-minded and self-reliant. The family's financial ruin clearly determined his early career choices and the lateness of his marriage to a wealthy widow, Marguerite Guiot, in 1615. He was to die in 1619 as the result of a duel, pre-deceased by his wife on 15 October 1618 and his infant son on 8 December that year.

The third child of the *grand prévôt* was Alphonse, born in 1582. He had been designated by the family for the bishopric of Luçon, one asset left by François which was to prove of unexpected value. The lucrative right to nominate to revenue-producing ecclesiastical benefices, like tax exemption for extensive monastic estates, had been a bargaining weapon between spiritual and temporal sovereigns since the emergence of the large nation states of the late fifteenth century. So too was the not inherently unreasonable wish of secular sovereigns to appoint seasoned, educated and able ecclesiastics to run their administrative and legal systems, with salaried deputies to take over their pastoral responsibilities.

At least half a dozen ecclesiastical lords chancellor, including Wolsey of England, du Prat of France and Cisneros of Spain, endowed with the plenitude of civil jurisdiction, were not only beneficed clerics, but were also made papal *legati a latere,* giving them full, if territorially circumscribed, papal jurisdiction, to avoid clashes between sacred and secular jurisdictions. The development of arrangements to use what were once ecclesiastical revenues to finance the enlarged secular administrations of post-Renaissance Europe, and of the theological and canonical arguments adduced to justify them, shows an unexceptionable pattern of negotiation between conflicting interests and rights, with, inevitably, quarrels and abuses.

In 1584 Henri III had granted to François the right to present a candidate to the bishopric, one of the less desirable episcopal benefices in France and notoriously described by Armand-Jean on becoming its incumbent as 'l'évêché le plus crotté de France'. The diocese was certainly run down, but Armand-Jean exaggerated. François had initially nominated for the bishopric his own father's brother, Jacques du Plessis, for royal and papal approval, while using a power of attorney to keep the diocesan revenues in his own hands. Jacques never entered his diocese, but François arranged a one-year exchange of its not negligible but multiple-sourced revenues for 10,000 livres.

Alphonse's entry sometime shortly after 1600 into the particularly austere Carthusian order at the Grande Chartreuse appears to have been the result of a genuine religious choice, no doubt conceived in the fervour of the purely religious branch of the Catholic revival.[17] It is likely that his decision was triggered by the sudden need to confront the imminence of episcopal responsibilities, but his choice of a contemplative monastic life did nothing to contribute to the financial situation of the family, as so many younger sons did by becoming clerics, whether to acquire a benefice or to avoid imposing on the family the need to buy an office or a commission for them.

After Armand-Jean, the fourth child and future minister, came Nicole, born in 1587, who married Urbain de Maillé, marquis de Brézé, but not until January 1618, when she was over thirty and when Armand-Jean was able to endow her with 62,000 livres. Another 18,000 came from Henri. The debt-ridden Brézé family contributed an august and ancient name. In 1617, before the marriage, the Brézé family declared debts of 107,000 livres, but Richelieu had cleared Brézé indebtedness to the extent of over

400,000 livres by the 1630s.[18] Nicole was to have three children
of which the third, Claire-Clémence, was on 11 February 1641
to marry the future 'Grand' Condé, soon to be celebrated for
his youthful generalship during the final stages of the Thirty
Years War.

The young Armand-Jean must have passed his infancy in the
Paris house, probably leaving only on 12 May 1588, when the
Parisians put up the celebrated barricades to cut communications
between the groups of mercenaries posted by the king. When
Henri III quietly galloped out of Paris for Chartres on 13 May,
and in October summoned a meeting of the estates at Blois, it had
been the duty of the *grand prévôt* to remain with him. His wife and
the children returned home to Poitou, where fighting and pillage
were still sporadically fierce. Armand-Jean therefore spent the last
two years of his father's life with his mother, brothers and sisters
at Richelieu until, after the assassination of Henri III, the transfer
of his father's allegiance to Henri de Navarre, and his father's
death, his mother was able in 1594 or 1595 to take the family
back to Paris. The return to a new house near the Louvre was
made possible by a reimbursement of 45,000 livres for the loss
of rights connected with an abbey of Saint-Urbain and by other
promises of Henri IV.

Armand-Jean's education began in Poitou, and was paid for by
Amador de la Porte, his mother's half-brother.[19] Richelieu was to
rely heavily on Amador, who was born in 1567 and died suddenly
in 1644, and to reward him richly in later life. Dispensed as early
as 1583 from the requirement of proving noble lineage to join
the order of Malta, he became its grand prior in 1640, eleven
years after the post had become vacant on the death of Henri
IV's illegitimate son, Alexandre de Vendôme. Amador was also
to be made governor of Angers, governor of Le Havre, both at the
time politically sensitive posts, a member of the powerful *conseil de
la marine,* and was caretaker for Richelieu in the governorships of
La Rochelle, Brouage, and the isles of Ré and Oléron. Called in
by Richelieu to fill posts in which he needed a reliable incumbent,
Amador remarkably seems to have escaped the opprobrium in
which Richelieu and most of his family were commonly held during
his years of power.

Amador's nephew, Charles de la Porte, duc de la Meilleraye,

also profited from Richelieu's patronage.[20] Born in 1602, he left the Huguenot religion to become *écuyer* to Armand-Jean when he was bishop of Luçon.[21] In September 1635 he had been made *grand maître* and captain general of the artillery. Richelieu also made him *lieutenant général* of Normandy, governor of Rouen, and acting governor of Nantes, with reversionary rights to the governorship into which he may have entered even before Richelieu died. Created a marshal of France, he acted as caretaker of Richelieu's Brittany governorship, which he purchased in 1637. Richelieu was to rely on and to exploit his family in order to safeguard and advance his own interests, but there is also an element of gratitude in his furtherance of the careers particularly of the La Portes, of whom Amador was elderly, and La Meilleraye a crassly incompetent general.

Hanotaux says in his biography of Richelieu that Armand-Jean was sent to the abbey of St-Florent at Saumur, forty kilometres from Richelieu as the crow flies, which means that he must have boarded. He was a bright, if sickly child, subject to migraine and sporadic fevers while still quite young. The choice of an abbey school, rather than private tuition from a local abbé, suggests only his mother's desire that he should be properly taught, not that he was destined for an ecclesiastical career. It is probable that Armand-Jean remained in Poitou, perhaps with Alphonse, three years his senior, until the family's return to Paris in 1594 or 1595, and also that income from the Luçon bishopric, held by Jacques du Plessis until his death in 1592, may thereafter have been applied to the upkeep of the household, although it appears to have been administered by Henri.[22]

Henri, born in 1580, was anxious to gain formal, legal independence, and may already by 1595 for some years have been a page at the court of Henri IV. Whenever it took place, his entry into the royal household argues considerable influence, no doubt of his father's friends, and possibly of the king himself. Henri was to become a *gentilhomme ordinaire* with a salary of 3,000 livres a year, and then a *mestre de camp* in the Piedmont regiment, before in 1617 becoming *mareschal de camp*.

By mid-1598 he had renounced his claim to inherit his father's estate and obtained royal letters of emancipation, freeing him to act in his own name, without the adult representation normally required until the age of twenty-six. This grant was registered at the Saumur *sénéchaussée* despite the recorded opposition of his mother, whom Henri was also in January 1610 to oblige to hand over to him the inherited *seigneurie* of Châteauneuf.[23] Perhaps, as head of the family successful in re-establishing its fortunes, he wished all its affairs to be under his control, but there may perhaps also have been legal considerations to do with keeping the Rochechouart inheritance out of his mother's hands and therefore away from his father's creditors.

The emancipation enabled Henri to act as his father's principal creditor rather than as heir to his debts, one tactic among several others which argues excellent advice and strong royal favour. Royal favour was probably also required to have the liquidation of his father's estate entrusted to the *grand conseil,* more likely to be amenable to royal influence than the normal civil courts. Henri is known in all to have bought in claims on his father's estate of about 192,000 livres or more.[24]

He bought only one property which had not belonged to his father, and managed to spend some 73,000 livres on land between 1602 and 1615, by which date he had redeemed all the family estates except Richelieu itself, not put up for sale until after Henri's death. It would be bought by Richelieu in 1621 for 76,000 livres. Henri's transactions were completed when, two days before his marriage to Marguerite Guiot in 1615, they made a mutual donation of lands. Since his wife predeceased him, dying on 15 October 1618, the properties he had ceded to her reverted to him, while he retained what he had acquired from her gift. The value of Henri's lands at the date of his death in 1619 was more than 200,000 livres, the capital raised for his purchases having been much augmented by the court favour he enjoyed when the crown redeemed with a capital payment some salt tax revenue and a *rente* from the general revenue which had been due to the *grand prévôt.*

From 1595 Armand-Jean was at the Collège de Navarre in Paris, finishing his secondary education with the expectation of a military career. At Navarre, one of the four colleges at which it was possible to study theology, the pupils spoke Latin. Armand-Jean may not even have finished the arts course, which ordinarily culminated in philosophy, rhetoric and graduation as a master of arts. He was sent in 1601 or 1602 to Antoine de Pluvinel's expensive academy, a military-style finishing school founded in 1594 for aspiring pages and courtiers rather like the Tudor Inns of Court in England. Young nobles were trained in horsemanship, fencing and music as well as military mathematics and manners. The education was physical, moral and social, impregnated with the code of honour prevailing at Henri IV's rather coarse court.

For a while Armand-Jean used the title Marquis du Chillou, after the estate brought into the Richelieu family by his great-grandfather's marriage in 1506, to distinguish himself from his brothers, and it is doubtless on his activities at this period that are founded the later accusations of womanizing levelled against him notably by Mathieu de Morgues, who had become a hostile pamphleteer.[25] In May 1605, he appears as a patient of the king's doctor, Jean de la Rivière, and in the *Ephémérides* of Théodore Turquet de Mayerne, as being treated, with a number of other eminent personages, for 'gonnorhea inveterata'. Armand-Jean's case had been given up as hopeless by a number of other doctors. Mayerne was the specialist, about to write a book of the disease.[26]

It was during his early Paris years that Armand-Jean formed his firm liaison with the Bouthillier family, four sons of a Paris lawyer who had worked for François de La Porte, and finally taken over the practice.[27] He also formed his relationship with Michel le Masle, three years younger than himself, who was to become his secretary and trusted man of business. Le Masle was already in 1600 the '*petit valet*' who carried Armand-Jean's papers to school. He was to stay with him all his life.[28] Armand-Jean was also very close to Jacques de Bourges, an *avocat* in the Paris *parlement* who acted for the La Porte family, and his wife, Jeanne de Saint-Germain, Mme de Bourges, daughter of an apothecary and widow of a *valet de chambre* of Henri III. He may have lodged with them for a while. None of his close friends was from a family of the *noblesse d'épée*.

It was when he was eighteen that Armand-Jean must have allowed himself to be put forward as the family candidate for the bishopric of Luçon, replacing Alphonse. The Richelieu family had managed in 1592–93 to impose as bishop in succession to Jacques du Plessis, uncle of the *grand prévôt*, the local parish priest of Richelieu, François d'Hyver, intending to keep him in the position until Alphonse should come of age. This arrangement encountered understandable resistance from the chapter and from

Rome, unwilling to endorse episcopal nominations by the Huguenot
Henri de Navarre between 1591 and 1596, particularly because he
was neither absolved until 1595 nor yet even securely king. Hyver,
whose episcopacy demanded both the registration of royal letters of
appointment and papal bulls,[29] did not go near the diocese, whose
revenues were paid to Henri. His episcopal bulls were received only
after the direct intervention of Henri IV, now a Catholic, in March
1599, and he was to resign to make way for Armand-Jean.

The cathedral chapter had resented the original 1584 grant to the
Richelieu family of the right to nominate to the see, and continued
to make difficulties, electing its own dean against a royal nominee,
and even inquiring about the legality of electing its own bishop. It
was the chapter which brought its guerilla war with the Richelieu
family to crisis in 1603, by extracting from the *grand conseil* the
previously ignored 1593 ruling of the Paris *parlement,* then sitting
in Tours, that a third of the episcopal revenues should be devoted
to repairs to the cathedral. Its various other tactics, like refusing
Alphonse a canonry, had all failed.

The family had to resort to seeking Alphonse's formal nomination to the see, and it was when faced with the immediate prospect
not only of pastoral responsibilities but no doubt also a revenue-
yielding career as an ecclesiastical statesman, that Alphonse decided
to enter the Grande Chartreuse. By February 1604 the papal
nuncio's correspondence reveals that the king was to nominate
not Alphonse but Armand-Jean as bishop of Luçon. The chapter
continued to fight sporadically during 1604, after which chapter
and family agreed to an arbitration which did not, however, put
an end to the chapter's discontent.

Armand-Jean du Plessis's acquiescence in his new career as a
bishop must date from late in 1603. It was made out of a sense
of family loyalty, and no doubt urged on him by Henri, to whom
Armand-Jean was to continue to pay 4,000 livres a year from the
revenues of the diocese. The finances of the arrangement will have
been worked out before the king was asked to apply for the papal
appointment, and Armand-Jean was taking a characteristic risk. He
knew he was opposed by the chapter, which had just won its
ruling from the *grand conseil.* Either the king or the pope could
be disenchanted at the switch of candidates from Alphonse to
Armand-Jean, particularly since Rome was beginning to react

firmly against family sees; and he was still seven years under the canonical age of twenty-six. None the less he immediately began to prepare seriously for an ecclesiastical career.[30]

Michel de Pure,[31] writing in 1656, tells us that Armand-Jean, now presumably bishop designate, returned not to Navarre late in 1603 for his philosophy, but to the Collège de Calvi, transferring back either to Navarre or to the Sorbonne for theology, but the records contradict one another. It is at least possible to read the documents as indicating that the MA studies were completed in 1604, save perhaps for a formal examination exercise. By late 1604 Armand-Jean was certainly studying theology, and in 1606 he was dispensed from normal requirements to proceed to the theology baccalaureat, no doubt because of the impending bishopric. He was described as a bachelor of theology at Rome in December 1606, but the evidence points to a trickle of examinations, dispensations and public acts which brought him the baccalaureat only in December 1607.

Almost all the early accounts of Richelieu's career mention his acquaintance, often as a pupil, with the better-known theologians of the Catholic revival in which he found his spiritual and theological roots. The revival was not yet distinguishable into the two main groupings which only gradually diverged, one mystical, devotional and institutional, the other papalist, pro-Spanish and political, but the relationship of Armand-Jean du Plessis to it shows an early aptitude for cultivating his peers. At this date the theologians were no doubt interested in him on account of his powerful connections, his reputation, his bishopric and his abilities. The most prominent theologian of the revival was the commentator on Aquinas, André du Val,[32] the master of both Saint-Cyran and Bérulle. As the movement's two principal branches moved away from one another, du Val's views were to be repudiated by Saint-Cyran's co-operator, Jansen, in the 1640 *Augustinus*, and Bérulle was to break with him. Richelieu's pastoral writings reflect theological positions not dissimilar from those of du Val, and he came to distrust the different but related spiritualities of both Bérulle and Saint-Cyran.

The literary and philosophical optimism of Renaissance France had stopped quite suddenly with the outbreak of the religious wars in 1562. The Renaissance itself had been as much a northern

European as an Italian phenomenon, although its altered perception of human potential was explored in literature and painting in different ways in different regions both north and south of the Alps. The philosophical sub-structure for the new value system had however been imported into the rest of Europe from Florence, where Cosimo de' Medici's protégé Marsilio Ficino had elaborated at Cosimo's request a new Christian philosophy from Plotinus's adaptation of Plato. He produced a 'theology' which supported the immortality of the soul, but also upgraded the powers of human nature to make instinctive emotional and physical love between human beings the starting point from which their highest spiritual perfection might be obtained.

During the French religious wars the development of this intensely optimistic neoplatonism was halted. It was not so much repudiated as given a stoic gloss. In their reaction to the blood-letting, French writers suddenly relied more on ancient stoic authors, especially Seneca and Epictetus, and introduced the mixture of intellectual relativism and Christian stoicism characteristic, for instance, of Montaigne. Montaigne himself simply laughed at Ficino's attempts to establish an ordered path from physical human love to the beatifying love of God.[33]

It is not without significance that Armand in his twenties was attracted to both Saint-Cyran, whose later spirituality he was to find dangerous, and Bérulle, a prominent and energetic reformer, but whose spirituality, full of neoplatonist exemplarism, was insensitive to the personal needs of his penitents and was fundamentally incompatible with Richelieu's own. The closeness of the relationship between Saint-Cyran's spiritual values and those of Bérulle is not yet widely understood,[34] but Armand-Jean du Plessis's formation in Paris shows him in his early twenties indiscriminately embracing representative figures and devotional forms from the Catholic revival which a later power of spiritual discernment would oblige him to repudiate.

This was not the only way in which the young Armand-Jean was to change. He was already endowed with the charm for which he became famous, and which he was soon to use to astonishing effect with both Paul V and Henri IV, but he had still to develop the sang-froid for which he is also known, and to conquer an excessive emotional instability, his mood swings and his vulnerability to depression. In Paris his principal intellectual mentor became Philippe Cospeau, born in 1571 and successively bishop of Aire (1607), Nantes (1621) and Lisieux (1636), well-known as a preacher, who was to give one of the funeral orations in Paris for Henri IV in 1610 and assist Louis XIII on his deathbed in 1643.

Armand-Jean is known to have taken his theological studies seriously, even if all the accounts we have of him at this date are designed, often with his own help, to flatter him. It is to be assumed that the king's first letter to the pope requesting Armand-Jean's appointment to Luçon dates from late 1603. He had received two small priories in the diocese of Tours from Alphonse, and in 1604 approached Del Buffalo, the nuncio, about the question of a dispensation from the canonical age of twenty-six required for bishops. The nuncio passed the request on, although he is likely to have known that Armand-Jean had been lying when, not yet nineteen, he had represented himself as twenty.

The papal secretary of state passed the request to Clement VIII, whose reply implied that the curia was waiting for Armand-Jean to 'solicit his bulls', which is to say pay up front. That would not have been an inexpensive matter, even without paying for the dispensation, the legal charges for which would have to be added. When the French ambassador raised the matter of the bulls with a new pope, Paul V, he got no more than a vague reply that he might hope for a happy outcome when he applied. In fact Armand-Jean achieved a reduction of 18,000 livres, which implied a negotiation by some powerful intermediary. The chapter was to claim in 1607 that the Richelieu family had not carried out its obligations under the 1604 agreement, and a new contract had to be signed in 1609. Armand-Jean agreed to pay a third of what was still required to restore the cathedral, which was still much less than the third of his revenues which the chapter demanded.

Du Plessis[35] began to take orders, and was a sub-deacon when he went to Rome in 1606, the only time in his life apart from the Avignon exile of 1618 when he left French soil. There had been more trouble with the Luçon cathedral chapter, who objected to his claim that, as nominee bishop, he had a right to the revenues accruing from the use at Luçon of the episcopal seal. The chapter took the matter to the *parlement,* where du Plessis won. Henri IV wrote further letters to the French ambassador and to cardinal

Joyeuse, and du Plessis was accorded his bulls on 18 December 1606.[36] The pope, who granted the age dispensation a week before he issued the bulls, is said to have joked about being lied to about the age.[37] The dispensation declares Armand to have been in his twenty-third year. In fact he was just beginning his twenty-second. He had been proposed in the consistory of 17 September 1606, and had been granted his dispensation on 1 December. His bulls contained a clause reserving 4,000 livres a year to Henri, providing that the new bishop was left with at least 3,000 livres for himself.

Du Plessis was ordained priest in Rome, and consecrated bishop there on 17 April 1607. On 2 June at Fontainebleau he took the oath of fidelity to the king to which the temporalities of his office bound him. Late that summer, after what must have been more short cuts or dispensations from the norm than have been recorded, he defended his theses in Paris, and on 29 October he received his doctorate of theology and became a *hospes et socius* (member and fellow) of the Sorbonne, which might mean the college or, equally, the theology faculty with which the college was colloquially but misleadingly identified.

From October 1607 to December 1608 du Plessis remained in Paris, exercising his charm, impressing the *dévot* party with a seriousness of religious purpose, becoming known for the sharpness of his intelligence, acquiring a reputation as a preacher, and becoming a member of the immediate entourage of the king. Even if we discount what was later written to please him or to flatter his memory, we know that the king referred to him as 'my bishop', and discussed the future of France with him, whether du Plessis's original introduction to court circles was due to his father's memory or to the good offices of Henri. His relationship to the king is a further testimony to his charm, as no doubt also is acquisition of new and powerful protectors, like Cardinal Du Perron, the ex-Huguenot archbishop of Sens who became the king's chief ecclesiastical adviser. It was to be December 1608 before the bishop of Luçon braced himself to take possession of his diocese.

3

The Rise and Fall of the young Bishop 1608–18

He was met at Fontenay-le-Comte in the neighbouring diocese of Maillezais by a deputation from the Luçon cathedral chapter, and conducted to Luçon in late December 1608. The migraines which his overstrung nerves would provoke for the rest of his life had begun to be severe in 1608, and only the distaste with which he confronted the lonely and hostile discomfort of Luçon explains his delay in taking up his appointment. He had turned twenty-three. At his induction he gave an address expressing his hope that the Catholics and the Huguenots of his diocese would live in harmony.[1]

He visited Paris at least annually, and from about 1611, when he was ill for much of the year, he stayed regularly with Henri Louis Chasteignier de La Rocheposay, coadjutor bishop at Poitiers in 1608, and appointed diocesan bishop in 1611. La Rocheposay's father had fought alongside the *grand prévôt,* and La Rocheposay himself governed his diocese as though he were its military commander. He liked military dress and kept military guards, although he was also a reforming bishop, bringing into his diocese five of the newly-founded religious congregations of the early seventeenth century.

It was both as warrior and as bishop in 1614 that La Rocheposay defended Poitiers against Condé, at that time allied to the militant Huguenots. Jean Duvergier de Hauranne, better known as Saint-Cyran after the abbey La Rocheposay was to bestow on him in 1618, wrote a pamphlet in La Rocheposay's defence, *Contre ceux qui disent qu'il n'est pas permis aux ecclésiastiques d'avoir recours aux armes en cas de nécessité.*[2] Saint-Cyran was known to du Plessis as a friend of both La Rocheposay and of Sébastien Bouthillier, already a canon of Luçon, and in 1614 to become dean of the chapter.

Du Plessis is not known ever to have used the dilapidated episcopal palace at Luçon. He sometimes rented accommodation, but his preferred residence was his priory at Coussay, quite near the Richelieu estate, and in the diocese of Poitiers. In Richelieu's correspondence, we find Mme de Bourges buying and selling things for du Plessis in Paris. His letters to her, obviously informal in tone and occasionally nearing amused self-caricature, exaggerate the pinches of financial constraint. He needs some silver plate to show off his noble lineage. He must have old episcopal vestments altered, as he cannot afford new. He cannot afford a pied-à-terre in Paris. He has no furniture there, but furnished lodgings are unpleasant, and unfurnished houses so expensive. He would still buy a house if he could find one cheap enough.

In 1609 he writes, 'I am lodged very badly. There is nowhere to make a fire because of the smoke . . . There is nowhere to walk, nor garden, nor avenue, nor anything else, so that my house is my prison.' One of the things about Richelieu which started early, never changed, but has never much been remarked upon, was his need not so much for the winds of open countryside, as for the fresh air of well-kept and extensive gardens, away from urban stench, a particular concern later in the construction of the Palais Cardinal.[3]

The diocese had been carved out of Poitou in 1317, and was geographically not inextensive, with at least 250 parishes, and perhaps almost double that number. It was certainly not rich, and the cathedral, erected during the fourteenth and fifteenth centuries, was in poor condition. The diocesan revenues, a miscellaneous bundle of *rentes* deriving from a patchwork of rights, were leased by du Plessis for nine years for 13,000 livres a year in 1610. Even if there remained the 4,000 livres to find for Henri, and the cathedral repair bill to pay, du Plessis did not suffer serious poverty.[4] Henri arranged for his brother to take over in 1608–1609 the abbey of Ile Chauvet, which was in his diocese, and represented an extra but unquantified source of income for him. The priories must have brought in some two or three thousand livres, and some help was to be forthcoming from Sully, the Huguenot governor of Poitou and the administrator who had brought order to Henri IV's financial affairs.

Du Plessis had scarcely got settled in to his diocese when Henri IV was assassinated. In 1609 Habsburg troops had occupied the quasi-independent Rhineland territories of Jülich-Cleves on the death of the duke, and on 13 May 1610 Marie de' Medici had been crowned queen of France so that she could act as regent while Henri IV led his army against the imperial forces. She was to have made her solemn entry into Paris on the Sunday, but on Friday 14 May, at about four in the afternoon, Ravaillac assassinated Henri IV because he was proposing to go to war on fellow-Catholics. The dead king's marriage to Marie de' Medici, brokered by Clement VIII, had resulted in six children, of whom the eldest, successor to the throne, was the future Louis XIII, born on 27 September 1601. He was not yet nine years old.[5]

Very swift action brought the regency to Marie de' Medici, before it could be claimed by one or other of the princes of the blood. But Condé, son of the king's late cousin, Henri I de Condé, was on bad terms with Henri IV and had taken refuge in Milan, a possession of hostile Spain.[6] Of the other two first cousins, the elder, François, prince de Conti, acquiesced in the regency of the queen mother, while the second, Charles, comte de Soissons, was out of Paris.

On the afternoon of the assassination, the *parlement* happened to be in session, although its first president and senior judge was at home with gout. He immediately came, summoning such representatives of the other five sovereign courts in Paris as could be found. The duc d'Epernon, captain-general of France's infantry, attended by right of precedence, and, although the proceedings had no constitutional validity, the ratification by the whole body of Marie de' Medici as regent by about half past six was a ruling by those in power and in Paris which was intended to be unchallengeable. Constitutionality was ensured next day by a *lit de justice* in which the king re-assumed all delegated authority in the kingdom. Conti and the six-year-old son of Soissons were there, with as many cardinals, bishops, and peers as could be assembled. No one listened to the eight-year-old boy king, but it was at his command that the chancellor,

Sillery, formally invested his mother, Marie de' Medici, with the regency.

The boyhood of the future Louis XIII had not been happy.[7] He was the eldest of the six children of his father to be born of Marie de' Medici, who was coarse, vulgar, rather unintelligent, and entirely lacking in refinement or personal distinction. She was also lonely except for her sole compatriot, Léonora Galigaï, and Léonora's Florentine husband, Concino Concini. She was, however, fertile. This was particularly important for the French monarchy, since not only had Henri IV's first wife, Marguerite de Valois, produced no children, but the queens of the three previous kings, Henri III, Charles IX and François II, had between them produced only one legitimate child, the daughter of Charles IX and Elizabeth of Austria, whose gender precluded her succession.

Richelieu's *Mémoires* tell us that he heard of the assassination at Coussay from Sébastien Bouthillier. He may truly have anticipated an outbreak of disorder in place of the smooth transfer to power which did take place, but the regent neither asked for du Plessis's help, nor wanted it. Others, too, like La Rocheposay, pressed on her their titles to appointment to her entourage by sending her reports of troop movements and gatherings of nobles. Du Plessis went so far as to send an unrequested oath of loyalty from his clergy and himself. When the time came, du Plessis, known in Paris as Henri's brother, 'le frère de M. de Richelieu', was to find his cause at court furthered more by Henri and by the husband of their sister Françoise, René de Vignerot, seigneur du Pont de Courlay, than by his own efforts to put himself forward. Henri de Richelieu was sensible enough not to deliver the grovelling letter or the oath written to Marie de' Medici by his brother, offering his services with his sympathies. Du Plessis's charm had been vanquished by ambition and was toppling over into obsequiousness.

Bouthillier wrote to tell du Plessis that he should say nothing, but could not prevent him from writing widely to the entourage of the regent to announce his intention of coming to Paris to present his homage. Bouthillier distributed the letters. Du Plessis did come to Paris, spending most of the second half of 1610 there, and was bitter at the absence of any intention to give him the appointment in the regent's court which he plainly thought he merited. He returned not to Luçon but to Coussay, and worked off his resentment by sending out churlish and ill-conceived letters to his grand vicars, his subordinates but his seniors, and organising a more controlled, but still enraged epistolary campaign to those who were, or might become able to advance his career.

Henri IV had been preparing not only to occupy Jülich, but also to support the duke of Savoy in attacking the Spanish-held duchy of Milan. With the exception of the capable but Huguenot Sully, Marie de' Medici kept the advisers bequeathed to her,[8] and, guided by them, contented herself with ending the imperial sequestration of Jülich on 2 September 1610, and withdrew altogether from the enterprise against Milan, forcing Savoy to take refuge under Spanish tutelage.

It is true that Marie de' Medici did not want the services which the young bishop of Luçon was pressing on her, but the ground was worth testing, and his advances were made at a moment when pensions were being doubled in the two years to 1611.[9] Personal ambitions were being satisfied on an unprecedented scale. Among those to benefit were Marie de' Medici's foster-sister, Léonora Galigaï and her Florentine husband Concino Concini, already, according to the Spanish ambassador, the favourite of Marie de' Medici by September 1610.[10] Concini was quick to seize opportunities for enrichment, purchasing the marquisate of Ancre, the lieutenant-generalship of Picardy to date from 9 February 1611, and the post of first gentleman of the bedchamber. By 1612, however, and in spite of the prodigal attempts to buy their support, the higher nobility were returning to their governorships and rallying their private armies, increasingly hostile to the regency.

Du Plessis had returned to Paris in 1611, renting a house from Denis Bouthillier.[11] He succeeded in getting the letters-patent for the establishment of a seminary registered by the *parlement,* and in resolving the succession to the recently deceased abbess of Fontevraud in his diocese, for which he required royal assent. For much of that year he was ill, but he also treated with Méric de Vic, the royal councillor charged with ironing out confessional disputes in Poitou. Paris officialdom, worried by the Huguenot assembly at Saumur in 1611, began to be approvingly aware of du Plessis's activities as diocesan bishop of Luçon.

Although the disciplinary decrees of the council of Trent[12] were not promulgated in Luçon until 1622, it was in their spirit that du Plessis governed the diocese. He wanted an instructed and reformed clergy capable of refuting Huguenot theological positions, and therefore needed some co-operation from the conservative chapter, which believed that the new bishop had usurped its own rights. Du Plessis proposed to found a seminary, was a tight and watchful administrator, authoritarian by disposition, but willing to work hard and to achieve his aims chiefly by charm. Meanwhile, his ambition, if it did not yet directly involve political influence for its own sake, certainly did include the acquisition of greater status and more money. He kept an ear open for better episcopal vacancies opening elsewhere.[13]

Many of the religious foundations within his diocese were controlled from outside it, some dependent on great abbeys, and others providing revenues, generally through agents, to some of the great families of France. The houses of the religious orders were exempt from his jurisdiction, but, like many of the reforming bishops of his generation, including La Rocheposay, du Plessis sought help through the importation of the newer non-exempt congregations designed, like the Visitation shortly to be founded by Jeanne-Françoise de Chantal and François de Sales, for specifically pastoral purposes.[14] In 1611 Bérulle, whose spirituality strongly emphasised the importance of the hierarchical priesthood and the concept of 'servitude', established the French Oratory as a group of non-monastic diocesan priests on the model established in Rome by Philip Neri. Disliking the traditional monastic vows, and the exemption of the monasteries from episcopal jurisdiction, he intended to provide for the education of priests, and du Plessis had immediately invited the French Oratory to establish a presence in his diocese. By June 1612 various Oratorians had become frequent visitors for five or six months at a time.

Du Plessis had also invited the Capuchins, a branch of the Franciscans, who eventually established houses at Les Sables d'Olonne in 1616 and in Luçon itself in 1619. Capuchins had been working in the diocese before du Plessis's arrival, and in 1610 they established a 'province', with its own regional superior, in Touraine. From 1613, its superior was the redoubtable 'grey eminence', Père Joseph (François le Clerc du Tremblay), already a friend of Bérulle and later to become Richelieu's close friend and principal adviser on foreign policy.[15]

After an initial, and poorly attended diocesan synod in 1609, du Plessis undertook the visitation of the parishes of the diocese, and in 1613 promulgated a number of synodal decrees, mostly dealing with dress, discipline, and those occupations or situations forbidden to clerics, but also laying down norms for behaviour, preaching, the conduct of services and the running of parishes. This was exactly what might be expected of a zealous young bishop anxious to implement the reforms of the council of Trent and charged with repairing the religious organisation of a diocese suffering from the ravages of the wars of religion, a build-up of vested interests and a great deal of neglect.

Much of what was stipulated about clerical dress and behaviour, female housekeepers, and jurisdiction to preach, to conduct marriages, or to hear confessions, merely reiterated universal provisions on clerical discipline, some of which had obviously fallen into disuse. On the other hand, du Plessis, sensitive to the danger of appointing incompetent and unworthy parish clergy, innovatively wished to open vacancies to competition, as recommended by the council of Trent.

Du Plessis was not always successful in attempting to vet candidates put forward by those in whose power it was to present parish priests, but the 1611 letters patent for the establishment of a seminary allowed him to make a levy of 3,000 livres on benefices worth more than 800 livres a year. A second set of letters patent of August 1613 extended the tax to all benefice-holders except parish priests, but the seminary, housed at du Plessis's private expense, scarcely got off the ground. The *parlement de Paris* refused at the instigation of the chapter, still resentful of the du Plessis appointment, to register the second set of letters patent. Its superior resigned, and du Plessis handed it over to the Oratorians, but the project gradually collapsed.

Du Plessis was also in these early years of his episcopate active in anti-Huguenot controversy. The Huguenots were strong in Luçon and aspired, for instance, to build a temple on a provocative site opposite the cathedral, and to bury their dead in Catholic cemeteries. From 1609, there was a small stream of appeals from Luçon to Paris to have the legitimate rights of Catholics respected, showing not only continued guerilla squabbling between the two communities, but also that in parts of the diocese Catholic worship had not yet been restored at all.

It is in this context that du Plessis's involvement with Richard Smith arose. A Catholic controversialist working in Paris and writing against James I of England, Smith was later to arouse the hostility of the Jesuits by attempting to override the exemption of their English mission from episcopal jurisdiction. Richelieu was in 1624 to make Smith the superior of the English mission of the diocesan priesthood, and employed him for a dozen years to assist him in anti-Huguenot controversy.

Du Plessis saw his religious pamphlets, and those which he inspired others to write, as an essential part of his pastoral activity, without conscious regard for the basis which they established for the further advancement of his career. The 20-page ordinances of 1613 appeared with a pamphlet for confessors signed by the grand vicar whom du Plessis later wished to make his coadjutor, Jacques de Flavigny. This was the 78-page *Briefve et facile instruction pour les confesseurs,* organised round the decalogue and the commandments of the church, insisting on the individual's obligations to God, church, prince and country. It contains the bishop's own doctrine. He recommends worship in the vernacular, is moderate on the Huguenots, but does not allow Catholic assistance at Huguenot ceremonies, mixed marriages, or ecclesiastical burial for heretics. Du Plessis takes the liberal view, which the Jansenists were later to attack, that sorrow for sin based on the fear of hell ('attrition'), while inferior to sorrow based on regret for offending God ('contrition'), is an adequate basis for sacramental absolution.

Most important is the treatment of gender issues in the *Briefve et facile instruction.* Coquetry is allowed if intended to lead to marriage, as are love letters. This was just four years after François de Sales had raised eyebrows by permitting make-up and dancing in the *Introduction à la vie dévote,* and including in that work a chapter 'De l'honnêteté du lit nuptial', a further instance of the humanisation of what had been the repressively anti-sexual spirituality of late medieval Catholicism, as well as of the burgeoning confidence in nature's instinctive potential for leading to virtue which is the dominant feature of the value shift which was taking place in French culture.

The *Instruction du chrestien*, which Richelieu was to write in 1618, was essentially a handbook for preachers centred on the essential points pertaining to the Christian life. Those concerning belief were laid down in the Apostles' Creed, and those concerning behaviour in the ten commandments and in the commandments of the church. The work points out how the Christian may obtain from God the strength to conform to both sets of norms. The underlying theology allows to Christians the power, by taking advantage of the grace of God, to determine their own permanent destiny after death.[16]

In 1618 du Plessis, faithful to the eucharistic devotion of the Catholic revival, also stressed the importance of frequent communion, of which Saint-Cyran, at first a strong advocate, later became a firm opponent.[17] Du Plessis was also committed to the promotion of devotion to the Blessed Sacrament which was characteristic of the celebrated convent of Port-Royal under Sébastien Zamet before Saint-Cyran took it over. Zamet had also founded a fashionable convent known as the institute of the Blessed Sacrament.[18] Frequent communion and the devotion to the Blessed Sacrament that went with it strongly coloured the public devotional aspects of the revival and were among the characteristics which were to be suppressed in Jansenist devotion.

After the initial failure to control the anger deriving from his frustration at failing to attract attention in the entourage of Marie de' Medici, du Plessis softened his approach to subordinates, referring to his health as if almost to excuse himself. The charm and courtesy having been re-assumed, respect within the diocese re-appeared. Du Plessis planned a further assault, but this time on political power. His démarche, no doubt guided by his brother Henri, was, as by now we might expect, not without risk.

Late in 1611, du Plessis attempted to secure election by the ecclesiastical province of Bordeaux to the assembly of the clergy which was to meet in Paris in May of the following year, writing twice to François de Sourdis, the cardinal archbishop of Bordeaux, and sending his friend Sébastien Bouthillier, now a canon of the Luçon chapter, to plead his cause. Du Plessis was not successful, although Bouthillier was himself elected to represent the lower clergy. Du Plessis had a lawsuit concerning episcopal revenues before the *parlement,* and was in Paris again early in 1612. He may

also in March 1612, a month during which du Plessis is known to
have preached before the court, have attended du Perron's council
at Sens called to condemn the forthright gallicanism of Edmond
Richer, head ('syndic') of the theology faculty since 1608, who
was aggressively determined to extend the claims of the French
church to autonomy from Rome.

Du Plessis appears to have left Paris suddenly, cancelling a
preaching engagement at the Louvre on Easter Sunday, presumably
to report on the threat of rebellion under the Huguenot military
leader Rohan, married to Sully's daughter. His brief return to
Paris in 1613, ostensibly to renegotiate with the Anglican divines
the terms of Richard Smith's appointment to his service, obviously
allowed him to reappear at court. He may have seen Concini. On
2 October 1614 the majority of Louis XIII was to be proclaimed at
a *lit de justice* within days of his thirteenth birthday. Mayenne, the
last great leader of the League, had died in 1611, and Soissons, the
youngest of Henri IV's cousins, in 1612. Late in 1611 the second
son of Marie de' Medici had died at the age of four. That left her
third son, Gaston, born in 1608, as heir presumptive until Louis
XIII should have direct male issue, with Condé, most disaffected
of the princes, second in line to the throne.[19] The continuation
of that situation until the birth of the future Louis XIV in 1638
was to exercise a determining influence on Richelieu's career and
policies.

In February 1614 du Plessis made his bid for political influence
by writing a letter of wholehearted support to Concini. The risks
he was running were great. There was still a serious chance
that Marie de' Medici would lose the regency to Condé, that
the country would be riven by civil war, or at least that the
scandalous advancement of so obvious a small-time adventurer
on the make as Concini, now a marshal of France, and the
ascendancy at court of someone so lacking in birth, upbringing,
moral or intellectual elevation, and personal distinction, would be
regarded as too intolerable to be sustained.

Du Plessis appears not so much to have aligned himself with
what he took to be the winning faction, as with the sovereign
endowed by divine anointment with the right to govern France.
The letter to Concini was a clear challenge to fortune, elegant,
daring, and not to be gainsaid if things went wrong, 'I ask you

only to accept that my promises will always be given effect, and that, while you continue to honour me with your affection, I shall devote myself worthily to your service.' Du Plessis was lucky. He was now to achieve the recognition he craved.

The princes, increasingly led by Condé, negotiated the treaty of Sainte-Ménéhould in May 1614, forcing Marie de' Medici to call a meeting of the Estates-General,[20] thereby humiliating her into submitting her administration to public scrutiny. She also had to pay the princes a large indemnity for their expenses in arming themselves against her, and to agree to the disbanding of her own forces in return for the dismissal of theirs. On 27 September Louis XIII reached his thirteenth birthday. The proclamation of his majority at Paris on 2 October automatically turned rebellion against him into high treason.[21] He charged his mother, Marie de' Medici, with continued responsibility for the administration of his kingdom. The regent had become the queen mother.

The Estates-General met in Paris at the end of October. La Rocheposay, helped by Duvergier, managed a successful campaign to have du Plessis elected to represent the clergy of Poitou. The first estate, the clergy, had 140 deputies, including five cardinals, seven archbishops and forty-seven bishops. The nobility were represented by 132 deputies, and the third estate by 192, of whom about a third belonged in fact to the nobility, while many of the rest possessed *seigneuries*. The simple peasantry was not actually represented at all.

The pressures on Richelieu were to increase, but from now on he gives no sign of any doubt about the congruence of his religious duty to support the king with his personal desire for wealth, recognition, power and preferment. He is clear that support for the king, still a semi-sacerdotal figure as well as temporal monarch, is his religious duty, and it is true that his loyalty to the king opened the path to great wealth and enormous political power. But his actions and attitudes subsequent to 1615 make apparent that ambition for power and wealth, even before 1615, was not likely to have been a motivation stronger than perceived duty. His father had managed well enough to reconcile dedication to duty with the path which, had he not suddenly died, would have led him to power and wealth.

Du Plessis was later to dismiss the Estates as merely a populist cloak with which to conceal the antecedent decisions of an elite. He might even have thought along those lines in 1614, but that did not mean that the Estates could not be useful to him. They could be exploited to prove his own usefulness to the clerical establishment which dominated the first estate, the cardinals and senior bishops.[22] Du Plessis, who had been considered for the opening address, was one of a number of bishops who negotiated with the representatives of the other two estates on behalf of the clergy, but his diplomatic missions were confined to minor issues, did not involve discussions with the court, and did not attract the attention of any of the foreign or domestic commentators.

It was on 15 January 1615 during the Estates that the marriage contract between Du Plessis's brother Henri, now *mestre de camp,* and Marguerite Guiot was signed in Paris. The fact that there were only two signatories for Henri, du Plessis and René de Vignerot, suggests that Henri's position at court was still too modest for him to afford much assistance to his brother in attaining his ambitions, but Du Plessis now found the break for which he had been looking. No doubt as a result of remaining publicly uncompromised over such issues as royal and papal sovereignties or the taxation of office-holders, and because he was *persona grata* with both the court and the most respected of the senior clergy, Sourdis and du Perron, du Plessis was able to secure for himself the task of making the final speech for the clergy on 23 February 1615, when he presented the clergy's *cahier* of petitions at the winding-up of the Estates.[23]

The fact that he spoke for more than an hour, depending for both views and arguments on widespread consultation and on the recorded intervention in the preceding debates by du Perron, but did not add anything identifiably original, confirms the view that what he sought was not change but some recognition for his own abilities. His most important points concerned the implementation of the decrees of the council of Trent in France.[24] He countered the gallican view that France's senior secular officials should not be appointed from the ranks of the clergy, liable to be too subject to Roman influence, and praised the queen mother, calling for restoration of the Catholic religion in Béarn, the native region of Henri IV. He also expressed approval of the marriage plans concluded with the Spanish royal house by which Louis XIII was to marry Anne of Austria, the Spanish infanta, while the elder of his younger sisters, Elisabeth, was to marry not the prince of Piedmont, to whom she had been promised, but the eldest son of the king of Spain, in due course to become Philip IV of Spain.

The princes had foolishly, but not quite incredibly, expected the estates to rise up against Marie de' Medici and her Italian favourite, and to prefer the old model of a council of nobles. They did not corporately realise how odious feudal social arrangements had become to the new bourgeoisie, and they did not corporately understand that they were in consequence provoking the legitimisation of a model for centralised power which would lead France into monarchical absolutism for almost two centuries.

On 24 March 1615, the chancellor delivered the crown's reply to the *cahiers* of the three estates. He announced the abolition of the sale and inheritance of offices, and the *droits annuels,* the tax payable annually by office-holders estimated to yield one and a half million livres, and thereby infuriated the sovereign courts, which depended on the stability of office-holding, and hence on the monetary value of hereditable offices. The number of pensions which were driving France into bankruptcy was to be reduced, and a new *chambre de justice* to investigate and control tax contracts was to be set up. It was not enough to satisfy the public. The higher nobility, with the notable exception of Guise, dispersed only to conspire against Marie de' Medici.[25]

In other ways the royal reaction to the estates' *cahiers* had been too much. On 13 May, in view of the reaction of the magistracy, the sale and inheritance of offices was restored with the *droits annuels* until at least the end of 1617. The *parlement* had already decided to make further representations, which contained an outright attack on Concini, and amounted almost to a factitious alliance with Condé, who in fact despised the *parlement,* in calling for a meeting of peers. The *conseil d'état* replied by reminding the *parlement* that its functions were merely judicial. It had no executive role, or right to express political opinions. And on 31 July 1615 Concini, now maréchal d'Ancre, was charged with suppressing the rebellion of the princes.

Condé now formed an alliance with the Huguenot leaders, and it was only the protection of the Guise army which allowed the queen mother to exchange her daughter for the Spanish infanta at the river Bidassoa, part of which demarcated the border between France and Spain. On the journey the court stayed for much of August and September at Poitiers, and was forced to leave the princess Elisabeth, who was ill, in du Plessis's care, affording the bishop ample opportunity to write a series of ingratiating letters to Marie de' Medici about her daughter's health. It was at this point that du Plessis, who had not attended the assembly of the clergy which met between May and August 1615, and was back at Coussay at the latest early in April, appears to have been promised the post of grand almoner to Anne of Austria. The promise was formally confirmed in November. The emoluments were only 300 livres, but the duties were not onerous, and the post established for its holder some footing at court.

The point has been made that the appointment indicates the only modest esteem in which du Plessis was held, since the post of grand almoner to Marie de' Medici herself was being kept vacant after the dismissal of cardinal Bonzi in 1615. It seems more likely that du Plessis was appointed to the household of Anne of Austria because, the post being newly created, no incumbent needed to be paid for it. In 1617 du Plessis was to sell the office of grand almoner to Sébastien Zamet, then bishop of Langres, for 60,000 livres in cash and goods worth in excess of 10,000 livres, using most of the proceeds to provide over three quarters of the dowry of his sister, Nicole, now twenty-nine, for her marriage to the marquis de Brézé in January 1618.[26]

The court stopped briefly again at Poitiers on the way back from the Spanish border in January 1616, but du Plessis played no part in the negotiations between the court and Condé which took place between February and May at Loudun, quite close to the Richelieu estate. Père Joseph, who had entered secular political life by mediating in 1615 between Condé and Marie de' Medici, was involved in the negotiations, and no doubt kept du Plessis informed of their progress. Du Plessis did follow the court back to Paris in May, after it had stayed at Tours and Blois, but in the first two months of 1616 du Plessis, or perhaps Henri, was complaining about the damage done to the family properties by Condé's forces.

Talks between Condé and the government, conducted by Villeroy, the secretary of state, took place between February and May 1616 and led to the treaty of Loudun of 3 May 1616 with terms favourable to Condé. Villeroy had in particular agreed to Condé's demand that Concini be removed from the post of lieutenant-general of Picardy and governor of Amiens and that Condé should himself be rewarded with one and a half million livres, a place on the council, Berry, and the fortress of Bourges. Concini immediately stripped Villeroy of his post as councillor, although it took from June to 9 August to relieve him of his functions.

Late in May du Plessis was made a *conseiller d'état,* an office for which he probably also did not pay, since it still technically belonged to Villeroy. On 16 May the chancellor, Sillery, who could not constitutionally be dismissed, was forced to hand over the seals, normally in the chancellor's custody, to Guillaume du Vair, a noted orator and neostoic moralist who had been rewarded by Henri IV in 1596 with the governorship of Provence. Puysieux, the chancellor's son, lost his position as secretary of state for foreign affairs.

These measures much strengthened Concini's position. He was appointed lieutenant-general in Normandy, of which Marie de' Medici was herself governor, and governor of Caen and Pont de l'Arche, with a *douceur* of 300,000 livres. When Condé moved to Paris in late July of 1616 and quickly dominated the council, his popularity, partly a function of the widespread detestation of Concini, was such as to make him a serious rival of Marie de' Medici for power. However, Condé lacked strong political allies, since the princes did not trust one another and, following the advice of Claude Barbin, the new *contrôleur-général des finances,* the queen mother had him arrested on 1 September. He was not to be released until October 1619.[27]

The queen mother then continued to rid herself of the advisers inherited from Henri IV, dismissing even du Vair on 25 November. The way had become clear for Concini to have his own team appointed. It included the bishop of Luçon, who had already since June been successfully negotiating with Condé on behalf of the court, and who by now had a residence in Paris in the rue des Mauvaises Paroles. The regent's promise of a significant role in the king's council had been kept.[28]

When the seals were taken from du Vair on 25 November, du

Plessis took over the vacated secretaryship of state and was given nominal responsibility for foreign affairs and war. This afforded him 17,000 livres, to which must be added the 2,000 livres he received as a member of the king's council, and a 6,000-livre special pension added by the king.[29] The Venetians, the Spaniards and the English ambassador thought the appointment a victory for the Spaniards and the pope, such was the association in their minds between du Plessis and the political wing of the leading figures of the Catholic revival, although du Plessis himself was determined to appear impartial in his attitude to both Spaniards and Huguenots. Although he was the most junior member of the council, he successfully insisted on an episcopal right of precedence.

As a minister, du Plessis was sensitive to France's interests in north Italy, but otherwise intent on promoting peace. He offered France's mediation in a variety of disputes, but was rebuffed by both Venetians and Savoyards unwilling to believe in the strength or stability of Concini's administration, and preferring other avenues of negotiation. There was also little he could do to prevent compensation prejudicial to the interests of France for the Spanish Habsburgs in return for their allowing the imperial crown to pass to Ferdinand of Styria and the Austrian Habsburg line. His principal task was reduced to reassuring neighbouring powers that the French regime remained open-minded, that the Spanish marriages did not mean a shared foreign policy, and to dissuading foreign Huguenot supporters from allowing mercenaries to be raised abroad by the French Huguenots.

Du Plessis probably wrote the king's letter of 17 January 1617, after the dissident princes had begun to assemble armies, in reply to a manifesto by Mayenne. The *Declaration du roy sur le subject des nouveaux remuemens de son royaume* of mid-February was certainly by du Plessis. Both pamphlets take their stand aggressively not on argument, but on absolute royal authority, the mystical quality investing legitimate monarchs. No open rift between the still adolescent king and his mother had yet appeared, although Louis XIII's dislike of Concini was becoming obvious.

However much du Plessis might have wanted recognition, wealth and a chance to exercise his talents, he was committing himself to establishing *de facto* the *de iure* authority of the legitimate monarch, whose personal inadequacies must already have been becoming clear to him. To that end early in 1617 he was correctly cultivating Claude Barbin, the *contrôleur-général des finances* who had persuaded him not to resign the Luçon see on his ministerial appointment of 1616, as Concini wanted, since the resignation would obviously make him uniquely dependent on Concini himself.

Concini, prickly and imperious, did not personally attempt greatly to interfere with the political decisions taken in the entourage of the queen mother. His interests were in money and power, not administration, and for much of early 1617 he was in Normandy. Du Plessis, providing he avoided giving overt offence to Concini, had a reasonably free hand, although the *Mémoires* reveal that he found Concini's moods tiresome, and it is not unlikely that, as some sources suggest, he and Barbin vainly sought permission from Marie de' Medici to resign.[30] At this date, perhaps still in order genuinely to serve the king, du Plessis made strenuous efforts to bring the three royal armies up to strength to confront the princes, and he was able to use his brother to convey the king's instruction to Montigny in charge in the Nivernais.

The nobles had started again to raise troops against Concini in January 1617. Some of them assembled at Soissons, Bouillon on 6 January 1617, and Nevers later that month. They were joined by Vendôme and Mayenne. But pacificatory sounds came from Marie de' Medici. No general uprising ensued, and the nobles came back to court after manifestos, protestations and parades of strength on both sides. Some of the declarations signed by the king were both written by du Plessis and, as secretary of state, also counter-signed by him.

Concini might still have survived, had it not been for the sudden rise of the duc de Luynes, the king's falconer, and the encouragement he gave to the young king, whose model, friend and intimate companion he had speedily become. The fifteen-year-old Louis XIII, prompted by the thirty-nine-year old Luynes, ordered the arrest of Concini in a *coup d'état* of 24 April 1617.

Concini was to have been tried by the *parlement*, but he was shot 'resisting arrest' in the head at close range by three pistol shots fired by the Marquis de Vitry, captain of the guards, and two other known officers, who then stabbed him and kicked his body aside.[31] Louis XIII wanted the body exhibited on a gibbet but, after a secret burial at Saint-Germain l'Auxerrois, it was disinterred by the crowd, castrated, pulled to pieces, and bits of it were burnt, thrown to dogs, and stuck on to pykes. Vitry was given Concini's post as marshal later in 1617.

Léonora Galigaï, brutally arrested weeping in bed and bundled to the Bastille, was indicted for treason with Claude Barbin. Léonora Galigaï was found guilty, with her dead husband, of *lèse-majesté*,[32] largely on account of the huge financial benefits that had accrued to her husband and herself and been partly transferred out of the kingdom rather than for any specific illegalities, but also for exercising a sorcerer's maleficent influence on Marie de' Medici. She was beheaded on the day of her condemnation, 8 August 1617, and her wealth, like her husband's, confiscated to the crown.[33]

Louis XIII almost immediately donated it to Luynes, ostensibly as a reimbursement of loans. Barbin's trial was transferred to the *grand conseil,* and, although found guilty of treason, he was condemned with comparative leniency only to confiscation of goods and exile abroad. He had to sell his office of *intendant-général de la reine,* and was still being held in the Bastille in October 1619. The assassination of Concini was the act by which the young king, who was entirely under the sway of Luynes, seized power from his mother.

Léonora Galigaï was accused at her trial of procuring for du Plessis the post of grand almoner to Anne of Austria. It is not improbable that she did, although there is no evidence.[34] The general tone of obsequiousness, and later of gratitude, in du Plessis's relationship with the volatile Concini had persisted, but in order to explain the inclusion by Concini of du Plessis in his ministry of November 1616, some role must be assumed to have been played by the well-connected Henri. What it was has never been unravelled, but it would not be surprising if Henri had energetically furthered his brother's cause with the queen mother rather than with Concini or his wife. Henri had served Marie de' Medici on the 1610 mission to Lorraine, and again in a military role against Condé in 1615, and he is known to have looked with pleasure on his brother's appointment as almoner to Anne of Austria. Although apparently without any official appointment in the entourage of Marie de' Medici, du Plessis had since the autumn of 1616 also been acting as a senior official in her household.

It was Luynes who saved du Plessis from immediate dismissal by the king in the general hysteria immediately following Concini's assassination. The king was standing on a billiard table and had shouted du Plessis's dismissal at him, when Luynes spoke in his favour.[35] Du Plessis was more fully disgraced than he immediately realised. The king sent him to attend the council, where it was made clear to him by those of Henri IV's advisors to have survived that he was no longer welcome. It was in effect a dismissal.

Villeroy, Sillery, Puysieux, Jeannin and du Vair were recalled. The armies dispersed, and the nobles drifted back to court to be amnestied by the king, now openly hostile to his mother, with whom he would not communicate for nine days, during which she was shut in the Louvre. Du Plessis's offer to act as a go-between was accepted, and it was his usefulness in negotiating the conditions for her internal exile which postponed and mitigated his own fate. It was agreed that Marie de' Medici should retire with a small entourage to Blois, and that Barbin's life should be spared. Luynes wanted du Plessis to act as court informant from the entourage of the queen mother, and thought he had a title to du Plessis's gratitude, although Richelieu was to contribute much to his later vilification.

The queen mother left for Blois and exile on 3 May 1617, in political disgrace on account of her patronage of Concini and her hostility to the princes, but retaining her offices, income and the governorship of Normandy. As she left, the king made an embarrassed formal farewell. Du Plessis was in the last carriage of her party. With the court's approval, he was to be made president of her council, keeper of her seal and intendant, in the hope of effecting a reconciliation, although he did not succeed in the risky attempt to dominate her Italianate entourage, and he was not alone in the ambition to be chief mediator between the queen mother and all other parties. Furthermore, any reconciliation between the king and the queen mother would necessarily endanger the position, and perhaps even the life, of Luynes. It would not easily be effected.

Du Plessis was genuinely concerned to promote and protect royal authority, and that for the moment meant co-operating with Luynes, to whom he started by faithfully reporting. He was sensitive to his vulnerability to the intrigues at the queen mother's court, and the threats he perceived in all directions were he to be toppled from his tightrope provoked in him shrill outbursts of near-paranoia unrecorded of him either earlier or later.

The queen mother disliked being spied on, and the king's court had no confidence that du Plessis would not attempt to make himself the impresario of a come-back. Genuine hostility to him at Blois pushed him to the point of panic, and there are signs of self-pity in the letters. On 11 June he left suddenly for Coussay, wrongly alerted by his brother Henri that a coup against him was to be attempted. He probably hoped that, should the alarm prove to be false, he could quickly return, ostensibly after a brief absence on business or recuperation. The queen mother did urgently invite him to return, but he had made it too easy for others to remove him. The king wrote on 15 June commending him for returning to his pastoral duties and commanding him to stay in his diocese.

Du Plessis, never slow to spot an opportunity, now undertook to refute a Huguenot reply of mid-July to a series of court sermons preached by the Jesuit Père Arnoux and dedicated to the king. His 1617 polemical *Principaux points de la foy de l'église catholique défendus contre l'escrit addressé au Roy par des quatres Ministres de Charenton* is a response to the letter addressed to Louis XIII by the Huguenot ministers of Charenton. It shows du Plessis to be modelling himself consciously on cardinal du Perron, but the most important feature of the work is its focus on the falsity of the contention that the Huguenots were loyal to the French monarchy. Their most serious fault in his eyes was already political. Du Plessis was thanked by the Jesuits and congratulated by the Sorbonne.

It took him six weeks to produce the *Principaux points de la foy catholique,* which he also dedicated to the king,[36] insisting above all on obedience to the king as God's anointed ruler and to the Catholic adherence to that doctrine. It was the key to attitudes which have often puzzled commentators, but which were at once political and religious, as attitudes had so often been during the days of the League, and continued to remain during the Catholic revival. The anointing of a secular sovereign was not at all, in the early seventeenth century, merely symbolic of the sacerdotal function which the rite conferred, but was itself the bestowal of divine spiritual authority.

The queen mother softened her resentment at du Plessis's desertion, and at Henri's role in it, and asked Luynes to allow him to return to her. Du Plessis wrote a series of excessively deferential letters to Louis XIII and undertook a series of other approaches, partly through Père Joseph, which simply irritated the king's court, still unnecessarily afraid that du Plessis could broker an alliance between the queen mother and Condé. Du Plessis had some grounds for reiterating his stream of complaints that his principles were not understood. They were in their practical, applied way not only as religious, but as mystically rooted as those of Père Joseph, Bérulle, Vincent de Paul and François de Sales.[37]

On 26 October 1617 du Plessis was ordered from Coussay to Luçon. He removed his possessions from Blois, rented a residence belonging to the Luçon chapter, and resided in his diocese from November 1617 until April 1618, negotiating for preachers, for the seminary, and for a hospice with Bérulle and the Capuchins. In February du Plessis's brother Henri and his brother-in-law, René de Vignerot, who had been handling du Plessis's business and keeping him informed of events in Paris, were ordered back to their estates. On 7 April 1618, after Rome had been considered and discarded as offering too much scope for intrigue, they were ordered with du Plessis himself to the papal enclave at Avignon. The *Mémoires* improbably attribute that move to various intrigues, but it is more likely to have reflected Luynes's persistent fear that du Plessis might become an agent in the rehabilitation of the queen mother, now under close military surveillance at Blois. Luynes was controlling membership of her household.

Du Plessis left Luçon hurriedly on Good Friday, and took a month to get across France. The papal curia had not been consulted, obviously disliked the removal by the secular power of a bishop from his diocese, and feared that it might itself be drawn into France's internal domestic quarrels. Rome, like Paris, broadly but wrongly suspected du Plessis of real or potential conspiracy.

It has been said that du Plessis's strident attempts at self-justification exacerbated Luynes and made du Plessis the architect of his own further disgrace after a period of relative grace during the period immediately following the *coup d'état*. His behaviour was certainly found irritating and met with suspicion, but in fact it was made necessary by the need he felt to vindicate his principles. He was not intriguing against the king. At no time had he betrayed his patriotic and religious duty to work for the true

interests of the divinely ratified monarch, and of that of those who
served him.

On 15 October 1618 Henri lost his wife, whom he had had to
leave behind at Richelieu, giving birth to his son, who died on 8
December. The court had taken seven months to grant his request
to return to care for her and the infant son whom he was never
to see. After the deaths, he wrote a will leaving virtually his whole
estate to a variety of religious orders, which he was to revoke a
few days before his own death the following year. Both brothers
had seen their ambitions crumble. They were in their mid- to late
thirties, and no prospect was on the horizon. Each of them had
reached his moment of deepest despondency, and there appeared
to be nothing to hope for.

All three of the exiles, du Plessis, Henri and René de Vignerot,
had made frequent requests for permission to return home for
short periods. Both Henri and René de Vignerot eventually had
their requests granted. One day, perhaps, permission for the
bishop of Luçon to return to his pastoral duties could usefully
be employed by the court as a bargaining counter to extract a
favour from Rome. Meanwhile du Plessis, whose letters to the
chapter at Luçon themselves began to show a new spiritual fervour,
completed at Avignon the *Instruction du Chrestien,* his most important
pastoral work, begun about 1609. He also made a will, leaving his
silver to the cathedral at Luçon and his library and 1,000 livres to
the seminary.

4

Rehabilitation and Red Hat

Du Plessis's career was at its nadir early in 1619, even if his disgrace, like that of the queen mother, was relatively mild. He was thirty-four. The court, dismissively referring to him as 'Luçon', was mentally reducing his status to that merely of a provincial bishop. He had been useful for a few weeks in helping to settle the queen mother into exile, but both that activity and the association with Concini also made him suspect, a possible dissident, and potentially a political danger to Luynes, who was systematically humiliating Marie de' Medici. Although the threat that he represented to Luynes seemed slight, and counter-balanced by the possibility that he could be useful in any negotiations which might be necessary with Marie de' Medici, du Plessis could usefully be parked at Avignon and forgotten about.

We have only superficial clues about his state of mind. Du Plessis had at Luçon thrown himself into his role as reforming bishop, devotional writer and Catholic controversialist. Even after the setback which had brought him to Avignon, he might realistically have hoped for a distinguished career as an ecclesiastic. The disgrace was real, however, and the repeated rejections of his requests to be allowed to return were dispiriting. He had after all tasted the satisfactions afforded by admission to the *conseil d'état* and experience had shown him that he possessed practical skills in both politics and diplomacy of a higher order than he had exhibited when he had first urged his services on the newly widowed regent. He must on the other hand have known that the exile, which was unlikely to be permanent, still left him with a range of choices.

There had been no confiscations, and the worst du Plessis could expect was to be sidelined until Luynes's distrust evaporated, as it surely would, perhaps after an eventual reconciliation between the queen mother and her son. Even if Luynes was likely to oppose du Plessis's return for any foreseeable future, the pope was not going for ever to acquiesce in the exile of a bishop which prevented him from exercising his pastoral responsibilities, particularly in view of the exalted position which du Plessis, however briefly, had played in his country's affairs, and his open advocacy of the Tridentine reforms. There would eventually have to be a negotiation.

The indiscriminate way in which du Plessis had fired off gloomy letters from Luçon before the exile to Avignon denoted determination as well as need for support and, if possible, mediation. The nuncio reported to Rome du Plessis's loss of authority at court, and Paul V had shown signs of sympathy, if not of action. Du Plessis was noted for the enthusiasm of his pastoral and polemical activities. He had recently in the 1618 *Principaux points* published an eirenic, perceptive and highly esteemed account of the religious situation in France and its roots in theology and jurisprudence, defending the view that religious toleration should be restrained at the point at which dissent leads to political action. He was sufficiently removed from despair at Avignon to continue his pastoral work by writing the *Instruction du Chrestien*.

As had been intended from the beginning, the almonership to the new queen, itself a sinecure, had facilitated an important political position in the entourage of the young king's mother. Although Marie de' Medici had at first resented what she took to be du Plessis's desertion in June 1617, she had relented, and it must have been obvious to him that the fixation on Luynes of the youthful monarch he knew to be violent and unstable would not last. Ultimately a reconciliation between the queen mother and her son, opening the way for his own return, seemed more than likely. If for the moment there was no immediate tangible hope of continued political or ecclesiastical preferment, the worst thing about du Plessis's situation was the frustration imposed by the need for patience.

Then, on 22 February 1619, Marie de' Medici escaped from Blois. The plot was conceived by one of her Italian attendants, Ruccellaï, who invited the former favourite of Henri III, Epernon, now sixty-five, to lead a rebellion against Luynes to reinstate the queen mother. Louis XIII was still only seventeen. The escape was like an episode in a Dumas novel, and still has the astonishing air of one of those *coups de théâtre* which, throughout Richelieu's career, suddenly changed the apparently predictable course of future events.

In February 1619 Epernon left the town of Metz for the Angoulême district. He was governor of both. In Angoulême he raised a cavalry troop which he took to Loches, where there was a defendable fortress about sixty kilometres from Blois. At Blois one of Epernon's men put a ladder from the road against the cliff face of the château, leading as far as the rampart, and then a second from the rampart to the queen mother's room, 120 feet above the road.

The portly forty-five-year-old clambered out of her window, and down the ladder to the rampart, but could not face the second and steeper ladder. A slide, with cords attached to a cloak, was improvised. Marie de' Medici was got down and, accompanied by two of Epernon's men, walked the few hundred metres to the Loire bridge. They passed soldiers going the opposite way who took her for a prostitute with a pair of clients, before they safely joined Epernon and his son La Valette, the archbishop of Toulouse, with a hundred and fifty horsemen.

The court was at Saint-Germain and panicked at the possibility that the *grands*, as the mostly dissident nobles were called, might move towards civil war, or that there might be a Huguenot rising, or that Spain would throw itself behind the queen mother, or that more than one of these things might happen, spontaneously or in concert. Louis XIII wanted to capture his mother by force, but Luynes insisted on a less violent approach, and wanted to send du Plessis's dean, Bouthillier, to control Marie de' Medici. Bouthillier asked for du Plessis to be allowed to help, and Luynes, finally persuaded that du Plessis had not counselled the queen mother to rebellion, consented. Père Joseph, like Bouthillier, had been active in du Plessis's interests during the exile, and it was the Capuchin's brother, Charles du Tremblay, who took to Avignon the royal

command for du Plessis to resume his functions at Angoulême
in the entourage of the queen mother. Du Tremblay arrived at
Avignon on 7 March.

Du Plessis left immediately, was briefly arrested by the governor
of Lyons, unaware of what was happening, and had arrived at
Angoulême by 27 March. Bouthillier and the Jesuit confessor of
Marie de' Medici had already visited her, and had been followed by
a delegation consisting of Philippe de Béthune, younger brother of
Sully, and Bérulle, vainly charged with distancing the queen mother
from Epernon. Instead, she wrote a series of letters to her son
justifying her escape, and giving her views about the government
of the kingdom. The court nevertheless found it possible to regard
her escape as an abduction by Epernon, which allowed them to
negotiate with her.[1]

When du Plessis arrived, he went straight to Epernon, who was
by then looking for a political ally against Ruccellaï. Epernon took
du Plessis to the queen mother, whose entourage regarded him
with suspicion. They had remained with her at Blois, and had
had to endure accusations of treachery, whereas du Plessis now
came as an envoy from Luynes and the opposing camp. As a
diplomat, however, he was the only professional among them,
and he was invited to join the queen's council and given the seals.
Ruccellaï disliked the immediate ascendancy of du Plessis, and to
Epernon's pleasure walked out when du Plessis said that he would
have given the queen advice different from that which she had had
from him.

Seconded by Bérulle, du Plessis quickly negotiated an agreement
which neither abandoned Epernon nor renounced the hope of the
queen mother's eventual return to court. It was signed on 12 May,
and gave Marie de' Medici the right to a 'place of safety', for which
she had to surrender Normandy and accept the governorship of
land-locked Anjou and of the towns of Angers, Chinon and
Ponts-de-Cé. They were of strategic importance on account of
their bridges across the Loire, but du Plessis would have preferred
her to have been given Nantes, offering possible escape by sea.

Du Plessis then encouraged Marie de' Medici by concluding a
memorandum with the statement that, if she lived without intrigue
in her chosen place but was still persecuted, he would then be
foremost among those arguing that France's government was being

sacrificed to private interests, with the implication that the king would thereby have forfeited his authority. That memorandum is important partly because it assuaged bellicose sentiments in the queen mother's entourage, and partly because it shows that du Plessis, far from being a power-hungry conspirator, was ensuring that, before implementing his undertaking to abandon dedication to the mystically constituted monarch, the continued unwarranted persecution would have given him a morally valid reason for doing so.

There had been clashes between the du Plessis party, now firmly in charge, and the queen mother's old entourage at Blois. Du Plessis arranged for his brother Henri to be made governor of Angers in place of a close friend of Ruccellaï. Another of Ruccellaï's associates, Charles de Lauzières, younger brother of Antoine, marquis de Thémines, captain of the queen's guards and equally angered at the appointment of Henri to Angers in place of his own elder brother, provoked Henri during a casual street encounter on 8 July. Swords were drawn, and in what was as much a brawl as a duel, Henri was mortally wounded.[2]

Richelieu, as du Plessis now became, was deeply distressed at Henri's death both at the time and for the rest of his life. For a while he even thought seriously of turning away from politics. In the short term, however, he turned to his family, not so much to advance their stations as because he badly needed support from those he could trust. Richelieu remained publicly deferential to Epernon, but swiftly replaced Ruccellaï, Thémines and other Blois relics of the Concini era with his own relations, friends and others on whom he knew he could rely. Amador de la Porte was made governor of Angers, and Richelieu's sister Nicole's husband, Brézé, captain of the guards, from which post he was to be promoted in steps to become a marshal of France.

What could by this date be seen unequivocally as the political Catholic party in France urgently favoured a reconciliation between Marie de' Medici and Louis XIII.[3] Its most active member was Bérulle, but it also included Père Joseph and the Jesuit confessors to Marie de' Medici and Louis XIII, Père Arnoux and Père Suffren. The reconciliation was symbolically sealed by a carefully engineered but emotionally frigid meeting between mother and son at Couzières, near Tours, in September 1619.[4] Meanwhile Richelieu was coming to play an increasingly important role in the affairs of the queen mother, winning concessions from the court on detailed matters of money, offices and garrisons, and establishing for himself the political base which he had hitherto lacked in the domination of the queen mother's affairs, appointments, policies and expenditure.

Richelieu's *Mémoires* blame on Luynes both the continued failure of Marie de' Medici and her son to reach an agreement which gave the queen mother a share in government, and also the continued suspicion under which Richelieu himself laboured. They do, however, contain more special pleading than reliable information. There was a delay in paying off the queen mother's debts which delayed a final settlement, and both the appointment of a new governor for Gaston, her second surviving son, and the marriage of her daughter Christina to Victor Amadeus I, duke of Savoy, seem to have been decided without reference to her. In all three matters, Marie de' Medici may well, however, herself have been to blame. But it was the release of Condé from Vincennes, where he had been moved on 15 September 1617, and his absolution from all blame in October 1619, which really irked her exiled court and the *grands*, since it left Marie de' Medici stained with abuse of power for imprisoning him in 1616.

Luynes had been created duke and peer by an emotionally and politically dependent seventeen-year-old king in August 1619, and his brothers were made peers soon afterwards, following on hugely beneficial marriages, and the appointment of one of them, Cadenet, as a marshal of France, a minister and *intendant des finances*.[5] From April 1620, the *grands* increasingly rallied in support of Marie de' Medici, whose court had settled at Angers. Condé was the new and belligerent ally of Luynes, who tried to counter the defection of the *grands* by bringing three of them, Guise, Nevers and Bellegarde, into the council.

As tension between the king and his mother escalated rather than died down, Luynes offered concessions, but classically too little and, above all, too late. He also instructed his emissaries to Angers to pin the blame on Richelieu for the rejection of the proferred concessions as inadequate. Richelieu was still striving for a full reconciliation. His exhortation to Marie de' Medici not to oppose her son seems to have been authentic and sincere,[6] but her failure to take his advice only resigned him to the inevitability of the armed engagement to come. He therefore put in place the necessary finance, partly by having crown revenues seized, and may well have exercised some of the skills in military generalship whose development his change of vocation in 1603 had denied him. The Huguenots, in whose interest a rebellion lay, sought to participate in any conflict between mother and son. This prospect alarmed the clerical party, and cardinal du Perron led an impressive delegation of clergy to Angers, seeking to avert a serious armed clash.

It was the king, now eighteen, with the encouragement of Condé and in spite of the hesitations of Luynes, who decided at a council meeting on 4 July to use arms against his mother to quell dissidence in Normandy. It was his first intervention in council. Rouen and Caen fell without an engagement, and the king, leading his troops, turned to Angers, where his forces won an untidy skirmish in stifling heat at Ponts-de-Cé on 7 August 1620. The queen mother's army of three thousand infantry, four hundred cavalry and three cannons was to be dispersed by the king's army on the following day in what was to become known as the *drôlerie* of Ponts-de-Cé. The chateau of Angers surrendered on 9 August, and on the following day the king and his mother concluded a peace treaty.

The king, with an army in existence and prompted by Bérulle, decided that this was the moment to incorporate into France the territory of Béarn, part of the buffer state of Navarre in the south-west where the edict of Nantes stipulating toleration did not apply, and which was linked to France only because they had a king in common. By September Louis was in Bordeaux, and on 14 October made his entry into Pau, capital of Béarn, from which he proclaimed the annexation of that part of Navarre north of the Pyrenees, including Béarn, which still remained outside France. Catholic worship was reinstated amid a flurry of triumphalist documents and procedures, but with the Huguenot pastors given pensions. By early November, Louis was back in Paris.

Negotiations with Marie de' Medici had continued, with Luynes more eager than ever for a peaceful settlement, although the queen mother was not accorded the place on the *conseil d'état* which she solicited, and she continued to maintain cordial relations with the Huguenot leader, Henri de Rohan, and his brother, Benjamin de Soubise, both of whom Luynes considered to be dangerous. Marie de' Medici and her son were formally reconciled, and the king adopted Richelieu as a French candidate for the sacred college, writing to request the red hat as early as 29 August 1620. In August 1620 Bouthillier was sent to Rome, possibly by Richelieu but with a mission endorsed by the king, to hasten negotiations. He swiftly realised that to further Richelieu's elevation, he had to present him otherwise than as a representative of the queen mother's camp in the struggle with her son, especially since Marie de' Medici, like her son and the nuncio, Corsini, judged it more important in late 1619 that La Valette, already once denied a red hat early in 1618, should be reinstated as France's prime candidate for membership of the sacred college, if only as a recompense for the services of La Valette's father, Epernon.[7] Louis indicated privately to Rome that the red hat requested for Richelieu had no urgent priority. In the end both La Valette and the nuncio Bentivoglio were elevated in Paul V's final creation, early in January 1621. It was to be September 1622 before Richelieu was finally made a cardinal.

Luynes had supported Richelieu, and to symbolize and cement the new relationship, the marriage was arranged of Luynes's nephew, the Sieur de Combalet, to Richelieu's favourite niece, Marie, daughter of his elder sister Françoise, the future duchesse d'Aiguillon. The wedding was celebrated with much ceremony at the Louvre in late November 1620. Marie de' Medici gave the bride a handsome present. Then, having successively been made *connétable* and keeper of the seals in the course of 1621, Luynes died suddenly of purple fever that December, precipitating another change of course in Richelieu's career.

Louis XIII, born within a year of the marriage of Henri IV and Marie de' Medici, was brought up not only with his father's other legitimate offspring, but also with his father's three illegitimate children by Gabrielle d'Estrées, who had died in 1599, two other illegitimate children by the marquise de Verneuil, one by the comtesse de Moret, and three by Charlotte des Essarts. The surviving mistresses and the divorced queen Marguerite lived at court with the new queen, Marie de' Medici. As his illegitimate siblings were born, Louis was informed, and made conscious very young of the distinction between legitimacy and illegitimacy, and of the fact that he was heir to the throne by right of birth.

He had an artistic temperament and an extreme sensibility which was feminine in character. Although he was highly strung, impetuous and wilful, and in consequence moody, ill-tempered, imperious and sometimes violent, the disastrous philosophy governing his childhood was based on character-formation by physical coercion. Often written off as merely the unenlightened attitude of the age, it was in fact abnormally brutal, the subject of serious contemporary critical comment, notably by the Venetian ambassador. Louis's father bullied him, thinking to develop his masculinity. From the age of two he was frequently beaten, sometimes by Henri IV himself. His governess, Mme de Montglat, was ordered to beat him as often as possible, and on 23 October 1604, when Louis was just three, we know that an enraged Louis scratched, kicked and hit her. It has been alleged that an enduring addiction to childhood pursuits constituted an early sign of psychological retardation. Louis certainly enjoyed making things, drawing pictures, writing music and shoeing horses as well as hawking.

All his life, Louis was subject to bouts of gastro-enteritis, and by his early twenties he had developed what is now thought to have been the tuberculosis from which he was eventually to die. The serious hypochondria which led him in one year to have himself bled 47 times, purged 215 times, and to take 212 medicines,[8] was parallelled by the damagingly obsessive scruples which infected his devotional life, and by a strongly masochistic tendency born of the feelings of inadequacy beaten in to him. Richelieu went so far as to say he had never seen the king ill other than as a result of emotional agitation.[9]

Louis was a potential athlete. Pluvinel's academy had turned him into an excellent horseman. He enjoyed hunting, aspired to military success, was inured to hardship and indifferent to danger in the field, was at ease with the common people, and was happiest when leading his armies. On the other hand, he was timidly uncertain of himself at court functions, stammered, and, no doubt because lacking in self-confidence, was obstinate, touchily suspicious, and proud, easily conquered by kindness but stiff-necked in the face of any challenge to his regal prerogatives.

The name by which history has sometimes known him, 'Louis le Juste', was invented, according to a letter of Malherbe, the leading court poet, of 17 October 1617, to avoid 'Louis the stammerer', which Malherbe would not have mentioned if he had not heard it used. Marie de' Medici, in spite of sporadic bouts of sentimentality, devastatingly failed to display any affection towards him. At the age of one month he was removed from Fontainebleau and taken to Saint-Germain-en-Laye, and he was six months old when, on 16 March 1602, he was first fondled by his mother. She clearly preferred her youngest son, Gaston. It was this, more than anything else, which accounted for Louis's tortured psychology, although it did not help that Concini treated him with contempt, wore a hat in his presence, had him beaten, sat on his throne and kept him short of money.

The psychology of Louis XIII is important not only to explain the vicissitudes of his relationship with Richelieu, on whom at one period he was also to become emotionally fixated, but also because the whole future of France depended on his ability to generate a male heir in the direct line. To appreciate the currents of European diplomacy in the first half of the seventeenth century, one does not have to subscribe to the Cleopatra's nose theory of history, as understood by Pascal when he suggested that it was a sign of our pettiness that Cleopatra's sexual attractions, symbolised by the length of her nose, changed the course of human history. The relatively trivial circumstance of the succession to the French throne of Gaston d'Orléans, or of any son of his, or failing which of a Condé, may not in retrospect much have changed the whole subsequent history of Europe's political arrangements. The identity of monarchs seldom does. It looked, however, at the time as if it might.

In August 1612 Marie de' Medici's ministers had agreed to the double marriage, between the king and Anne of Austria, the Spanish infanta, born five days before Louis on 22 September 1601, and between Louis's eldest sister and the future Philip IV, king of Spain, which took place by proxy in October 1615 at Bordeaux and Burgos and incidentally alarmed the United Provinces, the German princes and Venice. The princesses were exchanged with elaborate ceremony in the middle of the Bidassoa on 9 November and, as time passed, Louis XIII's failure to produce an heir with his wife, Anne of Austria, understandably gave rise to increasing anxiety.

Nothing written at the time of Louis's sexual activities and his emotional entanglements by the diarists and authors of *mémoires* is free of personal prejudice, and contemporary source material, often tinged by a detestation of Richelieu, is largely distorted by malicious gossip, or is too overtly protective of the royal reputation. Much material, including letters from the French court, or about it from ambassadors, was intended to create a specific effect outside France. There were, however, a whole series of generally older men for whom Louis formed firm attachments which, according to Tallemant's *historiette* of Louis XIII, went beyond the bounds of simple friendship:

'The king began to show affection for someone else starting with his coachman, Saint Amour. Afterwards he showed indulgence for Haran, keeper of the kennels. The Grand Prior of Vendôme, the commander de Souvray, and Montpouillan-la-Force, a young man of wit and warmth, but ugly and red-headed . . . were removed by the queen mother one after another. Finally came M. de Luynes. We have spoken of him elsewhere . . . We shall speak of the others as they come.'[10]

From adolescence therefore, Louis was prone at the very least to emotional fixations on men, often his seniors. Some of these obsessions were certainly tinged with masochism. Earlier biographers have argued that the pattern of Louis's life suggests that he could enjoy strong but platonic affection for women but that he never overcame a repugnance at the idea of physical intercourse either with his wife or with any other woman.

We know more about his sexual relationships than might be expected because of the extreme public importance that his marriage should be properly consummated, and that it should produce an heir. Until it was consummated, there was no sacramentally valid marriage, and the bond uniting France and Spain was not religiously forged. Spain demanded that the marriage should be consummated, Louis's contemporaries teased him about it, the *machismo* of court culture required it, and the establishment of a dynastic line and a national French identity depended on it. If there were no sacramental marriage, or even if no male heir were forthcoming, both Condé and Vendôme could eye the throne in the light of the dubious case made out to legitimise the annulment of Henri IV's first marriage.

Louis had given every indication of looking forward to the wedding, behaving with some bravado when it appeared that Condé's forces might prevent him from entering Bordeaux on the way to it. He had entered the city in full military apparel, with a bright-coloured scarf, at the head of a cavalry troop. But the wedding night in 1615 was traumatic. Bride and groom were scarcely fourteen, but political urgency dictated no delay, and Marie de' Medici was there to see that duty was done, taking her son to his wife's room herself.[11]

Héroard, Louis's doctor, tells us that he was there for two and a half hours, of which he slept for one, but that he said he had done his duty twice and had blood to show for it. Tallemant, always well informed but never entirely to be trusted, tells us that Louis had announced that he was merely 'going to piss into her body', and reports the widely repeated rumour that 'he produced nothing but clear water'. That he did not suffer from erectile dysfunction is also clear from one of Tallemant's coarser anecdotes that can be interpreted as asserting that the king derived sexual stimulation from being beaten.[12]

After the wedding night Louis slept alone, not even eating with his wife for six months, although calling on her each night before going to his room. Anne on the other hand was flirtatious, and enjoyed the company of male courtiers. After a year the Spaniards sent back the French retinue of Elisabeth, and the French retaliated by depriving Anne of her Spanish household, leaving her to make what she could of life at the French court.

It was not until Friday 25 January 1619 that Héroard reports of Louis:

> 'Put to bed. Prayed to God. At about eleven M de Luynes comes to persuade him to sleep with the queen. He resists strongly and resolutely, even crying, but is carried, put to bed, forces himself, as they say, but *haec omnia nec inscio* (these are things I know nothing about). At two o'clock he comes back . . .'[13]

This time, we have a formal letter from 'Frère Joseph, unworthy Capuchin' dated 14 February 1619 to an unknown addressee, but intended for the eyes of Philip III of Spain, in whose hand it is initialled 'seen':

'I beg your Reverence to allow me to rejoice with him at the happy outcome brought about by the achievement of a marriage ordained by God for the good of his church and his greater glory . . . The Most Christian[14] king passed the very day on which he had fulfilled his duty to the queen in great devotion, and in an emotional transport which God alone could produce . . . Their Majesties, on their knees beside the bed, prayed for a long time before going to bed. Several other things show clearly the work of God. The morning after that first night the king promised the queen in a vow that he would be faithful to her, and would never love any other woman.'

The Spaniards had not, it appears, been impressed by the reported exhibition by Marie de' Medici of the blood-stained sheet nearly four years earlier. From this point on Héroard puts into his diary 'significant numbers' whenever the king visits the queen, or when she comes to him. These enigmatic marks and numbers have been taken to indicate if, and sometimes how often, the king and queen made love. Even those historians who, perhaps precipitately, take this view of their meaning allow that marital relations between Louis and Anne were largely over by 1622, and entirely finished by 1626. Héroard died in 1628, but the diary peters out rather earlier. From 1622 it is scrappy and brief, with entries missing, but it is a privileged document, and it reads without exhibiting any obvious signs that details have been cosmeticised.

All that can be said is that Héroard's private information about what took place between king and queen when they are known to have been together has to have been supplied by one or other. Nothing said to have been reported by nurses or ladies-in-waiting left with the couple in a curtained bed can reasonably be trusted any more than Marie de' Medici's exhibition of the sheets. Louis was well aware of the pressures on him to produce a male heir, and no one doubts Anne's willingness at least in the period from 1619 to 1622, when she had a miscarriage on 16 March. Accounts of exactly how it happened vary, but Anne was playing some sort of game which involved racing, sliding and possibly jumping in the Louvre with Luynes's wife and one of Henri IV's illegitimate daughters. She fell heavily. Since she knew she was pregnant, and how important it was that she should come successfully to term, she was at best being preposterously negligent.

Historians have, not surprisingly, felt the force of a general consensus in interpreting the facts with an eye to maintaining the plausibility of Louis's paternity of the sons born to Anne in 1638 and 1640, of whom the first became Louis XIV. There was some cynicism at the time, and a questioning attitude has recently become again discernible. The argument that Louis XIV could have had no other father than Louis XIII, and therefore did not, is beginning to look thin. The question of whether someone other than Louis XIII was responsible for the pregnancies which resulted in Anne of Austria's miscarriages of 1622 and 1626 may also need to be re-opened. Some historians mention a series of miscarriages, gleaned mostly from court gossip collected by the memorialists, although there is no firm evidence for more than those two. The difficulty is that so much of the evidence that can be harvested from chronicles and memoirs reads like special pleading or a cover-up to protect belief in Louis XIII's paternity of Louis XIV.

Richelieu, whom some historians have suspected of being in love at different times with both Marie de' Medici and Anne, left, as might be expected, nothing at all to indicate any such feelings, and it is extremely unlikely that his intimacy with each in turn extended to any impropriety leading to an infringement of his sacerdotal obligations.[15] More important is how much he knew of the private affairs and even feelings of both queen mother and queen, even when he was no longer close to either, and how he used the knowledge that he possessed.

The relationship between Louis and his first chosen mentor, Luynes, became intense, and as early as the end of 1614 began to worry his mother and Concini. It was Luynes who persuaded Louis to take over his royal powers, first exercised in the decision to remove Concini and in the decision of 4 July 1620 to used armed force against Normandy.

Born in 1578, Luynes married Marie de Rohan, daughter of the Huguenot leader, only on 13 September 1617, several months after he had come to power. Always indecisive, he called back the ministers who had been in post at the assassination of Henri IV seven years earlier.

In 1620 Luynes had moved personally closer to Richelieu and the queen mother, although his support for Richelieu's cardinalate moderated during 1621, as he discovered the strength of the opposition in both France and Rome. Luynes took part, however half-heartedly, in the king's anti-Huguenot offensive of 1621 which the king regarded as a sacred duty, although he also clearly enjoyed cutting a dash at the head of his troops.

The king left Paris in late April 1621. Then, during the siege of Montauban, Luynes died on 15 December, and Louis was obliged to return home after failing to force Rohan to surrender the town. He arrived back in Paris late in January 1622, having shown both atrocious, if sporadic and off-hand, cruelty, as well as an occasional desire to be regarded as the merciful father of his people. Louis left Paris once more in March 1622 to sweep down the west coast, achieving the renewed successes which would leave the Huguenots with only La Rochelle and Montpellier. The siege of Nègrepelisse, where the citizenry had butchered a royal regiment quartered there, led to the worst atrocity of the war. Louis allowed his troops simply to sack the town because his royal dignity had been outraged.

During these king's campaigns, Richelieu had kept a resolutely low profile, and we know correspondingly little about his day-to-day activities. There is, however, evidence from the *Mémoires* and elsewhere, that he later became concerned to conceal what his attitudes and actions had been at this point in his career. He had established excellent relations with Luynes, appeared detached at being kept waiting for his red hat, and sent Louis de Marillac, a prominent councillor of the Paris *parlement,* as a permanent emissary to the peripatetic court, which was following the king. He had had time to negotiate the return to Paris of the queen mother and for her re-admission to the council. None the less, the queen mother was to be allowed to attend the council only on specified occasions, and she was not to confide in Richelieu concerning the king's business.

Richelieu's belief in policies of pacification and tolerance, and of confrontation with the Habsburgs rather than the Huguenots, underwent a setback when the Huguenot Soubise suddenly led a new rebellion in January 1622. With Luynes dead and the queen mother in active commerce with her son's Huguenot adversaries, Condé's hopes of leading a party against her, perhaps provoking another civil war, and of dominating the council looked as if they might be satisfied.

By the early summer of 1622, the tide had begun to turn. Luynes had been dead for six months. The court's considerable hostility to him had continued after his death, notably concentrated in such works as the 1622 *Chronique des favoris,* written by the fiercely anti-clerical, pro-Huguenot admirer of Henri IV, François Langlois de Fancan, a pamphleteer who supported and was subsequently employed by Richelieu. Pamphlets promoting or attacking individuals or policies were the ordinary means of drawing the attention of the literate public to issues about which those who had the means to employ pamphleteers, or the ability themselves to compose and publish pamphlets, felt strongly enough. They were normally sold in the streets and were often anonymous or pseudonymous, as well as frequently libellous.

Louis's suspiciousness of Condé increased, and he became friendlier to Richelieu, accepting his usefulness in controlling his mother's urges to regain political power. By the end of April, Richelieu was France's sole candidate for the cardinalate. The pope, now Gregory XV, promised that Richelieu would be included in the next promotion, and the announcement was made on 5 September. When Richelieu formally accepted the red hat from the king at Lyons in December, in the presence of the queen and the queen mother, he laid it at the feet of Marie de' Medici.

From 1620, Richelieu had envisaged his future as linked to that of Marie de' Medici. Indeed in 1621 it was recommended to him that he should renounce all personal political and ecclesiastical aspirations, to live as almoner to Marie de' Medici, seeking only to obtain satisfaction for her needs. It was not ambition that prevented him from following this advice. It would have meant renouncing the element of divine vocation in directly serving the anointed monarch in the constitution of a powerful and integrated France. He was nonetheless Marie de' Medici's *surintendant des finances* from 1619, her chaplain from 1621, and president of her council from 1623. In 1620, he had seen that his future excluded a return to pastoral work in his diocese. While it still seemed unsafe to resign his see, he did in 1620 seek to have his vicar-general made a suffragan, able to undertake full pastoral responsibility for the diocese. He himself finally resigned the Luçon see in May 1623, after the Tridentine decrees had been accepted in his diocese, and after his return to Paris with the queen mother, and her readmittance to the council.

Richelieu had been busy accumulating benefices since 1621, acquiring five abbacies by 1623, Saint-Benoit-sur-Loire, Redon, Pontlevoy, Notre-Dame du Vast and Saint-Pierre de Chalons.[16] Only Redon was in the gift of Marie de' Medici, and the Roman curia made no difficulties about authorising the necessary spiritual jurisdictions. There were other, lesser benefices, but Richelieu tripled his ecclesiastical income, and began investing in land. With the Richelieu name, he now inherited the family duties Henri had assumed, the Richelieu lands, and the estates and debts of both his father and his brother.[17] His first purchase was the *seigneurie* of Richelieu itself, auctioned off in February 1621 to satisfy his father's creditors. In early 1623 he bought for 270,000 livres the *comtés* of Limours and Montlhéry in the neighbourhood of Fontainebleau. The following year he bought the Paris house he was eventually to turn into the Palais-Cardinal. And in 1621 he made the first of his many and increasingly large investments in 'domain', a source of revenue consisting of estates, the revenue from the acquisition and disposal of offices, legal and other fees, tolls, sometimes hunting or wood-felling rights, and charges imposed when fiefs changed hands.

A pension of 10,000 livres a year was accorded to him by the crown shortly after his elevation to the sacred college, and by 1624 his income from all sources is estimated to have been around 85,000 livres, over three times its level three or four years previously. He began to acquire a reputation for a splendour, eventually to reach unprecedented proportions, but also for greed. Not only did his wealth increase, but so also did the extent of his interests. In 1622, on the death of Henri de Gondi, second cardinal de Retz, Richelieu applied for the position of *proviseur* of the Sorbonne, an office to which he was elected at meetings on 29 August and 2 September by members who were naturally aware of the proximate announcement of the cardinalate.

Richelieu took the office seriously, as he had taken seriously his episcopal obligations at Luçon. Although the college was only the principal meeting place of the teaching members of the theology faculty, 'la Sorbonne' had come to mean not only the college, but also the faculty, by no means all of whom were members of the college. The post of *proviseur* nevertheless conferred some degree of supervisory authority over the public teaching of theology in Paris outside the Jesuit Collège de Clermont,[18] esteemed by Richelieu and, like the Collège Royal, later the Collège de France, kept by him independent of the university.

Just as in the *Principaux points* Richelieu had distinguished between liberty of conscience and civil dissidence, so in his position as *proviseur* of the Sorbonne, he showed sensitivity to the distinction between his ecclesiastical authority, which did not as a cardinal include any formal ecclesiastical jurisdiction at all, and what was to become his civil jurisdiction as a minister. He took care in deciding in what guise to present which disputes for settlement by the jurisdiction he considered appropriate.

From the beginning Richelieu realised that religious discord was also a social and political issue as well as a doctrinal matter, while gallicanism raised theological as well as domestic political concerns. Richelieu's fastidious observance of the distinction between the two sovereignties, sacred and secular, and his ability to exploit it in the interest of creating a unified nation, were among the pillars of what in 1622 was still his coming political success.

When, for instance, the Jesuit Santerelli was condemned by the *parlement* for maintaining that the pope had the spiritual power to depose a temporal sovereign, Richelieu took the side of the *parlement*. Temporal sovereignty came directly from God through anointment in a ceremony in part scarcely distinguishable from an ordination. On the other hand Richelieu defended the Dominican Jean Testefort, censured by the theology faculty in 1626 for allowing too much power to the papal magisterium in interpreting the scriptures.[19] The teaching *magisterium* belonged exclusively to the spiritual sovereignty. In a way interesting for the relationship between secular and ecclesiastical authority even as late as this, Richelieu had the Sorbonne's theological censure against Testefort annulled not by Rome, but by letters patent signed by the king on 14 December on the grounds that the theology faculty, itself a secular, not an ecclesiastical body, had created civil discord.

Richelieu took a papalist stance, too, in the matter of the gallicanism of Edmond Richer, chair of the faculty. Supported by the *parlement,* terrified of any doctrine of the spiritual primacy which might lead to justifying such regicides as that of Henri IV, Richer had published in 1612 a *Libellus de ecclesiastica et politica potestate,* condemned in the same year by provincial synods at Sens and Aix. Controversy spluttered on as Richer's views flowed into a current of hostility to the regular clergy, and their exemption from diocesan supervision. The elderly Cardinal La Rochefoucauld, himself recently recruited to the king's council and partly responsible for ensuring that the king had a Jesuit confessor, was behind the appeal to Richelieu's intervention in February 1623.[20]

Richelieu, himself under attack by 1625 for anti-Habsburg policies and alliances with Protestant forces for political purposes, reacted by obtaining a decree from the council on 7 November 1626 which annulled a decree of the *parlement* of the 24 July and allowed the doctors of theology from the religious orders to vote in the faculty. Since they were overwhelmingly papalist in inclination, Richelieu was able to obtain on 27 December 1629 what amounted to a retractation from Richer, who said he had never meant to attack papal authority. It is again characteristic of Richelieu to keep firmly separate in his mind the issue of spiritual authority, on which he sided with the pope, and the objectives which made his alliance with foreign Protestants necessary for the protection of French interests in the purely temporal political order. As early as 1625 he had a pamphlet attacking the alliances as a betrayal of the church censured by the faculty.

During 1621 and 1622 Richelieu's headaches had got worse, and he showed symptoms of exhaustion, no doubt caused largely by the restraints he imposed on himself by the need he correctly perceived to keep the lowest possible political profile, undertaking only what could be passed off as domestic chores for the queen mother, and giving only what could be passed off as her opinions. Unhappily, all he could do as head of the queen mother's household and in the matter of his own advancement was not enough to absorb his nervous energy, although there was the building and decoration of the queen mother's Paris residence, the Luxembourg, to oversee.

That included the delicate matter of commissioning Rubens to paint his famous series of pictures celebrating the queen mother's life in such a way as to satisfy her greed for glory without being politically offensive to her son.

Richelieu was successful enough for the mistrust of his political ambitions to wane during the course of 1622. He admits in the *Mémoires* that he aspired to succeed to Henri de Gondi's place on the king's council when Gondi died in August 1622.[21] The need to appoint an ecclesiastic was generally agreed, but Richelieu had to be content with succeeding only to the cardinalate until the war-mongering anti-Huguenot policies now championed by Condé, from the beginning intent only on his own political aggrandisement, began to lose their persuasiveness. Condé had left the king's entourage for self-imposed exile in Italy even before the treaty of Montpellier of 18 October 1622 extricated Louis XIII and Rohan from situations from which they both sought to escape.

During the period of France's internal religious disputes, the Habsburgs, in apparent pursuit of European hegemony, had made serious inroads into France's external security. By the treaty of Paris of 7 February 1623, France allied with Venice and Savoy. The prospect of a renewed alliance with the Protestant Dutch was certainly discussed. The militantly anti-Huguenot strategy which had been advocated by Condé was being discredited, with the result that Condé's opponents were able to secure appointments to the council.

Marie de' Medici had returned to court and begun to regain confidence. Her relations with her son improved to the point at which little trace remained of the former hostilities. Foreign emissaries began to hope to use her influence, gradually discovering that her policy insights and advice had in fact been those of a self-effacing Richelieu, whose potential role in governing France in place of the 'greybeards', as they were called, became apparent to them. Louis XIII had meanwhile left the business of governing France to his ministers during the anti-Huguenot wars of 1621 to 1623, so that there was going to be a change of ministers as well as a change of policy.

Nicolas Sillery, the chancellor, and his son Puysieux, principal secretary of state, both opponents of Condé, concluded a private alliance with Marie de' Medici, and were briefly victorious in the struggle to obtain control of the council from late in 1622. It was their candidate, La Vieuville, who was made *surintendant des finances* in January 1623. After the 1622 peace of Montpellier, the need for military finance lessened, and La Vieuville found it relatively easy to cut back on royal expenditure. Until mid-1624 he was backed by the king, by disposition frugal to the point of meanness, in his efforts to cut back even the pensions paid to the old nobility.

La Vieuville, however, whose ineptitudes outside finance were soon obvious, wanted more complete power over the council than he was to be allowed. In the process of trying to acquire it, he was prepared to bring Marie de' Medici back to the centre of affairs, and, perhaps at her prompting, made overtures to Richelieu. It was La Vieuville, almost certainly with the complicity of Richelieu and Marie de' Medici, who finally encompassed the dismissal of Sillery and Puysieux to their estates early in 1624.

Pamphlets critical of Luynes had continued to appear, and Fancan issued a series of virulent attacks, including *La France mourante* of 1623 as well as an attack on the financial management of La Vieuville.[22] Sillery, who had remained titular chancellor, had regained custody of the seals on the death of Luynes. He had succeeded in undermining the authority of Schomberg, responsible for both war and finance, who was dismissed in late January 1623, but by late in 1623 Sillery had himself been forced by the intrigues of his quondam protégé La Vieuville, to return the seals.

Acting with ostentatious independence, Louis bestowed the keepership of the seals on Etienne Aligre, a former protégé of Schomberg, on 6 January 1624. Ministerial responsibilities were re-arranged to maximize the control exercised by La Vieuville, who wanted control of foreign affairs as well as finance. He was ready to offer Richelieu the chair of the *conseil des dépêches,* charged with co-ordinating foreign affairs, in February 1624, but Richelieu refused, arguing that such a body needed a representative on the *conseil d'état* itself.

Externally, things were going badly for France. Its representatives failed to stop, or even to perceive, the creeping augmentation of Habsburg control when, for instance the French ambassador to Rome agreed with the pope to concede to the Spaniards the right of passing through the strategically important Valtelline valleys in north Italy, so allowing them freedom of movement between

Lombardy and the Rhine and Danube basins. Foreign ambassadors in France began to wonder what was presaged by the more active political role the king apparently proposed to take for himself.

In fact the king knew perfectly well that the advice proferred by his mother came from Richelieu, and at Compiègne on 29 April Louis announced the admission of Richelieu to the council, with the restriction that he should not actually handle France's affairs outside the council chamber. The promotion was presented as being due to the need to replace the ailing Cardinal La Rochefoucauld, who none the less continued to act as president when he was again able to attend.

Richelieu successfully insisted on 9 May on the precedence over other members of the council to which his cardinalate entitled him, but otherwise adhered to the irksome constraints of his low profile. La Vieuville, who appeared to have been Richelieu's advocate, meanwhile made further damaging mistakes, playing into the hands of those who suspected him of moving France closer to the Protestant powers. He concluded a semi-secret agreement that a private promise rather than a public guarantee by James I to tolerate English Catholics would be enough to clear the way for the marriage of Henrietta-Maria, the king's youngest sister, to the prince of Wales, later Charles I. The pope had refused to sanction the mixed marriage without something stronger, and La Vieuville was making the fatal mistake which Richelieu was always careful to avoid. He acted without the king's authority.

Richelieu was made a member of the commission appointed to negotiate the conditions of the English marriage. He was partly responsible for having his former adviser, Richard Smith, made bishop of the English church, so that he had a knowledge unequalled in France of the mind of English Catholics. He also drew the king's attention to the way La Vieuville was acting without royal authority on matters other than those concerning James I and English Catholics, and he appears to have been privy to Fancan's two fierce pamphlet attacks on La Vieuville, *Le Mot à l'oreille de M. le marquis de la Vieuville* in May, and *La Voix publique au roi* in August 1624.[23] Louis changed his attitude to La Vieuville, but his lack of confidence in himself had forced him to become good at dissimulation, and he did not reveal his intentions until the moment of La Vieuville's arrest and imprisonment at Amboise on 13 August.

From then on Richelieu was the most important minister in the council.[24]

There was no dramatic or immediate change of policy, but Richelieu took firm control. He had reached the position from which he could achieve his life's ambition, the creation of a national identity for France.

5

First Minister: Strategies 1624–9

In the first chapter of his unfinished *Testament politique* addressed to the king, to guide Louis XIII in the conduct of state affairs after his death,[1] Richelieu gives a perceptive analysis of the ills of France in 1624. In particular, he points out that the Huguenots were 'sharing the state with the king', that the *grands* were behaving as though they were not the king's subjects, the provincial governors as though they were sovereigns in their own right, and that, with private interests being given precedence over public welfare, the role played by France in the world's affairs had diminished.

The *Testament* declares that Richelieu promised to employ all his efforts 'and all that authority that it pleased the king to give him' in the threefold undertaking to destroy the Huguenot party, to humble the pride of the *grands,* to bring all the king's subjects back to their obligations, and to raise the king's name abroad to its rightful position.[2] If, as seems probable, this was indeed Richelieu's recollection in about 1635 of what he had thought in 1624, then these three things summed up what then appeared to him necessary to restore order to the kingdom, but they did not constitute a structured policy. Meanwhile his letters show that in 1624 he favoured the use of gentler pressures on the Huguenots over any policy of suppressing them by force, and that he was aware of the need to relieve the ordinary people of the burdens currently imposed on them.

Richelieu knew Louis was insecure, of uncertain judgement, readily upset and easily influenced. He had seen Louis's emotional dependence on the older Luynes, and on the young male favourites mentioned by Tallemant, to whose list must at this date be added François de Barradas, elevated to first gentleman of the chamber, captain of the royal château of Saint-Germain, and lieutenant-general of Champagne, dismissed for mingling in politics in 1625, and for challenging to a duel his successor in the royal favour, Claude de Rouvroy de Saint-Simon. Saint-Simon, father of the memorialist, had been discovered as an adolescent page in the royal stables, and was to remain favourite until 1636. The lands he had been given were raised to a *duché-pairie* in 1635.

Louis's relationship with him excluded neither a platonic relationship with Marie de Hautfort, a court beauty and lady-in-waiting to Anne of Austria, nor, among his seniors, Richelieu himself, on whom for a period the king was to become emotionally dependent. Richelieu also knew that, if he could succeed in winning the king's confidence, he could not only personally achieve grandeur and enrichment, but that he could find the policies which would restore religious peace and some degree of social harmony among the peasant population. Uprisings against the tax regime were already beginning sporadically to break out. His inclination was never towards avoidable violence, and his memoranda to the king invariably set out a reasoned case for leniency in those great trials of the reign which at the king's insistence ended in executions.

Although Richelieu's constitution was strong, he was driven by his nervous intensity to bouts of tears, which he found humiliating. He suffered intermittently from his migraines and from neuralgia. The feverish illness to which he had succumbed in 1611 began sporadically to reappear from 1621. His skin became increasingly subject to ulceration, and he suffered severe pain from haemorrhoids, which intermittently made him unable to travel except lying down. Later on, from about 1632, he was troubled by retention of urine, and two years afterwards also by rheumatism and toothache.[3] There were periods of respite, but part of what appeared to be Richelieu's ascetic hauteur was the consequence of a refusal to surrender to physical infirmity and a desire to suppress its outward manifestations. He ate little, and preferably alone, although his official table was normally set for fourteen guests, invariably of high rank.

Richelieu did not avoid or deserve the reputation he acquired for coldness or arrogance. It was the price he had to pay for keeping his thoughts to himself, covering his tracks by ensuring that his private documents, including intelligence reports, did not survive for posterity, and appearing assiduously to be merely the executive rather than the originator of royal policies. His method of controlling political decisions comprised the frequent submission of clear political memoranda to the king, which the king marked with comments and returned. Richelieu further protected himself by sheltering behind his unattractive public image of contemptuous duplicity.

What the *grands* saw was largely the prince of the church and in effect the principal minister of the state, sole confidant of the king in political matters, who was aloof, inscrutable, powerful and ruthless. His outstanding qualities were in fact patience, subtlety, self-control, an acute political awareness, an intense psychological acumen, and a very strong determination to achieve greatness for his king, appropriate standing for himself, and glory for France.

He resisted receiving official visitors when he could. When he could not, he could be the embodiment of graciousness, simplicity and charm. We have the testimony of scores even of Richelieu's opponents testifying to his affable, modest demeanour, gentle, considerate, courteous and even warm. His household was devoted to him, and even Tallemant, who detested him, commends his loyalty to friends, allies and staff. His staff were in return remarkably loyal to him. It mattered to him that his aristocratic lineage, his ecclesiastical status and his position as the king's first minister should be publicly displayed and acknowledged, but his public image was also a mask which he put away when he could.[4]

Unfortunately it is difficult to know which of the many stories about Richelieu's informal behaviour might be true. The stories relating that Richelieu donned fancy dress to amuse Anne of Austria are clearly malicious in inspiration. Tallemant is a major source of anecdote, but he relishes long-winded gossip and often, as in relating the final dismissal of Richelieu's literary secretary and general factotum, Boisrobert, caricatures the truth. Boisrobert apparently admitted a well-known Parisian prostitute and former actress to an all-invitation rehearsal of *Mirame* in 1641 in the smaller of Richelieu's private theatres in the Palais-Cardinal, and she had made sure that her presence was noticed by Gaston, who had also arrived uninvited. The first night itself was gate-crashed by a number of ladies giving names they knew would be on the invitation list, and were shown to seats. The king, in the presence of Gaston, teased Richelieu about the women who had been at the rehearsal, and Gaston then said he had even seen the actress there. Tallemant says, admitting hearsay, that Richelieu was furious. Tallemant's intention is only to make Richelieu look ridiculous, or at worst hubristic, and he tells us that it was the duchesse d'Aiguillon who insisted on Boisrobert's dismissal, but it is difficult from his account to know exactly what happened or whether Richelieu or his niece over-reacted.[5]

Unfortunately for Richelieu's image, Philippe de Champaigne did not paint Richelieu pottering in his garden or stroking the cats of which he was fond, and we are unlikely ever to know quite how far he relaxed in intimate company. As often as he could, he retired to his spectacular country estate at Rueil, about eight kilometres from Saint-Germain. In 1633 he acquired for 105,000 livres the château and dependent farms, in one of which he often stayed during the re-building, and in 1635 for 216,000 livres he bought the *seigneurie*. The duchesse d'Aiguillon, to whom Richelieu left the property and from whom Louis XIV was to consider purchasing it, claimed that Richelieu spent 780,000 livres on enlarging the château and laying out its famous formal gardens, in which the cardinal delighted to walk up and down, talking, generally before and after dinner at midday and supper.[6] He enjoyed music and the company which he found entertaining, like that of Boisrobert, who amused him, or in which he could relax as with equals, like that of a handful of senior ecclesiastics. He could be witty and cordial while remaining dignified and, although he could be angry, he was never discourteous. He did not avoid ostentation, but the quality most alien to his character was vulgarity. There was style in everything he did.

There is little point in rehearsing the accusations of amorous liaisons levelled against him. There are a score of named women, including the queen, the queen mother, Marion Delorme and Mme de Chevreuse, the remarried widow of Luynes. There is not only the inherent unlikelihood that Richelieu's developed sense of personal honour would have allowed him a sexual dalliance after his ordination, but there is no evidence, however circumstantial, to support even the slightest flicker of reasonable suspicion. Some of the alleged liaisons are clearly impossible.[7] The most persistent allegation in the memorialists and pamphleteers is that of an affair with Marie de Bragelogne, wife of Claude Bouthillier, brother of Sébastien. It could chronologically and geographically have happened. It is virtually certain that it did not.

Richelieu introduced Claude into the household of Marie de' Medici and raised him to be a secretary of state in 1628. The king appointed him *surintendant des finances* in 1632. The Bouthilliers' son Léon, comte de Chavigny, later a minister and secretary of state, was rumoured to be the son of Richelieu and Mme le Bouthillier. But, at the date of Léon's conception, Richelieu had much to be grateful to Sébastien for, and a liaison between Claude's wife and Richelieu which produced a son, for which there is no evidence at all, would have involved a quite implausible degree of concealment or connivance by Claude's three brothers, Sébastien, Victor and Denis. It must be regarded as certain that this allegation, too, is part of the malicious gossip to which Richelieu was continuously subjected.

The allegations of Richelieu's atheism can be similarly discarded. They are evidence only of the wildness of the accusations made against him, and of the strength of the right-wing Catholic commitment to an anti-Huguenot ideology which could corporately fantasise to such an extent in order to discredit Richelieu. What has occasioned less comment is the regularity of Richelieu's religious life, for which we have reliable evidence from sources outside as well as within his household. He was sensitive enough to the delicacy of his position to solicit from the pope a dispensation to allow him to discuss in council the need for going to war, which required the shedding of blood, and, he likewise wrung from an unwilling pope a commutation recently denied to a Spanish cardinal of his priestly obligation to recite daily the breviary office. It would have taken him about an hour. He heard mass most days, himself celebrated on big feast-days, and confessed and communicated weekly. He liked to retire to a monastery for Easter.

Richelieu's position in 1624 was none the less difficult. Aligre became chancellor on the death of Sillery in October 1624, and

Schomberg was reinstated as *surintendant,* although with lesser powers. Richelieu arranged for two other *surintendants,* Michel de Marillac and Bochart de Champigny, and himself retained ultimate responsibility for both finance and foreign affairs. He had achieved his cardinalate and his position in the *conseil d'état* in spite of his strong association less than a decade previously with Concini, and then with Marie de' Medici. His penetrating intelligence was recognised, but, however cogent his advice appeared, Richelieu knew that he needed to deploy immense self-control and abnormal amounts of patience, delicacy and tact if he was going to persuade the king to trust him.

He was also under threatening pressure from the pro-Spanish clerical party led by Bérulle to cement the alliance with Spain, to suppress the Huguenots, and to break off Protestant alliances outside France. This group, political descendants of the old Catholic League, attached itself initially to Marie de' Medici, and at first included Père Joseph, Anne of Austria and the Marillac brothers.[8] Richelieu now saw how that policy would necessarily lead to a Habsburg Europe in which France might at best play some role as a Spanish satellite. Relevant to the difficulty of reducing the Huguenot strongholds on the west coast, which could hope for supplies and reinforcements to arrive by sea, was Richelieu's further realisation that France could never regain the status of a dominating European power without a maritime strength to protect its coasts and secure its commerce, not only off the west coast, but in the Mediterranean, the English channel and the Baltic.

The arrest of La Vieuville on 13 August 1624 had left Richelieu much the strongest member of the *conseil d'état.*[9] Before the arrest the other five had been the queen mother, the cardinal La Rochefoucauld, born in 1558, Lesdiguières, the converted Huguenot *connétable,* Aligre, keeper of the seals, and La Vieuville, the *surintendant des finances.* Meetings were attended by four secretaries of state who opened the day's reports, informed the king and prepared the replies. In principle, executive orders became valid when countersigned by the king, whose signature was authenticated by the relevant secretary.

When the king was absent, the chancellor took the chair and sealed documents. If the chancellor was in disgrace, as Sillery was in 1624, his function, but neither his title nor his authority, was transferred to the keeper of the seals. Votes were taken, but were binding only in the absence of the king. Apart from the queen mother, the chancellor and the *connétable,* no other member of the council took precedence over any other, unless by formal royal *brevet,* such as Richelieu obtained by virtue of his cardinalate and on the intervention of Marie de' Medici. He gained precedence behind La Rochefoucauld but before chancellor and *connétable.* When Schomberg was brought back to replace La Vieuville on 16 August, he was referred to as 'third minister', and Aligre, to become chancellor on the death of Sillery in October 1624, as 'second minister'. A hierarchy of members independent of seniority by appointment was thereby established, although technically Richelieu's title remained for four more years Secretary of State for Commerce and Marine.[10]

Richelieu's promotion in 1624 was popular at court and with foreign diplomats. The prohibition laid on him in March preventing him from receiving foreign ambassadors had to be lifted in May, when they began to insist on seeing him. His attitude to the king, his mother and the secretaries of state remained appropriately deferential, and he did not assert himself obtrusively in the official business of the crown. The king, however, did connive at a private correspondence between Richelieu and France's ambassadors, senior administrators and influential figures at home and abroad. This network included several Capuchin friends of Père Joseph, himself sent by Richelieu to Rome in 1625, ostensibly to attend the general chapter of the Capuchins, but in fact primarily as his private correspondent there. It was the depth of information and the clarity of Richelieu's judgement which finally ensured his leadership of the council.

It was by virtue of the impression made on foreign ambassadors as much as on his fellow-councillors by Richelieu's extensive knowledge of the major issues and the clarity of his mind that Richelieu took power in the council during the course of 1624. As early as May 1624 Richelieu had been asked to preside over a meeting with the ambassadors of Savoy and what was not yet formally the Swiss confederation.[11] He marked his coming ascendancy by holding it at his own residence. His first major diplomatic success, the marriage of Henrietta-Maria to the prince of Wales, marked the revival of a seriously thought-out French foreign policy, almost dormant since the death of Henri IV, who first thought of the desirability of the marriage.

Negotiations were helped by Marie de' Medici's continuing enthusiasm for the marriage. The difficulty lay in obtaining papal consent to the mixed marriage without a firm English commitment to lift all persecution of Catholics. Urban VIII had succeeded Gregory XV in 1623. A Barberini from Florence who had served as envoy and later nuncio to Henri IV, his sympathies, fortified by fear of a Habsburg domination of the Italian peninsula, remained pro-French. He was none the less unsatisfied with soon-to-be-forgotten verbal assurances which were all the English were prepared to give. In the end, although James I wanted to break off negotiations, Richelieu obtained the necessary formal treaty through the English privy council, a procedure which inevitably caused difficulties when James I confronted his parliament with the *fait accompli.*

He also contrived to make the English accept an episcopal chaplain for Henrietta-Maria, with twenty-eight French ecclesiastics and a hundred French citizens in her household, so satisfying the pope and the French Catholic party. It was foreseeable that they would cause much nuisance and fail to convert England, as they were supposed to, but Richelieu rightly saw that France needed the marriage, especially as the Spanish had wanted to marry one of their princesses to the prince. The Anglo-Spanish marriage contemplated in 1623 would have been yet another way of consummating a Habsburg hegemony in Europe. It was essential for France that England should remain at least neutral if any part of western Europe north of the Alps was to remain strong, independent and not effectively subject to Habsburg control.

The contract was signed on 17 November 1624, and Bérulle sucessfully extracted from the pope in January the necessary dispensation for the mixed marriage, extravagantly celebrated in Paris in May. Marie de' Medici gave a magnificent entertainment for the two courts in the gallery of the Luxembourg, where Rubens's recently completed set of twenty-one paintings for her now hung.[12] James I had died in March, and the duke of Buckingham, whose good looks, breeding and manners had brought him the favour of James I and dominance in the English royal council, came to Paris on 24 May to escort the new king's bride to England.

The failure of the projected Spanish marriage for the English heir has been attributed largely to Buckingham's swash-buckling arrogance in Madrid. In Paris he cut a dashing, stylish figure, and is reported to have worn twenty-seven sets of clothes in three days. Rubens painted him. His intimacy with Anne of Austria became court knowledge and then common gossip. She had allowed him into her bedroom in 1623, while he was accompanying Charles to Spain, and incurred a strong outburst of anger from her husband. When the flighty twenty-year-old Anne had had the miscarriage of 1622, caused by the fall on 14 March while indulging in what has always been regarded merely as giddy horse-play in the Louvre with Mme de Chevreuse and Mlle de Verneuil,[13] Louis had called on her two days later, before departing for his campaign in the south. Strangely, if Anne was carrying his child, and quite possibly the dauphin for which all France had been waiting, the king was not told what had happened until a week after the fall.

In 1625 Marie de' Medici and Anne accompanied Henrietta-Maria with Buckingham as far as Amiens, where Buckingham and Anne contrived, probably with the assistance of Mme de Chevreuse, to be left alone in a trellis garden by the Somme. Anne's lady-in-waiting, Mme de Motteville, whose memoirs go out of their way to protect royal reputations, reports that Anne screamed and reprimanded her equerry for having discreetly withdrawn.

After leaving with Henrietta-Maria for Calais, Buckingham impetuously invented a pretext to return to Amiens with a message for Marie de' Medici from Charles I, and was introduced into Anne's bedchamber, where all we are told is that he threw himself to his knees and made the violence of his passion obvious, although the pair are not reported to have been alone together. Both the king and Richelieu were informed. The equerry was dismissed, as was the *valet de chambre* who had delivered to Anne the letters of Mme de Chevreuse encouraging Anne to accept Buckingham as a lover.[14] Buckingham was not to be allowed to return to France. The result was the creation in Anne of an antipathy for Richelieu which was to have serious political consequences lasting until Richelieu's death.

From 1626, when Anne suffered a second miscarriage in the autumn, the king's attitude to his wife suddenly changed in a way quite different from that following the explosion of anger he had undergone over the 1623 episode with Buckingham. Whether this was because of an onset of jealousy, or because of the setback in producing an heir, we can only conjecture. No longer was Anne made regent for northern France when the king was absent, or placed above his mother in hierarchy of personal esteem. Héroard's diary notes show an abrupt diminution in his normal visits at the end of the day before going to bed. It is possible that the rumours of other miscarriages before that of 1626 were loyal smoke-screens put up to conceal the real state of the king's relationship with his wife. The state of the king's marriage was certainly court gossip, and it was to play an increasingly determining role in the establishment of Richelieu's policies.

Buckingham, whose perceived improprieties aggravated the French in 1625 as two years earlier they had annoyed the Spaniards, was himself hurt by the rebuffs with which his anti-Spanish diplomacy was met in France. Richelieu had refused to be drawn into Buckingham's schemes for an assault on the Spanish Low Countries and for an English recovery of the palatinate,[15] whose electoral prince Frederick was the son-in-law of James I.

Matters were complicated by the Spanish need for their forces to have free communication between Lombardy, which they controlled, and the imperial Habsburg armies north of the Alps. Richelieu needed the English alliance, which was not calculated to improve his relations with Spain, but he had also to balance the need to respect the pro-Spanish feeling in the entourage of Marie de' Medici against the increasing urgency of containing Spanish rights in the Catholic Valtelline, gateway to the Alpine passes separating the Habsburg-dominated Po valley from the Habsburg territories in the Rhine and Danube basins. Richelieu did not succeed in reconciling the contradictory constraints, and relations with England were further to deteriorate during 1625 when Buckingham, now favourite of the new English king, tried to save Charles I from embarrassment in front of parliament by declaring that the commitment to restore civil liberties to Catholics had been no more than a sham to enable the pope to give the dispensation for the marriage.

Meanwhile Henrietta-Maria and Charles found their marriage uncongenial, and the queen blamed Buckingham for attempts to curtail the size and activities of her French household. Richelieu's political strategy was further disturbed by Buckingham's failed expedition against Cadiz in October 1625, which he capped by a widely reported disparaging remark which he made in The Hague about the powerlessness of the king of France. Politically, France's situation was worsening as relations with both Spain and England deteriorated.

By the end of 1624, Richelieu as the king's chief councillor, had four main areas of political concern. Two of them were domestic and undramatic, but vital. Richelieu needed firstly to strengthen the reform of France's administrative system with a view, particularly, to diminishing the remnants of feudal power inherited or presumed by the *grands,* and he needed secondly to establish in the population at large a sense akin to his own of obligation to the crown which took precedence over any other political loyalties.

The problem of the *grands* came increasingly to centre on the figure of the king's younger brother, Gaston, feckless and disloyal, but heir presumptive until Louis should fulfil his duty by generating a male heir in the direct line. The second need, to establish a sense of national unity, involved Richelieu in the creation of his cultural propaganda machine. Both of these concerns need to be treated in the most appropriate chronological context. The other two areas of concern, the tensions which were to lead to war over northern Italy, and the policy towards the Huguenots were equally vital, but led to more dramatic and more immediate events.

The Valtelline was a problem which Richelieu inherited. Geographically, the Valtelline is the hundred kilometres of the upper Adda valley starting about twenty kilometres east of the northern tip of Lake Como and extending due east to Tirano, but in the seventeenth-century it was taken also to include the upper reaches of the Adda north-east of Tirano, the county of Bormio, the forty kilometres stretching due north from Lake Como to the Splügen pass, and the valley leading east from Chiavenna to Maloja. North of the Po, the Spanish-controlled territory of Milan bordered that of Venice, but only the Valtelline allowed the Spaniards to avoid Venetian territory in crossing the Alps from Lombardy to the Tyrol through St Moritz or Chur, from where the Rhine flowed to Lake Constance, and out westwards to Basle through Schaffhausen. The strategic importance of the Valtelline was immense, since whoever controlled it could either allow or block communications across the Alps.

The difficulty was compounded by the religious issue. North of the comparatively rich and Catholic Valtelline lay the relatively poor, mountainous and aggressively Protestant Grisons (Graubünden), a confederation of three leagues into a Bund which for complex historical reasons laid claim to the overlordship of the vassal Valtelline, to which the Grison leagues and the Spaniards had direct access, as did the Venetians threatened to the west and north by Habsburg forces, and to the east from the Dalmatian coast. Under Henri IV in 1602, France had negotiated with the Grisons at substantial cost freedom of passage for French forces through the four major alpine passes leading down to the Valtelline. The conflict of political interest between Spain on the one hand and, on the other, France, Savoy and Venice, was complicated by the clash of religious allegiances involved in the alliance between Catholic France and the Protestant Grison leagues.

Venice bribed its way into a similar treaty with the Grisons in 1603, thereby stinging the Spanish governor of Milan, Fuentes, into closing the route from Milan to the Grisons and erecting a large fort at the mouth of the Adda. The disruption of supplies of salt and grain was catastrophic for both Lombardy and the Grison leagues, within which an intermittently violent conflict arose between pro-Spanish and pro-Franco-Venetian parties. In 1617 the Grisons, threatened with starvation unless they allowed passage to the Spaniards over the passes to the Tyrol and the upper Rhine, counter-attacked with a Protestant missionary campaign in the Valtelline, in turn provoking a massacre of some 400 Protestants on 19 July 1620 by Catholics armed by the Spaniards.

By October the Spaniards had themselves overrun the valley and were erecting further forts including two in the valley at Morbegno and Sondrio, and one at Riva, barring the route north to Chiavenna and the Splügen pass. A month later, in the early stages of the Thirty Years War, the forces of the Elector palatine, who had accepted the throne of Bohemia, were destroyed at the White Mountain outside Prague, leaving the Habsburgs now also supreme along the Rhine, and increasing the importance to them of control of the Valtelline and the passes to which it afforded access.

On 26 April 1621, by the treaty of Madrid, the Valtelline was restored to the Grisons with permission to be granted for Protestant worship there, but discontent on all sides led to further warfare, and to Spanish-Austrian control of the whole area, Valtelline and Grisons, sealed by the treaty of Lindau in September 1622. Six weeks later, on 19 October, the peace of Montpellier, regarded by the political Catholic party as a sell-out, was signed in France between the king and the Huguenots. The council could now turn its attention away from Louis's anti-Huguenot campaigns towards the menace of Habsburg encirclement.

Richelieu, already speaking powerfully through Marie de' Medici, was urging the deployment of all diplomatic means to reinstate the provisions of the Madrid settlement. In 1623 both Richelieu and Marie de' Medici took part in the negotiations leading to the treaty of Paris of 7 February which pledged France, Savoy and Venice to work for the surrender of the Valtelline forts and the liberation of the Grisons. A week later the Spanish minister, Olivares, agreed, with French consent, to hand the Valtelline forts over to papal troops, whose instructions were to offer free passage to all. The papal occupation was fixed at four months, and the forts were to be razed.

Gregory XV died in July 1623, and Urban VIII was persuaded to keep his troops in the Valtelline, although he resented the cost and kept the garrison to a minimum. Richelieu regarded the papal decision to allow the Spaniards free passage through the Valtelline as a dangerous betrayal, and La Vieuville sent the marquis de Cœuvres, brother of Gabrielle d'Estrées, to collect an army of Swiss mercenaries to occupy the valley. By late 1624 Cœuvres, with the help of Venetian siege guns, had taken back the Valtelline and all but two of the forts. In order to lessen the affront to the pope of his attack, Richelieu allowed the papal troops to retire with dignity, and Cœuvres negotiated the right for the Valtelline, against payment, to impose their own civil and criminal jurisdiction, and to exclude Protestant worship, thereby disillusioning the Grisons.

Richelieu might successfully have pursued his policy of gaining exclusive control of the Valtelline and the mountain passes if, in January 1625, the French Huguenots under Soubise, supported by Spanish money, had not renewed the civil war inside France by seizing the Brittany port of Blaret and the royal ships it contained. Negotiations involving the Valtelline had now to be conducted solely by diplomatic means, while Richelieu mustered still limited French financial and military resources to deal with the renewed threat to the unity of France. Circumstances were again forcing him to react to urgent immediate constraints when he would rather have pursued a grander long-term strategy.

This was the moment at which Père Joseph was despatched to Rome, but he was unsuccessful in reaching agreement. Urban VIII sent his nephew, cardinal Francesco Barberini, to Paris as legate for three months in the summer of 1625 to argue that the pope was in earnest in refusing to subject the Catholic Valtelline to the Grison leagues, and insisted that France's promises to the Grisons were abrogated because a Catholic sovereign could have no obligations to heretics.

Louis XIII was throughout the negotiations over the Valtelline more inclined to belligerence than Richelieu, who later said that he had never felt nearer to death than during the legate's visit to Paris. Despite the best efforts of numerous pamphleteers to show how French policy was compatible with Catholic loyalty, Richelieu experienced as the determining point in his political career the convergent burdens of the king's trust, the widening distance between his own political thinking and the views of Marie de' Medici, rooted in the political Catholicism inherited from attitudes formed during the ascendancy of the League, and the need to decide whether to take the interests of France to the point of armed conflict with the pope. He had formerly spoken with the voice of Marie de' Medici, after having first put his ideas into her head. Henceforeward he was to form an analogous relationship with the king, carefully taking instructions from him to execute the policies he had himself inspired and initiated. Louis was more apt to assert his independence than his mother had been, and occasionally Richelieu would fail to moderate the king's outbursts of violence.

Both Bérulle and Père Joseph argued Richelieu's position against the king, but to no effect. Finally, after powerful arguments put to the council by Marillac, Richelieu was obliged to concede enough to the French pro-Spanish faction to negotiate in May 1626 the Franco-Spanish treaty of Monzón which restored the Valtelline only nominally to the Grison leagues, but permitted the exercise only of Catholicism and, with much difficulty, preserved

France's monopoly rights of access to the alpine passes. Surrender of rights to the Spaniards to use the passes would also have harmed the Dutch, themselves resisting Habsburg domination, on whom Richelieu was by now relying to borrow the ships he needed to defeat the Huguenots. France's allies, however, including the Dutch, were considerably angered by the terms of treaty, and it did not go far enough to appease domestic opposition from the political Catholic faction.

Richelieu's opposite number in Spain was Gaspar de Gúzman, count-duke of Olivares (1587–1645), practically Richelieu's exact contemporary, and for twenty-two years prime minister of Philip IV, who was eighteen years younger, and with whom Olivares had a subservient but gubernatorial relationship in many ways similar to that of Richelieu and Louis XIII.[16] Olivares needed peace in order to turn his attention to consolidating the Spanish positions in the Low Countries and the palatinate, and he could allow the matter of the passes to lapse for the moment.

Richelieu, for whom the treaty represented a measure of diplomatic success, went to extraordinary lengths to keep the negotiations secret from Venice and Savoy, whose safety he was putting at greater risk from Habsburg attack, until he could present them with a *fait accompli* with an apologetic reference to reasons of state. The French ambassador in Madrid was to assume personal responsibility for what he had agreed to, and, in the event of failure to achieve the monopoly rights in the Valtelline which France required, to return home, and to make sure that no piece of paper relevant to the discussions was left in Madrid to show that the French king had authorised negotiations behind the backs of his allies.[17]

The revolt of Rohan's brother, Benjamin de Soubise, in January 1625, ultimately leading to the siege of La Rochelle, and supported only by exceptionally militant Huguenots, can be seen as the opening of the final postlude to the religious wars which had brought Henri IV to the throne. The 1622 peace of Montpellier had scarcely been observed, and tension had led to sporadic violence in a number of towns. Richelieu had consistently advocated moderation and the avoidance of civil war, but Soubise's action finally persuaded him that Huguenot dissidence needed to be crushed.

Soubise wanted to create a diversion to distract the Spanish from

besieging the Dutch at Breda, and seized the west coast town of
Sables d'Oleron with Blaret. There were six galleons in Blaret
harbour, including the splendid eighty-gun *Vierge* built in Holland
for the duc de Nevers who, with Père Joseph, wanted to transport
a crusading army to release the Christian prisoners of the Turks.
On 18 January 1625 Soubise anchored his ten ships alongside the
galleons, which they boarded and seized that night. Rohan rose
again in Languedoc, and the citizens of La Rochelle joined Soubise,
who had occupied the islands of Ré and Oléron off La Rochelle.

Early in June, only weeks before his arrest, La Vieuville had
concluded a treaty with the Dutch, paying them 2,200,000 livres to
enable them to continue their war against Spain in return principally
for putting twenty warships at the disposal of the French. The
Dutch, in consequence, now found themselves supplying the arms
with which Richelieu was fighting their coreligionaries. They were
reluctant to open fire on Soubise's fleet until it started to use
fireships against them. The English, supporting the French attack
on Spanish forces in Genoa, refused on religious grounds to be
diverted to attack Soubise, but Montmorency was able to gather
a large enough fleet to defeat Soubise at the isle of Ré and chase
the remnants of his fleet to Falmouth. Charles I put pressure
on the French to respect the treaty of Montpellier, recalled his
ambassador from Paris, and dismissed a large portion of Henrietta-
Maria's French entourage.

Richelieu, himself undismayed by the contradictions in policy
which forced him to advocate the crushing of the Huguenots in
France while supporting Protestants against Spaniards in the United
Provinces, was none the less forced by the pro-Spanish Catholic
party in France to tread warily. His memoranda to the king in early
September show how aware he was of increasing opposition, and
the council meeting at Fontainebleau on 29 September 1625 showed
that Marie de' Medici sympathised with it to the point of defending
the attitude of the departing papal legate, Francesco Barberini,
the pope's nephew, sent to persuade the French to abandon the
Grisons and grant right of passage through the Valtelline to the
Spaniards.

Richelieu won the day with a point of casuistry adduced by
cardinal La Valette who had been assured in Rome of the duty
of subjects to obey their rulers, from which it followed that the

Spaniards were merely using religion as a subterfuge to justify their opposition to returning the Valtelline to Grison control. It is true that Olivares was no more reluctant than Richelieu to support Protestant military activity where he saw that political advantage might be gained. There followed a pamphlet assault on Richelieu's policies, another postlude to an earlier battle in which it was argued that the spiritual sovereignty could abrogate the jurisdiction of temporal sovereigns. Richelieu's own pamphleteer supporters had an easier task in replying,[18] and on 5 February 1626 he made peace with the Huguenots, restoring Rohan and Soubise to favour and allowing La Rochelle to keep its religious privileges with regard to the Protestant cult.

Bassompierre, a former ambassador to Spain and the Swiss federation who was created marshal on 29 August 1622, was sent to England in the summer of 1626, where he temporarily smoothed matters over. However, that November Epernon seized in Bordeaux an English fleet carrying a year's supply of claret, which provoked a riposte from England ordering the confiscation of all French ships, many of which were taken in the Channel. Charles I was preparing for broader hostilities which were to break out in 1627 when Soubise and Buckingham arrived before La Rochelle, landing a garrison on the Ile de Ré.

Meanwhile, by the end of 1625 Richelieu had drawn up broad plans for the reformation of the administration of France, widely consulting with France's ambassadors, merchants and financial officials, and sending special commissioners to check on the state of coastal defences. This information, much of which found its way into the *Mémoires* and the *Testament politique*, was compiled into a constantly revised and refined series of memoranda, many of whose recommendations were put into effect even before the *Assemblée des notables* which Richelieu persuaded the king to convoke in December 1626.

Richelieu's ideas for administrative reform at this date were obsessed by maritime and commercial issues. He had had himself created *Grand Maître et Surintendant Général du Commerce* in January 1626, adding *et de la Marine* in October that year, when he effectively superseded the two admirals of France, Montmorency who administered the fiscal jurisdiction of the west coast, and Guise who had the same rights in Provence. An edict issued at

Saint-Germain in October 1626 created a new department of state, governing trade, shipping and the colonies without reference to the *parlements* holding jurisdiction over the coastal regions.[19]

In 1625 the French government possessed no vessels based on the Channel or the Atlantic ports, and only ten galleons in the Mediterranean. All merchant ships were armed, however, so that the difference between merchant and military vessels was not great, and the whaling ships built at Saint-Malo had specially reinforced hulls, which made them particularly easy to convert into military vessels. Richelieu now expedited the founding of merchant and military fleets, and encouraged the formation of trading companies like the *Compagnie des Cent Associés de Morbihan,* constituted on 31 March 1626 by four founding associates and Richelieu, and given the monopoly of trade with the east and west Indies, Canada and the Levant. Not suprisingly, Richelieu's pamphleteers were put to work to justify the prelate's association with commercial activities normally prohibited to ecclesiastics.

Meanwhile the *parlements* had succeeded in preventing the formation of other similar trading companies whose privileges necessarily infringed their rights, and made difficulties about registering the Saint-Germain edict of October 1626. The Paris *parlement* took until March 1627, and the *parlements* of Rennes and Rouen until April. Rennes registered the edict only with important reservations, and Bordeaux took until May. The *parlements* of Aix and Toulouse did not register it at all. It remained without effect in their territories until 1631. None the less, by 1635 France had three squadrons in the northern seas, and a squadron and twenty galleys in the Mediterranean.

Before the *Assemblée des notables* had approved the project, Richelieu had put in hand the building of eighteen large ships in Normandy and Brittany, and early in 1627 he ordered another six, buying materials from Holland. When that proved too expensive, he tried to restore commercial relations with Sweden and Danzig, trading salt, wine, vinegar and spirits for timber, hemp and resin. France also ordered vessels to be built in Holland, five in 1626 and twelve in 1627. At the siege of La Rochelle in 1627–28, Richelieu would have a squadron of thirty-five ships.

Richelieu's first administrative priority was to remedy France's commercial weakness, which he rightly considered to derive from her lack of maritime resources. To proceed further with the radical re-organisation of France's economy and administration which he had begun to envisage, he needed a more widely based authority than that of the king and his *conseil d'état,* or even than that of the extraordinary council which had met in 1625. The *Assemblée des notables,* scarcely distinguishable in function from a much enlarged council, was a gathering, traditionally of important office-holders, invited by the king, and not mandated as were the delegates to Estates-General. Such an assembly had been held in Rouen in December 1617 to discuss the implementation of the demands of the Estates of 1614–15 while Richelieu was in exile at Luçon.

In 1626 invitations to attend an *Assemblée des notables* were issued in the name of the king to thirteen members of the clergy, thirteen nobles including his brother Gaston, and twenty-nine office-holders, mostly senior members of the magistracy. The queen, in spite of her right to be present, was not there, no doubt on account of her enduring quasi-disgrace. Richelieu's preparation had been meticulous, with precise information about French trading conditions available from agents in Madrid, Brussels and London, together with news of vexations placed on French commerce everywhere, duties levied and goods dumped by foreign merchants in France.

The assembly met at the Tuileries from 2 December 1626 to 24 February 1627.[20] Richelieu, with the help of Schomberg and Michel de Marillac, was unostentatiously planning nothing less than a thoroughgoing and radical overhaul of the whole governance of France. A commanding part in the proceedings was played by the marquis d'Effiat, a courtier and diplomat who had strongly supported Richelieu since 1624. He became *intendant de commerce* in January 1626 and *surintendant des finances* on 9 June that year.[21]

The agenda was dominated by the newly disastrous financial situation in consequence of the recent civil wars. The assembly attacked the financiers and recommended a drastic diminution in royal spending, but authorised the building of forty-five ships. Explicit proposals covered commerce, marine power, expenditure, fiscal reform, and the venality of offices, although this last item was quietly dropped from the final memorandum on account of the cost it would impose on the exchequer. In the light of Richelieu's own penetrating analysis of the political situation in

Europe, he formulated his proposal to conclude an alliance with Catholic Bavaria, partly because it made strategic sense, and partly to parry ideological objections to his Protestant alliances and to provide a counter-weight to some of the constraints in his dealings with Olivares.

Richelieu, not at all insensitive to the suffering of the peasantry, spear-headed the refusal to raise taxes. The assembly duly approved his own principal plans which they had in fact been convoked to ratify, although the polite fiction that Richelieu and the king needed the advice of the notables was courteously maintained. Richelieu's plans involved strengthening France's trade, building canals between the Seine and both the Loire and the Saône, redeeming mortgaged royal property, and diminishing royal expenditure.

If France had the six years of peace which Richelieu's speech implied that he needed, it would emerge with a balanced budget and with the peasants relieved of oppressive taxation. Only the members of *parlements* remained unhappy, because Richelieu's *intendants,* answering directly to him, meant that Richelieu's administration could increasingly ignore the established powers of the provincial courts, particularly because matters of financial administration would no longer require to be registered by them. However strongly he felt about the autonomous wielding of feudal powers by the *grands,* whose subjection to royal authority he regarded as imperative, Richelieu was not opposed to the nobility as a class. Indeed, he remained touchily keen to be regarded as belonging to it by right of birth. The group whose power Richelieu was most keen to prune was the magistracy.

His mostly temporary commissioner *intendants* not only provided Richelieu with powerful instruments for centrally directing administrative and fiscal measures, but they also much increased the immediacy of appropriate political or military response wherever dissidence threatened or financial necessity dictated. Under Richelieu, too, such matters as the upkeep of the roads were removed from the regional taxation authorities, the *généralités,* and transferred directly to central officers of the crown. The result was an improved road network for the movement of goods and also, from 1630, a national postal and stage-coach service, with properly organised tariffs and time-tables.

In the event, there was no six-year period of peace, and Richelieu's strategic planning was again and again to be frustrated by pressing constraints whose greater urgency pushed aside its implementation. He had no realistic opportunity to propose the wide-ranging internal political reforms which he envisaged. They involved the creation of four separate councils to assist the king, promulgating throughout France those decrees of Trent which did not infringe gallican privilege, the abolition of traffic in offices, and the severe punishment of atheists for the civil offence of 'blasphemy'. Richelieu, like his predecessors, would have to resort to borrowing from the financiers. A series of royal edicts on financial administration was none the less issued and capped by the *Code Michaud* of January 1629, largely drafted by Michel de Marillac. It considerably tightened the regime for tax farmers, abolished claims for tax exemption based on spurious titles to nobility, much strengthened financial accountability, and instituted a more intense scrutiny of public expenditure.

It is easy to derive a misleading impression from Richelieu's slow progress from 1624 to 1626 as he gathered in the reins of power, centralised it in his own hands, gained the confidence of the king in whose name he was conscientiously careful always to act, and moved through the creation of a navy and the promotion of commerce to achieve the endorsement of his policies by the *Assemblée des notables*. It may look as if Richelieu's first two years as chief minister consisted, if not in the smooth execution of a well-considered overall strategy, at least in the avoidance of major pitfalls into which less thorough, less well-informed, and less astute French ministers might have fallen. In fact the radical reforms which Richelieu's informed political imagination projected, the clarity of his vision, the energy with which he pursued it, and his refusal to give way to pressure groups and policies which would have led France to disaster were also together stacking up serious dangers. There was still also a copious list of mistakes to be made with the English marriage, in the Valtelline, with the Huguenots at home, and in France's relationships with Spain, England, the pope and the United Provinces in the Low Countries.

On 25 April 1626 the king's brother, Gaston, duke of Anjou, became eighteen. He was his mother's darling, debauched, feckless and dissolute, but ambitious and reasonably entitled, like his

mother, to a place in the *conseil d'état*. He was also the heir
presumptive to the throne and old enough to be married. It
was looking increasingly likely that he himself, followed by any
legitimate eldest son, might become king of France. That year,
Anne of Austria became twenty-five. Her marital relationship with
the king, whatever it might have been before, had dwindled away
certainly to almost nothing after the miscarriage of 1622, and the
miscarriage of 1626 was not to occur until the autumn. Early in
1626, the prospects for a male heir in the direct line looked slim,
and the question of Gaston's marriage accordingly took on political
importance.

If Gaston remained a bachelor, the throne would revert, possibly
after his own reign, to Condé, known as 'Monsieur le Prince', or
his successors. That possibility looked like the path to political
instability and a series of ill-considered foreign or domestic disputes
which might undo all that Richelieu was carefully trying to achieve,
making France a dependency of Spain. Gaston was ambitious to
seize power, but lacked any personal trait in which he might have
anchored Louis XIII's scrupulous sense of religious vocation as the
divinely anointed sovereign of the French people. If, on the other
hand, Gaston married and had male issue, might Richelieu not
only lose his own position, but also owe allegiance to a feckless
and petulant monarch in love chiefly with his own aggrandisement?
Richelieu was slow to make up his mind in favour of seeing Gaston
married.

Shortly after Gaston's birth, and two years before his own death,
Henri IV had selected as Gaston's bride Marie de Bourbon, duchesse
de Montpensier, one of the richest heiresses in France.[22] She had
come into her fortune, and her mother, after her father's death,
had married the duc de Guise. Gaston found Marie de Bourbon
unappealing. The comte de Soissons, denied the hand of Henrietta-
Maria to which he had once aspired, had subsequently hoped to
marry her. Condé was naturally against a marriage which was likely
to dilute the chances which his line had of one day succeeding to the
throne. Anne of Austria felt that any male child of Gaston would
imperil her own position.

Marie de' Medici strongly favoured the marriage of her favourite
son to Marie de Bourbon, but as soon as Richelieu began pressing
for it in the spring of 1626, there grew up at court around

Soissons and Condé a 'party adverse to the marriage', collecting the sympathies of a group of disaffected nobles, whose aversion to Richelieu was growing. From early in 1626 the government knew that it was menaced by a huge conspiracy. Its members included Montmorency and Nevers as well as Conti and other princes of the blood, Vendôme and the grand prior of the order of Malta, Alexandre, the illegitimate sons of Henri IV always hostile to the king.

They were in touch with the English, whose attitude to Richelieu had become frosty, and the Dutch, who felt let down by the treaty of Monzón. Some of them, for their own different ends, wanted to put Gaston on the throne. Too many provincial governors were sounded out for the matter not to get back to Richelieu, and a large amount of incriminating material was found among the papers of Gaston's governor, marshal Ornano, who had already caused trouble by demanding admittance to the council to accompany his charge, the heir presumptive, even if he was made to stand, like the secretaries of state.

A conspiracy aimed at the removal of Richelieu, which appeared not to involve treason, was formed. Near its centre was Mme de Chevreuse, intimate friend of the queen, who was privy to it, hostile to Richelieu, lover of intrigue, and perhaps, since she was born a Rohan, hoping to achieve something for the Huguenots. According to Mme de Motteville, Anne of Austria asked Mme de Chevreuse to persuade Gaston's governor, Ornano, that it would please the queen if her brother-in-law could be persuaded not to marry Mlle de Bourbon. Should the often sickly Louis XIII die, Anne of Austria would then marry his successor, Gaston. In the end the conspiracy's principal victim was to be the dispensable marquis de Chalais, said by Tallemant to have been a handsome young man who had recently killed a rival in love on the Pont Neuf, and who was willingly enough seduced by Mme de Chevreuse who needed him for the execution of the plot.[23] Mme de Chevreuse ensnared, seduced and incriminated Chalais, making him jealous, according to Mme de Motteville, by telling him that Richelieu was in love with her.

Ornano, whose distinguished career had brought him the marshal's baton, had been Gaston's governor since 1619. La Vieuville had dismissed him, and a disrespectful letter to the king had put him in the Bastille, but Richelieu, who had rehabilitated him on La Vieuville's fall, now suspected him of unwarranted self-importance and undue influence on Gaston, whose marriage he opposed. Richelieu probably failed to quieten Gaston's resentment, when, at a council meeting in November 1625, Gaston's peremptory demand to be appointed head of the army to subdue Soubise met with the robust rebuff that he should confine himself to hunting. If Bassompierre's *Mémoires* are correct, Ornano may even have thought that he was serving the king by opposing the marriage.

It is probably because of the polarised opposition of the views of the queen and the queen mother that Richelieu's memorandum to Louis XIII on the advantages and disadvantages of the marriage was more than usually non-committal. Richelieu knew proof of the conspiracy was necessary, but, according to Richelieu's pamphleteers, Louis XIII acted precipitately. He asked Ornano to come to Fontainebleau on the evening of 4 May 1626 and had him arrested together with his two brothers and an associate. Richelieu later loyally said he had approved the arrest. Ornano was kept in the dungeon at Vincennes, which, according to Mme de Rambouillet,[24] was worth its weight in arsenic. He duly died there on 2 September of an illness of eleven days essentially caused by the damp. His lungs had simply been destroyed. The king regretted that there had not been time to put him on trial to dispel rumours that he was the victim of a plot.

Gaston, upset at the arrest, protested to Aligre, the chancellor, who dissociated himself from Richelieu's action, and Gaston is reported to have sworn vengeance against Richelieu, who had always been extremely circumspect in his dealings with him. Louis XIII defended the need to arrest Ornano to his brother and, no doubt at Richelieu's prompting, now ordered the seals to be taken from Aligre and given to Michel de Marillac, a leader of the pro-Spanish Catholic party and former member of the Catholic League whose appointment was proposed by Richelieu and welcomed by Marie de' Medici. Aligre was obliged to retire to his estates. Richelieu suggested that Condé should be allowed to return from Italy, where he had been since defeat in 1622. He had long wanted to return, and Richelieu was able to satisfy a distrustful Louis that the cordial assurances Condé had given him were entirely satisfactory.

It is possible that the original or final intention of some at least of the members of the conspiracy had been the assassination of the king with the support of the Huguenots and the duke of Savoy, and his replacement by Gaston, but at this point, the cabal made Richelieu its target and its object the release of Ornano. Among Ornano's papers a letter from Vendôme had been found offering not only support for Gaston's aspirations to replace Louis XIII, but also urging Ornano to 'use menaces and violence against Richelieu'. Other letters from Vendôme and his brother, Alexandre, complain about their treatment since the death of their father, Henri IV, and confirm their readiness to conspire with England, and even to attack Louis XIII. Chalais later confirmed much that was discovered in Ornano's papers, and admitted that a plot was devised to kill Richelieu by arranging for Gaston and his suite to ask unheralded for hospitality at the house where Richelieu was staying, at Fleury-en-Bière, about four kilometres from the forest of Fontainebleau, and then over dinner to contrive a quarrel which came to blows, one of which would kill Richelieu. Vendôme is reported to have preferred a simple ambush.

Chalais, a one-time favourite of Louis XIII who had been ousted by Barradas and had been involved in the plot by Mme de Chevreuse, leaked details of it to an uncle, Valençay, a commander of the knights of Malta. Valençay reported them to Richelieu, who, when Gaston's officers came to announce Gaston's impending arrival next day, went to Fontainebleau at daybreak to await Monsieur's awakening. He expressed his regrets that he had not heard earlier of Monsieur's intentions, but he was that day moving to another property nearby, and would be unable to receive him. Chalais had been brought to Fleury and confessed everything. According to Fontenay-Mareuil's memoirs, Vendôme now set about activating his own plan, but Bassompierre recounts that Louis XIII, whom Richelieu had informed, had immediately sent him a personal guard of sixty horsemen and sixty foot soldiers.

On 31 May Gaston was forced by his mother to sign an oath of loyalty to his brother. Richelieu retired unwell to Limours. The king, with a small army behind him, convoked the Vendômes to Blois where, after characteristically entertaining them for two days without giving any indication of his intentions, he had them arrested on 13 June at 2 a.m., when they were asleep, only subsequently telling Richelieu what he had done. The Vendômes, as half-brothers of the king, were too grand to be tried. They were put in Vincennes. Alexandre died in prison in 1629, while César was released the following year. Brittany was given to Thémines on Richelieu's recommendation, in spite of the duel in which his younger brother had killed Henri on account of Richelieu's preferment above Thémines. Gaston thought of escaping from Blois and raising the standard of rebellion, of which, it later appeared, there had been real danger. The rebellion would have led to the marriage of Gaston with Anne d'Autriche, perhaps after an annulment of the king's marriage on grounds of impotence.[25]

Richelieu was sufficiently upset by what had happened, and by the accusations and threats breaking against him from so many quarters, that he wanted to resign. He had tried before, but been held back by Père Joseph. This time, his request, sent via Marie de' Medici, was turned down, and he received from Louis a famous letter of thanks and commitment signed at Blois on 9 June and personally delivered by Marie de'Medici, 'I have every trust in you and truly I never met any man who served me so much to my liking . . . I will never forsake you . . . Remain assured that I shall never change, and that no matter who attacks you, I will be your second.'

A royal pension of 60,000 livres had been bestowed on him on 16 January. From now on he was also accorded the rare privilege of an armed guard, otherwise legitimately enjoyed only by the king, his mother, his brother and provincial governors.[26] Richelieu disliked the sacrifice of privacy, but recognised the necessity of 'saying goodbye to freedom', 'The more they seek my life, the more I will seek to serve the king'.[27] Co-operation had become very close, with interviews of two hours taking place regularly between king and cardinal.

When Richelieu was ill, only the king was permitted to visit him. When necessary, the council met at his bedside. Louis became increasingly restless without Richelieu, whom he needed to draw up notes on all policy decisions. But the formalities were always observed. It was left to the king to take, or at least to promulgate, all decisions. Important letters always went out in the name of the king, and Richelieu never let slip the observance of formal deference. While the secretaries of state were willing to take orders from Richelieu, the cardinal was careful never to give them more than suggestions or drafts for their approval, never to assume an authority not officially bestowed, and never to usurp the responsibilities of ministers or ambassadors.

Louis took Gaston with him to Nantes by river, arriving on 7 July. The Brittany estates professed their loyalty. Chalais was arrested on the 9th, and Louis XIII interrogated Gaston in the presence of his mother, Richelieu, Schomberg and Marillac. Gaston revealed everything, exculpated himself, and affirmed his readiness to marry Marie de Bourbon. She was given a strong escort in case Soissons attempted an abduction.

On the morning of 5 August the contract was signed; in the afternoon the betrothal was celebrated, and the forms of consent were exchanged in the evening. Louis and Richelieu were present at the nuptial mass on 6 August.[28] Mme de Chevreuse was exiled to her estates, but preferred to flee to Lorraine. Gaston was elevated to the duchy of Orléans, given Chartres and Blois, and a great deal of money. Ten months later, on 4 June 1627, his wife died giving birth to 'La grande Mademoiselle', who would play an important role at court under Louis XIV. Richelieu had received Gaston and his bride sumptuously on their way back to Paris. He had been warned by the *procureur général* of Rennes that he was himself to be waylaid on his way back from Nantes, and travelled with nearly a hundred guards provided by the king. It was the third project to assassinate him.

A special commission of magistrates from the Brittany *parlement* was appointed to try Chalais, a silly but tragic scapegoat. His execution would not involve royal blood, but would send the desired tremors through the *grands*. The interrogation lasted several weeks, and involved three visits to the prisoner by Richelieu, who was later to charge Anne of Austria of connivance with the plotters. She denied conspiring to change husbands.[29] Whatever the previous state of the king's marriage, it was from now on no more than an empty charade.

The king made it known that he would commute Chalais's mandatory sentence for those found guilty of *lèse-majesté*, which involved dismemberment of the corpse, exhibiting the pieces, confiscation of all goods, and debarring his posterity from nobility.

The verdict of guilty was reached on 18 August. Chalais was to be beheaded, but might then be buried in consecrated ground. The excutioner, probably bribed by Gaston, did not turn up, and a shoemaker due to be hanged was offered a pardon to undertake the beheading in the late afternoon of 19 August. He notoriously failed to sever the head with a Swiss sword, turned to a cooper's adze, and took over thirty strokes. Chalais was still conscious enough to murmur 'Jesus, Mary' after the fourth.

6

La Rochelle, Mantua and the Crisis of Confidence

By the end of 1626, Richelieu had reached the point at which, with almost religious devotion, he could pursue his great ambition to build a great and unified France. It was to be done through and in the name of a king who now depended on him, and Richelieu's mind was clear about the immediate objectives to be achieved. The king's authority still urgently needed to be enhanced, that of the older landed, and largely dissident nobility to be diminished, that of the Huguenots crushed, and that of the Habsburgs circumvented. France still needed a national identity, and none of its leading figures yet understood Richelieu's slowly developing vision.

Richelieu himself had not yet foreseen the cost in deaths, suffering and deprivation which his cultivation of internal unity and external grandeur would impose on the people of France, or the pain he would himself be caused when it became apparent that he needed to force the king to choose between Marie de' Medici, who was the king's mother and his own benefactress, and himself. It was in the end the queen mother's presumptuous behaviour which constrained Richelieu to impose that choice on the king, although his own partly religious ideology could not have withstood any analogous need to choose between his essentially chivalric notion of the grandeur of France and the mystical concept of the divinely underwritten authority

of its monarch. He successfully avoided being confronted by
it.

Louis XIII was not always to take Richelieu's advice, but he never
renounced Richelieu's aim of promoting the greatness of France or
forced him to choose between loyalty to his person and loyalty to
his kingdom. Ideologically, the greatest concession that Richelieu
was forced to make concerned the clear distinction in his mind
between the pope as the unique source of spiritual jurisdiction
and the autonomy in temporal matters of Europe's independent
political sovereignties, of which the nation states were only the
largest.[1] However unremarkable that distinction may seem to us,
Richelieu took it to an extent virtually unconceived of by most
of his contemporaries, of whatever religious commitment. For
Richelieu, France's interests took priority over religious allegiances
in everything but the transmission of spiritual powers and of strictly
spiritual jurisdiction.

The pivot of his confrontation with the nobility was not chosen
by Richelieu. It was the issue of duelling. Ever since his brother's
death, Richelieu had felt strongly about the waste of life occasioned
by duelling, but it would have been uncharacteristic of him, certainly as early as 1626, to allow his personal feelings to determine
his political attitudes. Legislation forbidding duels had long been
in place, if rarely enforced. Richelieu, believing that its severity
was the reason for its non-enforcement, even pushed through
its liberalisation against a reluctant *parlement,* restricting the death
penalty in February 1626 to those whose duels actually resulted
in death, or whose seconds also duelled with one another.

The *parlement* had to be forced to register the new edict on
24 March. Other duellists would be deprived of office, and the
duellist who issued the challenge exiled for three years, but the
laws began now sporadically to be enforced, and the *noblesse
d'épée* was infuriated at a sprinkling of deprivations of office
and banishments. In his own mind, it was on behalf of the
aristocracy that Bouteville-Montmorency set out deliberately to
outrage the king. He was France's champion dueller and had
fought twenty-one duels, in one of which two people had died.
One of his own seconds had recently been killed, and Bouteville
prudently removed himself to Flanders with his cousin and other
second, Rosmadec des Chapelles. The king eventually let it be

Richelieu's works were predominantly dictated. He was a dedicated pastoral theologian and reforming bishop.

François du Plessis de Richelieu, military captain, grand prévôt, in confidence of Henri III and Henri IV, and father of Richelieu.

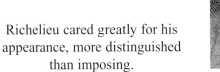

Richelieu cared greatly for his appearance, more distinguished than imposing.

Successively queen to Henry IV, regent and queen mother, Marie de Medici presided over the ascent of Richelieu, quarrelled with him and died in misery, poverty and exile.

The original caption says that Marie de Medici is returning from Ponts-de-Cé, where in fact she lost the battle. Rubens here undertakes to save her dignity. The angel carries the victor's crown.

Declaration of the majority of Louis XIII on 2 October 1614. The boy was just thirteen and has been given a beard. He asked his mother to continue governing, but the proclamation and delegation of authority turned rebellion into high treason.

Louis XIII, king of France and Navarre, in 1643. The original caption proclaimed him to be on earth what the sun was in the sky. Weak and petulant, the divinely anointed monarch had to be given mythological stature.

LOVYS DE BOVRBON ROY DE FRANCE ET DE NAVARE

Voyant cet Alcide à la guerre
N'auoir d'egal en ces bas lieux,
Dis hardiment qu'il est en terre
Ce qu'est le Soleil dans les cieux.

Mich. van Lochom. gand.

LOUIS XIII EN 1643

D'après Mich. Van Lochom.

Anne of Austria in 1642, infanta of Spain, queen of France, fun-loving, lonely and unhappily married to Louis XIII.

HENRY II DV NOM DVC DE MONTMORENCY ET DE DAMVILLE PAIR ET
MARESCHAL DE FRANCE CHLR DES ORDRES DV ROY GOV DE LANGVEDOC

Henri du de Montmorency, widely supposed to have been the queen's lover, rebelled on behalf of the rights of old nobility, was defeated and executed.

Giulio Mazarini, naturalised as Jules Mazarin in 1639, successor of Richelieu and lover from an uncertain date of the queen, Anne of Austria.

Gaston, brother of Louis XIII and heir presumptive from 1611 to 1638.
The presumption hardened to near certainty before the queen gave birth to her
first child, a son, at thirty six.

VRAY·PORTRAIT·DV·R·P. IOSEPH·CAPVCIN
FONDATEVR·DES·RELIGIEVSE·DV·CALVAIRE·

Père Joseph's Capuchins gathered invaluable information for Richelieu, while
Père Joseph himself, for whom Richelieu wanted the cardinalate, dreamed of
an old-fashioned crusade against the Turks.

known that Bouteville might return to France, but not to Paris or to court.

The baron Beuvron wanted to avenge Bouteville's last victim, but at the instigation of Louis XIII a reconciliation seemed to have been arranged over a dinner in Brussels after which, however, Beuvron issued his challenge. Bouteville, furious at the king's decree, agreed to fight, but in Paris, in daylight, with seconds fighting, and in the Place Royale, the recently built most fashionable, expensive and beautiful square in Paris,[2] scene of a famous carousel to mark the king's betrothal in 1612 and of an even more brilliant tournament won by the king in 1620. The fact that the seconds also fought ensured that any conviction would attract the death penalty, even if no one died as a result of the duel. The assumption was that Louis XIII would not dare go so far as to have a Montmorency executed.

The duel took place at 2.00 p.m. on Wednesday 12 May 1627. Chapelles, seconding Bouteville, killed one of Beuvron's seconds, Bussy d'Amboise, so ending the encounter, and one of Bouteville's seconds was seriously wounded. The king was livid. Beuvron fled to England with his unwounded second, but Bouteville and Chapelles were caught at Vitry-en-Perthois, on the way to Lorraine, having been discovered at a posting-inn by two emissaries of the dead man's mother, sent by her to guard property which had belonged to him. The pair were arrested, and the king sent a troop of 320 horsemen from Paris to meet them. They were already accompanied by 140 horsemen stationed locally. The Paris *parlement* showed no reluctance when the king commanded an immediate hearing, and the couple were condemned to death.

Bouteville had not, said Condé, as reported in the *Mercure français,* done more than indulge his need to defend his honour, the highest value acknowledged by aristocratic society. The *Mercure* did not point out how paranoid that need had become for Bouteville, or that he held a duelling school in his Paris house. Richelieu replied to a petition for mercy that he neither could nor should intervene. In spite of numerous pleas from the higher aristocracy for mercy, sentence was finally pronounced at 1.00 p.m. on 21 June, the execution graciously and unusually postponed for twenty-four hours.

To the king, Richelieu, whose letters show him still much later to have been concerned about the circumstances in which duelling was morally permissible, put forward reasons for and against clemency, concluding with a not too firm recommendation for the commutation of the sentence to life imprisonment, but advising the king to resolve according to the needs of the state.[3] Louis XIII, touched but unable to overlook the affront to his dignity, and knowing, as Richelieu had pointed out, that clemency could only lead to continued contempt for royal authority, walked away from the five of the grandest ladies of the French court who had come in person to make a final petition.[4] The pair were beheaded in the Place de Grève, on 22 June, at 5.00 p.m. Their opponents were harmlessly hanged in effigy.

Meanwhile, the Huguenots were rallying in France, and France's relations with England, where Soubise was now a refugee, were deteriorating. Buckingham, only partly motivated by the wounds inflicted by Richelieu on his vanity, was having ships armed in an effort to pre-empt Richelieu's effort to make France a major maritime power.[5] On the west coast both Catholic and Huguenot communities needed to be reassured that they would not lose trade to the merchant maritime companies being formed. Richelieu's letters show him seeking to allay their alarm in February 1627, relaxing a little in March, but resuming urgency in April with warnings alerting to possible sea-borne attack. Partly through Père Joseph's Capuchins, Richelieu was exceedingly well informed of the potential for mercantile enrichment in north and south America offered by mastery of the seas. It is even possible to see the religious bitternesses as simply the touchpaper which lit the smouldering antagonisms bred of commercial rivalry.

At this juncture Richelieu played what at first looked like one of his master-strokes. Warned by the comte du Fargis, the French ambasador to Madrid, that Rubens was in Madrid ostensibly to paint, but in fact in his capacity as one of Olivares's agents in the Spanish Low Countries, Richelieu uncovered a projected peace between the Low Countries and England and attempted to forestall it with a Franco-Spanish offensive alliance aimed against England and dated 20 March 1627.[6] Unhappily, it was to prove of no deterrent value at all.

Richelieu, informed in great detail about English preparations and intentions, had heard in May that English ships were being loaded with corn. He himself gathered an army which was put under the overall generalship of Gaston, the king's brother, in Poitou, but effectively commanded by the duc d'Angoulême.[7] Although there was no formal war with France, it was clear that English action would be directed against La Rochelle and the off-shore islands of Ré and Oléron in an attempt to reignite Huguenot insurrection in France. Throughout the early spring of 1627 Richelieu organised defensive forces, borrowing on his own account to pay for what was necessary, and spending a sum said to be in the neighbourhood of two million livres of his own, added to four million collected privately.

On 19 June, Buckingham issued orders for several infantry regiments to be transported to La Rochelle, wrongly supposing that they would be welcome there. The ships would land the garrison and go on to release the captured English wine-ships, still at Bordeaux and still the cause of much irritation. On 27 June Buckingham sailed with 98 ships, of which 74 were combat vessels and the others carried supplies. He had 4,000 naval personnel and carried some 8,000 men, declaring that his aim was to make the French king respect the rights of the Huguenot citizens of La Rochelle.

The departure of the English fleet from Portsmouth had been known at Paris on 30 June, three days after it sailed. A little later a report arrived that it had been sighted off Brest. Meanwhile Rohan had been collecting a Huguenot force in the south. Louis XIII and Richelieu themselves had left Paris on 28 June for the southwest, when Louis XIII fell seriously ill at Villeroy, the second overnight stop. Richelieu himself was riddled with perpetual migraines and he was feverish, but he spent day and night at the king's bedside, personally nursing him. The two men had come to depend on one another in joint pursuit of their great nationalistic enterprise, which by this date depended on both, and Richelieu could never for an instant be unaware that the death of Louis XIII would entail the accession of his brother.

Admiring tributes to the focus and intensity with which Richelieu unstintingly poured every reserve of nervous energy into the conduct of affairs were commonplace. During one four-week period he sent out couriers at the rate of more than seven a day. Many of his subordinates were ecclesiastics with a talent for

military organisation who combed the coast for every coracle that
floated and could be used to relieve Saint-Martin, the larger of the
two forts on the Ile de Ré. If the Ile de Ré fell, the Ile d'Oléron
could not be defended, and if that fell, La Rochelle could not be
blockaded from the sea.

It was on account of the king's illness, probably a particularly
severe recurrence of his constant intestinal troubles, but certainly
aggravated by anxiety about the political and military situations,
that Angoulême was given command of the army, some twenty-
thousand strong, surrounding La Rochelle. News was kept from
the king, because it could only excite him. For general matters
leadership devolved on Marie de' Medici, previously charged with
government north of the Loire, to free the king to lead the
campaign. Schomberg was in charge of military arrangements,
and Richelieu of maritime affairs and the general defence of the
western seabord.

On the morning of Tuesday 20 July Buckingham's fleet appeared
off the Ile de Ré, garrisoned by a thousand troops commanded
by Toiras, an able *maréchal de camp,* with two forts. One, Saint-
Martin, was fully operational and virtually impregnable, but the
other, la Prée, was still in a state of unpreparedness. In spite of
months of English depredations, Richelieu had gathered a fleet of
fifty ships.

On 21 July the English opened fire on the two forts. Toiras
was unable to prevent Buckingham from disembarking 2,000 men
at Sablanceaux, at the extreme east of the island, at its nearest
to La Rochelle, and was forced to retreat. By 27 July he was
obliged to take refuge in Saint-Martin, leaving the rest of the
island to Buckingham, who had now landed the rest of his forces.
Buckingham granted Toiras a truce to bury his dead, and gallantly
paid tribute to them. There was a purely chivalresque courtesy
exchange of melons and scented orange water.[8] Toiras had in fact
lost some two hundred men, including his own brother. He now
faced a siege, with access to Saint-Martin blocked both by sea and
by land.

Toiras was short of supplies, ill, and his troops were becoming
demoralised. The situation was sufficiently desperate for him to
send three swimmers to the mainland, all with the same urgent
threat that he could no longer hold out. Only one arrived, but

Richelieu managed to organise a fleet of fifteen small ships, of which thirteen managed to get through with supplies on the high tide in the early hours of 7 September. At the next lunar tide, on 7 October, the English were waiting and a battle took place. This time twenty-five out of thirty-five ships got through with provisions and reinforcements. Richelieu and Schomberg, knowing that Toiras could not hold out beyond mid-November, then conceived the daring plan of landing from the Ile d'Oléron 6,000 men, 300 horses and six canon, to be commanded by Schomberg.

The English were alerted, and frightened into making an inadequately prepared attack on the fort on 6 November. It was repulsed, partly because the ladders were too short. When Schomberg landed with fifty-four boats on the night of 8 November he found the English in full retreat from the island. Over fifteen hundred English troops were killed before the remainder could sail away, taking Soubise with them, saved by a favourable tide. Marillac published a *Relation* giving Richelieu the major part of the credit for the victory. Richelieu had himself directed the final assault on the island wearing a black soutane, a cuirass, a starched collar and a plumed felt hat with a rapier under his red cardinal's cloak.

When Buckingham had first arrived, Soubise had gone to La Rochelle, where his mother, the duchesse de Rohan lived, to sound out the town itself. He was at first refused admittance, and begged by the mayor to go away, but finally split the population into two parts, those, mostly merchants and office-bearers, who wanted peace, prosperity and nothing to do with the English, and those, led by their pastors, who wanted the establishment of a theocracy. It was from their ranks that a new mayor was chosen. Eight hundred citizens went to offer their services to Buckingham, and La Rochelle passed the summer warily assessing the situation, and seeking to exploit it for any religious advantages that could be gained without compromising continued commercial prosperity.

It was presumably the success of Richelieu's penetration of the maritime siege forces at the Ile de Ré on 7 September which on 10 September incited the Huguenot forces within La Rochelle to fire on the French troops preparing siege works round the town, instituting open hostilities between the town and the king. The Rochelais still regarded themselves as loyal to the king, but they had allied themselves with the English, whose potential exploitation of La Rochelle as a bridgehead Richelieu was determined to prevent. He explained his policy in a letter of 8 October to Condé, charged with suppressing the uprising in Languedoc. In spite of the crusading fantasies of Bérulle, elevated to the cardinalate in 1627 on Richelieu's recommendation and at the king's request, and of Père Joseph, Richelieu made clear that his concerns were not religious, but political. The Huguenots had become a threat to the unity of France.

The king was by now recovering, but the escape had been narrow and his doctor, successor to the elderly Héroard, was still cautious. Strategy was still in Richelieu's hands, although from August 1627 orders were sent as 'given in the presence of the king'. Richelieu was also put in direct command of the army. Like his generals, Louis de Marillac and Bassompierre, Richelieu preferred not to attempt a direct assault in favour of a plan put forward by Métezeau, the king's architect, to cut the town off from the open sea by building across the bay, but out of range of the town's guns, a 1500-metre mole of stones, masonry, and blockships with guns mounted on floating platforms attached to it and a gap on which artillery was trained and through which only small craft could pass. The royal fleet would be stationed nearby. The plan was successful, and by January 1628 the blockade was effective by sea as well as by land.

A set-back in the king's health prevented his rejoining his army, but he was able to return to Paris, make the queen mother regent in his absence, and leave for Blois on 20 September, where Richelieu joined him on 1 October, meeting him again on 7 October at Parthenay to travel with him to La Rochelle, where they arrived on 12 October. Richelieu immediately set about organising everything necessary for the siege, from vessels from Spain and the Low Countries, to guns, men, money and clothing from all over France. Richelieu himself made further loans, but progress with the long line of forts surrounding the town was slow, and the triple pay required by the 4,000 men to recompense them for the ardours and the dangers they were incurring was difficult to fund. Furthermore, Gaston, unhappy that Louis had taken over command, retired to Paris, and for a period Bassompierre refused to take orders from Angoulême.

For his personal residence Richelieu had chosen a small château by the sea, Pont-de-Pierre, so exposed and isolated that the

Huguenots thought it possible to hire a squad of adventurers to attack it and abduct him. They underestimated the security provided by Richelieu's information service, and the night they came, they found no cardinal, but a troop of musketeers and several companies of cavalry. Père Joseph, who had made his home in one of the château's garden pavilions, had been informed by one of the Rochelais Catholics.

Louis had to be stopped from going to the Ile de Ré with a shipment of troops, and spent his time riding up and down, examining, reviewing and exercising his troops. Nothing, he wrote to his mother on 25 November, would give him peace until the enterprise was finished. However, he fell ill again, and had to withdraw from the front, becoming depressed when he received news that the Rochelais had broken through to take French prisoners, or that a shipload of provisions had reached the town. Asked to provide a general account of the situation, Richelieu had to inform the king that an anti-French alliance was being formed between Huguenots, England, Savoy, Lorraine and the emperor, Ferdinand II. For Richelieu, who had now staked his future and his dream on the pre-emptive crushing of Huguenot opposition in France, the necessary prelude to the creation of a national culture, the only possible solution lay in expediting the surrender of La Rochelle.[9]

Black in mood, annoyed with Richelieu, mentally depressed and physically sick, the king withdrew to Paris on medical advice, persuaded by Richelieu to leave him in full command, with the title of 'Général de l'armée du Roi devant La Rochelle et provinces circonvoisines', and with two secretaries of state. Louis left on 10 February, breaking into tears immediately after taking leave of the cardinal and leaving an emotional message of gratitude and concern for him, insisting that he should stay away from danger, and writing the same evening to assure him of his enduring affection and sense of loss at being deprived of his guidance. Richelieu, who had immediately relapsed into a fever, was touched, and, on receiving his letter, wrote an equally emotional message to the king. He followed it up with a series of detailed reports, annotated on reception by Louis.

The campaign was not going well. Richelieu's army was falling to pieces, demoralised, and Huguenot sorties were becoming more frequent and successful. On 12 March 1628 an unsuccessful attempt was made to create a breach in the town walls at a gate used by boats collecting salt from the marshes. The breach, at the Porte Maubec, would have been above a network of canals about which Père Joseph had been informed. Richelieu himself had waited all night with some five thousand men, ready to enter the town, but the group with the explosives had lost their way.

Richelieu's domestic enemies tried to detain the king in Paris, leaving Richelieu to his fate on the presumed failure of the siege, but Louis kept his promise to return early in April, and arrived back at La Rochelle on Easter Monday, 17 April, pleased at the progress on the mole. Marie de' Medici wrote to Richelieu how pleased the king was with all he had done. When an English fleet appeared in May to re-provision the beleaguered town, Louis XIII had to forbid Richelieu to sail into battle on one of the French ships. The English fleet retreated before canon fire from the guns along the mole. After no more than a token effort to succour the starving Rochelais on 16 May, the English fleet inexplicably withdrew on the 18th.[10]

The Rochelais pinned their faith on a huge fleet of over 150 vessels which Buckingham was said to be preparing. Then came the news of Buckingham's assassination on 23 August by John Felton, a Puritan subaltern who had served under him and whose grievances were partly religious and partly personal. The fleet arrived none the less, 114 vessels, on 28 September. Two days later, the English deployed fireships against the guns on the mole. Richelieu and the king themselves fired canon from exposed positions against them. On 3 and 4 October there was a naval gun-fight, then a four-day storm, after which the English ships withdrew before French forces, which were by now superior. It was at this point that La Rochelle decided to negotiate. The *Mercure* reported that the inhabitants had been trying to digest leather stewed in tallow. Dog meat and donkey meat had been luxuries. More than 13,000 people had died of hunger. The capitulation was signed on 28 October.

Liberty of cult and a general amnesty were granted, with less than a dozen of the leaders exiled for six months, and no property confiscated. Catholicism was restored, and one of the churches designated a Catholic cathedral. Père Joseph declined the offer of a new bishopric of La Rochelle. The ancient privileges and governmental structures of the self-governing town were abolished, and an *intendant* responsible to the crown was put in charge of finances, the courts and the maintenance of order. The walls and forts, other than those on the ocean side of the town, were to be destroyed. Richelieu, in favour of co-existence with Huguenots wherever it did not generate political dangers, and whose primary concern was now to encourage the Languedoc Huguenots to surrender, thought the agreed measures too severe. When French troops occupied the town on 30 October, there were only 5,400 inhabitants left out of 28,000.[11] Over a hundred died from the instant effects of a normal diet on their digestive systems. Louis XIII made his entry on 1 November, and Richelieu abandoned military apparel. On 10 November the English fleet disappeared. A week later Louis returned to Paris, and a peace treaty with England was signed on 20 May 1629.

In the meanwhile Richelieu's skill, courage and energy won universal plaudits. In Louis's attitude there was clearly affection, if also a wary concern for the supremacy of his own authority, and an insecure need to manifest it. When Richelieu stopped work on the destruction of the walls of La Rochelle, Louis made obvious his annoyance, and Richelieu acknowledged to petitioners that he was lucky if half the propositions he put to the king were accepted. None the less, the king was now totally dependent on him, and the role played by Richelieu in the formation of official domestic and foreign policy was finally paramount. No formal changes were made, but Richelieu began to be able to issue orders on the king's authority which formerly would have been communicated by the king to the appropriate secretary of state. The other secretaries of state welcomed Richelieu's clear, well thought-out and coherent instructions. He had in fact become chief minister, however careful he remained not in any way to wound the king's paranoid sense of his own dignity, and not to forget the formalities, 'It will please Your Majesty to order . . .', 'It will please him to have a letter written saying . . .'[12]

Among the effects of the protracted siege of La Rochelle was the need for Richelieu to defer attending to other matters, in particular to the consequences of the death of the childless duke of Mantua, Vincenzo II of Gonzaga, on 26 December 1627.

In spite of its tangle of domestic, dynastic, commercial and religious feuds, the western European political situation was dominated by the struggle between the Austrian imperial Habsburgs and their Catholic Bavarian, Rhenish and Spanish allies, and the northern German Protestant princes with their Dutch, Danish and English allies for dominion over central, and especially German-speaking Europe. France's interests would have been adversely affected by the outright victory either of the Protestant forces or of the Habsburgs. Luckily, neither was likely, but the death of Vincenzo nevertheless left Richelieu with some difficult decisions. They were further complicated by the plans of the widowed Gaston who, having lost his first wife in childbirth on 4 June 1627, had fallen in love with Marie de Gonzague, daughter of Charles I, duc de Nevers, claimant to the Mantua duchy, and of Catherine de Lorraine, who had died in 1618.

Vincenzo, the dying duke of Mantua, had been persuaded by emissaries from France and Mantua itself, sent largely at the pope's instigation, to sign a will for the smooth transfer of his territories of Mantua and Montferrat to his French cousin, the duc de Nevers. Nevers's son, the duc de Rethel, was hastily married at the pope's prompting, with a necessary papal dispensation from the impediment of consanguinity, to Marie de Gonzague, Vincenzo's niece and only close relative, on Christmas Day 1627, the day before the duke died.[13] Spain and Savoy, both urging claims, appeared to have been outwitted, but Mantua was an imperial fief, and could pass to Nevers, who was not an heir in the direct line, only if the emperor invested him with the duchy, which Ferdinand II, who wanted the territory himself, was not about to do.

By this date the tiny marquisate of Montferrat, close to Piedmont, was more important than Mantua itself, and it could pass through the female line, giving the duke of Savoy's grand-daughter, Marguerite, a title. However, Mantua and the duke of Savoy had already agreed to divide the territory between them. They signed their treaty on the day Vincenzo died. Although in formal alliance, Franco-Spanish relations had been strained by the probably deliberate failure to send Spanish naval assistance to arrive in time to help the French at La Rochelle. The Spaniards had now begun to besiege the chief town of Montferrat, Casale, which dominated the upper Po and the road from Genoa to Milan. It was defended by a Mantuan garrison and French troops under the command of the duellist Beuvron, now anxious to restore his name.

In France the political Catholic party, still led by Bérulle, recently introduced to the council at the request of the queen mother, and commanding the support of Marie de' Medici, both Marillacs, Michel and Louis, and Père Joseph, regretted that the La Rochelle Huguenots had not been more severely punished and forbidden to exercise their cult.[14] With the exception of Père Joseph, a friend of Nevers, they wanted Louis XIII to turn immediately to the suppression of the Huguenots in Languedoc. Richelieu on the other hand was persuaded in December 1628 that the siege of Casale could speedily be raised and that Languedoc should be left until the spring of 1629. The king, he thought, would still be back in Paris by August.[15]

At a council held in Paris on 26 December 1628 at which the queen mother, Richelieu, Michel de Marillac, keeper of the seals, Schomberg, and Bérulle were present, Richelieu expounded his view that France's political advantage demanded the immediate Italian expedition, already promised some months previously to the Venetians. Bérulle and Marillac, supported by the queen mother, who hated Nevers and had not forgotten his rebellion under her regency, thought it more urgent to crush the Huguenots in the name of religion. It was an important meeting because it marks the formal break between Marie de' Medici and Richelieu. Louis XIII accepted Richelieu's advice, was asked by the cardinal to take three days to consider the matter, and after that period reaffirmed his decision to give priority to the situation in the Italian peninsula. Gaston had asked to be appointed commander, but whether out of jealousy or out of disapproval of his brother's marital intentions, the king decided a week after Gaston's appointment to lead the army himself.

Before the king left, he held a *lit de justice* commanding the *parlements* to register the 'Code Michaud', which until Michel de Marillac's fall was to tighten the country's administration, but widen access to noble status. Richelieu also wrote a memorandum for the king dated 13 January 1629, setting out his recommended programme, which included putting an end to the political insurrection of the Huguenots in Languedoc, a relaxation of taxation of ordinary people, abolition of the *paulette,* diminution of the political pretensions of the *parlements,* build-up of sea-power, fortification of France's external frontiers but demolition of internal fortifications, avoidance of open war with Spain, but gradual territorial extension of France towards Strasbourg, Geneva and Neuchâtel. He also advocated the eventual annexation of Navarre and Franche-Comté, since he considered them rightly to belong to France, such operations to be undertaken over a long period, unobtrusively, and with great care.[16]

Louis made his mother regent and left on 15 January 1629, reaching Grenoble on 14 February. The duke of Savoy had blocked the passes that Louis was going to use, successfully hoping to raise the price of passage. Richelieu was in the vanguard and wrote to the king at Oulx from the frontier at Chiomonte that his marshals, Créqui and Bassompierre, were going to force a passage to Susa at dawn the following day. The king received the letter at 23:00, rode through the night, and was present for the attack at 07:00 the following morning, 6 March, when with some courage he led the main body of troops. The price for Savoy's co-operation in opening the passes, negotiated on 11 March, was the town of Trino and 45,000 livres in *rentes.* The Spaniards lifted the siege of Casale on the night of 15 March. The king stayed briefly at Susa, where he was visited by his sister, Christina, princess of Piedmont, married to the heir of the duke of Savoy and pregnant at the time, and then left Richelieu with part of the army to settle unfinished business while he went back to Languedoc.

The principal Huguenot communities in the south of France were at Privas, Alais, Uzès, Castres, Nîmes and Montauban, and Richelieu had worked out in which order to take them. Both Rohan and Soubise were being supported financially by Spain, where, like Richelieu, Olivares would cover his political aims with a religious motivation always and only when it suited him. Louis XIII started as planned with Privas, to which he laid siege on 14 May, but felt in urgent need of Richelieu, who arrived on the 19th. Privas opened its gates on 21 May. The tactic was to destroy houses, trees, crops and gardens on the outskirts of towns, showing seriousness of intention but sparing the inhabitants the much worse horrors being inflicted on capitulating towns elsewhere in Europe. Richelieu was ill, and had some trouble in restraining his victorious troops from massacre. Père Joseph led a team of missionaries which procured mass conversions.

Seeing d'Estrées ready to attack Nîmes, Condé Montauban and Ventadour Castres, the Huguenot leader, Rohan, gave up, accepting Richelieu's moderate terms, and the edict of pacification was signed at Alès on 28 June. There would be an amnesty, but fortifications and walls were to be destroyed by the inhabitants, and at their expense, and freedom of cult and conscience were restored. Their churches were restored to the Catholics, and on submission the larger towns were spared the aggravation of a garrison. Rohan was awarded 300,000 livres in reparation for damage done to his property and exiled for a period. He was later to become one of France's great generals.

The king left Richelieu, with Bassompierre, Schomberg and Louis de Marillac, the marshal, to restore order, and departed for Paris, where it was cooler, on 15 July. The governor of Languedoc, Montmorency, was to assist Richelieu, who offered the terms of the pacification in return for submission town by town. At the most stubborn, Montauban, Richelieu was eventually accorded a solemn entry, accompanied by two archbishops, seven bishops, sixty other ecclesiastics, and followed by 1,200 horsemen, of whom 1,000 were from the regional nobility. He refused to be treated with the royal honours offered to him, but offered to have the ruined main church rebuilt at royal expense. The pacification edict was duly registered by the *parlement* of Toulouse, and throughout the south Richelieu was everywhere regarded as the hero of the hour.

He was again receiving urgent messages from the king to rejoin him, but his health had suffered, and he was delayed at Pézenas by a series of fevers which could have proved fatal. Throughout August he received letters from the king and others, saying how grateful the king was, how much he had relied on Richelieu, and how great his affection for him was. Richelieu, knowing the king's proclivity to tantrums and tetchiness, his capacity for petulance and displays of temper, was almost exaggeratedly careful to retain an attitude of submissiveness and respect. The floweriness of his expressions of devotion to the king and acknowledgements of appreciation of the royal affection suggest an awareness that there would be moments when the king resented his dependence on Richelieu, indulging what Richelieu called his 'petits dégoûts' of which the king did not himself know the cause. Foreign diplomats knew perfectly well how easily the king could reduce Richelieu to tears.

Occasionally Louis rejected Richelieu's advice. Once, Richelieu so far forgot himself as to accept the king's decision to go back to the cool of Paris from Nîmes 'provided that it please your majesty to make a [solemn] entry into Nîmes first'. 'Provided that' was a mistake, and provoked a predictable outburst of childish irritation. Richelieu was referred to as 'His obstinacy', and had to think up a compromise whereby the king would accept the invitation to make a formal entry, but would then be called away at the last moment. Louis agreed, then next morning came into Richelieu's room to announce that he had changed his mind, and would after all make his solemn entry. He owed it to his *gloire,* although he did not put it like that, and was as resolved today to do it as he was resolved yesterday not to.

Anecdotes of this sort have a moral. It is not so much the scandal that Europe's political future, and the well-being, indeed the lives and deaths, of hundreds of thousands of people depended on the petty resentments of ill-behaved but divinely anointed monarchs of arrested development, but that Richelieu, in his changing circumstances, and drawing on immense reserves of patience, self-control, psychological powers of penetration and cunning, could so manage the interplay of power, personalities and potential as to create a nation aware and confident of itself.

By the summer of 1629 Richelieu could no longer command the backing of a unified council. The emperor had still not agreed to invest Charles I of Nevers, cousin of Vincenzo of Mantua and the father of the duc de Rethel, with the duchy of Mantua. Richelieu's well-founded view that France's current priority had to be the situation in north Italy had cost him the support of the political Catholic wing, and his situation was complicated by the widowed Gaston's determination to marry Nevers's daughter, Marie de Gonzague, against the determination of Marie de' Medici to prevent him.[17] Although relations between Richelieu and the queen mother had remained cordial until late summer, by September, when Richelieu returned to Fontainebleau in triumph, she was insultingly cool, congratulating only Louis de Marillac.[18] The king twice attempted a reconciliation, but the estrangement was becoming clear enough for Richelieu formally but vainly to offer the king his resignation.

Of the political Catholic party, Michel de Marillac, an ex-league member prominent in the foundation of religious houses earlier in the century, habitually and profusely professed the highest esteem for Richelieu, who reciprocated. A letter from Marillac to Richelieu of 11 August 1629 does, however, suggest that there had been some altercation, and rumours of a possible discord had to be denied by Richelieu.[19] With Bérulle, the situation had become more difficult. He owed his position on the council to Marie de' Medici and, according to Richelieu's *Mémoires,* his cardinalate in 1627 to Richelieu, who rightly perceived that he was 'gently and persistently obstinate'.[20] Richelieu was irritated by Bérulle's not infrequent recourse to private divine 'revelations', as about God's intention himself to bring about the surrender of La Rochelle, so rendering the siege works otiose, or about the need to turn against the English in the summer of 1629 rather than conduct the campaign in Mantua and Montferrat.

Bérulle and Michel de Marillac both separately tried to prevent the expedition to relieve Casale, but Richelieu may have underestimated the strength of the trio Bérulle made with Michel de Marillac and Marie de' Medici in the pursuit of what were basically political goals for ostensibly religious ends, well after Richelieu himself had learnt to keep them separate. According to Montglat, Michel de Marillac and Bérulle roused the queen mother to jealousy by pointing out how far the king's chief minister had moved from his former closeness to her and how totally the king had come to rely on him. Bérulle's letters to the king in the spring of 1629 treacherously encouraged him to discount seeds of doubt about Richelieu planted in his mind by letters from his mother, which he and Marillac had in fact themselves inspired in her. Marie de' Medici's religious inclinations were easily exploited by Bérulle and Marillac, and she was naturally adverse to any attack on Savoy, about to be ruled by her son-in-law. Richelieu meanwhile was naturally aware that the measures he was taking in support of Nevers would promote his own goal of unifying France, since the French Huguenot leaders would enthusiastically back any move against Spain, such as those implied in support afforded to Nevers.

Matters were not helped by the increasing antipathy of Gaston d'Orléans, still only twenty, for Richelieu, in spite of the cardinal's successful support for his appointment as commander of the army for the Italian expedition to reinstate Nevers. Marie de' Medici, whose dislike of Nevers was compounded by an unfavourable comparison he had once made between the origins of the Medicis and those of the Gonzagas, and who wanted Gaston to marry her niece, sister of the grand duke of Tuscany, thought that Richelieu was abetting Gaston in thwarting her will. When Richelieu modified his attitude and appeared to take her side, she thought him simply insincere.

Indeed, Gaston's promised appointment to the Italian army, appearing to favour his marital ambitions, was probably the cardinal point at which Marie de' Medici's attitude toward Richelieu finally changed to hostility, although resentment at the way Richelieu had usurped her primacy in the council had been building up for months. None the less, she had made him a present of Bois-le-Vicomte and given him 180,000 livres on his success at La Rochelle. Richelieu was desperate on 30 April 1628 to make her believe that he had no greater care even for his salvation than he had to please her.

When the king took command of the army for the Mantuan expedition himself, instead of remaining in Paris to kindle support for his strategy, as Richelieu had originally hoped, Gaston became resentful. He had already been made to promise publicly to renounce his intention to marry Marie de Gonzague in the presence of Louis XIII, his mother, Bérulle, Marillac and others. Marie, motherless at six, had been brought up largely at the French court, lodged by her father with his sister, Mme de Longueville. Nevers now ordered his daughter to return home, and sent an emissary to fetch her, but Gaston was planning to abduct Marie de Gonzague with the complicity of her aunt. His mood changed to fury when he learned that his mother had sent an armed party to Mme de Longueville's château at Coulommiers and virtually imprisoned Mme de Longueville and her niece in the king's apartments at Vincennes to prevent Gaston from taking her off to the Low Countries. With more passion than logic, Gaston's rage now turned against Richelieu, to the extent that the cardinal improbably thought that the quarrel between Gaston and his mother must have been merely a blind for what all along had been intended as an alliance between Gaston and his mother against him.

Richelieu wrote to cardinal de la Valette[21] that he was merely supporting the king's own opposition to Gaston's marriage, and Marie de' Medici announced herself satisfied. On Richelieu's return, Gaston withdrew to Lorraine. Since he was the heir to the throne, he could virtually demand rehabilitation on his own terms, which were the government of Orléans and 200,000 livres. He left Nancy for Paris on 2 January 1630, and remained there in *de facto* charge while Louis campaigned and his mother spent the year in Lyons as regent.

Meanwhile Philip IV's council in Madrid advised him to repudiate the agreements over Casale and Susa. The Spanish general Spinola, who at Richelieu's invitation had admired the siege works at La Rochelle, was appointed commander of Spanish troops in Italy and began again to besiege Casale, where Toiras was the French commander. The emperor, annoyed at the refusal of Nevers to submit to his commissioner's jurisdiction, sent twenty thousand troops up the Rhine, through the Grisons, and over the Splügen pass, to lay siege to Mantua and to invade Venice. They were joined by a Spanish army, bringing the total to 44,000. The pope, alarmed, sent 11,000 troops to the Mantuan frontier.

It was again with difficulty that Richelieu persuaded the king in council in late November of the need to send an army to Italy. He spent the last months of 1629 in Paris, where he had acquired the ground on which he was to build the Palais-Cardinal, gave an ostentatious Christmas fête for the court, and on 29 December, having taken leave of the king and the two queens, Marie de' Medici and Anne of Austria, left for Italy with cardinal de la Valette, Montmorency, Schomberg and Bassompierre as his lieutenant generals.

By 18 January he had reached Lyons and by 1 February, Grenoble. He was much concerned in the organisation of troops, supplies and strategies. At Turin, where the expected opposition was not met, Richelieu dressed in gold-stitched soutane, cuirass, plumed hat and sword, with pistols in his saddle holsters, to ride with the cavalry before taking again to his carriage. The king was to take over the command as soon as matters had been settled with his brother in Paris. That was to take until 18 April. Louis left on 23 April, arriving at Lyons on 2 May, having left the two queens and the council at Dijon.

Charles-Emmanuel, the duke of Savoy, had been paying only lip service to his obligations towards France, and did what he could to hinder French progress. Richelieu, still the advocate of minimum violence, but not of a 'shameful' peace, took from Savoy the town of Pinerolo, southwest of Turin. It has been said that this was the decisive step which rendered war with Spain eventually inevitable.[22] The pope sent an agent to demand the return of Pinerolo to Savoy. His name was Giulio Mazarini and he was secretary to Panciroli, the papal nuncio in Turin, charged with making peace among the Catholic princes.

Both the king and Richelieu considered the pope's terms quite inadequate. Pressure in France against the expedition was none the less mounting, and the pamphlet war was intensifying. Although Louis XIII, advised by Richelieu and all his senior officers, now invaded Savoy to take Annecy and Chambéry, he felt obliged to send Richelieu to Lyons to expound the situation to Michel de Marillac and Marie de' Medici, who remained unconvinced. The centre of Marillac's argument had shifted from the need to protect and extend political Catholicism to the now pressing need for internal reform in France, where poverty, misery, affliction and real starvation lay behind intermittent uprisings.[23] Richelieu's answer was that the king had chosen 'le parti le plus généreux'. The word 'généreux' is significant. For Descartes at this time, 'générosité' was the chief of all the virtues, the epitome of 'gloire', the heroic quality denoting personal honour, normally without any ethical content, whose acquisition was the highest moral goal of the early seventeenth century in France.

Marie de' Medici twice refused to come to Grenoble or Vizille, a few kilometres to the south, for further discussions, and the king finally ordered Richelieu to accompany him back to Lyons where a council was held. Marillac's tone was sufficiently insolent for the king to walk out. By 24 June Louis was back at Grenoble, and, convinced that Marillac had to be separated from Marie de' Medici, had ordered Marillac to follow him. Marillac who, as keeper of the seals, was supposed at all times to be physically close to the king, took his time, and pleaded that his health prevented him from proceeding beyond Grenoble. Richelieu was under strong pressure from the queen mother and her entourage to allow the king, ostensibly for the sake of his health but in fact to abort the campaign, to leave the army for Lyons. Richelieu realised that the king's departure would mean the army's disintegration, and the king's doctor agreed that the king's lodgings at Saint-Jean de Maurienne were better for his health than the king's lodgings at Lyons would be in June. Meanwhile, plague demoralised the army.

Charles-Emmanuel of Savoy was, however, to die in July, and his son and successor, Victor Amadeus, was strongly pro-French and married to Christina, sister of Louis XIII. Imperial troops were meanwhile arriving to assist Charles of Lorraine, and threatening France's eastern border. Montmorency had managed to emerge victorious over a Savoy army from an ambush northwest of Turin, but Wallenstein himself, the imperial general, was now coming to Savoy's support with imperial troops. Mantua fell on 18 July 1630 and was pillaged by the mainly Protestant troops of the Catholic imperial army, and both Nevers and Rethel were taken prisoner.

Richelieu was finally obliged to advise the king to return to Lyons, while he himself stayed at Saint-Jean. When the plague broke out there, the king ordered Richelieu, too, to return to Lyons, where he arrived on 22 August, having been kept informed by Bullion, the future joint *surintendant des finances,* of the feeling being whipped up against him in the entourage of Marie de' Medici. He had nevertheless continued to cultivate her good offices, sending small presents and expressions of devotion. She had replied only through a secretary until the king made her write herself. Richelieu was consoled only by a stream of affectionate letters from the king.

In Italy the situation was improving. Casale had been relieved. To please Marillac and the queen mother, whose coldness towards him continued, Richelieu had persuaded the king to appoint Louis de Marillac, half-brother of the keeper of the seals, to command alongside Schomberg in Piedmont, since Montmorency was ill. Mazarini, the pope's emissary, now mediated an arrangement whereby, pending a final setlement, the town of Casale was to belong to the imperialist party, while Toiras retained its citadel.

The emperor had called the electors together at Regensburg on 3 June in order to have his son named as his successor. Richelieu had sent Père Joseph to negotiate, although France's official plenipotentiary was Brûlart de Léon, the French ambassador to Switzerland. Père Joseph, carrying credentials signed by the king, held extensive talks with Wallenstein, and arrived at Regensburg on 29 July. Brûlart had two sets of instructions, one public and the other private. The public set gave him power to negotiate a general peace in Italy and to commit France to it.

For Richelieu, Brûlart's mission was primarily to disrupt the emperor's plans for the imperial succession and to limit the emperor's quest for allies to his war with the German Protestants. But Mantua had fallen on 18 July, and Brûlart's instructions could be read as authorising a settlement of the Mantuan question, perhaps against French concessions elsewhere. On 11 August, Brûlart and Père Joseph were told that any Italian settlement was contingent on the abandonment by France of commitments to Venice, the Low Countries, Denmark and Sweden. Brûlart replied that for such a treaty he needed further powers.

Richelieu had become unwell and Louis very ill indeed. Brûlart and, at the emperor's insistence, Père Joseph, signed a treaty on 13 October by which the Spaniards would withdraw from Casale and the imperial forces from Mantua pending the emperor's decision about the succession. Nevers would be invested with the duchy but would not fortify Casale, and the French would retain in Italy only Pinerolo and Susa. France would not assist the emperor's enemies. Although Brûlart, Père Joseph and, in France, Richelieu and Bouthillier were well pleased with the first account of the treaty which they received on 20 October, Richelieu was outraged two days later to read its full text at Roanne, and especially at the commitment to remain neutral in Germany. The treaty could not be ratified, as the king tartly informed Brûlart on 22nd. In fact, it did not need to be. Mazarini negotiated a satisfactory settlement in Italy. The Spaniards would withdraw from Casale and Montferrat if the French evacuated the citadel and restored to Savoy the territories they had occupied.

Without needing help from Père Joseph, the German princes had encompassed the dismissal of Wallenstein and had not underwritten the imperial succession. Wrangling about whether or not the Regensburg treaty was binding or needed ratification continued between the interested parties, ever more like some monstrous board game, with diminishing relevance to real politics. There were no real winners. Sadly Nevers, who had once built and equipped five magnificent galleons for a crusade, found his new duchy reduced by sack and plague to 25 per cent of its former population. Both his sons died of the plague, and he had to borrow furniture for his palace. Mantua's currency collapsed, and Guido Reni refused to paint for him because the fee was too small.

Louis XIII had left Saint-Jean for Lyons on 25 July 1630, having avoided infection with the plague, and having survived his doctor's stern regime of bleedings and purges. He was lost without Richelieu. He renewed the subsidy to the Dutch who were fighting the Habsburgs, but was cautious when Gustavus Adolphus asked for a full alliance with Sweden. Richelieu was torn between the need to direct operations in Italy and the desire to stop the king from succumbing to the atmosphere at Lyons hostile to his political strategy. On 13 August the king's doctor wrote to Richelieu that the king was well, and on 22 August Richelieu arrived at Lyons.

On 22 September the king became feverish at a council meeting, and Richelieu took him back across the Saône to the archbishopric, where he was put to bed. The fever got worse and was not responding to the daily bleedings. The queen mother attended the bedside, and the doctors began to fear for the king's life. Louis had asked his confessor to tell him if he was about to die, and Père Suffren let him know that there was some anxiety. The king made a general confession and asked for the last sacraments. The cardinal archbishop of Lyons brought communion.

On the 29th, Louis was worse, and in pain. He was anointed and prepared for death, making peace with his mother, and asking for his subjects to be told that he asked their forgiveness. At 10 p.m. what we now know to have been an intestinal abscess burst in a great discharge of blood, pus and dysentery. The doctors did not expect the king to live through the 30th. He called for Anne of Austria and embraced her, then whispered something to Richelieu. By now the haemorrhage was lessening and the pain receding. Convalescence was normal and swift. Richelieu had been in tears, and his letters to Schomberg and Effiat show the intensity of his emotions. He was naturally blamed for having endangered the king's life with the expedition to Savoy, and plans were being made for the council after the king's death and Gaston's accession. Might Anne of Austria marry him? Would Richelieu be exiled, imprisoned or executed? There is documentary evidence that all these possibilities were canvassed, and some probability that Richelieu was preparing his flight, probably, it was thought, to Avignon.

As the king recovered, his mother tried to speak to him about Richelieu and appears to have been the cause of the king's relapse into fever for a week. His reaction, when she returned to put pressure on him, was what it had been in August, that Richelieu was the best servant France had ever had. Louis postponed all discussion until he had returned to Paris. He left with Richelieu on 19 October, receiving at Roanne the text of the Regensburg treaty. Louis decided to continue his journey, leaving Richelieu to wait for the queen mother, Marillac and Bouthillier to hold a council. Marillac wanted the treaty ratified, but the majority was against him. The treaty would not be ratified. The king's doctor wrote regularly to Richelieu, and then the king himself, who was well enough to gallop back to Paris from Versailles.

Richelieu accompanied Marie de' Medici by boat and the pair got on well. The queen mother invited Richelieu into her carriage. The military memorialist Fontenay-Mareuil rightly thought she was dissimulating. We know from her correspondence that she was demanding Richelieu's disgrace. On 5 November Richelieu was at Fontainebleau. Marie de' Medici returned to Paris to plot with Marillac Richelieu's downfall. Richelieu went to Saint-Germain while the king stayed at Versailles, where he hunted and warned Richelieu that his mother had not modified her attitude. The Louvre was being repaired. Marie de' Medici went home to the Luxembourg.

On 9 November Richelieu sought an interview with the king, but was told to wait. The king himself went to Paris, staying next to his mother in the rue de Tournon, and Richelieu, gnawed through with anxiety, went to the Petit Luxembourg. Presenting himself to Marie de' Medici, he found her again cold. On Sunday 10 November the king called on his mother, who ordered all the doors to be locked.[24] She then demanded Richelieu's dismissal, saying that the king must choose between Richelieu and herself. While she was in full flight alone with the king, Richelieu entered without knocking.

Richelieu had of course been warned that the king was alone with his mother and immediately knew that Marie de' Medici must be demanding his dismissal. She had herself dismissed all members of her household placed there by or on account of Richelieu, including his niece, Mme de Combalet, whom Richelieu had already met leaving in tears. He knew the geography of the building well from his period in the queen mother's service, and was still its *surintendant*. Three contemporary accounts tell us that he guessed that a first-floor door from behind the staircase leading up from the chapel would not have been locked.[25]

Mme de Motteville gives a splendid account of the queen mother's fury, and the tornado of insults and wild accusations she emitted. Richelieu was overcome with emotion, fell to his knees and wept. He went as far as to offer to make public apologies for faults he had not committed, and reiterated his gratitude for all the queen mother had done for him. Refusing to be silenced, she asked the king whether he preferred his valet to his mother. None of the memorialists is completely reliable, but three of them, Brienne, Fontenay-Mareuil and Vittorio Siri, deriving from Saint-Simon, inform us that Richelieu offered there and then to resign.

The king finally succeeded in stopping his mother, and ordered Richelieu to stand up and leave. He then made his own departure, ignored Richelieu in the courtyard, and left in his carriage. Marillac headed a whole group of courtiers into the Luxembourg where the queen mother told them of her ultimatum. Either she went, or Richelieu did. It was a day of congratulations and relief. The queen mother's victory seemed assured.

Richelieu thought so, too, and made ready to leave for Le Havre, of which he was governor, announcing his decision to Mme de Combalet and to Bouthillier. He intended to start out that evening for Pontoise. According to Tallemant, supported by Brienne, Montglat and Fontenay-Mareuil, La Valette arrived with wiser counsels. Richelieu should go to Versailles where he could defend himself or if, as la Valette supposed, the king was favourable to him, Richelieu could strengthen his resolve. Others arrived, agreeing with la Valette, when suddenly a message arrived that the king wanted to see Richelieu.

The king had left the Luxembourg to return to the rue de Tournon where he threw himself on his bed, traumatised chiefly, according to Mme de Motteville, by his mother's failure to observe protocol in his presence. He then prepared to go to Versailles, still a simple hunting lodge standing where the marble court is now, sending Saint-Simon to the Petit Luxembourg to tell Richelieu to call on him there. Saint-Simon gave the message to la Valette, who delivered it, returning with Saint-Simon to the rue de Tournon, where the king was calmer. At Versailles the king with Saint-Simon and two gentlemen-in-waiting were expecting Richelieu and la Valette. Richelieu dropped to his knees, thanked the king, who raised him up affectionately and told him how much he appreciated all Richelieu had done for his mother, and how he was now determined to defend Richelieu against the cabal which had taken advantage of his mother's good will.

Richelieu knelt once more and cried when the king said that he intended to retain his services. Louis lifted him up again, asked him to stay the night, and dismissed everyone else. Richelieu later confided to two of his collaborators, Sirmond and Guron, that he told the king that, in spite of his immense gratitude to the king, he would prefer to retire, to avoid responsibility for any deterioration in the relationship between the king and his mother. The king turned this offer down, partly because Richelieu's advice was more valuable to France than his mother's, and partly, he affected to believe, because the damage was being done not by his mother, but by the cabal which surrounded her, with which the king was prepared to deal. The next day Richelieu wrote emotionally confirming his devotion to the king and accepting the order to remain at his service.

The king now appears to have acted entirely on his own initiative, calling ministers and secretaries of state to see him. Marillac thought he was being summoned to receive Richelieu's position, but Louis told his council that Marillac was at the root of the trouble, that he would be spared punishment on account of his age and his service, but he would be stripped of his position and exiled. Together with Saint-Simon, la Valette, Bullion and Bouthillier, the king decided to give custody of the seals to Laubespine, sieur de Châteauneuf, and that the first president of the Paris *parlement* would be Nicolas le Jay. Both were friends of Richelieu. Michel de Marillac, finally realising what was happening, wrote a letter of resignation from nearby Glatigny, where he had been told to wait, and was attending mass when called on to return the seals. When mass was over, he was told he would be accompanied into the place of exile chosen by the king, but was not told where he was going. He was to be made to borrow 1,600 livres from relatives in order to pay for the journey, but was not allowed to communicate to anyone on the way, nor take anything with him. The destination turned out to be Châteaudun, where he would die on 7 August 1632. After his departure the queen mother was informed of what had happened, and caused consternation. Guillaume Bautru, satirist and diplomat, coined the term 'Journée des dupes' to designate the universal surprise at the way the king had turned the tables.

Meanwhile Louis de Marillac, the half-brother of the keeper of the seals, had at his command an army which he might have rallied to the support of Marie de' Medici, of Gaston and of other actual or potential dissidents and enemies. He needed to be apprehended in Italy, preferably before he had heard of what had happened in Paris. The courier managed to reach the three marshals, Schomberg, La Force and Louis de Marillac at their camp in Italy at midday on 21 November, before the news of 10 November had reached them. Schomberg read the despatch, and summoned the guards to arrest Marillac while the three marshals dined. A further despatch a fortnight later ordered Marillac's transfer to Sainte-Ménéhould, halfway between Verdun and Reims. The king, seeking to justify the arrest, primarily intended to prevent the marshal from turning troops against the king, had launched an inquiry which revealed that Marillac had been guilty of the usual peculation in the construction of the citadel at Verdun years previously.

Thirteen counsellors of the Dijon *parlement* were appointed to a special commission to try him at Verdun in July 1631. Marillac dragged out his defence, and the king moved the trial to Richelieu's favourite retreat, Rueil, near Saint-Germain, naming Châteauneuf president of the commission. Additional judges were appointed, making twenty-three. On Saturday 8 May 1632, they condemned Marillac to death by thirteen votes to ten. Comment has understandably been aroused because Richelieu ostentatiously took care to be seen to have refused to have anything to do with the arrest and trial, and no written evidence remains to connect Richelieu with the trial although it was held in his own château.

An intercepted series of letters from Lorraine and Brussels, however, led Richelieu to write a memoir for the king in March 1632 pointing out the danger to France from enemies both outside and inside the country. He drew attention to the need, among other things, to hasten the settlement of the Marillac case.[26] The series of small, but cumulatively substantial legal improprieties to which Richelieu resorted to achieve the condemnation are a measure of the urgency he attached to it, although he contrived to leave the impression that he did not want the death penalty implemented. Marillac was executed at the Hôtel de la Ville on the afternoon of 10 May, having been told of his sentence only on arrival that morning at the place of execution.[27]

7

The Defence of Victory

After the events of 10 November 1630, Richelieu appears from various ambassadorial accounts to have been not at all elated, but on the contrary, severely depressed, particularly on account of his rupture with the queen mother. Bullion, sent by the king to test the ground, told Marie de' Medici that the cardinal was unrecognisable in his distress. We have the account of Bullion's visit in a letter to Richelieu of 18 November. When the king saw his mother on 19 November, she was adamant that she would have her revenge, and that she would not tolerate Richelieu in her presence. In a routine meeting with a delegation from the *parlements*, the king let slip his determination that, while paying due respect to his mother, he also intended to defend Richelieu against her animosity. His words got back to Marie de' Medici and drove her to new pitches of fury against Richelieu, who summoned a platoon of powerful intermediaries to assure the queen mother that he neither inspired the king to make his declaration, nor knew that he was going to.

Richelieu continued to make efforts to placate her, and to prevent a breach between Marie de' Medici and Louis, which might well, it seemed, have fractured the political unity of France itself, particularly if Gaston d'Orléans were to move to rebellion.[1] It was largely due to Richelieu, and at some cost to himself, that France's unity was maintained. He wrote to the half-dozen of his relatives whom he had placed in the queen mother's household and whom she had dismissed, asking them to obey her wishes and to remain silent. The nuncio Bagni, recently created cardinal and about to return to Rome, tried to mediate, and succeeded in getting the queen mother to meet Richelieu in the council. She received Richelieu icily, then asked him to call on her on 15 December, when she burst into tears, declaring she had never wished to separate Richelieu from the king.

By now, Gaston's record had made it obvious as well as inevitable that the apparent reconciliation would break down. Gaston, more than ever the favourite son, was still twenty-two at the end of 1630, and knew that it was increasingly likely that he would remain heir to the throne. There was indeed every likelihood that he would succeed his elder brother. He was in a position to marry if he pleased, and start a civil war if he wanted, although he was counting on more support from the old aristocracy than was actually forthcoming. Whatever he did, his status as Louis's heir would continue to give him virtual impunity.

For a few days he hesitated. Having congratulated his mother while the wind was blowing behind her and against Richelieu, he now called on Richelieu to congratulate him. When the outrageous requests he made for those closest to him, a dukedom for his companion, Antoine de Puylaurens, and a red hat for his favourite, Le Coigneux, were inevitably paid off with lesser promotions,[2] Gaston called on Richelieu on 30 January 1631, revoked his offer of friendship, and left the court for Orléans, before moving a few months later to Spanish-ruled territory at Besançon. Richelieu alerted the king, who came from Versailles to reassure Richelieu and to reaffirm his determination to protect him.

Ambitious, debauched and unencumbered by his brother's religious scruples and sense of divine mission, Gaston's position was strong, as Richelieu was well aware. Richelieu's position, on the other hand, was still weak. He was burdened by the ever-present physical danger of assassination, by a debilitating sense of responsibility without the certainty of enough power to give him real control, and by the headstrong moods of the king. It is difficult, in the face of the prodigious efforts Richelieu made to preserve peace between the king and his mother, to blame him for what now looks like a miscalculation, but he uncharacteristically overreacted.

He was backing an assertion of royal authority which went too far. Bassompierre was put in the Bastille in February 1631 on the strength of a suspicion bred of his new cordiality with Louis de Marillac, as shown in an intercepted letter. He was not released until after Richelieu's death. The opposition was being driven from aggravating dissidence into open rebellion, and the king, guided by Richelieu, risked making himself vulnerable by alienating significant sources of national and international sympathy.

Richelieu, as always extremely cautious not to appear to presume in his relations with the king, wrote him a careful, controlled memoir, very long and quite free of spite, but firmly pointing to the conclusion that Marie de' Medici must be removed from any position from which she might cause damage. The king, now totally reliant on Richelieu's friendship as well as his advice, was not unwilling to ask her to leave Paris for Moulins, of which she would be made governor. He decided himself to take her to Compiègne, away from the politically corrosive forces to which she was subject. He arrived there on 12 February and pleaded with his mother, who adamantly refused to appear at council meetings. Louis left to return to Paris on 23 February. Marshal d'Estrées, the former marquis de Cœuvres, was to guard her. The queen mother's doctor and confidant, Vautier, also close to the Marillacs, was sent to the Bastille. Three duchesses close to the queen mother and the Princesse de Conti, who was to die a few days later, were all exiled.

Marie de' Medici agreed to go to Moulins, as the king had instructed, but asked if she might be allowed to wait at Nevers for the town of Moulins to be cleared of a rampant infection, and for the château to be repaired. Permission was given, but she remained at Compiègne. When on 20 March the king wrote saying that Moulins was now ready, she found endless reasons for delaying the move to Moulins, apparently afraid that she might be taken back to Florence. By May Louis was offering his mother Angers or Blois, and rumours were reaching Richelieu that the king's mother was preparing an escape.

The guard had been relaxed in order to avoid giving the queen mother the impression that she was imprisoned. Then on the evening of 18 July, Marie de' Medici did leave Compiègne, where the liberally bribed guards failed to stop the dramatic deployment of empty vehicles and lame excuses for the late-night comings and goings of carriages. There were improbable assertions that one carriage was going after hunting spoils, that another contained an eloping lady-in-waiting, and a third the lady-in-waiting's luggage. Highly penetrable disguises were being used.

His mother's disappearance provoked from Louis a series of defiant assertions of his commitment to Richelieu, of which the climax was the erection of the Richelieu estates into a *duché-pairie* in August, making Richelieu a duke and peer. The queen mother had intended in her flight to stay on French territory at the frontier town of La Capelle, temporarily under the charge of the son of marquis de Vardes, baron du Bec, a friend of Gaston who promised to open the gates for her. Richelieu got wind of the plan, and sent Vardes back to his post just in time to frustrate the queen mother's attempt to enter La Capelle.

Marie de' Medici, whose escort was frightened of probable pursuit, was forced to carry on across the border. She arrived at Avesnes, the nearest town on Spanish soil, on the evening of 20 July, subsequently moving within the Spanish Low Countries to Mons, then Brussels. She wrote Louis violent letters accusing Richelieu of everything she could think of, and even arraigned Richelieu before the Paris *parlement* essentially for subverting the power which belonged to the king, his mother and the princes of the blood. The king had to go to court on 12 August and deny what the queen mother had asserted. Marie de' Medici's flight incidentally removed Louis de Marillac's last hope of escaping the axe, which was reprieve as part of a bargain between the queen mother and the king. Marie de' Medici's life from this point becomes a sad story of illusion, decline and poverty. Nowhere was she more than briefly welcome, neither in the Low Countries, nor in England, nor in Holland, nor in Germany. Louis XIII cut off her revenues and never allowed her back to France, even when she was in financial straits in Cologne, a decision endorsed by the council in 1639.

Gaston, meanwhile, was fortifying Orléans, against which Louis marched, starting out on 11 March. On the 26th, at Dijon, he declared his brother's supporters guilty of *lèse-majesté,* and on 3 April he received a letter from Gaston, still at Besançon. Gaston, too, initiated proceedings against Richelieu, suppressed by order of the council on 12 May, and on 31 May he wrote his most violent letter of all against the despotic tyranny which Richelieu exercised over the king. On the approach of his brother with his army, Gaston fled first to Spanish Franche-Comté, and then to Lorraine.

The queen mother's flight incidentally resulted in a rapprochement between the *parlement* and the king, who had held a *lit de justice* in May at which he exiled several magistrates, although they were allowed back on Richelieu's intervention. As Richelieu had foreseen, the king needed the *parlement* to register a declaration against Gaston, and now also the queen mother, in order to make their adherents guilty of *lèse-majesté*, and to confiscate his mother's offices and revenues. The king conceded the re-establishment of the discontinued *paulette* for members of the *parlement*, making their offices again heritable and saleable. He also took the opportunity to opine that members of the *parlement* 'maliciously exaggerate the misery and want of my poor people, who matter to me more than anything else'.[3]

Once the queen mother had crossed on to Spanish soil, she was not herself a real threat to the king, who, on the other hand, needed at all costs to neutralise Gaston in Lorraine. The duke there, Charles IV, was giving assistance to the emperor. Of his two sisters, one, Henriette, had taken Gaston's companion, Puylaurens, as a lover, while the other, Marguerite, had fallen in love with the easily captivated Gaston, who wanted to marry her. Richelieu was naturally well informed about the intrigues with which Nancy, Lorraine's capital, was overflowing, and he also saw that France needed to secure Lorraine for itself, partly to prevent the emperor from using it as a way in to Champagne, and partly because Richelieu foresaw the possible need for France to have at its disposal Lorraine's easy access to Alsace.

An army under the command of Louis XIII and Richelieu forced the imperial garrison stationed at Moyenvic in Lorraine to withdraw in December 1631, and by the treaty of Vic of 6 January 1632, the duke of Lorraine had to concede to the French freedom of passage and the fortress of Marsal for three years. What nobody knew when the treaty was signed was that Gaston had been secretly married to Marguerite for three days, before going to join his mother in Brussels, where he conspired with her to lead into France an army provided by the Spaniards and the duke of Lorraine. Details of the plotting, probably including rumours of the marriage, were inevitably being passed to Richelieu by his network of informers. The rebels hoped to attract the support of Henri II de Montmorency, governor of Languedoc, whose sister was married to Condé. One of her maids, as might almost routinely have been expected, was also one of Richelieu's informers. Montmorency was a marshal of France, although to his resentment the title of *connétable* held by his father had not been bestowed on him.

In 1631 popular uprisings, partly occasioned by the results of a particularly poor harvest, had in fact occurred in Paris, Bordeaux, Poitiers, Marseilles, Orléans and Aix. Languedoc's disaffection arose also on account of the administrative reforms which Richelieu was trying to impose.[4] Montmorency had offered refuge to Richelieu when he had appeared to be in danger during the king's illness at Lyons in 1630. He had not objected to the introduction of the tax-gathering royal commissioners in Languedoc even before a compromise was agreed whereby their activities were made contingent on letters patent issued by the provincial estates meeting at Pézenas on 12 December 1631. But his wife was a niece of Marie de' Medici, and she encouraged her husband, himself a friend of Gaston, to become enmeshed in the plans for rebellion being hatched by Gaston. Richelieu taxed Montmorency about his attitude to the potential disloyalty of Languedoc, and was content to accept his reassurance.

What finally moved the thirty-seven-year-old Montmorency to commit himself to the rebel cause was the treatment of the Marillacs. He is also generally assumed to have been the lover of Anne of Austria. Montmorency's decision must essentially have been a reaction to Richelieu's attitude to the *grands*. He talked even of offering his services to the Protestant Gustavus Adolphus if the plot failed. He was a fearless commander, the most powerful member of the old feudal aristocracy left, and the last of his line. His was not a local grievance, but a stand taken alongside those who detested chiefly the king's preference for Richelieu over those who thought themselves entitled by right of birth or marriage to participate in government.

Montmorency bade Gaston to await his signal before moving troops to Languedoc, but Gaston impetuously moved within a week of Marillac's execution, assembling a force of about 2,500 horsemen at Trier before enlisting the renewed support of the duke of Lorraine. A loyal French force immediately marched on

Nancy, and was to force Charles, the duke, to ask pardon personally from Louis XIII on 8 July. In mid-June Gaston had marched on Dijon with a mercenary army, calling on the kingdom to rise and deliver Louis XIII from the 'tyranny' of Richelieu, 'disturber of the public peace, enemy of the king, subvertor of the state . . . tyrant and oppressor'. It was a serious miscalculation. The city and the *parlement* of Dijon, like most other towns, remained loyal to the king, and denied entry to Gaston's forces. Gaston himself rallied some of the gentry in Auvergne, but his sole real hope now was Languedoc, which he entered on 22 July, meeting Montmorency's army at Lunel on 30 July.

Montmorency had deliberately provoked the Languedoc Estates, meeting on 22 July, by inviting the deputies in the name of the king to approve the appointment not of commissioners, to which they had agreed, but of the king's *élus,* which Richelieu was again seeking to impose, having already failed two years previously, and to which Montmorency knew that the deputies were firmly opposed. When the taxes were finally levied by the *élus,* the deputies protested, while at the same time inviting the duke to join with them in a declaration of commitment to the king's service and 'the relief of the province', hiding the declaration of independence under a loyal verbal formula.

Montmorency intentionally exacerbated feelings further by having the deputies arrested together with the archbishop of Narbonne, a Richelieu supporter who was to preside over meetings of the Estates. At Toulouse, the *parlement* simply rejected the declaration of the Estates and remained loyal to the king. The bishops of Albi, Lodève, Uzès and Saint-Pons offered to open their cathedral cities to Gaston's troops. By the summer of 1632, Richelieu distrusted Montmorency, but a plan to capture him at Montpellier was leaked, and Montmorency eluded capture.

The rebellion itself was soon over. The king at a *lit de justice* ordered the Paris *parlement* to register an edict making treasonable any assistance given to Gaston, who was himself offered the restoration of revenues and privileges if he submitted and disbanded his army. Montmorency was declared a traitor, and his vast properties were sequestrated. In mid-August the king led an army southwards, hearing on 1 September before he had reached Lyons of the victory of his army of better disciplined and trained

troops under Schomberg at Castelnaudary, where Schomberg, with
not quite half as many troops as were in the rebel armies, had
engineered a confrontation. The king's half-brother, the comte de
Moret, son of Henri IV by Jacqueline de Bueil, who had joined the
rebel forces, was killed, and a severely wounded Montmorency,
after his own troops had failed to retrieve him, was taken prisoner.
He is said to have had twenty-four wounds from seventeen blows,
with his teeth knocked out by a bullet, but to have broken through
six ranks of Schomberg's troops, and to have killed men in the
seventh row.[5] Rebel officers were summarily hanged.

Gaston, locked into Béziers, tried to negotiate while hoping for
help from Spanish troops whose route Schomberg had blocked.
Louis XIII and Richelieu took over the negotiations in Montpellier.
Gaston momentarily escaped to a fortress near Carcassonne, but
was predictably forced on 11 October to sign a submission, the
Béziers 'articles of peace', in exchange for a pardon which extended
only to Gaston himself, to the household which accompanied him,
but neither to Montmorency nor to Gaston's supporters in Brussels.
Gaston had bargained in the hope of saving Montmorency, but was
forced to abandon him to his fate. An associate of Condé dined
with Richelieu and reported from Montpellier on 30 September
that Richelieu held out little hope of mercy.[6] Gaston was forced
to declare that he would break his alliance with Lorraine, Spain,
other foreign princes and his mother. He promised to remain on
good terms with Richelieu. His only private satisfaction was the
ability to confirm to his brother that the duke of Lorraine's sister
was already his wife.

The king pacified Languedoc, abandoning the *élections* which
Montmorency had used to provoke anti-royal sentiment, and, when
Montmorency had recovered, he had him taken to Toulouse, the
capital, where the *parlement,* with special jurisdiction conferred by
direct commission of the king, was ordered to institute proceedings
against him. Montmorency, as a peer, had a right to be tried by
the supreme court of the Paris *parlement.* His capital, Toulouse,
might actually have been more sympathetic to him than Paris.
Châteauneuf, the keeper of the seals in succession to Michel de
Marillac, who had presided over the trial of Louis de Marillac, was
personally to preside.

The death penalty for treason was inevitable, but intense pressure

for a reprieve was brought to bear, among others by Anne of
Austria, a miniature of whom Montmorency was wearing in a
diamond bracelet when he was wounded, as Richelieu informed
the king. Others to intercede were Montmorency's wife, an Orsini
niece of Marie de' Medici; his sister who was Condé's wife; the
duc d'Angoulême, who was the illegitimate son of Charles IX and
one of the king's commanders at La Rochelle; Gaston, who at first
tried to make Montmorency's reprieve a condition of submission;
Marie de' Medici; the duke of Savoy; and the pope.

Both Marie de' Medici and Gaston sent threatening letters to
Marillac's executioners in an attempt to discourage those who had
been going to carry out Montmorency's execution, which none the
less took place in the courtyard of the Toulouse Hôtel de Ville on
30 October 1632. A primitive form of guillotine was used. Louis
allowed as a final privilege that the executioner should not be
allowed to touch or bind him, and at Montmorency's request the
execution was brought forward from five o'clock to three, the hour
of the death of Jesus. His preparation for death was devout, and he
slept peacefully for six hours the night before he was to die. Among
the bequests Montmorency was allowed to make was a painting
which he left to Richelieu, the *Saint Sébastien mourant* now in the
Louvre.[7] On his deathbed in 1643, Louis XIII said the denial of a
reprieve to Montmorency was the action he most regretted.

Richelieu had appeared to favour clemency, but the *Mémoires*
and other sources make clear that, like Marillac, Montmorency
was sacrificed at Richelieu's instigation to give public notice that
the fate of the individual was subordinate to the interests of the
country, the famous 'raison d'état'. The highest officers concerned
in the successful campaign against Gaston and Montmorency were
promoted, and Schomberg was made governor of Languedoc. After
the execution, the court undertook a triumphal progress through
the south, in the course of which it learnt in November that Gaston
had once more fled to join his mother in Brussels, feeling that the
execution of Montmorency had released him from the obligations
imposed by the Béziers articles. A sharp letter to the king of 12
November was immediately printed and publicly distributed.

The presence on Spanish-controlled territory of the heir to the
French throne was a serious blow to France. His recent rebellion
had been backed by Spanish troops on the orders of Olivares.

Though cool towards Gaston, the elderly Spanish governor of
the Low Countries, the Infanta Isabella, daughter of Philip II of
Spain, but also granddaughter of Henri II of France, had been
obliged publicly to support him, and had in fact lodged him at
her own expense in the apartments of her late husband. Olivares
had made a large sum available to her to have troops for Gaston's
rebellion raised in Alsace. War between Spain and France had
looked quite probable on the eve of Gaston's rebellion, and his
renewed presence in Brussels had effects not only on Richelieu's
foreign policy, but also on the tightness with which administrative
control needed to be imposed on France itself. Gaston might yet
have split the country.

    After the execution of Montmorency, and no doubt partly
because of the nervous exhaustion resulting from that event,
Richelieu had been seriously ill at Bordeaux in November 1632.
His health had held up well between 1621 and the 1628 bouts
of fever, which recurred in 1629 and 1630, when they had kept
him at Saint-Jean de Maurienne,[8] but now his rheumatism became
chronically painful, and he experienced a life-threatening retention
of urine, apparently the consequence of an anal abscess painful
enough to prevent him from sleeping for six days, and which kept
him in Saugeon, near Saintes. He could be moved only by stretcher.
After the 1632 crisis, he was able to travel again in January 1633,
when he returned to Paris through Brouage and La Rochelle, in both
of which he now needed private business managers to oversee the
receiving and reinvestment of the income from his marine rights.

    At Cadillac Richelieu had stayed with the now aged Epernon
sufficiently briefly for him not to have needed to risk eating
anything. He left Epernon very early, having taken only a bowl of
soup 'which had not come from Epernon's kitchen.' Epernon had
been among Richelieu's sickbed visitors at Bordeaux, and Richelieu
had feared capture and abduction by him and others in the queen's
entourage. Châteauneuf, now lover of Mme de Chevreuse, recalled
as lady-in-waiting to the queen, had made no secret of the hope
he had shared with her, and with Anne of Austria, that Richelieu
would not recover. He is said to have danced for joy in the next
room as Richelieu's health deteriorated, while also accepting the
honours prepared for Richelieu in the towns between Bordeaux
and Paris, and generally acting as if he had already succeeded

the first minister, about whom his letters in cipher to Mme de Chevreuse were contemptuous. The king expressed his outrage in a letter to Richelieu of 4 February 1633 when he heard. The cardinal was aware of the barely concealed hostility and the physical danger it entailed.

Châteauneuf had become suspect, and Père Joseph had been trying for a month to turn the king against him. Père Joseph had worked well. The king came from Paris to meet Richelieu, telling him that he had decided to dismiss Châteauneuf, allowing Richelieu the chance to appear to question the wisdom of such a move. Richelieu had the correspondence of Châteauneuf and Mme de Chevreuse seized and found the anticipated disobliging references to himself in what Mme de Chevreuse had written, as also letters of complicity from Henrietta-Maria, the king's sister, now queen of England. Châteauneuf was arrested on 25 February 1633. He was to stay in the Bastille until after Richelieu's death. Sympathisers with the cardinal's ill-wishers were punished in effigy, a freely and frequently dispensed warning to miscreants to stay away. Mme de Chevreuse was exiled to Touraine. The cardinal had reached the apex of his power.

Late in 1631 he had begun construction of a magnificent new château at Richelieu with plans by the architect Jacques Le Mercier, who had previously drawn up plans for the Louvre for Louis XIII, and worked for Richelieu on the Palais Cardinal and the Sorbonne. Richelieu had started work on his father's old château soon after he entered government, spending 24,595 livres on construction in 1625 and 1626, but intending even as late as 1630 to do no more than finish on a reduced scale the building his father had started. He visited the château for two or three days in 1626, returning in October 1627 to receive Condé there, and was later to insist that most of his father's château should be incorporated into the new residence, in spite of the difficulties which that created for the alignment of the facade. Le Mercier did his best to disguise with ornamentation the fact that it was out of true.

Work took place under the general supervision of the archbishop of Bordeaux, Henri de Sourdis.[9] In May 1631, before the erection of the estate into a *duché-pairie* in August, Richelieu had been granted letters patent to construct a walled town adjacent to his château, with four annual fairs, like the already well-established town of

Niort, the residents to be freed of all taxes until the first hundred houses had been built. To annex a small new town to a newly built château was of course the most grandiloquent of opulent gestures, but it had been done before, by Sully at Henrichemont and Henri IV for the Place Royale.

Like them Richelieu could not find the cash resources he needed, and financed his gesture by pre-selling building plots. Le Mercier drew up the plans for the small town although, since the residents of the fourteen houses planned for each side of the principal tree-lined avenue had themselves to have their houses built to a uniform plan, Richelieu was to have considerable difficulty in recruiting them. Sourdis reported that the main street was still five houses short on 30 July 1633. Most of those who came aimed to please the cardinal, presumably for profit, and the majority left after his death.

To add lustre to his town, Richelieu would even install a printing works and on 20 September 1640 would obtain letters patent for an academy, called 'royal college', for members of the French and foreign aristocracy where Latin, Greek and French law would be taught, as well as the exercise of arms 'fitting for the nobility'. He also built a hospital and a church, staffed by four priests from the new missionary order recently founded by 'Monsieur Vincent', Saint Vincent de Paul.

To erect this ensemble in the middle of rural Poitou made a statement with nuances of meaning which it is easy either to exaggerate or to gloss over. There was obviously family *pietas* in finishing off what Richelieu's father had started, and there was also in the sheer immensity of the project a clear intention on Richelieu's part to reflect his own personal standing. But the relatively lavish provision of devotional and health-care facilities of the highest quality reflects Richelieu's seriousness about religion and his no doubt too infrequently expressed sense of social responsibility. The idea of an academy reminiscent of Pluvinel's, but intended for an international clientele of aristocrats and potential rulers, neatly encapsulates an inherited elitism of outlook together with a serious interest in intellectual formation, which must be viewed in the wider context of Richelieu's later such projects.

By 1631 Richelieu had bought up a score of neighbouring fiefs of different sorts to augment the dignity of the original *seigneurie*. By July 1633, Sourdis could inform Richelieu that the duchy was capable of bringing in 55,000 livres a year, and in that year Richelieu set aside 60,000 livres for the building works. When Gaston d'Orléans, about to build at Blois to plans by Mansart, visited the new château in 1635, Léon Bouthillier could report in a letter to the cardinal of 28 May that, when all was finished, he would have the most magnificent residence in Europe, Fontainebleau alone excepted.[10] In 1663 La Fontaine was to write that Richelieu's concept for his mansion and town was worthy of someone whose place in history would be greater than that of thirty popes. Unhappily, almost nothing remains. The park was broken into parcels when the family could no longer afford the upkeep, and the mansion was itself finally bought in 1835 to be broken up and sold for its stone.

The hospital was much used, and much of the town must have been inhabited by domestic staff attached either to the great house or to the households of the grand avenue. These houses were affordable only by prosperous merchants, administrators, financiers, members of the magistracy, or crown employees, none of whom was likely to make a house at Richelieu their ordinary residence. The concept of Richelieu town was essentially urban, and houses in the country made real sense only if there was land attached and farming to be pursued.

At the end of December 1636, the bishop of Albi was to deliver two paintings by Poussin for the 'king's apartments' at the château, which already had two Mantegnas set into the wooden panelling. As in only the greatest palaces of the period, the Louvre and the Luxembourg, and some of the Loire châteaux, there was to be a gallery of paintings. The collection was to contain works by van Dyck, Rubens, Dürer, Caravaggio and Perugini, with others then attributed to Raphael and Titian. At the ends of the gallery were equestrian portraits of Louis XIII and Richelieu.

Very little is known about the painter, Nicolas Prévost, but there were twenty of his canvases, of which twelve are now at Versailles, devoted to the exploits of the reign of Louis XIII.[11] The decoration also included tributes to the queen, to Marie de' Medici and to Gaston, with many antique marble or bronze busts, sculptures, and medallions bought for Richelieu by agents in Italy.[12] There were portraits of the cardinal's mother, his father and his grandfather in the ante-chamber to his own room, inside which was a copy of a Michelangelo given to him by Montmorency.

The cardinal never visited Richelieu again after his three-day stay in 1632, although he did think of going around the feast of All Saints in 1640, and again on his return from Perpignan in 1642, when his doctors thought it preferable for his health to go to Bourbon 'on account of the waters'. Aubery recounts that the cardinal had said that, were Richelieu to be only ten leagues from his town, he would not have the least temptation to go there if the king's business called him elsewhere. Yet he showed the same prodigious attention to detail in the planning of the layout, construction and decoration of palace and town at Richelieu as he did with everything else, from the exact measures taken to deploy troops and provisions at La Rochelle, to the precise provenance and destination of small groups of troops and horses to be dispersed among the three commanders of the armies of the Mantuan expedition. We know that in 1633 the pontifical authorities allowed a consignment of sixty statues and as many busts, two heads and five vases to be loaded on to empty galleys returning from Civittà Vecchia to Marseilles, from where they were transported to Richelieu. Two breakages were reported to the cardinal. In 1639 he had 'fifty or sixty' statues in Rome destined for Richelieu. He can never have seen them.

Just as his attention had been too obsessively absorbed by the delicate intricacies of his political involvement for him to preside over his mother's funeral in November 1616, only eleven days before his entry into the council, so he was also too taken up with the mind-challenging intricacies of the diplomatic background to the Thirty Years War to have time to visit his shatteringly grand mansion. He did, however, effortlessly master the last detail of the difficulties in supplying water to the park after the gradient had been miscalculated, and three alternative draft plans had been sent for him to choose between them. The cardinal certainly supervised decisions taken about the height, number and positioning of the hardwood saplings planted in the park, and the spacing of the elm avenue leading to the house.

Richelieu's attention to detail was no doubt a function of his nervous intensity. When he was marrying off his three cousins on the same day in 1634, he took the trouble personally to order three parasols, red, violet and blue, of the finest and lightest silk to be found in Genoa. They were to be decorated in gold lace. Admittedly, they were ordered through the secretary of state for foreign affairs, the comte de Chavigny, and the French ambassador in Genoa, but attention to the minutiae of such arrangements manifests not only the importance Richelieu attached to ordinary domestic arrangements, but also the extraordinary power of his mind, concurrently devoted to directing the destinies of France, with everything which that entailed. Devoting his staggering intellectual powers to getting domestic details exactly right afforded him relaxation and great personal satisfaction.[13]

The taste of the mansion's decoration was not his. Prévost was a protégé of the bishop of Albi, and his work is not considered to be distinguished. But the function of the mansion, the town and the dukedom was neither to be aesthetically satisfying, nor even to symbolise political power. It was to reflect an imposing personal grandeur, tempered perhaps only by a genuinely personal enthusiasm for laying out grounds. It did betray a need to render illustrious the family from which he came, and whose future social standing he was attempting to assure, but this does not mean that Richelieu aspired to join the *grands,* whose families had once shown the military prowess in the monarch's service which had entitled their ancestors to a share in the country's rule.[14] It was much more a statement that the old social system which made political power dependent on heredity had been abolished.

Personal grandeur, the non-ethical quality which the seventeenth-century called 'merit', no longer depended exclusively on lineage or on outstanding military qualities.[15] In no sense did Richelieu set out to rival the *grands,* whom he regarded essentially as relics of an era in which the sacerdotal character of the anointed king was taken less seriously than he took it. If he exercised his architectural patronage at Richelieu largely to manifest his personal standing, he also donated a new building to the Sorbonne, and joined with the king in building a church for the Jesuits. His greatest creation, the Palais-Cardinal, was left in gratitude to Louis XIII.

Any attempt to understand Richelieu's decision around 1631 to transform the modest family château into the prodigiously imposing house, park and town he created leads to the conclusion that Richelieu drew much satisfaction from manipulation, meticulously mastering vast organisational complexities. It was an ability which reflected the devastatingly impressive speed and range of his intellect, and it left room neither for sentimentality nor for humour. The obsessive grasp of detail shows throughout the vast volumes of published letters.

If Richelieu was readily moved to tears, it was not on account of any unusual sensitivity of feeling, but the simple result of nervous stress, a consequence of the intensity with which he committed himself even to minutiae in the management of affairs. Richelieu was easily moved to sometimes strong emotion, although he generally concealed it, but there was little room for tears of tenderness in a temperament so totally dominated by so penetrating an intelligence. It is rare even to find occasions on which Richelieu felt any clash between propriety and expedience. Expedience easily erected itself for him into a strict moral imperative, especially when the needs of state dictated the neglect of the rights of the individual.

From the moment of his re-appointment to the council, Richelieu had begun to acquire land. In 1623, the year after his elevation to the cardinalate, he sold a family property at Ansac, west of Limoges, and bought the château of Limours, south-west of Paris, which had once belonged to Diane de Poitiers, and which Louis XIII bought from the cardinal at the end of 1626 for the eighteen-year-old Gaston. In 1628 Marie de' Medici gave Richelieu Bois-le Vicomte at Mitry-Mory, which today is at the south-east corner of Charles de Gaulle airport, north-east of Paris but for Richelieu the wrong side for proximity to the court. The cardinal was to exchange it in 1635 for Champigny-sur-Veude, which was close to Richelieu, and could be incorporated into the *duché-pairie,* while he himself rented Fleury-en-Bière, near Fontainebleau.

In August 1633, he acquired Rueil, convenient for Paris, Saint-Germain-en-Laye and Versailles, immediately adding to it adjoining lands and purchasing the feudal rights, spending nearly 800,000 livres in all.[16] Within the rebuilt château, Richelieu had apartments built for his niece, the duchesse d'Aiguillon, as well as quarters for his personal guards, and a theatre. While work was going on, he would stay in one of the estate farms. Visitors to Rueil have left few details about the château, but were astonished at the wonders of the gardens. Built into a hillside, they contained grottos, waterfalls, fountains, a lake, a wall painted with a trompe-l'œil arc de triomphe, and a stream, composing a picturesque fairy-tale landscape such as was newly fashionable in Italy. Richelieu had exotic chestnuts planted round the lake, with tulips in the parterres, giving detailed directions to his head gardener, Jean Maignan. He was proud of the revenue yielded by the vines he grew.

For his town house, known successively as the Hôtel Richelieu, the Palais-Cardinal, and after his death as the Palais-Royal, Richelieu bought on 9 April 1624 what had been the Hôtel de Rambouillet, just to the west of the Louvre, giving on to the rue Saint-Honoré, the new east-west axis of Paris which was altering the shape of the town.[17] He also acquired a further property, the Hôtel de Sillery, whose demolition was intended to improve his view, and gradually bought further properties to the west, beginning in 1628 to build a wing along the west side of the garden to plans by Jacques Le Mercier. The first-floor gallery, known as the *Galerie des hommes illustres*, exhibited paintings by Simon Vouet and Philippe de Champaigne of great servants of France, including the king, Marie de' Medici, and Richelieu himself.

Richelieu's nomination as director-general of fortifications in 1631 allowed him to pull down at public expense what was left of the old town ramparts, and made possible the acquisition of further properties to the west, as far as the present rue de Richelieu. To finance his building, in 1636 the cardinal sold forty-two building sites on the northern and western edges of his property, with building restrictions to preserve his own gardens from being overlooked, bringing him an annual rental income of 10,500 livres. The large-scale building operations on the site, eventually to result in the completed Palais-Cardinal, seem to have been conceived in 1633.[18] By 1639 the palace was finished, and the cardinal had already moved there from the Petit Luxembourg, the house next to the Luxembourg palace given to him by Marie de' Medici when he was her *surintendant*. In 1639 he signed a contract with the king's painters, Jean Blanchard and Henri Mauperché, to execute for the Palais-Cardinal large paintings of 'La Ville et château de Richelieu' and of Rueil, a smaller painting of his second *duché-pairie* of Fronsac, acquired in 1633 for 600,000 livres and left to his sister's son, Armand de Maillé de Brézé, together with four other paintings, one of the Sorbonne, one each of the two hospitals Richelieu built, and one of the door to the Jesuit church.

Architecture had become a political and cultural tool.[19] Its new status was symbolised by the erection of the statue of Louis XIII in the Place Royale and of Henri IV in the Place Dauphine, commemorating the urban renewal which took place under both monarchs. Richelieu's own architectural patronage drew on his own funds for public purposes, but also utilised public funds for personal property, and it is impossible to distinguish rigorously between Richelieu's patronage and that of the state or of the king. Nevertheless, Richelieu's early architectural endeavours were undertaken on his own initiative. He was thrilled by the 'folly' of his purchase of Limours in 1623, on the eve of his re-admission to the royal council, even before he had gained the confidence of Louis XIII.

Richelieu also had the Sorbonne building physically rebuilt to plans by Le Mercier which were shown to the fellows on 20 June 1626. There were protests, but Richelieu had been to considerable pains to ensure that the fellows' way of life and day-to-day convenience should not be disturbed, and a contract was signed on behalf of the cardinal on 30 July 1626 with the entrepreneur Jean Autissier describing in detail the building to be constructed. It was expected to cost two million livres, and an enthusiasm among the fellows for the new building was suddenly ignited when, on 8 August 1628, the foundation of a Jesuit college was laid just across the rue Saint-Jacques.

Richelieu was stretched for money by the siege of La Rochelle and the need to lend to the king. Such funds for the project as Richelieu could make available had first to be spent on the acquisition of buildings to be demolished, and do not show in the builders' accounts. Building at the Sorbonne was therefore slow. Work was supervised by Sublet de Noyers, the devout and austere secretary for war from 1636, author of military and monetary reforms and a brilliant administrator, who also assumed responsibility for public buildings.

The foundation stone of the new church, within the Sorbonne precincts and also by Le Mercier, was laid on 15 May 1635. It was to contain Richelieu's tomb. In 1639 the church was 'fort avancé', but it was not until March 1642 that the whole site for the new building was acquired. Richelieu wrote to Sublet as late as 22 September 1642, ten weeks before his death, thanking him for clearing away the buildings ruining the view from the chapel and making way for the square. His will specified that the Sorbonne should be given priority in the expenditure of the two thirds of his revenues made available to his niece and residual heir, the duchesse d'Aiguillon, intended to pay his debts and complete his unfinished projects. Six days after his death, on 10 December his heart and organs were taken to the still unfinished chapel, where the body was to be formally received on 13 December prior to its entombment.[20]

8

Religious and Cultural Background

By 1634, the year in which he was forty-nine, Richelieu had slowly gestated within himself a perception of the means by which his ultimate personal dream of an independent and glorious France might be fulfilled. Before the crisis of 1630, he had been only instinctively groping towards a definition of his aims. The strategy which he hoped would allow him to implement his vision became clear against the optimistic move towards the cultivation of the heroic which the culture of literate France was undergoing in the first thirty years of the century.

The exploration of the heroic ideal in novelists like Camus and Gomberville, in playwrights like Pierre Corneille and Scudéry, in poets like Malherbe and Chapelain, and in painters like Poussin and Claude goes hand in hand with a resurgence in France of the pastoral convention, exploited by the poets and painters of the Renaissance, but neglected in France during the religious wars. The primary function of pastoral conventions in the imaginative work of early seventeenth-century France was the moral upgrading of behaviour, including sexual behaviour, which, because it is both natural and depicted in a natural setting, takes on a life-enhancing innocence alien to the late medieval Christian tradition.

While, elsewhere in Europe, and particularly in Italy, Spain, England and perhaps the Catholic parts of the Empire, the changes in cultural values which we refer to as the Renaissance had continued to examine the enhancement of human moral potential, the damaging civil wars had forced the examination of personal and social attitudes in French culture into its defensive position, neostoic and relativist. While some poetry remained bucolic in setting, very few truly pastoral pieces emerged from France during the period of the wars. With their end, the French exploration of heroic moral values immediately accelerated in a movement made more pronounced by its contrast with the cultural tone predominant during the preceding period. For the first three or four decades of the seventeenth century it was as if France, as it recovered from its late sixteenth-century despondency and erratically fought off threatening political disintegration, was catching up with Italy, Spain and England.

The cultivation of the heroic was to be abandoned in the France of the 1640s, but the exploration of the innocence of instinctive behaviour was to be taken much further, as the partisans of the *modernes* conquered the admiration for Homeric and Virgilian norms of violence and versification admired by the defenders of the *anciens* in the *querelle des anciens et des modernes* in the late seventeenth century, leaving the eighteenth to produce the joyousness of rococo and the idyllic fantasies of Fragonard and Boucher, with quasi-philosophical support from Jean-Jacques Rousseau.

Following on Richelieu's youthful personal success in Rome and Paris, an early ambition to ingratiate himself with the powerful had given way firstly to a diminished obsequiousness and then to the more assured certainties of the pastorally committed if still ambitious anti-Huguenot bishop, enduringly fastidious but now less unctuous. The concern with religious apologetic marking this period subsequently waned, although Richelieu was still to finish writing his important work of pastoral and devotional theology, the *Traitté de la perfection du chrestien,* on his last journey early in 1642, the year of his death. The concern to demarcate the stages on the path to Christian perfection did not dwindle. By 1615 the juvenile piety which had involved promising God good deeds in return for divine favours had disappeared,[1] but Richelieu had still to free himself from the need to cultivate a La Rocheposay or a Bérulle. As late as 1634 his devotional life was still to deepen.

Richelieu's personal religion was to become more concerned with spirituality and less with propositional credal statements, more deeply aware of the distinction between spiritual and temporal realms and the deference proper to the different norms which governed each. Politically, Richelieu moved cautiously during the first years of his re-admission to the king's council, from 1624–1626, but what the *Testament politique* says about the need Richelieu felt in 1624 to address the problems raised by the Huguenots, the *grands,* and France's external glory was a later reminiscence, and was anyway not an ordered statement of political aims. It was in response to external stimuli and instinctive feeling, rather than to any earlier defined hierarchy of strategic goals, that Richelieu found himself strongly advocating that the north Italian campaign be undertaken before addressing the problem of France's internal cohesion, and later still that it became clear to him that the consolidation of a united France demanded an anti-Huguenot civil war.

By the time of the crisis occasioned by the Mantuan succession, the link between Richelieu's private values and the political priorities which he was to impose on France was already discernible, and circumstances were obliging him to force the king to choose between the pursuit of France's independent grandeur and the desire of the political Catholic party for peace with Spain and a subordinate position for France in Catholic Europe. Only by about 1633, after the *journée des dupes* and the executions of Montmorency and Louis de Marillac, were Richelieu's private values and political aims, domestic and external, totally clear and integrated, although Richelieu did not yet fully realise what domestic miseries they would entail for the nation. Richelieu was reluctantly to prove willing to impose on France's people painful sacrifices analogous to those he imposed on himself in the interests of achieving glory for France.

Historians have often been dazzled by the accretion of power and the magnificence of the display of wealth, while remaining puzzled by the cardinal's austere but enigmatic exterior. They have sometimes adverted to Richelieu's vulnerabilities, but seldom penetrated to the core of the devout but insecure personality. Richelieu only slowly achieved sureness of touch, and had to force himself to offer to Louis XIII the firm advice recorded in the letters, which certainly before 1630 sounded more decisive than was warranted by their author's vision at the time.

Vociferous enemies among Richelieu's contemporaries created the image of a merciless tyrant who ruthlessly enforced his power over the king and the country. The nineteenth century reversed this picture, and the post-romantic view has inclined to see in Richelieu the subtle and penetrating mind which aroused admiration among his contemporaries, and which was the source of the vision, and the administrative mechanisms necessary to realise it, from which pre-revolutionary France was to emerge. None the less it may well be true that it is impossible to name any historical personage in French public life who has provoked more hatred than Richelieu.[2]

Whether interested in the concentration of power and the politics of princes, or in the statistics of starvation, what many historians have missed or misread is the nature of the moral background developed among the educated elite after Henri IV had, if not actually ended the religious wars, at least reduced them to a smoulder. La Rochelle and the alliances between the Huguenots and the *grands* show that the smoulder was still dangerously capable of bursting into flame.

Although, even after La Rochelle, France was not truly to enjoy internal peace until the 1650s, it did generate during the first third of the century an unprecedented surge of cultural optimism, most clearly shown in the intensity and quality of its interest in literature and the visual arts, and in the personal and social values they explored. The most advanced artistic achievements of the age were probably to be found in the visual arts, often, even generally, depending on a sophisticated knowledge of the myths of classical antiquity. Artists and poets used them not only to enhance the dignity of Louis XIII, but also to elevate attitudes towards all instinctive human behaviour to the heights they had enjoyed in the mythology of classical antiquity as adapted by the painters and authors of early seventeenth-century France.[3]

Until relatively recently literary historians were not much concerned about the period between Montaigne, who died in 1592, and the beginnings of Pierre Corneille in the early 1630s. But much of what Richelieu believed in derived from the principles enunciated in the moral treatises of d'Urfé, who went on to probe them in his hugely popular novel *L'Astrée,* or in those with stoic resonances in their titles by du Vair, the keeper of the seals whom Richelieu replaced on the council in 1616.[4]

Theologians have not generally emphasised the truly astonishing nature of François de Sales's radical optimism. Literary historians have failed to do adequate justice to the heroic values explored on the stage by Corneille to upgrade human potential, or to the immense optimism about human nature examined in fiction by authors like d'Urfé, Gomberville and La Calprenède. Few students of Descartes have adverted to the breathtakingly optimistic assumptions behind his life-long attempt to unify all non-empirical forms of human knowledge into a deductive system based on an absolute metaphysical certainty which would support belief in the immortality of the soul. In 1637, Descartes thought it possible to show that both ethics and medicine were exact sciences whose logically demonstrable conclusions could lead to the greatest virtue and happiness of which human beings were capable.[5]

The philosopher who came nearest to summing up Richelieu's ethical values, and whose expression of his moral ideal certainly derived from du Vair, was Descartes, born in 1596 who was Richelieu's nearly exact contemporary.[6] Before he devoted himself single-mindedly to the establishment of his philosophical system, apparently under the influence of Bérulle, Descartes led the normal life of a patrician youth. Like Pascal, he gamed, and he appears to have fought a duel over a woman.[7] Richelieu, in his subordination of all personal interests to those of the state, was the ultimate product of the culture of *gloire*, whose underlying ethic had been elaborated by du Vair and then Descartes. Richelieu was among its principal non-military exemplars, openly embracing the heroic ideal in all its quest for grandeur and identifying the manifestations of *gloire* explored by imaginative authors and dramatists with the desire for virtue.[8] What Richelieu's policies did to France in the half-decade after 1635 was for a period to wreck the underlying optimism of the culture of which he was the product.

It has always been at least one of the principal functions of the historical study of literature to identify the value systems of the society which produced it, and to see how the desirability or undesirability of potential alternatives was explored. By extension, the same can be said of other culturally conditioned genres, most notably the theatre, which before the age of nearly universal literacy largely filled the function later to be assumed by imaginative literature. At least in western Europe, a similar reassessment of cultural values appears in the history of spirituality, for present purposes comprising the forms taken by Christian religious devotion during the Catholic revival. It may be noted that Catholicism, especially in Spain but also in France, allowed its devotional forms to be adapted to the baroque much more easily than did those associated with Huguenot belief, no doubt because since the Renaissance Catholicism had more readily adopted an optimistic view about natural human potential.

The 'Catholic revival' had a much broader base than the political pro-Spanish party which emerged from the discredited League in the 1590s. Whether their spirituality was contemplative, like the Carmelites, or their purpose the relief of distress, like the Visitation and the foundation of saint Vincent de Paul, or missionary and educational, like the Jesuits, many of the new religious congregations in France were quite uncommitted to political wrangles involving secular support for foreign co-religionists. The Jesuits already had a wide international base. Bérulle, himself one of their pupils, set out not to found a new order, but to reform the French diocesan clergy, regarding the hierarchical priesthood as imposing a more important spiritual status than the vows taken by members of religious orders.[9]

Common to the mystical sources of Bérulle's spirituality was the belief that human spiritual progress consisted in the abnegation, then the annihilation, of human nature, to be replaced by a divinised and beatified personality joined to God, analogous to the way in which the incarnation joined the human personality of Jesus to the divine. The devout soul might share Mary's love of her son, and express the renunciation of all personal desire in the notorious 'vow of servitude' to the virgin taken by Bérulle's Oratorians on 8 September 1614, followed by the vow taken to Jesus on 28 February 1615. The vows of servitude were extreme expressions of baroque emotional attitudinising, but Bérulle was insensitive enough to attempt to impose them on the Carmelites, to whose more contemplative spirituality and developed religious sensitivity they were quite foreign.

Founded no doubt on heroic religious dedication, it is nonetheless not difficult to realise how fraught Bérulle's spirituality was with dangers of self-delusion, mental instability and even paranoia. Apparently religious phenomena could be, and were, induced by the imagination, with sometimes horrific results, as with the phenomena widely interpreted as diabolic possession or witchcraft.[10] It was during the 1620s that the necessity of nature's annihilation and replacement by a divine spiritual principle began to develop in the entourage of Bérulle into what would become the pessimistic religious basis for Jansenism, a spirituality developed by Jean Duvergier de Hauranne, abbé de Saint-Cyran, whom Richelieu was to have imprisoned.

Saint-Cyran had studied with the Jesuits at school and then at Louvain, although he finished his theology in Paris where, about 1610, he met Cornelius Jansen, with whom he shared living quarters, and with whom he moved to Bayonne. Their close association was carried on by correspondence after Jansen's return to the Low Countries as professor of scripture in 1614. Saint-Cyran's mother and sister were among the many accused of witchcraft in the wake of the notorious condemnation of Marthe Brossier for diabolic possession. Bérulle shortly after his ordination had published an already neoplatonist *Traité des énergumènes* in 1599, maintaining the reality of the possession. Marthe Brossier escaped to Rome, but there were some 600 burnings in Bayonne, including three priests among the victims.

Richelieu must first have met him after Saint-Cyran became closely associated with Henri-Louis de la Rocheposay, coadjutor of Poitiers from 1608, and bishop of the diocese from 1611. It was he who had led troops in the defence of Poitiers against Condé in 1614. Saint-Cyran was ordained so that he might take possession of his abbey in 1618, and it is important in view of his later spiritual teaching that even into the 1620s he followed contemporary eucharistic piety, again in all its baroque exaggerations, in particular desiring to celebrate mass and receive the eucharist as frequently as possible. Then for most of 1622 Saint-Cyran spent nearly an hour a day discussing Bérulle's spirituality with him. In 1623 Bérulle's defence of his vows of servitude in the *Discours de l'état et des grandeurs de Jésus* appeared. It was dedicated to the king, and 'approbations' to it were signed by an imposing and unnecessarily large array of theologians, including Richelieu and Père Joseph.[11]

In 1625 Saint-Cyran published the first two volumes of an intended four-volume attack on the Jesuit François Garasse's *Doctrine curieuse des beaux esprits du temps*. Saint-Cyran intended chiefly to rebut the element of trust in human nature in Jesuit spirituality, and dedicated his work with a rhetorical flourish to Richelieu. The controversy it aroused ensured that the third volume was suppressed and the fourth published only in synopsis. It is important as a precursor to the later views of human nature implicit in Saint-Cyran's spiritual rigorism, and as an early forewarning of the crisis to come in a cultural confidence which was still ten or a dozen years from reaching its peak.

Richelieu had by 1625 mentally broken with Bérulle on both the theological and the political fronts, although at the date of his return to power he may still have harboured interior uncertainties. Theologically he had embraced the Jesuit view that, always with the aid of God's grace and in spite of a universally admitted 'predestination', human beings were capable of accepting or refusing God's proferred grace, and consequently of determining their eternal fate. For Bérulle and Saint-Cyran, human nature was radically flawed, so that the life it sustained needed to be excised in favour of the life of grace.[12] Almost symbolically, Philippe de Champaigne, whose portraits were increasingly stripped of all decoration, was by 1640 becoming the Jansenist painter *par excellence*, while the Jesuits still preferred to use the resplendently baroque Rubens for their churches and for the woodcut frontispiece of their self-congratulatory centenary volume, the *Imago primi sæculi* of that year.

Richelieu first adverted to the serious danger posed by Saint-Cyran's spirituality of trepidation and its denial of liberty to fallen human nature when, by a series of machinations, Saint-Cyran succeeded in imposing himself and his spirituality on two rich and fashionable Paris convents, a recently founded institute of the Blessed Sacrament and the Cistercian monastery of Port-Royal. He had become a close collaborator with Bérulle, helping him with his literary activities, as well as writing his own anti-Jesuit pamphlets under the name of Petrus Aurelius and organising the Oratory in the Low Countries for Bérulle.

The superior of Port-Royal ousted by Saint-Cyran, Sébastien Zamet, himself a friend of the Oratory, although neither of Bérulle nor of the Carmelites, had persuaded the abbess, the celebrated Angélique Arnauld, to transfer Port-Royal from its Cistercian obedience to what in practice amounted to himself as its constitutional superior. Zamet was closely associated with the newly-founded lay Compagnie du Saint-Sacrement, dedicated not only to charitable works, but also to the rigid enforcement by civil authority of Christian moral norms. Incense, flowers, perfume, breeding, good manners, dowries and clean linen played an excessive, and characteristically baroque part in the spirituality of his convents.[13] Mère Angélique took Saint-Cyran's spiritual doctrine of self-abasement to the opposite extreme, to the point of cultivating bodily vermin.

The Jansenist-Jesuit disputes, no doubt reflecting the disputes about the workings of grace in the soul at the turn of the century, nonetheless originated in a strongly polarised difference of spirituality and devotional practice before they resulted in the seventeenth-century doctrinal confrontation. The ultimate religious question for any Catholic was to know whether the human soul could or could not by its behaviour on earth affect its eternal fate, or whether this fate, as the Jansenists and strict Calvinists believed, was simply the result of a predestinatory decree, from which no human being could escape.

Saint-Cyran, first inspiring and then himself led on by Angélique Arnauld, broke with the eucharistic spirituality of the new institute from which he ousted Zamet and, as her spiritual director, authorised Angélique Arnauld to abstain from communion from Easter to the Assumption (15 August) in 1635.[14] As he focused more intensely on attacking the Jesuit belief in the human capacity for self-determination and on devotional attitudes primarily based on a sense of guilt, a series of quarrels broke out in 1636 between Saint-Cyran and Zamet which came to involve the titular foundress of the institute of the Blessed Sacrament, the daughter of Condé and Charlotte de Montmorency later to become Mme de Longueville, and a sister of the chancellor, Pierre Séguier, both of whom cast doubts to Richelieu on Saint-Cyran's orthodoxy.

In 1630, Saint-Cyran chose the party of Marie de' Medici, and would have been arrested after the *journée des dupes* if he had not left Paris. His association with Jansen, author in 1635 of the *Mars gallicus,* a pamphlet against Richelieu's Protestant alliances in the Low Countries, further aggravated Richelieu, and Richelieu was seriously alarmed when, at the end of 1637, a prominent young barrister, Antoine le Maître, nephew of Angélique Arnauld, noisily renounced his career in an open letter to Séguier, and went to live an austere life of prayer in Saint-Cyran's Paris apartment. He was to become the first of the male *solitaires* associated with Port-Royal. At the same Saint-Cyran had collected round him a group of small children from leading families, entrusted to him for their religious and moral formation as well as for secular instruction. They constituted the nucleus of the school he intended to found.[15]

Then in 1638 Richelieu, advised by Père Joseph and alarmed by the extent of Saint-Cyran's religious influence almost as much as by his views, seized his chance and arrested Saint-Cyran when he attacked the king's prayer to the Virgin for the protection of France, which had been published on 10 February. Richelieu had him released from the dungeon to milder imprisonment at Vincennes, but not before he went blind there, and he is another of those who was freed on Richelieu's death. However, his association with Jansen, who had died bishop of Ypres in 1638, and the support for his spiritual attitudes given by Jansen's theology, ensured that Richelieu would work for the suppression of theological Jansenism when the *Augustinus* appeared, especially when six Parisian doctors had given their approval for the Paris edition of 1641. Shortly before his death, Richelieu arranged for the *théologal* of Notre-Dame, Isaac Habert, to preach against Jansen. Three sermons were actually preached, the first before Richelieu's death. Jean-François de Gondi, the archbishop of Paris, then forebade further sermons on grace.

In spite of his devoutness, Richelieu himself had little that was spiritually new to offer to his contemporaries, certainly not in comparison with such great spiritual figures of the Catholic revival as François de Sales, who introduced the central spiritual tenet that human beings even in their present fallen state had a natural inclination to love God. Richelieu respected the authority of the pope in religious matters, and he favoured the Jesuit belief in an autonomous power of spiritual self-determination. He promoted their educational activities exempt from episcopal control, and their spiritual mission, but not apparently on grounds of any deep theological reflection. He was not himself a profound metaphysical theologian, although his contribution to pastoral theology and apologetics were both substantial. His attitude towards Saint-Cyran's spirituality derived as much from its potentially destabilising social impact as from seriously thought-out doubts about his doctrinal orthodoxy.

Spiritual attitudes concerning the ways in which human beings could attain their spiritual perfection in this life and enhance the intensity of their eternal beatitude after death were naturally of paramount importance in Catholic cultural life. But the moral optimism of the Jesuits, to be brilliantly satirised by Pascal in his *Lettres provinciales,* as much as the pessimistic view of human nature underlying Bérulle's *vœux de servitude* (vows of servitude), were related to France's baroque secular culture by their elements of stylised exaggeration. The burden of Pascal's satire is what he calls the *extravagance* of Jesuit confessional practice as much as the doctrine of grace it promoted. Bérulle's *vœux* (vows) and Pascal's Jesuit targets are important here not only because of Richelieu's attitude to each, but also because they provide examples of how cultural values, themselves subject to development, insidiously but relentlessly permeate every aspect of any society's value system. Neither religious devotion nor political ambition escaped the intense and ubiquitous pressures of ambient cultural values.

In the early years of the century what we call the performing arts, including drama, had still scarcely been elevated above popular street entertainment. Drama was left to strolling players who relied on the biannual Paris fairs, were lucky if they could find or afford a hall or a *jeu de paume* to hire, and whose performances were entirely distinct from the neoclassical or biblical pieces used to teach rhetoric to adolescents in the few humanist colleges. In Paris and its environs the Confrérie de la Passion still held the monopoly of dramatic performances. Their religious mystery plays had been turned into excuses for debauched popular festivities and had been banned in 1598. The Confrérie occasionally let out its hall, the Hôtel de Bourgogne, or collected royalties for use of their monopoly from troupes which played elsewhere, and there was a French company, variable in composition, which played sporadically between 1606 and 1625. The audience, mostly servants, soldiers and the occasional young aristocrat, did not include socially respectable women.

Richelieu's desire to promote and sanitise French drama is documented only from the 1630s, but must have existed prior to that. It is, for instance, strange that the last payment to any Italian company in or around Paris at this period was the 24,000 livres paid to Martinelli on 17 December 1624, just after Richelieu had gained power. However, in January and February 1622 Louis XIII attended twenty-three performances given by the Italian *commedia dell'arte* company under Martinelli, relying on mime and improvisation, and he insisted that the company should stay on through the carnival, following the court to Fontainebleau and back to Paris. The next recorded appearance of an Italian company was on 13 June 1644. It had been invited back by Anne of Austria and Mazarin, and opened just eighteen months after the death of Richelieu. It looks very much as if Italian comedy had been effectively suppressed by Richelieu.[16]

In 1624, the date of the last payment to Martinelli, there were four theatrical troupes in Paris,[17] and the most popular and prolific French dramatist during the first three decades of the century, Alexandre Hardy, appears to have written over 600 plays, of which we have the texts of thirty-four and the titles of eighteen more. He entitled them tragedies, tragi-comedies, dramatic poems and pastorals, with an occasional comedy, and, when indoors, they will have been played on the apron of a stage in front of a series of curtain-booths depicting different scenes. Only the appropriate curtain was drawn back to depict the relevant setting.

On the other hand, the court ballets became increasingly elaborate entertainments in which the very great took part.[18] Bassompierre tells us that Marie de' Medici was so fond of them as to have them danced on Sundays, even while still in mourning for Henri IV. We know of a ballet partly by Etienne Durand, the queen's 'poète ordinaire', *La Félicité de l'âge doré,* for the opening of the *salle des fêtes* in the Arsenal on 6 December 1609. Malherbe wrote on 28 February 1613 that he had never seen anyone laugh so much as the queen at the comic act of a shepherd called Maret who led a man dressed as a dog.[19]

On 19 March 1615 the *Ballet du Triomphe de Minerve* was danced to celebrate the Spanish marriages and involved not only Durand, but also a librettist, a machinist and three musicians. The principal poets, librettists and musicians held what were virtually court posts and were expected to provide large numbers of ballets. By 1617 the court was expecting to see its ballets exploit mobile floats, turn-tables, perspectives, elaborate costumes and imposing scenery. That year on 17 January Louis XIII himself danced two roles in *La Délivrance de Renaud*, with Renaud danced by Luynes. The role played by mythological wonder-workers, by what was known as the 'Christian marvellous', and by heroic poetry in these ballets is no doubt connected to the widespread fear and persecution of their obverse, witchcraft and sorcery.[20] By 1635 the occasional live horse appeared on stage.

The ballets also had overt political implications. In *Le Ballet d'Apollon* danced on 18 February 1621, Luynes danced and was allegorically identified with Apollo, but the lines given to the smith, danced by Louis XIII, emphasised his royalty and made a clear allusion to Concini's fall, while the *Ballet du soleil* danced less than two weeks later rectified the emphasis, making Louis XIII the true image of the sun, with overtones of divinity. By 1632 the *Gazette* had begun to appear, and it reported that there were five thousand spectators at the Louvre alone on 7 March 1632 for *Le Ballet du château de Bicêtre,* also danced at the Arsenal.

We know that Richelieu built a theatre at Rueil, and what we know about the two theatres built by Richelieu at the Palais-Cardinal shows that he went to immense expense to accommodate the stage machinery required for the most elaborate court entertainments, ballets, court ballets, comédies lyriques, or comédies-ballets, as they were indifferently called. The first and smaller theatre with six hundred places was completed about February 1636 and the larger, designed by Le Mercier and improbably said to have seated three thousand spectators, was inaugurated with *Mirame* played before Louis XIII and Anne of Austria on 14 January 1641 to celebrate the marriage of Richelieu's niece, Claire-Clémence de Maillé-Brézé to the duc d'Enghien, later the 'grand Condé' and at this time fifth in line to succeed to the throne.[21] It was estimated in 1640 that the equipment for the large theatre, including stage machinery for elaborate effects installed for *Mirame,* would cost 100,000 livres.[22] *Mirame,* described as a *tragi-comédie,* was signed by Jean Desmarets, Richelieu's preferred author of entertainments, but was probably written, or at least had its action designed by Richelieu himself.[23]

When Richelieu had earlier adopted a set of five specific authors with whom to collaborate, only two, Rotrou and Pierre Corneille, were primarily authors of straight scripted drama. The rest were primarily poets or authors of libretti.[24] Richelieu was to create his own court, with his own poets and librettists. Jean Desmarets was his early favourite, to enter his service in 1634, and soon on his own to replace the group of five authors sponsored by the cardinal. He was a remote relation of the baronne du Vigean, herself passionately attached to Richelieu's favourite niece, Mme de Combalet, made duchesse d'Aiguillon in 1638.[25]

Richelieu's interest in drama was not dependent on its potential for political propaganda, although he cannot have failed to notice it. Montmorency had used it to good effect when Jean Mairet, the household dramatist at the family seat of Chantilly, inserted an attack on Gaston's 1626 marriage to Marie de Bourbon-Montpensier in his pastoral tragi-comedy *La Sylvie*, the poetic name of the duchesse de Montmorency. The play was both popular and influential when performed publicly in Paris, which suggests that the marriage, with all its dynastic implications, met with no great popular enthusiasm.[26] When, on 28 November 1634, his three cousins married,[27] Richelieu put on a great spectacle of theatre and ballet in the Arsenal *salle des fêtes*, which included plays by Corneille and Georges de Scudéry. In February 1635 he followed it by *La Comédie des Tuileries*, the first of the three plays by Richelieu's 'five authors', although again in fact largely the work of the cardinal himself. It was his initial move in promoting the elevation of scripted drama.[28]

Richelieu's interest in scripted drama was strong, although his court entertainments were not simple dramas. They were grandiose affairs, invariably involving music, dancing, elaborate scenery, exotic costumes, amazing stage effects and mythological settings for allegorical plots. He made scripted drama respectable by his patronage, by his open expressions of displeasure at pulpit denunciations of the Italian comedies, which were often bawdy, and by promoting the social rehabilitation of actors. He both sketched some plots himself, and made very perceptive comments about others. He also commissioned the abbé d'Aubignac, whom he had made tutor to his nephew, to write a report about the condition of the theatre and to make recommendations.[29]

Richelieu was himself especially interested in correct usage, proper versification, and the austere linguistic norms introduced into French by Malherbe's reforms of vocabulary, grammar and versification. He annotated himself a copy of Chapelain's *La Pucelle*, noting its defects in the margin. When Chapelain composed an ode in his honour, Richelieu asked to see the manuscript and suggested ameliorations. He clearly had firm personal literary views, but his aim in founding the Academy was not simply to promote them.

He understood the power of propaganda, and wanted to acquire control for the state over all cultural activity, both for the aggrandisement of France as a centre of literary activity and eventually also of learning, but also for the ability it would give the state to manipulate the personal and social values of France. The Academy was not only the first step to creating a cultural identity for the country, but also a means of ensuring what attitudes that identity would comprise. After Colbert had reformed it in 1673, the Academy together with its newly founded satellite academies for non-literary activities, would come near to achieving this goal.

According to his biographer de Pure, Richelieu had once in Paris shared lodgings with Cospeau, who formed part of the network of bridges between Richelieu and the sophisticated *mondain* world of Mme de Rambouillet, of whom Cospeau was an intimate friend as well as notoriously the subject of one of the more elaborate of her practical jokes.[30] The frequenters of the celebrated salon of Mme de Rambouillet, the *chambre bleue,* were a mixture of the high-born and the better-known and wittier members of the Parisian literary world. They looked down on the more earnest interests of the members of the academy which Richelieu was to found, although some of them also frequented the salon, and they were on the whole inclined to be politically hostile to Louis XIII and his minister. Tallemant was an *habitué.* But Mme de Combalet, the niece closest to the cardinal and from 1638 duchesse d'Aiguillon, was among the inner circle of those who frequented it, like her close friend, Mme de Vigean.

Like Cospeau they provided a link between Richelieu, through the Rambouillets, to the Condés, who came to dominate the salon. Such informal social networks were to be valuable to Richelieu especially as a means of gauging opinion at moments of political tension in France, but Richelieu had grandiose plans to establish what in fact was to become the French Academy we know. His desire was formally to bring under his personal control the cultural interests of the increasingly important newly educated but non-learned bourgeoisie, and incidentally to standardise the written language. The original members of the academy he subsequently sought to establish, formed a group of wealthy bourgeois inspired by the linguistic and poetic reforms of Malherbe, France's most distinguished court panegyrist. They may have been meeting as early as 1629. Richelieu was eventually to intend the academy to become the principal engine for the unification of all cultural activity in France.[31]

Around 1630, there were several groups of educated but not learned bourgeois meeting regularly but informally to discuss cultural matters more seriously than in the often frivolous *chambre bleue*.[32] One in particular, interested in a vernacular 'art de bien écrire' and keen to pursue Malherbe's line of poetic reform, gathered round Valentin Conrart and met in his house. Conrart was a relatively rich Huguenot who knew Spanish and Italian, but neither Latin nor Greek. He was the 'tendre ami' or *galant* of the writer Madeleine de Scudéry, sister of the dramatist, Georges. Her well-known novels were later to explore the possibility of a type of love devoid of physical passion.

The group was mockingly referred to by Camus, bishop of Belley, as 'l'académie des puristes'. Its members differed in religious and political affiliations, but shared an enthusiasm for vernacular language and letters. The group was essentially private and had agreed not to divulge their discussions. They were mostly young and reasonably well off, and some had reason to be hostile to Richelieu. Two were Huguenots, Conrart himself and Gombauld, the oldest member of the group and an intimate of Marie de' Medici. His pension was twice reduced by Richelieu. Malleville's employer, Bassompierre, was in the Bastille, and Serizay was the manager of the La Rochefoucauld estates. The four best known, Godeau, Gombauld, Chapelain, and Conrart were, like Malherbe himself, received by Mme de Rambouillet, and were no doubt on that account considered by Tallemant worthy of one of his malicious *historiettes*.

Malleville is said to have mentioned the meetings to Faret, best known for his *L'Honnête homme, ou l'art de plaire à la Cour*, dedicated to Gaston d'Orléans in 1630, and in a revised version to Pierre Séguier, the new chancellor from 1633.[33] He may have read portions to the group for discussion, and let the group's existence be known to Desmarets, the author of court ballets, and Boisrobert, a converted Huguenot and virtually Richelieu's literary secretary, licensed by Richelieu to be more forward than any other member of his entourage, and the only person who could be guaranteed to restore Richelieu to good humour. Desmarets, eventually to replace Boisrobert on his disgrace, was invited to join the gatherings, and read there the first part of his 1632 novel *Ariane,* but it was through Boisrobert, who informed Richelieu about the group's existence, that Richelieu established control.

In 1633 Boisrobert published *Les nouvelles Muses,* an anthology of poems by five members of the group. Through Boisrobert, Richelieu offered the group official status and letters patent constituting them into a formal consultative group. Its members, with the exception of the sycophantic Chapelain, were reluctant to accept. Chapelain's *Ode à Richelieu,* as corrected by Richelieu himself, had been published in 1633, and he was receiving a half-yearly payment, to become an annual pension in 1636. His argument that resistance would lead to suppression carried the day, and the group elected Conrart as its secretary although, since he had just got married, it could no longer meet in his house. Charged with compiling its famous dictionary, the Academy got bogged down in a protracted discussion about the gender of the letter 'a' for the first article of all.

Meetings were held weekly, and later more often, generally at the residences of members, but from 1643 at the residence of the Academy's protector, the chancellor Séguier, elected to succeed Richelieu on his death. From March 1634 a register of proceedings was kept, and in that year Richelieu personally emended the formal project to found the Academy sent to him on 22 March, and then corrected the revision. The number of members had been raised, first to thirty and then to forty, and Richelieu's ambitions for the Academy are clear from the privileges granted to its members, hitherto enjoyed only by princes of the blood, *ducs et paires,* officers of the crown, and holders of the great offices of state. He himself insisted on becoming its first protector.

Formidable pressure was put on the *parlement* to register the letters patent of 25 January 1635. The Academy wrote, Richelieu wrote, and the king issued *lettres de cachet* on 30 December 1635, ordering the registration, but all to no effect, even when Richelieu threatened to take the matter out of the jurisdiction of the *parlement* by putting it into the hands of the *Grand Conseil*. The *parlement*, like the original members of the group, feared the creation of an organ of cultural absolutism. Its opposition was as determined as Richelieu's resolution. What it feared is clear from the rider it added when the letters finally were registered. The Academy should limit its concerns to the 'ornamentation, embellishment, and growth' of the French language, and to the books only of its members and any others 'who wanted or desired it'.

The statutes themselves restricted the purposes of the Academy to rules of language and specified its tasks of producing a dictionary, a grammar, a rhetoric and a poetics, but they had also endowed it with inchoate powers of non-linguistic censorship. In what was to turn out to be an important provision, works by Academy members only might be considered for approbation, although 'if [the Academy] be obliged for some reason to consider other works, it will give only its opinion without any condemnation or approbation'. Richelieu had not yet succeeded in giving his academy the authority he wanted it to have.

He had taken under his wing not only Boisrobert but also Rotrou, a lawyer who made his living in the theatre until, no doubt aided by Richelieu, he bought himself an administrative charge. Richelieu's patronage was also assiduously courted by Georges de Scudéry, who succeeded neither in becoming one of the five authors nor a member of the Academy, but remained in Richelieu's employment until the cardinal's death when, like Desmarets, he gave up writing for the theatre. Mairet, too, was to give up writing for the theatre after the death in 1637 of his patron, Belin, but, like Scudéry, he played an active role in the famous *querelle* surrounding Pierre Corneille's play *Le Cid*. It was that controversy which enabled Richelieu to get the Academy registered by the *parlement*.

Desmarets was quickly replacing Boisrobert as Richelieu's impresario of ballets, even before Boisrobert's disgrace. He was concerned in the creation of the ballets danced on the occasion of the triple wedding of 28 November 1634 and wrote at least three more danced at the carnival of 1635, one with 26 *entrées* for the carnival of 1636, followed a week later by a comedy with twelve *entrées,* part of an entertainment which included a collation, music between the acts, a ballet and a concert. Like Rotrou, Scudéry dedicated a play to Richelieu, the tragedy *La Mort de César,* published in 1636 with two long poems, one of which was the *Discours de la France à Mgr le cardinal duc de Richelieu.* Scudéry's theoretical writings are facile, contradictory and certainly not derived from any serious reflection on dramatic principles.

At the end of 1636 relations between Mairet, Scudéry and Corneille did not appear strained. They had contributed preliminary verses to one another's published texts. D'Aubignac was setting out to become the theatre's reformer and law-giver.[34] Richelieu was trying to upgrade scripted theatre, changing the emphasis from spectacle to script, and from court entertainment to drama, which was only just becoming a literary genre in its own right. Louis XIII had begun in 1619–20 to remove for individual actors the prohibition preventing them from holding public office. On 16 April 1641 Louis XIII's declaration that actors on the serious stage belonged to an honourable profession, and removing from them civil disabilities was still felt to be necessary. The church was still refusing ecclesiastical burial to actors, although the church of Saint-Eustache, which refused ecclesiastical burial to Molière in 1673 until Louis XIV personally intervened to have a nocturnal burial sanctioned, afforded it by some commendable feat of ecclesiastical casuistry to the Italians Fiorilli and Biancolelli.

Pierre Corneille's *Le Cid* opened on Friday 2 or Friday 9 January 1637, described until 1648 as a *tragi-comédie.* The hero, Rodrigue, has just had to avenge an insult to his father by killing the father of Chimène, the heroine, in a duel. It is a sign of the diminution in exuberant cultural optimism that the lines guaranteeing their future marriage which caused the furore were cut from the play in 1660.[35] In 1637, however, the play was an immediate and immense success. Richelieu liked it, and it was played three times at the Louvre and twice at the Palais-Cardinal within its first month at the Marais, with Montdory in the lead. But Richelieu saw his chance. By having the morality of the play immediately and publicly questioned, Richelieu could force Corneille, on pain of forfeiting present and future professional or financial favours, to 'desire' it to be referred to the Academy, thereby erecting the Academy into the moral arbiter of printed or staged material and obliging the *parlement* to register its letters patent.

There were still difficulties to overcome, but Richelieu was helped by the way in which Corneille overplayed his hand. He had already showed his spikiness in a reference to people jealous of him in the 'Au lecteur' of his first play, *Mélite*. Although some evidence comes from partly scurrilous pamphlets and parodies, it seems certain that Corneille had a reputation for meanness. It is alleged in a pamphlet by Mairet and another probably by the satirist Scarron that, in view of the box-office success, Corneille demanded supplementary payment around 20 January. He certainly breached the custom of allowing the performing troupe monopoly rights to the play for four weeks by applying for a *privilège,* allowing him to sell the rights to a publisher, as early as 21 January. Above all, Corneille inexcusably published in February or early March the *Excuse à Ariste,* based on something he had written in Latin three years earlier, boasting with unpardonable arrogance his superiority over other dramatists.

Corneille's prickly self-esteem provoked a forceful riposte from Mairet, staying in one of Belin's houses in Maine, conscious of his poverty and his fading authority in the theatrical world. Mairet attributed Corneille's success to the use of his Spanish original. The attack, purely personal, had nothing to do with the morality of *Le Cid.* It was circulating in Paris in March or April, and provoked from Corneille the immediate and unpleasantly personal *Rondeau* contemptuously referring to Mairet, his senior by one year, as a 'young novice'.

The quarrel, which Richelieu cannot have foreseen and which was a disgrace to both dramatists involved, nonetheless further enhanced public awareness of the issues raised by *Le Cid.* Some three dozen fly-sheets were published at the rate of about one a week, although many confined themselves to the polemic between Corneille and Mairet without seriously addressing the issue of the morality of *Le Cid.* Although Corneille had left the group of five authors, Richelieu continued to pay him a pension, but kept Mairet waiting on Belin's death, and paid him only a small pension after Boisrobert, Rotrou and Chapelain had interceded on his behalf. The *achevé d'imprimer* or publication date of the text of *Le Cid* is 23 March and Richelieu had *lettres de noblesse* awarded to Corneille's father. They were signed by the king in January and registered at the Normandy Cour des Aides and Chambre des Comptes on 24 and 27 March. It is therefore clear that Richelieu personally, at least at first, did not think that Corneille had breached the norms of propriety or taste.

Nonetheless, Richelieu certainly inspired Scudéry's *Observations sur Le Cid.*[36] Pellisson is unreliable at this point, but can be believed when he suggests that Scudéry was writing at the cardinal's request, if not partially at his dictation, and that Richelieu was pleased at being able to submit the issue of propriety to the judgement of the Academy. The Academy demurred and tried to avoid accepting the official status that inevitably went with undertaking the task, but Richelieu brushed aside all their objections except that forbidding the group to consider works not by its own members. That could be got round by obtaining Corneille's consent, a task managed with difficulty on Richelieu's behalf by Boisrobert.

Corneille argued against the referral, but Boisrobert 'gave him well enough to understand his master's wishes', and Corneille gave his consent from his home in Rouen with the worst possible grace, 'The gentlemen of the academy can do what they like. Since you write to me that Monseigneur would be pleased to see their judgement and since it would amuse his Eminence, there is nothing I can say'. Chapelain's letters make it clear that the referral was the object of a concerted campaign orchestrated by Richelieu. Pellisson remarks that Corneille's letter, dated 13 June, was sufficient to confer jurisdiction on the Academy, 'at least in the cardinal's opinion'. The Academy first discussed *Le Cid* on 16 June. On 9 July the *parlement* registered its letters patent. Richelieu had finally achieved the creation of his instrument for cultural control.

The *Sentiments de l'Académie,* written chiefly by Chapelain, were revised by Richelieu himself, who made comments in the margin. He had 'a few handfuls of flowers' added to the draft, and then removed from a further version. The *Sentiments* are ponderous, high-handed, judicious and long-winded, supporting Scudéry's repudiation of the morality of the marriage and his argument that what is probable and fitting should take precedence over historical accuracy. The 'patricide' of Chimène in marrying her father's killer should have been avoided either by suppressing the historical fact of the marriage, or by the discovery that the dead man was not the true father of Chimène, or that after all he had not died of his wounds.

The following year Scudéry wrote *L'Amour tyrannique,* dedicated to the duchesse d'Aiguillon, to demonstrate how *Le Cid* should have been written, with two heroines who are anti-Chimène figures and whose passion is confined to the legitimate limits of marriage. 'L'amour raisonnable' takes precedence over 'l'amour tyrannique', and there is predictably no shred of Corneille's imaginative vigour, only an obsessive pastiche of his style and echoes of his words, but with unmotivated changes of fortune, disguises, daggers, imprisonments, poisons, mistakes and implausibilities. The duchesse d'Aiguillon was to stage a children's performance with the assistance of Montdory before the cardinal on 3 April 1639 with Pascal's sister, Jacqueline, in the role of Cassandre, after which Richelieu took the thirteen-year-old Jacqueline on his knee and rehabilitated Pascal's father, disgraced for complicity in the Rouen bond-holders' protest at default in 1638. Richelieu's successful foundations for what Colbert would turn into cultural absolutism under Louis XIV did not preclude informal displays of warmth.

In the formal address to the Academy on his reception in 1655, published in 1656, Richelieu's doctor, La Mesnardière, relates that the cardinal had called him 'seven or eight times' in the last weeks of his life to see him at Narbonne, during what was to be the last of his restless journeyings. In spite of the pain from which he was suffering, he wanted to discuss his plans for founding at Paris a 'great college' with 100,000 livres a year for the study of 'les belles sciences'. It would attract the greatest men of the century, and would be run under the direction of the Academy which Richelieu had already founded. Tallemant tells us that Richelieu had already bought a property which would become the Academy's permanent seat. Members of the Academy would have received a salary, would have appointed the 'illustrious' professors who would confer glory on the new college, and would have been charged with judging their abilities, merit and the salary of which they were worthy. It seems likely that eminent practitioners of the physical sciences would have been included.

The Collège Royal, into which the *lecteurs royaux* founded in 1530 had been formed in 1610, had always had some difficulty in preserving independence from the university, and it is apparent that, shortly before his death, Richelieu was planning, or at least dreaming of, a much bigger role for his Academy than it had so far achieved, and one which would truly have turned it into a body overseeing cultural and scientific activity in a France which would have threatened the autonomy of the universities themselves.[37]

9

The Thirty Years War

Richelieu was still sensitive about the social standing of his family, and believed, with most of his generation, that personal merit needed to be reflected in external display, in which he therefore magnificently indulged, collecting, building, creating gardens and constituting himself patron of art and literature. He was not immune to the desire to amass wealth, but by temperament he was ascetic. The jovial Boisrobert was retained until his disgrace largely to amuse him, but Richelieu, neither frivolous nor self-indulgent, was not easily amused. Too nervously intense, poor in health, and alert to the perpetual dangers to his person attendant on his position, he did not find it easy to relax other than by briefly walking in his garden, and derived personal satisfaction almost only from political analysis and successful political manoeuvering, whether in a domestic or in a larger European context.

Towards the end of 1636 a particularly virulent thousand-line poetic attack, the *Milliade,* rattled Richelieu more than others had done. France was by then at war, and Richelieu was accused of amusing himself by writing for the boards.[1] The accusation was unfair. Richelieu's exploitation of the theatre had a serious political purpose, as did his ostentatious display of power. Both were rooted in his desire to propagate the values which underlay the principled choice he had made, more comprehensible to his period than to ours, to press the king to advance the glory of France rather than the living standards of its citizens. Popular uprisings suggest that he went too far.

On 9 May 1635, France formally declared war on Spain. Richelieu must have seen war as inevitable even before the day of dupes. He had started to employ Hercule Girard, baron de Charnacé, as ambassador to the courts of the Catholic Sigismund of Poland and the Protestant Gustavus Adolphus of Sweden as early as 1629, and Charnacé had succeeded in patching up a truce between them. Gustavus's image as a Protestant military leader put him in natural opposition to the Habsburgs, the close alliance of whose Spanish and Austrian branches Olivares was successfully promoting. In January 1630 Richelieu, about to embark on his Italian campaign, wanted the Swedes to create a diversion by moving against imperial Catholic forces in the north, but French and Swedish commercial interests and political aims diverged too greatly for Charnacé to obtain a formal alliance.[2]

Maximilian, duke of Bavaria, had pledged himself to support the emperor during what turned out to be the Thirty Years War in return for control of the Palatinate and the Palatine electorship, but, urged on by the pope, he made a defensive alliance with France at Fontainebleau in May 1631. France was therefore left with the incompatible obligations to protect Maximilian against Gustavus Adolphus, and to support Gustavus, who had agreed to respect the integrity of Bavaria only if it remained neutral. Gustavus, violent and unpredictable, went on at Breitenfeld on 17 September to defeat the Catholic army of Tilly, Wallenstein's successor and at once commander of Bavarian forces and an imperial general.

In May 1631 Tilly had besieged, stormed and taken Magdeburg, the only town to have declared itself for Gustavus. His army had behaved with unrestrained brutality, killing some 20,000 people, with the result that Protestant Europe rallied to Gustavus. The Swedes could reasonably hold that Bavaria had breached its commitment to neutrality, thereby releasing Gustavus from his undertaking to respect the territories of Bavaria and the Catholic league. That winter Gustavus sucessively entered Würzburg, Frankfurt and Mainz, while opposing forces laid waste whatever lands they could occupy in the effort to feed themselves, torturing, massacring, scavenging and plundering. The German countryside was reduced to a state of extreme distress and all continental Europe awaited 1632 in alarm for what Gustavus might do next.

Perhaps fortunately for Richelieu, Gustavus, who had proved

impossible to control, was to overplay his hand, and was killed in battle at Lützen on 16 November 1632. Knowing that France would not attack his rear, he had proposed to sweep Maximilian before him, to seize the fertile and still peaceful area between the Danube and the Alps, disregarding Swiss neutrality, and to advance on Vienna. He had taken Augsburg and Munich when Wallenstein, reappointed commander on Tilly's death, captured Prague on 15 May. Any truce between Wallenstein and the Saxons would threaten Swedish communications, and Gustavus was forced to move north. Richelieu was more concerned with Lorraine where, within three months of his submission to Louis XIII, the duke, with full Spanish support, was again conspiring with Gaston to put him on the French throne. Richelieu did, however, endeavour to strengthen French military presence in the Grisons, where Gustavus coveted the French stranglehold over the passes.

Richelieu, as usual, fought his battles with legal arguments wherever he could. His mind, in this perhaps affected by his ecclesiastical training, remained legalistically attuned to the niceties of formal procedure, even when what was at stake affected the lives, and deaths, of tens of thousands. The *Mémoires* make clear that Richelieu attached the greatest importance to keeping Pinerolo, as the key to a French presence on the Italian peninsula. Partly by trickery, hiding two hundred French troops in the cellars of the fortress at Pinerolo, and partly by the mediation of Mazarini, he had in 1631 succeeded in keeping Pinerolo for France, countering Spanish outrage with accusations that Spain had been breaking the treaty of Monzón by moving troops through the Valtelline. He moved to protect the passes, and invaded Lorraine to obtain the duke's second submission.

To secure French borders, Richelieu had obtained the agreement of the archbishop Elector Philip von Sötern of Trier to garrison the fortresses of Philippsburg and Ehrenbreitstein at the junctions of the Rhine with the Saal and the Moselle, currently in Spanish hands. Gustavus, pleased to promote conflict between France and Spain, sent troops to help oust the Spaniards, who were driven out of Trier in May. The Spaniards re-took the city to which the French then laid siege on 6 August, regaining it a fortnight later. Ehrenbreitstein had fallen on 12 June, although Philippsburg was to hold out for two years. But by the middle of 1632, therefore, military conflict had already broken out between France and Spain on the Rhine.

Richelieu was still able to avoid a general war, because the emperor was already over-stretched in defending his territory against Gustavus, and Spain had just lost twenty-eight ships captured from a fleet of thirty bound for Havana, including those carrying bullion, the third such loss in a decade.[3] The Spaniards could not afford an open war with France and restricted themselves to organising an attempt to drive the French from the Rhine and to supporting any insurrection which Gaston d'Orléans, with his mother in Brussels since November 1632, might mount. They also tried to topple Richelieu by means of canonical penalties for initiating an alliance with heretics against a Catholic prince. The likelihood that they would succeed would still have been nil, even if the peace-seeking Urban VIII had not at heart been a Francophile.

In fact the Spanish initiative was painfully lacking in finesse, crassly attacked the pope himself, and much cooled Roman attitudes towards Madrid. Père Joseph was still anxious to see the military confrontation as fundamentally sectarian, but Richelieu sent Père Joseph's brother-in-law to Gustavus, so that the occupation of Trier could be presented as a joint victory, and to Maximilian to present it as a defence of the lands of the Catholic Electors. He also discontinued the Swedish financial subsidy and made a small monetary gift to Maximilian, walking his tightrope with the practised sureness of a political acrobat.

When news of the death of Gustavus reached Madrid, there was much solemn rejoicing, and Olivares thought the time ripe to sow as much discord as possible in France, 'We must wish it all possible evil.'[4] Richelieu was ill at Bordeaux after the execution of Montmorency, but returned to Paris, writing a long memorandum to the king on 3 January 1633 arguing for a continuation of his policies. There was no need for direct French intervention, but continuation of the war in Germany was necessary if the Habsburgs were not to attack France.

Even before the death of Gustavus, it was known that Feria, the Spanish commander of the Milan district, was assembling an army to cross the Alps and march against the Swedes in Bavaria. Ultimately he was instructed to occupy the Rhineland. It was only the doubts of Isabella, Spanish governor of the Low Countries, about subsidising Gaston and Marie de' Medici which made Olivares hesitate, but in April 1633 Olivares instructed Isabella to pay Gaston 60,000 crowns a month for six months to raise troops, and in May to lend Gaston 6,000 troops in addition to the 7,000 to be provided by Wallenstein.[5] Richelieu naturally feared the inevitability of an invasion of France if, in addition to these 13,000 troops and to those to be recruited by Gaston and by the duke of Lorraine, Feria's army should reach the Rhine and become available to join Gaston.

Richelieu successfully persuaded the Swedes later in 1633 to draw off the duke of Lorraine's troops by attacking Alsace. They laid siege to Hagenau and were victorious over the duke Charles of Lorraine at Pfaffenhofen when he came to the town's relief. Richelieu could now organise another French entry into the duchy. Nancy was besieged, and on 20 September duke Charles came to terms at Charmes. His sister Marguerite, now married to Gaston d'Orléans, was to be confided to the care of Louis XIII, a hostage for the good political behaviour of her notoriously debauched brother, Charles.

However, Richelieu would have preferred to take Nancy without a siege, and another brother of Charles and Marguerite, François, cardinal of Lorraine and un-ordained bishop of Toul, was allowed to cross the French lines to negotiate with Richelieu on behalf of the duke. Dressed first as a cavalier to accompany her brother across the French lines as part of his retinue, Marguerite, met by three horsemen and a fresh horse in a wood between the French lines and Louis XIII's headquarters, was spirited off to Thionville. There she dressed as a maid to accompany a young aristocrat to Brussels. Couriers had been sent ahead to ask Isabella for asylum and to announce Marguerite's imminent arrival to Puylaurens, Gaston's intimate associate. Isabella rode out of the city to meet her, and took her in her carriage to meet her new mother-in-law, Marie de' Medici, before putting at her disposal the quarters of her late husband.

Richelieu was to be further outwitted in what became a farce of disguises and meticulous respect for legal niceties. Charles abdicated his duchy of Lorraine in favour of François, whom Louis XIII, as feudal overlord of the duchy of Bar, part of Lorraine, refused to recognise. Bar had been inherited by Nicole, the wife and cousin of Charles, and her unmarried sister Claude, naturally also a cousin of François. Under the pretext of protecting their interests, Richelieu decided to keep Nancy. By adding it to the famous fortresses of Verdun, Metz and Toul, he could consolidate the protection of France's north-eastern frontier. François, however, carried off Nicole and Claude to Lunéville, where Richelieu ordered the French La Force to seize all three of them.

With La Force approaching fast, François, twenty-five, a bishop and a cardinal but still without priestly orders or the vow of chastity implied in ordination to the non-sacramental sub-diaconate, conceived the idea of outwitting Richelieu by marrying Claude and claiming Bar in her name. To execute his plan, he needed two dispensations. The first, a dispensation from the publication of banns, he could, as bishop, grant himself. The other, to marry his first cousin, was ordinarily considered to need a papal rescript. François decided to grant it himself by virtue of episcopal jurisdiction arguably conferred by urgency, and to have it ratified later. The marriage took place immediately, but there was a further difficulty. It was only sacramentally valid when consummated. Claude exhibited inhibitions and wanted to wait for the papal dispensation, but Richelieu's general, La Force, was only hours, perhaps less, away.

Consummation, canonically required for sacramental validity, was therefore hastily accomplished. La Force arrived too late, but locked the newly-wed couple in separate rooms, and next day took the cardinal of Lorraine, bishop of Toul and duke of Bar presumptive, with his wife (subject to papal ratification of the second dispensation) and her sister to Nancy. François wrote to Richelieu in Paris, informing him of his marriage and signing himself duke of Lorraine. Richelieu ordered the newly-weds to be brought separately to Paris. The king's conscience would not permit Claude and François to be together until papal ratification of the dispensation from consanguinity had arrived.

François, however, had again outwitted Richelieu. The ratification was in his hands before Claude and her sister could be removed. A priest with the appropriate jurisdiction was awoken and the marriage service repeated at 3 a.m., after which both François and Claude slipped away separately, François disguised as a valet and Claude as a page. It was midday before the French governor, suspicious at their non-appearance, investigated their quarters to find that they had flown. Some weeks later Richelieu learnt that they were with Christine of Lorraine, sister-in-law of Marie de' Medici. The final twist came when Richelieu was unable to obtain for Père Joseph the cardinalate which François had to resign on marriage.

Richelieu continued to have the problem of wresting Gaston, still successor to the French throne, away from his mother and back to France. He was helped by the death of the infanta Isabella, governor of the Low Countries, two months after the arrival of Marguerite in Brussels, and the appointment by Olivares of the marqués de Aytona, one of his own placemen, as governor. The Low Countries would henceforward be more directly ruled from Madrid.

Gaston's treatment was down-graded. He was made to understand that he had to take orders from Madrid, and on 3 May 1634 in Brussels an attempt was made on the life of his companion, Puylaurens, in which the complicity of Olivares was suspected. Louis XIII was necessarily prepared to restore his brother's position in France, since he was heir to the throne, but consented to do so only if the marriage to Marguerite was annulled. On 12 May Gaston signed a treaty with Philip IV of Spain, discovered on a Spanish ship grounded by the Dutch some months later, which bound him not to treat with his brother, Louis XIII, without Spanish permission, and to side with Spain in any war which should break out between France and Spain.[6] Spain was to provide Gaston with 12,000 troops for an invasion of France planned for September 1634. The courier on whom the document was found was also carrying authority for Aytona if necessary to declare war on France.

Richelieu had promised Puylaurens a peerage if he persuaded Gaston to return, further encouraging him by the promise of marriage to his own cousin. What finally decided Gaston to return was the crushing victory of the Spaniards at Nördlingen on 6 September, and the possibility that he would be required in consequence to join them in invading France again, which he was now unwilling to do. On 2 October 1634, on pretext of hunting, he escaped with his companions, reaching the frontier at La Capelle at nine in the evening. When, after the arrest of the twenty-eight year old Puylaurens, Gaston went on an excursion down the Loire, Richelieu not only had him accompanied, but had the river guarded by six ships. It was on this occasion in 1635 that Gaston visited the great house the cardinal was building at Richelieu. He was presented with one of the recently imported garden statues installed there.

The legal grounds for rescinding the marriage of Gaston and Marguerite rested on an extension of the 1579 ordinance of Blois which gave Louis XIII the status of father and guardian of his heir and brother, who was treated as a minor. Gaston's marriage to Marguerite, which had not had the consent of Louis XIII, could therefore be treated as the 'abduction' of Gaston by the duke of Lorraine, making the duke, a crown vassal, guilty of *lèse-majesté*. The marriage would then have been invalidated by the 'abduction' in both French and canon law.[7]

Louis XIII succeeded in persuading the *parlement* to take this view on 24 March 1634, and, after the report of a commission of five bishops, the assembly of the clergy concurred on 7 July 1635, accepting that the withholding of royal permission for a marriage of the prince of the blood invalidated it according to the 'fundamental law of the realm' which, by prescription over many centuries, had also become church law in France. It is again important to notice that, at a period during which high-ranking ecclesiastics could also be chief ministers of princes and generals of armies, enormous importance needed to be attached to the legal niceties, and how easily the law, or more accurately the spectrum of relevant legal principles, civil and canonical, could be made to support irreconcilably opposed political claims.

As far back as 1625 Richelieu, in need of highly placed support on which he could rely, had persuaded the king to write to the general of the Carthusians, and levered his elder brother Alphonse out of his monastery to be made bishop of Aix, where he was unpopular. Richelieu then secured Lyons for him, where he was both popular and successful, and Louis obtained a red hat for him, to be bestowed on 7 January 1629 by the king, who also made him France's grand almoner in 1632. It was Alphonse who attended Louis XIII on what appeared to be his deathbed at Lyons late in 1629. To attack the validity of Gaston's marriage, Richelieu now had Alphonse sent as ambassador to Rome, where he was well out of his depth. Twenty years as a Carthusian had fitted him ill for the sophisticated subtleties of Roman ecclesiastical life. Among the difficulties of protocol and domestic management in which he became ensnared, he had unsurprising difficulty in persuading Urban VIII to give Cardinal de la Valette the dispensation necessary for him to raise his army. Alphonse kept a sumptuous table and entertained prodigally in the Farnese palace, but money from France dried up, and he naively made diplomatic blunders, unintentionally upsetting Filippo Colonna, the Roman prefect, and causing offence by refusing his proper title to the cardinal of Savoy. The Spaniards made sufficient difficulty over his absence from his diocese for his brother to insist that Alphonse should resign his bishopric.

Rome had continued to argue for validity of the marriage, since the conditions for sacramental validity could not be allowed to be determined or modified by the law of any state. Urban VIII, who felt that François had been wronged by France, did not pronounce a definitive judgement. Although Gaston did in fact accept the nullity of his marriage, signing the document in Richelieu's own study at Rueil in August 1635, Marguerite appealed to Rome, and Louis XIII recognised the marriage after the death of Richelieu.[8]

Between 1630 and 1635, Richelieu's foreign policy had been one of expediency, if also largely determined by the desire to keep Pinerolo as a French fortress guaranteeing entry into Italy. Richelieu retained his scrupulous concern to justify his political and military activities by recourse to systems of rights and obligation, often now in conflict with one another, although virtually all ultimately deriving from the canonical adaptation of Roman law in the high middle ages. It was only because, on account of the danger emanating from the Swedish clash with imperial forces, he was invited in 1633 and 1634 to afford French protection to towns of Alsace both north and south of the Vosges, that Richelieu authorised their occupation. It was not difficult to manipulate ancient rights or antique customs to justify expansionist instincts. In the year before he died, Richelieu even instigated an enquiry into French rights in Milan, Naples, Sicily and Piedmont.

In 1633 no-one knew whether, or how vigorously, the Swedish chancellor, Axel Oxenstierna, acting for the infant queen Christina, would continue the policies of Gustavus Adolphus after his death. Only in February 1634, a full year later, were the Dutch expensively persuaded by France to continue the anti-Habsburg war. Bavaria had been devastated, and its duke, Maximilian, had been forced to join the Habsburg camp, so that the neutral third force which he might have led could not now emerge.

Oxenstierna proved unamenable to French pressure of any sort. Wallenstein for a moment seemed willing to commit his army against the emperor in return for support for his pretensions to the Bohemian throne, but his treason to the emperor was discovered and he was murdered on 25 February 1634. Olivares failed to persuade the emperor to go to war against France, and it was only the death of the other leading imperial general, Feria, on 11 January 1634 that caused the Spanish state council to put off a declaration of war against France in April 1634, the month in which the secret Franco-Dutch alliance was signed. Olivares did not know of it until a courier was captured in July.

Richelieu's policy of controlling northern European, Protestant military action against the Habsburgs without himself going to war with Spain had failed. That summer matters became worse. An army under the brother of Philip IV of Spain arrived from Italy at Lake Constance, as Feria had planned, intending at first to move down the Danube. Another army under the emperor's son, the king of Hungary, sought to join it, moving up the river. The pincer movement threatened to sever the communications of the north German anti-imperial army which was south of the river, and immediately retreated northwards, trying to prevent the two pro-imperial armies from joining up. The result, at Nördlingen, was catastrophic. The anti-imperial forces were outnumbered and destroyed, leaving something over 12,000 dead on the field, with a further 6,000 taken prisoner.

Richelieu immediately discussed the matter with Louis XIII, and then with Père Joseph. There was no alternative but war with Spain, although its declaration could be left until the spring. Bullion, Séguier and Bouthillier also agreed, and Richelieu began his complex organisational preparation, helped by the arrival of delegates from Oxenstierna and the anti-imperial league, whom Richelieu, at his coldest and least charming, reduced to conceding all his demands without making any commitment for France to go to war. France was to have equal voice in the anti-imperial councils and the Swedes were to hand to France the territories they held in Alsace. Catholicism was to be restored wherever it had been practised before 1618.

Things did not go well for Richelieu during the winter of 1634. French forces moved successfully to relieve Heidelberg, but Charles of Lorraine re-took northern Alsace with an imperial army and surprised the French at Philippsburg, advancing to Speyer. Spanish troops entered Trier and took prisoner the archbishop Elector Philip von Sötern. Richelieu had already met and taken a dislike to Hugo de Groot (Grotius), now escaped from Dutch imprisonment and the author of the celebrated 1625 work of legal philosophy *De iure belli ac pacis,* dedicated to Louis XIII.[9] The pension promised by the king remained unpaid, and Grotius was treated dismissively by the king. He quarrelled with Père Joseph while Richelieu was frostily aloof. He left Paris in 1631, only to return at the end of 1634 as Oxenstierna's ambassador.

He was to stay nine years, but had to wait a month before Louis XIII would see him, and Richelieu repeatedly but vainly demanded his recall to Sweden. He arrived just when Paris was welcoming the Dutch envoys who had come to negotiate the details of the new alliance, and in honour of whom Louis XIII had written the Ballet of the Blackbird, danced at Chantilly on 15 March 1635, in which the king alluded in public to his own sexuality by appearing in travesty. Given the problem of his succession, his sexual orientation was the subject of widespread comment. Both gay and lesbian relationships were common at court, but that did not mean that they could openly be admitted.[10]

When Oxenstierna himself came to Compiègne, the dignity of his welcome could hardly have been surpassed. Richelieu, now dependent on Swedish goodwill, was at his most charming and witty, speaking Latin, as gracious as only he could be, but merely expediting matters so that he would not himself have to spend longer with the Swede than the business demanded. The treaty of Compiègne was negotiated. It committed both parties to war, with neither able to conclude a separate peace. Suppression of Catholicism would cease, but the Swedes were to retain the episcopal revenues of the territories held by them. Richelieu was unenthusiastic about both his allies and the need to share supreme command.

On 19 May 1635 the French herald attempted formally to notify the governor of Brussels of the French declaration of war on Spain. The governor did not make himself available for the purpose, and the herald had to affix the declaration to a post at the frontier. Spain's own declaration was made in August. Urban VIII and his agent in Paris, Mazarini, worked urgently for peace, and tried to call a conference. Even Richelieu and Olivares negotiated in private to avoid war. Richelieu's health had deteriorated since the hideous suffering wrought in Germany by Gustavus Adolphus's army, and he was becoming a permanent invalid. Personally, he told Mazarini, he would have given an arm or half his fortune to have avoided war.

However, the emperor was forced by his spiritual advisors to make peace with Saxony in Prague on 30 May 1635 in order to free his forces for action against the French, and there was now no alternative but war for the glory of France, and the preservation of its independence. Richelieu was not ready. The army still depended too heavily on mercenaries, and the organisation of a proper commissariat remained urgent until the task was taken over by Sublet de Noyers, a careful and industrious adminstrator who was made secretary of state for war in 1636, but was also intendant of finance, superintendant of buildings and fine arts, and became one of Richelieu's executors. At the peak of his power, he was controlling foreign trade, patronising Poussin, and saving Fointainebleau from ruin. Scarcely two months after Richelieu's death he was to be discreetly dismissed.

Richelieu disposed of several armies: 25,000 troops round Sedan under Brézé, 9,000 in Picardy, 15,000 under the seventy-seven year old La Force, 12,000 under Rohan, summoned back to service after disgrace for conniving with Gustavus Adolphus to enter the Valtelline, and a new force of 20,000 being formed at Langres by Cardinal de la Valette. Twenty-one new regiments were being raised, and 12,000 Swiss were recruited, with 15,000 held in reserve. Rohan's task was to clear Alsace, then block the Swiss passes from the Valtelline, and finally to lay siege to Milan.

The Thirty Years War was ugly. There were incidents of starvation-driven cannibalism, and others in which peasants were roasted. Brézé's army joined the Dutch and was guilty of desecrations and human atrocities. The army disintegrated, and the Belgians, siding against the Spaniards, sent revengeful sacks of severed human ears to a shocked Aytona. France's military position quickly became critical as Charles of Lorraine forced his way between the armies of La Force and la Valette. La Valette himself was forced to retreat, leaving the lower Rhine towns to imperial forces, and his troops to nourish themselves chiefly on vine-leaves, cabbage and such root vegetables as they could find. Strasbourg expelled three thousand starving soldiers to die in the fields. Deserters from each army marauded in the countryside, and Oxenstierna saw little profit for Sweden in coming to the aid of the French.

Louis XIII, demoralised, blamed Richelieu, who had to prevent the king from taking command of the Lorraine army himself. Contact with it would have made the king even more morose than did Richelieu's insistence that the king should appoint the comte de Soissons to command the frontier forces in the north-east. The king then himself led a column to St Mihiel, fifty kilometres west of Nancy, which had declared in favour of Charles of Lorraine, and which Soissons was besieging. Richelieu was too ill to accompany the king, but had him accompanied by Séguier and Léon Bouthillier, son of Claude and soon to become the comte de Chavigny, two ministers on whom he could rely. Soissons was displeased at the king's interference, but St Mihiel fell just in time to prevent a confrontation. Its thousand troops were condemned to the galleys, but seven hundred of them escaped to terrorise the countryside. The king himself was forced to retreat a further sixty kilometres west to St Dizier.

Things did not go much better in the south. In the Mediterranean the Spaniards roamed with twenty-two galleons off the French coast, occupying and fortifying the Iles de Lérins, just off Cannes. A scissors movement towards Milan was thwarted when Franco-Savoyard troops moving from Pinerolo to the west to join Rohan, expected to come from the Valtelline, were checked. Meanwhile Richelieu had to restrain the king from a potentially self-destructive explosion against the Paris *parlement* which was obstructing new war taxation with every legal weapon it could muster.

The *parlement* had been obstructive since 1630, mostly by holding up the registration of royal decrees, including that erecting the Richelieu estate into a *duché-pairie*. Richelieu's own position might well have been compromised if the *parlement* had been provoked into serious revolt, but he had succeeded in gaining some measure of support from it with a long harangue on 17 January 1634 in the wake of the dismissal of Châteauneuf. The need for war taxation, and the inability of the population to bear its burden, produced a new wave of protest late in 1635, and the king openly manifested outrage. The *parlement* had refused to register forty-two new edicts creating offices whose sale might have raised money, and the king resolved the matter by having recourse to his primacy of jurisdiction in a *lit de justice* in December.[11] Several members of the *parlement* were arrested in January 1636, and it needed all Richelieu's remarkable skill to avoid a confrontation so serious that it could have cost the king his throne.

He did on the other hand succeed in keeping the inner council of himself, Bullion, jointly *surintendant des finances* with Claude le Bouthiller since 4 August 1632, Sublet de Noyers, and Séguier united, although the king behaved tetchily towards him, increasingly demanding to interfere personally in routine business, and Bullion sometimes successfully appealed over Richelieu's head to Louis XIII. Louis for his part regarded himself as custodian of the nation's welfare, insisted on signing all important documents himself, and indulged himself in fits of pique, temper and depression.

The military situation further deteriorated when the Spanish army under Prince Thomas of Savoy marched on north-east France in July 1636, taking La Capelle on 9 July after a seven-day siege and, after a siege of only two days, Le Catelet on 25 July. In early August he crossed the Somme. Bridges across the Oise were destroyed, and the citizens of Paris suddenly felt threatened enough to rally strongly to the city's defence and the conduct of the war. The *parlement* voted financial subsidies, the craft guilds and the university offered their services and their treasures, and the districts conscripted all able-bodied men. The peasants of Guyenne, in revolt over taxation, offered to lay down their arms to release soldiers for the defence of Paris. Corbie, about 130 kilometres from the capital, surrendered after eight days, and Richelieu, whose garden at the Palais-Cardinal had demanded the demolition of part of the city walls, was near despair, and was sustained only by the spiritual exhortations of Père Joseph. Governors of the surrendered fortresses were condemned in absence and dismembered in effigy.[12]

Thomas of Savoy moved cautiously, thereby allowing time for La Force to muster a largely untrained force of 30,000 men. Gaston, by now once again enjoying authority in France, raised a further 4,000 men and was made commander-in-chief, with Soissons as general. He scored a victory at Roye in Picardy. Before long, however, the rains slowed him down, and he decided to lay siege to Corbie, now fortified by the Spaniards. At this juncture Louis XIII arrived to take over for the third time from his brother, to whom Richelieu wrote from Amiens, instructing Gaston to await Louis's commands. Gaston petulantly withdrew but was prevented by Richelieu from taking with him the eight hundred nobles whom he had brought. Richelieu himself took the capitulation of Corbie on 14 November, having two citizens who had collaborated with the Spaniards executed in the market place. Gaston, whose work it had chiefly been, was enraged at the credit taken for the capture of Corbie by Louis and Richelieu.

A plot was now conceived by a group of officers to assassinate Richelieu at Amiens. The instigators probably tried in vain to involve both Gaston and Soissons, who had ominously been summoned by the king. Gaston, who came to Paris to congratulate his brother, found Soissons there. Gaston knew what the summons meant, and both he and Soissons hurriedly decided to leave. Only subsequently did Soissons attempt to persuade Gaston to join him at the Sedan seat of Bouillon, son of the Huguenot general, but communication between Sedan and Gaston's palace at Blois had been cut by Richelieu, and several of Gaston's emissaries were captured.

The king wanted to be severe, but Richelieu counselled yet another reconciliation to prevent a further defection by either Gaston or Soissons, and granted Gaston most of a new list of requirements, including money to complete the Orléans wing at Blois. The king even offered to reconsider the question of Gaston's marriage to Marguerite, partly because he feared that it might in fact be declared valid, as Rome clearly thought it was, and in spite of the opposition of Richelieu, who managed to delay Marguerite's return to France from Brussels.

Soissons, treacherously encouraged by Gaston, made an agreement with Marie de' Medici and the governor of the Low Countries by which Spain would not make peace with France without satisfaction for herself and Soissons, and the removal from power of Richelieu. Since that agreement effectively gave the Spanish army access to the still intact agricultural production of Champagne and the Meuse valley, Richelieu realised that it was necessary to outbid the Spaniards for the loyalty of Soissons, although Louis XIII took much persuasion to sign an agreement with him in July 1637.

In the south Vitry, the captain who had killed Concini and was now a marshal and governor of Provence, was quarrelling with Sourdis, archbishop of Bordeaux and admiral of the Levant, more about the hierarchy of command than about the tactics of removing the Spaniards from the Iles de Lérins. An attempt at reconciliation ended when Vitry in a demonstration of contempt for what he regarded as clerical hypocrisy struck Sourdis. Richelieu was enraged with Vitry, who was sent to the Bastille, but Sourdis was blamed for failing to persuade the Genoese to allow him passage to relieve the duke of Parma, forced into a Spanish alliance early in 1637.

Various strategies for restoring peace were subverted. The pope called a conference at Cologne to which Richelieu sent Alphonse, who was not making serious progress with the annulment of Gaston's marriage, although Alphonse had got on well with the pope, who refused to receive his successor, d'Estrées, because he had once fought papal troops in the Valtelline. D'Estrées also behaved aggressively and upset everyone. Alphonse got as far as Lyons only to discover that his brother had replaced him in his mission to Cologne, and took up his position as grand almoner. The Cologne peace conference was postponed when the emperor called an imperial diet at Regensburg. Richelieu told Mazarini, in Paris as the pope's emissary, that the diet, actually convoked to have the king of Hungary made 'king of the Romans' and imperial successor, was invalid on four counts.[13] When the emperor, Ferdinand II' died two months later, Louis XIII refused to recognise Ferdinand III as more than king of Hungary, and would therefore not negotiate with the new *de facto* emperor.

Richelieu now started his own overtures to Olivares, intending to send Mazarini, still ostensibly in the papal service, to Madrid. He knew Spain and Spanish well, but Mazarini thought this was because Père Joseph, jealous of Mazarini's influence over Richelieu, wanted him out of the way, and found a way out of going. Further discreet intimations of a desire for peace passed between Olivares

and Richelieu, culminating in a draft armistice agreement sent to
Olivares, who then sent an emissary, Don Miguel de Salamanca,
dressed as a Frenchman and in great secrecy, to negotiate in
Paris on his way to take up a post in Brussels. He demanded
to see Richelieu himself, who eventually agreed to meet him in
a church at Compiègne. All we have as a result is the report of
the Spanish council of state for 18 June 1638 in which Olivares
strongly denounced Richelieu.

Two things now occurred which brought the queen and her conduct to Richelieu's pressing attention. The first and less important
matter concerns Richelieu's attitude towards her and her secret
commerce with Spain. The second matter of concern to Richelieu
relevant to the queen was of vastly greater importance. On 5
September 1638, Anne gave birth to a son 'a little later than
the doctors expected'. In fact the pregnancy is said by one
modern biographer to have lasted ten months and two days,
which would imply that conception could have occurred even in
early November 1637.[14]

Anne of Austria was fun-loving, irresponsible and Spanish, but
deprived of her Spanish entourage, which had been reduced and
then removed a score of years before. She was also rejected by her
husband, and neglected in the conduct of affairs. She was, however,
never short of serious admirers. Her close circle included Luynes's
wife, later to become duchesse de Chevreuse, and Mlle de Verneuil,
who was Henri IV's illegitimate daughter, as well as Antoinette de
Luynes, sister of the connétable but now Mme du Vernet, and
the fourteen-year-old princesse de Conti. Their corporate wildness
was matter for scandalized court comment. The nuncio reproached
Anne with the company she kept on 23 February 1622.

The duke of Montmorency's passion for the queen was the
subject of an open allusion in the ballet, *Les Bacchanales,* danced
on 26 February 1623 before the king, with whom Montmorency
subsequently had an altercation.[15] The execution of Montmorency
in 1632 was to be one of two defining events marking Richelieu's
victory in his battle to retain control of French policy.[16] It
was alleged by contemporaries that the reason why the king
uncharacteristically insisted on Montmorency's execution after
his rebellion and the battle of Castelnaudary in 1632 was the
bracelet containing a miniature of the queen which Montmorency

was wearing when he was wounded. It was given into the custody of the former chancellor Bellièvre, who unsuccessfully tried to keep the matter secret from Richelieu.

Within days of the arrival in Paris of the handsome duke of Buckingham on 24 May 1625, the court had been amused by the imprudent enthusiasm with which the queen received him. The memorialists go out of their way to explain the relationship so that it could be thought to have stopped just short of an affair. Anne was certainly later to seduce a not unwilling Mazarin, with whom her relationship became long-standing. Malherbe, who lived until 1628 and who once wrote love poetry on behalf of Henri IV, now wrote love poetry to Anne for Bellegarde, a senior courtier for both Henri III and Henri IV, whose lands had been made a *duché-pairie* by Louis XIII.

Anne of Austria was naturally distressed, not only by the breakdown of any meaningful relationship with her husband, but also by the political hostility to Spain. She had strongly resented Richelieu's refusal to let Buckingham back into France after the Amiens episode, but she allowed Richelieu, aided by his niece Mme de Combalet, to place in her service Mme du Fargis. Mme du Fargis, whom Anne of Austria came to trust, came from the milieu of political Catholics. She knew Bérulle, tried to reconcile Marie de' Medici to her daughter-in-law, and had been living with the Carmelites until she inherited and married. Her husband had been ambassador to Spain for four years, and fled with her to Brussels in 1631 when she became implicated in the conspiracy led by Marie de' Medici's doctor, Vautier, to aid the queen mother's escape from Compiègne.

Tallemant, relying on the *Mémoires* of La Rochefoucauld, recounts that Richelieu used the mediation of Mme du Fargis to propose to the queen that he should himself resolve the difficulties of the succession by fathering a dauphin. That, he argued, would prevent her from being sent back to Spain if, as seemed likely, the sickly Louis XIII came to die, and she would instead rule with Richelieu as her consort. The memorialist Montglat has no doubt that Richelieu and the queen had a liaison, although Tallemant says that the queen rejected Richelieu, restricting their commerce to 'quelque petite galanterie' and speaks of Richelieu's own resentment at being rejected.

We can with almost absolute certainty assume that there was no affair, and it is extremely unlikely that any proposition, however tentative, was ever made. That much is simple court gossip, probably deriving from malicious jokes at Richelieu's expense, and circulating in and around the *chambre bleue*. There may well have been some *galant* flirtation scarcely surpassing the effort to charm and the demands of good manners. *Mirame*, of which Richelieu is probably at least the principal author, however, was called by Montchal, the archbishop of Toulouse, 'la grande comédie de l'histoire de Buckingham', and the script certainly contains lines interpreted by the audience as alluding to the queen's feelings for the courtier.[17] Even though the lines were probably written by Desmarets, they may well represent Richelieu's modest revenge for the rejection of former playful advances.

A serious break between Richelieu and the queen certainly occurred in 1637, when Anne was discovered to be in secret correspondence with the former Spanish ambassador in Paris. Her correspondence was naturally as a matter of routine intercepted, copied and resealed, and there was nothing necessarily extraordinary in her frequent visits to the convent at Val-de-Grâce, but the convent, whose abbess, Louise de Milley, was a Spanish citizen from Franche-Comté, served as a clearing house for Spanish news, and was naturally under surveillance. One of the abbess's ladies-in-waiting, an informer for Richelieu, reported the regular visits, and the box brought from the garden into the queen's room when she was alone with the abbess.

Exactly what took place is not clear. One of Anne's officers, Pierre de la Porte, left *Mémoires* which Tallemant appears to have seen and in which he claims to have been the go-between for the queen's secret correspondence in Spanish with the former Spanish ambassador to France, Mirabel. After the police discovery of a letter from Anne to Mirabel, La Porte was sent to the Bastille on 10 August 1637. Louis XIII ordered a search to be made in the convent under the supervision of the chancellor, Séguier, but nothing was found. The abbess, who denied everything, was nevertheless removed the same night by the archbishop of Paris, who had accompanied the chancellor.[18]

Tallemant accuses Séguier of searching the queen personally and indecently touching her in the process, but the search of

the queen's person took place only later. It must be supposed
in view of the political letters to Mirabel and Mme de Chevreuse
delivered to Richelieu that Anne was also in communication with
the new cardinal governor of the Spanish Netherlands, who was
her brother, as also was the king of Spain, Philip IV. When
confronted by Richelieu, Anne was persuaded by the cardinal to
confess in detail to her involvement with the Spanish authorities,
and to reveal the convoluted channels of communication through
La Porte to the secretary of the English ambassador, who sent the
letters to his colleague in Brussels, who passed them to Mirabel, the
Spanish ambassador. The political action was aimed at preventing a
Franco-English alliance which would have been highly detrimental
to the Spanish cause. Anne had been advised by Mme de Chevreuse,
who was helped by Philip IV to flee in male clothing from Couzières
to Brussels, from where she went to England.

On 17 August the queen signed a confession, undertaking
henceforward to remain loyal to the king and to France. With what
remained his innate disinclination to impose more severe conditions
than he thought necessary, and with his political antennae at their
most sensitive, Richelieu restricted himself to demanding only that
the queen should cease corresponding with Mme de Chevreuse,
who did not return to France during Richelieu's lifetime, and that
she should have in her household only persons of whom Louis XIII
approved.

With regard to the birth of the dauphin on 5 September 1638,
so late in her marriage, the great national joy was naturally not
unmixed with much speculation at the time. The paternity of
Louis XIII, however astonishing, was equally naturally proclaimed.
It cannot be disproved, and historians have normally refused to
cast open doubt on it, but it would be easier to believe in it if
it were not so intrinsically implausible, and if historians generally
had not stretched credulity beyond breaking point to defend it. Is it
conceivable that Richelieu, increasingly infirm, facing the extreme
improbability of a legitimate heir in the direct line, and therefore
the overwhelming likelihood of Gaston's succession, might possibly
have engineered it? Unsettling although it may be, the answer to
that question is probably yes.

In 1624, Louis had fallen in love with François de Barradas.[19]
Montglat, from whom we have an account of the king's reluctance

to sleep with the queen, tells us that it was Richelieu who dismissed him. He finally married outside France, and was succeeded in the king's affections by Saint-Simon, who remained the king's favourite until his place in the king's emotional life was taken by Louise de La Fayette, born in November 1618 and first noticed by the king in 1635, although their closer relationship began only towards the end of 1636.

Another maid of honour, Marie de Hautefort, had earlier caught the king's eye.[20] After an initial period of favour, said to have started at Lyons around 1630 when Marie was fourteen, she was supplanted by Louise de La Fayette, pushed forward by the pro-Spanish party, and herself became very friendly with the queen. The king was to turn to her again in May 1637, immediately after the entry of Louise into the Visitation, and by August they were again very close, apparently with Richelieu's approval. Marie de Hautefort was to remain the king's intimate companion until October 1639, although Tallemant is at pains to emphasise the chastity of the relationship.

Louise de La Fayette, who replaced Marie in 1635, belonged to the group of political Catholics who disliked Richelieu, opposed the war and the Protestant alliances, and spoke movingly to the king about the miseries of the people and the plights of both his mother and his wife. Louis was seriously infatuated with her, although not apparently physically attracted to her.

Saint-Simon compromised his own position by suggesting that Louis should make Louise his mistress, but Louise became frightened enough of the position to talk of entering a convent, a solution which suited Richelieu. Louis once claimed to have cried all night at the thought that he might be the only man she would ever love, but was totally out of her reach. Her politically minded friends hoped to keep her out of a convent, so that she might be used to turn the king against Richelieu, who for the same reason encouraged her to take the veil.

Shortly after the Jesuit Père Caussin had been made confessor to Louis XIII on 24 March, ironically at Richelieu's instigation, Louise joined the Visitandines in the rue Saint Antoine on 19 May 1637. The king wept as she went. In the convent Louise acted in concert with Caussin to bring about the reconciliation of the king and his mother, but also to further the cause of the Spanish party in France.

Père Griffet's *Histoire de Louis XIII* recounts that Père Caussin was even privy to a project to replace Richelieu as first minister with the duc d'Angoulême.

Against Richelieu's expectations, the king was allowed to visit Louise. Although he did not avail himself of the privilege unique to the sovereign of entering the nuns' enclosure, we know of several four and five-hour visits to Louise in the convent parlour in the second half of the year. Montglat tells us that the visits occurred weekly for four months.

Richelieu appeared to hold Père Caussin accountable for these visits, and for the effect they were having on the king's conscience. In the end, Caussin, who had intervened to stop Richelieu's persistent attempts to make the queen reveal the contents of her secret correspondence with Spain, was summoned by Richelieu, rightly anxious in case the Spanish party was working through Louise on the king's religious scruples about his treatment of his now impoverished mother and the misery which the war was causing to the people of France. Caussin had also given the king three sleepless nights by informing him that salvation might depend on eliciting acts of the love of God which were totally devoid of personal, even spiritual self-interest, although that was not the Jesuit view.[21] This doctrine, too, was traced back through a series of ill-conceived notes appended by the Oratorian Claude Séguenot to a translation of Augustine's *De virginitate* published on 15 March 1638, to Saint-Cyran, who appears never to have held it.[22] Richelieu was in addition suspicious that Caussin was working on the king's latent animosity towards him.

The crisis had come when the king had wished to confess for the feast of the Immaculate Conception, 8 December 1638, and been lectured by Caussin on his filial duty to his mother and his responsibility for all the suffering and death caused by the war. He was given another sermon at the altar rails as he communicated. Next morning the king, clearly moved by what had been said, told Caussin that he was dining with Richelieu at Rueil, and that he wanted Caussin to argue his case with the cardinal. Caussin arrived first, was put in a waiting room, and not invited in to see the king, while Richelieu responded point for point to Caussin's views, successfully rebuilding the king's morale and his trust. Caussin was exiled from the court on 10

December and did not return to Paris until after Richelieu's death.[23]

The idea adopted by the king of consecrating France to the Blessed Virgin emanated from Richelieu, and it is important to realise that Richelieu's single-minded dedication to the glory of France, and to the defeat of the Habsburg desire to conquer Europe, was the result of a properly spiritual reflection. This was the period of Richelieu's *Traitté de la perfection du chrestien,* published only posthumously, and very near the Jesuits in spirituality.[24] It emphasises the importance they attached to devoting their attention to mundane matters while from time to time during the day consciously placing themselves 'in the presence of God', and holds their view that the love of God is manifested by obedience to his will rather than in any multiplicity of mental acts. It has a chapter on the utility of frequent communion, and regards the Christian life in the classic terms of especially the northern Renaissance as a spiritual combat. The work is dated in some of its spiritual perspectives, linking spiritual progress to dogmatic commitment, and identifying its stages, but advanced on the possibility of reuniting Catholic and Protestant communions.

The *Traitté* marks a serious examination by Richelieu of his own conscience and of the spiritual rectitude as well the temporal appropriateness of his policies, and it gestated the idea of consecrating France to the Virgin, and placing the country under her protection. The king proclaimed the act of consecration on 11 December 1637, promising to celebrate the principle feast of the Virgin, her assumption into heaven celebrated on 15 August, with a particular magnificence, and with a procession in Paris.

At this date the king's correspondence with Richelieu makes clear how troubled his conscience was, and how besotted he became when he returned to Marie de Hautefort. It is full of accounts about lovers' tiffs, and of the pain inflicted on Louis by Marie's moods, which show how prepared he was, at least on occasions, to reveal to his minister his most intimate feelings. By the end of 1637, the king was chronically ill with the tuberculosis of which he was six years later to die.

For the detailed account of what happened on the night of 5 December on which the queen's child is traditionally presumed to have been conceived, historians have invariably relied on the Jesuit

Père Henri Griffet's eighteenth-century three-volume *Histoire du règne de Louis XIII*.[25] Griffet draws on Montglat and Mme de Motteville, and recounts how the king used to come to Paris from Fontainebleau to visit Louise de la Fayette in her convent. 'At the beginning of December' the king left Versailles to visit Louise, intending to spend the night at Saint-Maur.[26] During his visit so bad a storm arose that he could neither return to Versailles nor proceed to Saint-Maur, where 'his room, his bed, and the kitchen staff ("officiers de sa bouche")' awaited him. He waited, but the storm got worse, and night grew near. His own apartments at the Louvre were being re-roofed, and he did not know where to spend the night.

Guitaut, captain of his guards, 'who was accustomed to speaking freely with the king . . .', 'told him that the queen was at the Louvre and that he would find in her quarters supper and lodging prepared'. The king declined the suggestion and waited further, but the storm only got worse. Guitaut repeated his suggestion, but Louis answered that the queen ate and retired too late for him. Guitaut promised him that the queen would adapt her arrangements to suit Louis, who finally consented to the suggestion. Guitaut galloped ahead to inform the queen of the time the king wished to sup. The queen gave orders for the king to be served as he wished, and they ate together. 'The king passed the night with her, and 'nine months later Anne of Austria brought into the world a son whose unhoped for birth caused the whole kingdom universal joy'. The queen did indeed give birth to the son who was to become Louis XIV 'a little later than the doctors had expected', on 5 September 1638.

The whole history of the king's sexuality and of his physical and emotional relationship with Anne of Austria must raise doubts about the historical accuracy of this account, as indeed must also its provenance and its literary fairy-story register. Modern biographers are circumspect,[27] and the length of the pregnancy suggests that it would have been at least possible to arrange for Anne to have attempted to conceive in the interval between the storm, if there was one, and the later date which would be appropriate for a pregnancy of normal length. Why was Guitaut so insistent that the reiteration of his advice to the king is recorded by Griffet a century later? Is it possible that Guitaut was under instructions to contrive some means to get the king to spend the night at the Louvre, that is under the same roof as his wife? There is only one person who could have given such instructions.

The stakes were high. The king was ill. There is no evidence and not much likelihood that penetrative sexual intercourse between king and queen had occurred since 1624, and the evidence that there had been any before that date might not be capable of surviving seriously critical examination. It depends chiefly on the jottings of Héroard, who was after all in the royal pay. Alternative possibilities for the paternities involved in Anne's two previous proven pregnancies, and for their unhappy terminations, may need re-examination. In 1637 only a male child could save France from all that would follow from Gaston's succession, which would certainly have involved Habsburg hegemony, the sacrifice of French national identity, and the reduction of France to a fiefdom of Spain. There is even an alternative potential candidate for the paternity of Louis in 1638 and his brother Philippe, born on 21 September 1640. Giulio Mazarini, later certainly the lover of Anne of Austria, was already clearly in love with her.

Mazarini, as he was later to be known in France, emerged into history as secretary of Panciroli, the papal legate in Turin, the capital of Savoy. Richelieu had learnt from Mazarini in January 1630 that there could be no peace in Italy unless Pinerolo were restored to Savoy. Instructed by the pope to restore peace in Italy, Mazarin had successfully negotiated with Louis XIII at Lyons, finally agreeing terms with the duke of Savoy and the Spanish commander which were acceptable to the French. He famously brandished them, crying 'Stop! Peace!', on 26 October after a furious gallop through the French lines to Schomberg commanding the French army, when the French were already within sight of the walls of Casale.

Mazarini, arriving as head of the papal peace mission to Paris in December 1634, defended the validity of Gaston's marriage to Marguerite de Lorraine and vigorously opposed France's formal entry into the Thirty Years War, calling for a peace conference and attempting to detach France from her Swedish allies. Despite this stance Richelieu, drawn by the brilliance of his intelligence, had come to trust him and rely on him.[28]

After France entered the war in 1635, Mazarin, by now very

close to Richelieu, became papal vice-legate in Avignon, and then a French agent in Rome, where he put together the statuary for Richelieu's château. It was only when he had left Paris that he received the tonsure and was made a Monsignor, a purely honorific dignity entitling its holder to wear the purple soutane of pontifical prelates. Richelieu even tried to send him to Madrid to negotiate and, in view of Urban VIII's reluctance to make Père Joseph a cardinal, put forward the name of Mazarini instead. Urban VIII liked this idea even less and, not knowing that Père Joseph had been seriously ill for a week, actually made Père Joseph a cardinal on Saturday 18 December 1638, the day he died. Richelieu then set about grooming Mazarini as his own confidant and successor.

Richelieu persuaded him to leave the papal service in 1639, to come to Paris, and to become a naturalised French citizen. He left Rome on 13 December 1639. In 1640 he negotiated the surrender of Turin to the French, and in December 1641 Urban was finally persuaded to bestow on him the red hat. Mazarin had never taken the sub-deacon's vow of chastity, nor received any of the degrees of the sacrament of order,[29] and he never held any ecclesiastical jurisdiction. It was he who, after Richelieu's death, persuaded the dying Louis XIII to make Anne of Austria regent.

It is usually supposed that Mazarini, still in the papal service although active on France's behalf, was in Rome at the date on which Anne of Austria conceived the heir to the French throne, possibly in November, but certainly no later than December 1637. He had been presented to her by Richelieu, who, according to Tallemant, said 'Madame, you will like him. He looks like Buckingham.' Tallemant also says that Richelieu noticed that Anne of Austria was immediately attracted to Mazarin.

Mazarini and Anne spoke Castillian together, and it was to fight for the Spanish cause in the Valtelline that Mazarini had joined the papal army in 1625. Tongues at court were certainly wagging by 1631, when there was a rumour of a new pregnancy. Richelieu almost openly alludes to Anne's passion in a letter of 27 January 1632. When on 5 December 1634 Mazarin called on Anne, he told her that she should have a dauphin as soon as possible, to which she replied, 'That is all I want.' As with Mme de Motteville's account of Buckingham's first visit, the modern reader does not automatically pick up the harmonics of that sort of period discourse, especially when it is complicated by formal court etiquette.[30] Given the public knowledge about the state of her marriage, Anne was being extremely forward.

The nature of the relationship even at this stage, well before they became lovers, is also clear from the presents Anne accepted from Mazarin, including a good night's gambling winnings, and the scented gloves, oils and perfumes he sent to her from Italy. That they did become lovers seems certain, although the camouflage was for centuries effective. They did not, on the other hand, secretly marry, although it has been suggested that they did. Mazarin's uncertainty even at the end of his life about whether or not he should get himself ordained was plainly genuine.

By the mid-1630s his relationship with Anne was heavily flirtatious. When did they become lovers? There would even have been time to bring him from Rome after a storm in November, although it might not have been necessary. Georges Dethan, believing that Louis XIII was indeed the father of Anne's two children, published in his 1968 study of Mazarin and his friends translations of a selection of Mazarin's unpublished letters. He includes one to Montagu, a British diplomat formerly stationed in Paris, dated 'Paris,16 September 1637', with a footnote to say that the place-name of the copy published, now in the French foreign affairs archives, was a simple error.[31] Was it?

It can be taken for granted that Mazarin himself gave the correct place as well as the right date. Had he been in Rome, he would have had no reason to conceal the fact or to pretend to be in Paris, and it would indeed have been a careless copyist who changed the place from Rome to Paris. It is even odder today simply to assume a copyist's error with consequences of that magnitude. The content of the letter does not help to pinpoint where it was written, and while there may have been a mistake or an attempt to mislead, neither is remotely probable and it is disturbing to stumble across *prima facie* evidence that Mazarin was indeed in Paris in the autumn of 1637. If he was, it would no longer be physically impossible for him to have been the father of Louis XIV, as of Anne of Austria's second son, born in 1640.

Louis XIII returned three times from the Picardy front during Anne's pregnancy, grumbling that the delayed delivery of her child kept him at court. He made Mazarin the godfather of Anne's elder son, to whom indeed Mazarin became a surrogate father, while Louis himself cared more for humiliating his wife after the birth of the young Louis than for the upbringing of her children. Before the birth, he imposed on Anne a governess she detested, and his will had to be broken after his death in order to free Anne from the council with which he had sought to bind her.

It may still be difficult to believe that Louis, who would have had to connive at any false paternity, would have let his distaste at the prospect of Gaston's succession outweigh his pride and jealousy. Louis, however, a prey to strong feelings of guilt, may possibly have been persuaded by a desire to disguise his homosexual behaviour, which he must have regarded as mortally sinful, and perhaps also by a wish to disguise not only his failure to sire a dauphin but also his possible inability to consummate his marriage in the first place. That, however, is not documented. All that can be said is that in late 1637 Louis was in emotional turmoil and afflicted by strong feelings of guilt.

The truth is unlikely ever to be known with certainty. Not only is it the nature of the matter that any alternative paternity to the king's would have been closely concealed, but, if Louis XIII was not the father of Louis XIV, anybody who knew it will also have had a strong interest vested in concealing it. What was at stake was the future of France. The congruence of dates, events, circumstances, constraints, and the characters of the principal personages involved itself conspires merely to suggest that it is not impossible that Louis XIII was not the father of Louis XIV, but also that Mazarin was.

Richelieu as military commander, still half attired as a cardinal, at La Rochelle. He was in his early fifties.

Louis XIII expresses his confidence in Richelieu's navigation of the ship of state.

Richelieu, cardinal and commander, at La Rochelle. The bearded figure behind him is Père Joseph.

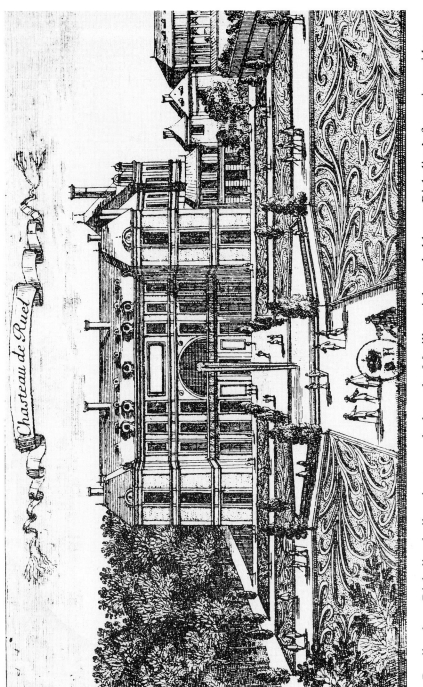

Chasteau de Ruel

Rueil, where Richelieu built a theatre and where the Marillac trial was held, was Richelieu's favourite residence.

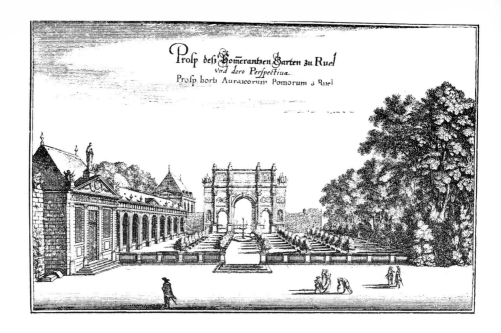

The water installations were the most luxurious and admired feature of the Reuil garden.

The Palais Cardinal from the street. Richelieu restructured the whole district, allowing no one to see into his garden.

The Palais Cardinal, built to be left to the king for the glory of France. Richelieu's rooms were austerely furnished, but he was proud of the garden.

The Château de Richelieu as left at the death of Richelieu's father.

At Richelieu, the grand avenue led to the semi-circular entrance shown in the lower print. The upper print shows the top quarter of the lower print. Richelieu never saw his meticulously planned château after 1632.

10

Domestic Affairs, Public and Private

The war was to continue until peace was finally concluded with the 1648 treaty of Westphalia after Richelieu's death. Meanwhile the cardinal, however much he affected to regard the provision of finance as the business of the *surintendants,* must himself be regarded as ultimately responsible for transmitting the cost of the war to the people of France. Inevitably, the cost of the war entailed increases in taxation. The war was leading the people of France to destitution, starvation and to sporadic rebellion.

Their uprisings must be seen in context. They were explicable in terms of a struggle based neither on caste, established by birth, nor class, established by social function. They were not limited to France, but blended into popular resentment at the refusal of princes and courts everywhere to abandon obsolete attitudes from the era of extensive feudal fiefdoms which pre-dated the large nation states. The old attitudes had been justified by the theologies, civil systems of rights and obligations, and the custom-based constitutional proprieties of the middle ages. The centralisation of French administration under Richelieu did not of itself entail any softening of feudal hierarchies. It merely made enforcement simpler, swifter, more efficient and more oppressive.

Popular disturbances as far away as India, China, Japan, Mexico and Russia have been seen as analogous in nature and cause. In France they were partly a reaction to the need perceived by Richelieu to tighten the administration of France, which meant centralising it for greater speed and accountability. Social consent was buttressed by the general view that divinely-ordained sovereignty had been bestowed in the tenth century on Hugues Capet's family and its successors, with the king seen as presiding over a hierarchical social order, but sharing elements of his sovereignty collegiately with his own caste. The theology erected to prop up this social order also maintained that any of those remotely in the line of succession, but especially princes of the blood, had the formal right to be consulted and heeded in the administration of the kingdom.

Those who became worse off in France as a result of the centralising regime required by the larger new nation state and relentlessly imposed by Richelieu's commitment to the glory of France included not only seriously distressed peasants, but also small-holders, artisans, merchants and the minor nobility. Insurgency, often thought of as rural, was also an urban phenomenon, breaking out where the aggrieved and the beggars existed in greater concentrations than in the countryside. Gaston d'Orléans, for good reason excluded from the inner circle of royal advisers but entitled under the old system to a senior role in government, was the natural focus for the leadership of those who resented Richelieu.

Furthermore, in presiding as sovereign over Richelieu's alliances with Protestant countries and his hostility to Catholic Spain, Louis XIII himself lay open to the accusation of heterodox repudiation of papal authority, which might have entailed consequent excommunication and deposition by the pope. The popes had not yet abandoned their right in theory to override secular sovereignty, to release the king's subjects from their duty of allegiance, and to impose on them the obligation of co-operation with any papal edict of deposition. Against these claims urged on behalf of the pope was a new stream of assertions of secular sovereignty. When the first pamphlets holding the canonical impropriety of co-operation with Protestants against Catholics appeared around 1625, the bishop of Chartres replied with an assertion of regal power which by this date was more baroque than medieval. He went so far as to say that the war against Spain was just because the anointed king had decreed it.

This was an exaggerated transposition of the late medieval anti-Aristotelian affirmation of God's transcendance. God himself, it was argued, was subject to no pre-existing laws. In the theology of the fourteenth-century *via moderna* stemming from Ockham, the moral law derived solely from the divine will, and acts were good or bad simply because God so decreed them.[1] The bishop of Chartres, by transferring to the anointed sovereign quasi-divine powers in the secular arena, and making legitimate that which the king decreed simply because he decreed it, was modifying Ockhamist theology to fit a secular context, and was also exaggerating Richelieu's view that the pope had no jurisdiction in temporal matters. The bishop's view was disavowed by the assembly of the clergy in 1626, and he was obliged to retract, although both clergy and the Paris *parlement* upheld his view of the independence of the king's sovereignty.

In the light of actions and attitudes justified by recourse to this type of ecclesiastical thinking, and of the humiliation of the *grands,* it becomes easy to understand how strong and socially widespread were the pressures of insurrection throughout Richelieu's period of power.[2] Not only did the dispossessed nobility and the lawyers from the *parlements* nurture thoughts of rebellion, but regional and local officials also experienced repugnance at the effect on the common people which the exactions which they were required to impose were having.

The rising waters of discontent manifested themselves in a sort of working to rule, with delays in the implementation of onerous decrees of whatever type or provenance, appeals against them, and amendments in the light of local circumstances. It comes as no surprise in the modern world to discover in the seventeenth century the widespread exploitation of tax loopholes by the rich, often through the purchase of offices more desired for the tax exemptions they carried than for the nobility they conferred.

Behind the 1632 rising of Montmorency was a history of poor harvests and growing resentment at the centralising activities of government. In 1629 Louis XIII and Richelieu had announced the intention of replacing the fiscal autonomy of Burgundy as a *pays d'état* with a system of centrally appointed *élus* with powers to levy taxes directly on individuals. Scarcely a year later it appeared that they intended to tax the production of wine, and both king and cardinal were burnt in effigy at Dijon on 1 March 1631. The city dignitaries and the military simply stood by and looked on until looting and arson took hold. The proposal to appoint *élus* was dropped and the abandoned *paulette,* allowing the sale and

hereditary transmission of offices, was restored. The interests of
the urban oligarchy had coincided with that of the peasants.

In Aix the attempt to replace regional autonomy by the system
of *élus* provoked a rebellion in the last three months of 1630.
An armed citizenry, encouraged by the magistracy, their officials
and the bourgeois merchants, swarmed through the streets on 19
September, and the provincial governor, the duc de Guise, whom
Richelieu wanted to demote from the admiralty of Provence,
did not act. A demagogic faction from the *parlement*, known as
Cascavéoux from their banner showing a bell on a white ribbon,
stirred urban artisans and rural labourers to insurrection, and a
march on 3 and 4 November led to attacks on the homes of the
parlementaires who opposed them, and whose banner was a blue
ribbon. The two factions of the *parlement* broke into open fighting
and the blue ribbon band sought an alliance with the queen mother.
In the end the uprising died away. Condé arrived with his troops,
ordered some hangings, and re-established peace. The king again
abandoned the project of *élus* in return for a considerable sum of
money, and the *paulette* was again re-established.

In 1631 there were popular uprisings in Paris, Bordeaux,
Poitiers, Marseilles, Orléans and Aix. More serious was the
Languedoc insurrection of 1632, when Montmorency hoped to
join in the major rebellion of Gaston and Marie de' Medici. The
towns were looking for compromise with Richelieu, and were
prepared to pay for their autonomy. The countryside, however,
suffered from the armies who billeted themselves, stole, pillaged,
destroyed farms and animals, frequently raping the women and
killing the men. There are scores of recorded incidents, not all
due to the measures taken to appease the huge need for money
generated by anti-Spanish hostilities, and not all directly due to
rural distress. But the need to raise more money was urgent, and
sometimes the rural situation was desperate. One or two of the
worst incidents between 1630 and 1635 left thousands of dead.

It was against this background that the sensitive and ascetic
Richelieu reasoned and prayed his way to formulating a policy
in which the glory of France came first by a margin which
appeared to him sufficient to justify the sufferings and deaths it
involved, both within the country and outside it. It was not only
the apotheosis of the cult of France's *gloire*, but also the result of

a calm decision reasoned out, and interiorly justified before God in conscience by an intelligent and devout theologian, perfectly conscious of his impending death, and prepared to be judged on what he did. Circumstances of upbringing and caste blended with the ethical values of an epoch of unrestrained optimism to produce Richelieu's spirituality, in whose genuinely Christian basis he himself wholeheartedly believed. Those who differed from him were frequently those who regarded the church's authority as extending further into the secular domain than Richelieu's only mildly gallican theology allowed.

In fact Richelieu acted with as much mercy as was compatible with not lengthening the war or worsening the economic constraints it imposed. He was capable of making examples of handfuls preferably of leaders of insurrections, and of allowing the relevant ministers and *intendants* to pressurise the populace to produce the money he needed to prosecute the war, but there is no evidence that Richelieu was himself ever guilty of entirely gratuitous cruelty. Indeed, he restrained Louis XIII who could react terribly to assaults on his pride, and sustain the harshest of attitudes in the name of his conscience. Richelieu could be cunning, threatening, unsure of himself, depressed, and privately subject to mood swings. He could browbeat, bully, and make himself feared, and easily be moved to tears, but after leaving Luçon he never in any serious public matter lost his icy self-control.

The government was convinced that the better-off citizenry was hoarding reserves of cash and that the monasteries were hoarding supplies of grain, but it was itself devaluing the offices which the king, generally in a *lit de justice,* was creating for sale. It was also creating the circumstances in which the currency would be debased and devalued, and in which profiteering in regions where the army needed horses or arms coincided with recession in others, ravaged by poor harvests or marauding troops. Corruption was inevitably widespread among tax gatherers, more concerned about the value of the coinage they received than of that which they passed on to central authorities.[3]

Shortly before the proclamation by Louis XIII of the solemn dedication of France to the Blessed Virgin, when Louis felt the need for divine aid with greatest intensity, he had asked the bishops to arrange for the 'forty hours' devotion to be observed in all France's churches. A characteristically flamboyant baroque development, this act of piety involved the exposition of the Blessed Sacrament to be adored continuously for forty hours in commemoration of the period between Christ's death at 3.00 p.m. on Good Friday until the resurrection, placed at 7.00 a.m. on Easter Sunday.[4]

Sermons were to be preached to remind the faithful that the object of the war was peace, which would lead to the restoration of prosperity. France may have had Protestant allies, but the religious nature of its struggle for self-assertion was something in which its leaders, including both Richelieu and Louis XIII, firmly believed. The underlying values might have been indistinguishable from those of the baroque cult of *gloire* and personal fulfilment, but here, as so often at this time, they were given a religious gloss which harmonised perfectly with the attitudes of baroque devotion coloured by the same values.

Where social unrest toppled over into insurrection, the social composition of the insurrectionary groups and their declared aims both show not only that the grievances of peasants and gentry were not very different, but also that neither was generally hostile to the king, the war or the church. Richelieu was regarded as a hostile figure because, although wielding virtually regal power, and recompensed accordingly, he was not God's anointed sovereign. The protests were against innovatory fiscal burdens, and therefore also against the removal of regional fiscal autonomy.

The worst of the uprisings were those of the *croquants* of Poitou in 1636 and of Périgord in 1637, and those of the *nu-pieds* in Normandy in 1639.[5] The first *croquants* were on the whole disciplined and organised. They objected even more to centralising government from Paris than to the basic taxes they had always paid, but they strongly objected to the pensions paid to the officers of the realm, including above all Richelieu, the council and the senior administrators of the kingdom. Willing to go back to the tax regime of 1610, at the death of Henri IV, their assembly asked that everything paid in excess since that date should be repaid.

This assembly represented the whole third estate, with its lawyers, landowners and merchants, who realised that their prosperity was linked to that of the kingdom and its sovereign. What is not clear is whether they realised that acquiescence even in their more reasonable demands, some of them purely local, would mean the end of the war and perhaps the Habsburg domination of France.[6] Concessions were made, and the compromises bought time and a measure of calm, but there were sporadic refusals to pay the basic *taille,* and local uprisings leading to murders, executions and quite serious armed skirmishes with up to fifty deaths.

The 1637 uprising in Périgord, where insurrection was virtually endemic, seems to have depended on the availability of migrant Poitou *croquants* who did not return home for the harvest after their defeat. Here the insurgents elected a noble as their leader, and a sizeable army was assembled to enter Bergerac, whose fortifications had been dismantled in 1630 after the Protestant defeat, and two thirds of whose citizens had died of the plague or of starvation in 1631. The insurrection was concerned primarily with fiscal matters, with the increase in the amount and type of exactions since 1610, with the devastation and atrocities of government troops, and with the interposition of fiscal officials between region and sovereign.

The insurgent force was disciplined, organised and devout, demanding respect for and co-operation from the clergy, but was overcome at La Sauvetat by an experienced force under La Valette, son of Epernon, the governor, who relied on surprise rather than waiting, as expected, for the arrival of his canons. A thousand *croquants* were killed, and La Valette lost two hundred men. After the defeat, and although the *parlement* of Bordeaux showed some indulgence, five *croquants* were decapitated, two hanged and one broken on a wheel.

Finally, the *nu-pieds* rebellion in Normandy was largely the economic result of the plague, which grew more severe from 1619, and whose ravages culminated in 1639, preventing both normal agricultural production and general commerce. Normandy on its own was expected to provide nearly a quarter of France's tax revenue, and from 1635 taxes were imposed directly from Paris, and not through the *Etats* of Normandy at Rouen, which did not meet between 1635 and 1638. From 1636 Normandy was a frontier province, obliged to nourish and sustain the ravages of large armies as well as to provide, uniform and arm its share of troops. In desperation, recourse was had to such innovative procedures as demanding advance payments before offices were due for renewal, and the wages of the military were in arrears. There were frequent uprisings, often supported by government officials, and on 21 November 1638 the people of Verneuil armed themselves against Richelieu's own light horse brigade. By 1639 only about half the payments were being made.

The *nu-pieds* got their name from the workers in the salt marshes of Avranches, who worked with bare feet, and their comparatively small-scale uprising is notable for the support of the other social groups who suffered from the government's desperate need for money. They included lawyers, merchants, priests, officers and a small but significant number of the minor nobility. Normandy was hit particularly hard by crushing poverty and the inequalities and inequities of the tax regime. There was notably little support for the uprising from rural workers.

The movement developed millennarian overtones aiming at the institution of Christian communities sharing possessions, although this goal was subordinate to the determination to get the government to modify the fiscal regime. Passions were aroused and fed by rumours and misunderstanding, and the *nu-pieds* left twenty-eight victims, most of them dead, before the royal army, which feared English intervention, suppressed the uprising in the last weeks of 1639, hanging a dozen of the insurgents and sending others to the galleys. The Rouen *parlement* was briefly dissolved, and a brutal repression was instituted throughout the province in 1640.

Richelieu was taken up by foreign affairs. His role in imposing the tougher fiscal regimes which undermined the *états* and *parlements,* was largely passive, and it was Séguier, the chancellor, who was sent into Rouen to repair its institutions, including the *parlement,* by a royal decree of 15 December 1639. His repressive activities, including a considerable number of executions, were over in three months. Exercising his supreme judicial power, he delivered judgements at Caen and Bayeux, then at Saint-Lô and Coûtances, ordering houses to be burnt and one whole village, Cérance, to be destroyed.

Cérance was not razed, although seven or eight ringleaders' houses were in fact burnt, and some leniency was allowed in the execution of sentences, especially in those affecting the property of nobles. Séguier returned to Paris on 27 March 1640, leaving the centrally appointed *intendant,* La Potherie, to oversee such further juridical measures as were necessary to ensure stability. The continued recalcitance of rural Normandy in paying taxes, abetted by both the nobles and the *parlement,* testifies that the brutality of the repression, however repugnant, was not at this period in gratuitous excess of what was required to put right the situation which had been allowed to develop, and which must largely be blamed on the time, attention and money required to implement Richelieu's foreign policy.

Quite apart from the domestic consequences of Richelieu's decision in conscience to promote the independence and grandeur of France, are the occasionally alleged failures of Richelieu adequately to restructure France's internal administrative arrangements. From the dismissal of Châteauneuf in 1633 and his replacement as keeper of the seals by Séguier, Richelieu had a royal council on whose ministerial members he could rely. It is true that his diplomatic abilities outstripped his administrative talents, but that is something of which he was aware and for which he attempted to compensate by leaving France's internal administration to the other appropriate members of the king's council.

Richelieu did not wish to rule France. There was an element of affectation in his deferring to the sovereignty of a pliant king. In fact he controlled and co-ordinated policy, but it suited him to take shelter behind divinely-backed royal authority, and to leave subordinates, known as his *créatures,* to determine and administer substantial areas of his general strategy.[7] This administrative structure had its failings, the most important of which was the tension between regional control and central policy. A royal army was the responsibility of the minister of war, but troops in any given province were the responsibility of that region, with administrative structures varying from region to region, depending on the presence of a *parlement* and the existence of regional *états.*[8]

Richelieu did largely succeed in letting the *grands* die out as provincial governors, although he did not exploit the alternative *intendants* as effectively as Colbert was to do in the reign of Louis XIV. Under Richelieu, they remained *commissaires,* with powers and appointments that were specific and temporary, although enough to make their holders loathed by the provincial *parlements,* since their arrival often heralded an increase in taxation or in its enforcement, and since they often had powers to register royal decrees, especially fiscal decrees, which meant suspending the sovereign jurisdiction of the *parlements* and their courts.[9]

Although Richelieu had maintained at the Assemblée des notables in 1626–1627 that no new taxes could be introduced because the people were simply unable to pay them, by 1637 he was forced to offer large subsidies both to the Swedes and to the Dutch without any real idea of where the money could come from.[10] France needed the Swedes to draw the imperial armies away from her eastern border and the Dutch to attack either Dunkirk or Antwerp. Bullion was unable to raise the money, and the subsidies were continuously in arrears. The *Testament politique* is explicit on the need to keep a due proportion between the economic charges on the populace, necessary in Richelieu's view to remind them of the subject status and to constrain them 'to remain within the boundaries of their obligations', and the ability of the people to bear the burden. When the state's need becomes urgent, it is to the rich that the sovereign should turn before any further 'bleeding of the poor'.[11]

When asking in the light of the social deprivation how it is appropriate to regard Richelieu's personal displays of magnificence, it must be remembered that *gloire,* although founded on personal merit, nonetheless required to be manifested by status, and its external manifestation, grandeur, itself looked on as a spur to virtue's achievement. Half a century earlier, *gloire* had ostentatiously been despised by Montaigne in the chapter of *Les Essais* entitled 'De la gloire', but du Vair had already regarded it as an incitement to virtue, no longer merely its own reward. As we enter the seventeenth century, Charron, whose 1601 *De la Sagesse* was heavily dependent on Montaigne, had looked on *gloire* as a synonym for honour. There are passages in the plays of Corneille where the constancy of the neostoic sage praised by Montaigne and du Vair is transformed on the stage into truly heroic moral elevation.[12]

Richelieu certainly was as wealthy as he was powerful, although it is almost impossible to put a meaningful figure on the realisable value of his estate, if only because the Palais-Cardinal and the surrounding land, intended to become a *quartier* or urban district in its own right, was designed as the royal palace it became, and no monetary value can meaningfully be assigned to so expensive but unsaleable an asset.[13] Richelieu had been accused by Gaston in 1631 of having plunged France into the Mantuan war for reasons of personal profit, although Richelieu had himself been lending money to the crown. He did, however, gain personal advantage from Gaston's flight to Nancy in 1631, taking for himself the governorship of Brittany, which he added to Le Havre, purchased in 1626 for 345,000 livres, a price probably reimbursed by the king. His personal lending to the state constituted no more than behaviour expected of persons much enriched by state appointments, and was always kept within manageable proportions, no doubt in view of the unlikelihood of repayment, at least after 1635. In 1640 he wrote to Bullion, the *surintendant des finances,* that his Paris collections of silver and jewelry were worth 150,000 livres each, and that, should it be necessary, they were available as security for state borrowing.[14]

Richelieu lived in constant danger of assassination, and was ill enough to have been unable to satisfy the demands put upon him without a medical staff in addition to a large household and military guards. Security in Paris was scarcely to be attained without a substantial personal troop of guards who needed to be housed and fed.[15] Security alone demanded a large and secluded household within a short distance from the Louvre. Richelieu also represented France to foreign diplomatic missions, and needed to project the visible image of domestic power not only to diplomats from elsewhere, but also to those who might be tempted to challenge royal authority.

As with the great mansion at Richelieu which the cardinal never found time to visit, so the Palais-Cardinal and the exterior trappings of Richelieu's way of life served a public and political purpose. In the minds of his contemporaries they did not conflict with Christian virtue, or even with humility, regarded by La Rochefoucauld, a little later in the century, as the true touchstone of authentic virtue. It is even probable that the need for public ostentation bred underneath the sometimes arrogant *persona* a deeper feeling in Richelieu of humility. He never gave any sign of regarding his personal merit as sufficient to warrant the outward display of his manner of life. He may have misjudged both the nature and the extent of the public perception of his ostentatious display, but neither the private greed nor the personal self-indulgence alleged against him seem justified accusations.

Richelieu was inclined to exaggerate both his early poverty and the subsequent expenses it was necessary for someone in his position to incur, declaring for instance in 1629 that, while his expenditure had quadrupled, he had not during the preceding decade succeeded in boosting his income significantly beyond 50,000 livres a year. It is now clear that during that period his income had at least quintupled. During the last six years of his life Richelieu can be shown to have received from known sources an income of between 900,000 and 1,100,000 livres a year, while he incurred annual household expenditure of about 500,000 livres.[16]

The *chambre des comptes*, a sovereign court which audited the accounts of the king's financial officials, later regarded 1630 as the turning-point of the country's finances, after which they became disastrous. According to Montglat, Bullion, defending his stewardship of the finances to the king during the 1630s, claimed that there were three abysses in the French financial administration, the navy, the artillery and 'the cardinal's household'. All three were under Richelieu's direct charge, but Bullion's accusation was unfair.[17] We do have most of Richelieu's household accounts for the year 1639. A few sheets have been destroyed, but what the accounts show is a total expenditure in line with that of other important figures of the period.

Their editor, Maximin Deloche, is probably correct in regarding the document as Richelieu's answer to Bullion, and to the widely believed allegations which exaggerated the splendour of Richelieu's manner of living, and contrasted it with so much real misery among the people of France. Richelieu may well simply have had a minutely accurate, authenticated and somewhat formal account of his expenditure drawn up primarily for the attention of the king to refute the allegations. There is no indication that the 1639 document is a single stray survival from a whole series of annual accounts, although such accounts must have been drawn up, if in a noticeably less formal manner, and with less meticulous care to justify each item.

Richelieu did, however, remain true to his belief that secrecy is the most essential condition for success, and the accounts for 1639 reveal no payments other than those of a normally expected type. They do not record any payments to informers, spies, or to any of those who performed discreet missions for Richelieu whether at home or abroad.[18] What they reflect is much more the concern for value which occurs obsessively in his early letters to Mme de Bourges, in the terms of contracts for supplying the army at La Rochelle, and even in his 1631 offer to God to found a Sunday mass in perpetuity if he is delivered of his headache 'within eight days'.

Mathieu de Morgues,[19] having turned hostile to Richelieu after living in the entourage of Marie de' Medici since the 1617 flight to Blois, was in a position to know intimately the details of Richelieu's private life and style of living. Well informed, he was also not totally wrong in his observation that Richelieu 'wanted to know everything, without learning anything from anyone'. Richelieu always maintained a watchfully suspicious eye on the motives and purposes of those with whom he came in contact, and of the cost of services and supplies, whether for himself or for the state, so that reserve and even dissimulation came in spite of the charm to dominate his behaviour. His early indigence also led him to draw attention to such later extravagances as were involved in increasing the size and dignity of his household, or having his letters sent by personal courier, so that he laid himself open to criticisms at the same time of flamboyant opulence and the penny-conscious meanness noted by Tallemant.

In fact Richelieu's measured gestures of generosity stem more from his continuous attention to detail than from any avariciousness. Without departing from his own formal, subservient public role, he could nevertheless characteristically see that the king was suitably advised on which diplomatic visitors to entertain, and how well, and ensure in detail that preparations, down to the furnishing and decoration of rooms, were adequate for the entertainment by the king of important visitors. He did not much trust the king to preserve a suitably formal demeanour. Chavigny and de Noyers were, for instance, told to make sure that the king understood how important it was that maréchal Horn, commander of the Swedish army in Germany, should be well received.

Louis's own meanness was proverbial. He quite typically hesitated to accept the dedication of Corneille's *Polyeucte* because of the present he might be expected to give. It was Richelieu who was concerned at the king's informal style of life when commanding his troops, who expressed harsh misgivings in the *Testament politique* about the upkeep of the dignity of the royal household, and who saw to it that France's honour was safeguarded when Marie de' Medici came to die, himself sending 100,000 livres to pay off her debts and her staff, and making arrangements for the return of her body to France and its reception by the king.[20] There are ways in which, while preserving all the decorum of deference, Richelieu was showing as well as instructing the king what his style of living should be.

Morgues's populist series of pamphlets against Richelieu from 1631 created the climate under which popular criticism was able to flourish. Alongside insinuations about Richelieu's relationships with women, and decently veiled cynicism about his religious belief calculated to breed mistrust in the religiously scrupulous Louis for his minister, Morgues was trying to engineer a break between Richelieu and the king. Congratulating the king on his 'careful housekeeping', Mourgues played on the king's latent hostility to his moral mentor, and it is largely due to Morgues's informed and intelligently plausible efforts that Richelieu's historical image has for so long remained demonised. In this he has been helped by the failure of any subsequent era to understand the system of values which swept through France in the first third of the sevententh century.

What might be considered the ordinary household of a senior administrative official can be gathered from Richelieu's well-known efforts in 1636 to restrain the spending of his nephew François de Vignerot, marquis de Pont-Courlay, younger brother of the duchesse d'Aiguillon and son of Richelieu's sister Françoise. Pont-Courlay had been made acting governor of Le Havre in 1631 and *général des galères* in 1635, and ought, Richelieu thought, to have had a sufficient income. By 1634, however, Richelieu was clearing Pont-Courlay's recently incurred debts of 200,000 livres.

In 1639 Richelieu stripped his nephew of the generalship of the galleys when paying off a further 247,000 livres of debt, deploying his legendary cunning by turning the sum into a loan, remitting the interest due, and making the capital gift only in his will. In attempting to enforce an end to prodigality, Richelieu as usual entered into considerable detail. His letter of 10 July 1636 on the subject is severe, admonitory and sarcastic, allowing a household of 28, each with named functions, after doing away with intendant, steward and some stable staff.[21] He even laid down the appropriate establishment of 16 for his nephew's wife and her two young daughters when Pont-Courlay was absent. She should be allowed one riding horse and four horses for her coach. The detail is extraordinary, and the hostility to extravagance obvious. 'If you need six secretaries,' wrote Richelieu, 'you must be busier than me, as I only have two. You have six *valets de chambre* and I have never had more than three.'

His own household, size and complexity apart, was nonetheless in several ways remarkable, and accurately reflects his character. He insisted first that his ecclesiastical status be reflected in the norms to be observed in his household. There was nothing of the bawdy roughness of the court of Henri IV to which, naturally, Marie de' Medici had been accustomed. Richelieu successfully created a family atmosphere in his household, keeping many of its members for protracted periods, some of them from his student days until his death, and recruited chiefly from his home region. If possible he engaged whole families in different capacities, so that his household staff was closely bound to him and dependent on him. This involved some risk on their part. When Fancan was dismissed in 1628, his two brothers had to go, too, one to the Bastille and the other to exile, simply because they had become potentially hostile.

Tallemant tells us that Richelieu was a difficult master, and Morgues of his sudden changes of mood between gloom and gaiety. His attitude towards those closest to him altered violently and unpredictably. He could be teasing and playful, biting or even cruel, and his anger could be frightening. But if he insisted that his orders were to be obeyed to the letter, he also attracted dedicated loyalty from his staff, and needed the affection of its members. Indeed, he depended on the ability to retire into the company of those on whose love and admiration he could rely. It was both his great personal weakness and his most attractive trait, although it fitted well into the pattern of large households, where heads and staff, seldom forgotten in wills, were expected to cultivate bonds of reciprocal affection.[22] Richelieu was particularly assiduous in seeing that his senior household officials were provided with appropriate benefices and other offices.

He was always loyal, and could be warm, as he had been when he took the young Jacqueline Pascal on his knees after her performance in Scudéry's *L'Amour tyrannique* to bring about the rehabilitation of her father. We should not be misled by the cold imperiousness assumed for the full-length portraits by Philippe de Champaigne. In familiar company Richelieu liked to play practical jokes, as with his pages or in the company of his favourite niece, Mme de Combalet, whom he called 'La Combalette'. He addressed Boisrobert as 'Le Bois' on account of rights over some Normandy woodland given to Boisrobert by Châteauneuf in return for services in respect of 'certain women of his acquaintance'.

Tallemant, whose *historiette* of Boisrobert is particularly brilliant, recounts how much Boisrobert was allowed to get away with in telling Richelieu what he did not want to hear, simply because he found it so easy to make Richelieu laugh. Boisrobert, Tallemant writes, 'knew Richelieu's weakness' and saw rightly 'that his Eminence liked to laugh'. Richelieu did not laugh at matters of state, and he took his ecclesiastical status seriously, but he certainly laughed at Boisrobert's skit on *Le Cid,* and several sources contain an anecdote about Richelieu's doctor, Sitois. During Richelieu's final illness, when he asked for something to relieve what must have been great pain, Sitois is said to have replied that the only efficacious remedy would be would three spoonfuls of Boisrobert after meals.

Richelieu went as far as to allow Boisrobert to tease him about the imprisonment of Vitry for striking the archbishop of Bordeaux, at the time a close friend of Richelieu. Vitry had invited Boisrobert to dine 'very well' in his rooms at the Bastille, more often a place of simple confinement than a true prison,[23] and proved to him from the Fathers of the Church that hitting a bishop was not a crime, asking Boisrobert to present the theological arguments to Richelieu.

Richelieu's first *maître de chambre,* the abbé de Marcillac, was normally in charge of ordering the household, of the cardinal's alms-giving, and of the petty expenditure of which he was expected to give a rigorous and documented monthly account. In 1626 he signed the alms accounts, but in 1627 was chosen by Richelieu to ensure the revictualling of the Ile de Ré garrison 'at whatever the cost'. Richelieu jotted down a reminder to himself to send Marcillac a note expressing his satisfaction, and Marcillac was also sent to commandeer vessels for the siege of La Rochelle. His reward was the bishopric of Mende to which he was appointed in March 1628. Richelieu was to use him again between 1635 and 1638 to find provisions for the armies in Lorraine and Alsace, but grew suspicious, telling the *surintendants* in August 1638 to pay nothing before they had seen authenticated accounts, and recommending again to Bullion in October that nothing should be paid before the submission of proper accounts.

Marcillac's successor as Richelieu's *maître de chambre* was also an ecclesiastic, the abbé de Beauveau, who first appears in the context of provisioning the Ile de Ré and the army at La Rochelle with victuals and munitions. He appears to have become *maître de chambre* in 1631, when he was rewarded with a priory before being made bishop of Nantes in 1635. The *Testament politique* makes clear that Richelieu's use of ecclesiastics in the role of military *intendants* was deliberate, a first step in the up-grading of the direction of the commissariat by confiding its principal functions to those who appeared disciplined and trustworthy rather than, as hitherto, to be left in the care of the scurrilous and the corrupt. One of Richelieu's achievements was to be the radical re-organisation of the *intendance* of the army.

After Beauveau, the post was occupied by the abbé de Cinq-Mars, whose father, Charles II de Broc, sold the Cinq-Mars fief to d'Effiat, the *surintendant des finances* from 1626 to his death in 1632 and close friend of Richelieu. Richelieu had a score of connections with the Broc family, and the marquis de Cinq-Mars later to be the king's last young male partner was the son of d'Effiat the *surintendant*. Deloche quotes a number of instances in which the marquis and the abbé were confused, and rightly draws attention to Richelieu's successful efforts at placing persons on whom he felt he could rely in the king's service.

The abbé, to whom Richelieu confided diplomatic and military missions, was already, by favour of the king, abbot of Fontenelle in the Luçon diocese, and in 1637 he was nominated to the lucrative bishopric of Auxerre. From this point he adopted the style M. d'Auxerre although he received his bulls only in January 1639 and was not consecrated until 4 March 1640. Although the new bishop continued to oversee the household expenditure during 1639, Richelieu treated him as more elevated in rank than either of his predecessors and entrusted him with the functions of inspector general of the army both in 1638, when the king and Richelieu came to Amiens and Abbeville to supervise operations, and in 1640 at Arras.

The household also included not only a chaplain, but also a confessor, Jacques Lescot, a known theologian appointed in 1639 on the death of his predecessor at the end of the preceding year. Here, too, the task was more than it seemed. Richelieu's confessor needed also to be a personal theologian of sufficient authority to quell the king's bouts of scruples and to resolve disputed cases of conscience.[24] Lescot, later to become bishop of Chartres, did fulfil the proper functions of confessor at Richelieu's deathbed, hearing his confession, bringing him viaticum, witnessing his will, saying mass in his presence, supporting him in his final agony, and even, at Richelieu's insistent request, assuring him of his salvation, which in the end was all that mattered.

After the two major ecclesiastics came firstly Richelieu's 'secretaries', of whom the principal was Michel le Masle, just three years younger than Richelieu. His role was rather that of *intendant*, business manager and steward, although Richelieu always referred to him in written documents as a 'secrétaire', and in 1626, the only year of which we know anything before 1639, he drew up the household accounts. In 1622, he had been sent to inspect and regulate spiritually and temporally the abbeys of Redon and Pontlevoy, and in 1630 he had to busy himself with the affairs of the priory of Marcigny, while in 1632 he was helping to oversee the construction of the town of Richelieu itself. He was rewarded with the priory of Roches, and then with a canonry at Notre-Dame, but continued to oversee the disbursements from Richelieu's private purse, which included the enormous loans to the government, and it was to him that the silver plate was to be entrusted if, in emergency, Bullion should need it as security for the 200,000 livres that might be borrowed against it.[25] In 1642, before Richelieu left for the army at Roussillon, he gave le Masle power of attorney over his affairs. Unhappily, many of the papers concerning Richelieu's private life, left by le Masle, were burnt in the fire which ravaged the Paris Hôtel-Dieu in 1871.

Richelieu never slept alone. There was always at least a servant in his room, and the fiction relates that a 'secretary' was always to hand. It is not clear whether the secretary replaced the 'servant', but the truth is almost certainly that the household member sleeping in Richelieu's room was part of his medical team, headed by a doctor, and including an apothecary and a surgeon, still scarcely more than a barber, perhaps also required to read to him during bouts of sleeplessness.[26] It is generally believed that the secretary would take dictation after Richelieu had slept from about 11.00 p.m. for three or four hours unless the cardinal was not ready to dictate, or preferred to compose or correct texts, or on his own to minute documents to which he intended to reply in the morning. Avenel prints one letter to Servien dictated at Rueil in the middle of the night of 4 January 1636 'in the hand of the night secretary' giving detailed instructions for several army matters, including the reduction of companies to be effected in nine regiments. Richelieu would then sleep for another hour or so from 5 or 6 a.m., rise and pray, and then call for his secretaries.[27] This is the picture painted by Richelieu himself and, as far as it goes, is no doubt true.

It is, however, clear that Richelieu was anxious to keep any manifestation of his infirmities as private as possible, and his sleeping pattern suggests that the middle of the night, when he would anyway require attention, was the most appropriate moment for medical care to be given and for dressings to be replaced. We know from his letters that he sometimes had himself bled at night, and there are few references to medical treatment by day. The bleeding procedure required a team of at least three. Mourgues does make jibes about the cardinal's debilitated physical state, but since he almost alone of Richelieu's enemies had had privileged access enabling him to know the pattern of medical care, his references merely confirm that Richelieu normally sought to keep the details of his medical treatment private.

Richelieu's night 'secretary' is almost certain to have been his domestic apothecary, who would certainly have needed an assistant. This may have been the secretary, probably without medical skills, to whom he dictated and who read to him. The literacy skills required of dictation secretaries were esteemed less than might today be supposed, and ordinary secretaries enjoyed a status little different from other servants, a situation which Richelieu wished to redress. There is an account of a visit paid to Richelieu during the night in the memoirs of La Porte. While Richelieu was on a chair having his haemorrhoids dressed, a candle was held for him to read the letters La Porte had brought from the queen and Mme de Chevreuse.[28]

During the 1630s Richelieu's health had not been steadily declining, but the haemorrhoids had more frequently been giving trouble.[29] During these crises Richelieu could only bear to be moved from place to place lying down, and in June 1635, although cured, he needed lengthy recuperation, being able to walk only very little in the garden at Rueil, and to take the air only sitting at a window. He twice became ill sitting in the garden, and complained that year of rheumatism affecting different parts of his body as well as of his migraines. It must be the result of a conscious decision that from 1636 the correspondence published by Avenel contains no further references to Richelieu's health until 1642, the year of his death.

Richelieu paid his apothecary and his surgeon 150 livres in 1639. His five *valets de chambre* were that year paid 100 livres, although they could also earn more from outside activities. They were the successors of the medieval 'écuyers', entitled to be called 'sieur'. They mixed socially with the cardinal's visitors, were smartly turned out, were generally left to their own devices or given other functions, sometimes of considerable responsibility, once they had seen to Richelieu's clothes and appearance, and could be treated with familiarity by him. They were treated like the pages of noble blood. Tallemant even records a rare practical joke played by the cardinal on his *valets de chambre* involving his pretended annoyance at the disappearance of one of two pieces of cloth given to him by Mazarin which he had persuaded the bishop of Chartres to take away. The pages were as furious as Richelieu intended them to be when the bishop duly returned two days later wearing it.

However it happened, Desbournais, the *valet de chambre* who stayed with Richelieu from his student days to his death, was in a position to lend Mazarin 10,000 livres, and others appear to have lent their name to transactions financed by Richelieu with which he did not wish his name to be associated. He used them as fronts. One, particularly gifted, ran several businesses of his own, including a bakery, and obtained the catering concession for Richelieu's household as well as hiring out horses to the stables and contracting to provide fodder. He appeared on the admiralty pay-roll, but not in Richelieu's will, presumably because he had been well rewarded in other ways. He is said by Mourgues to have had an annual income of 10,000 livres. The other *valets de chambre* in Richelieu's service at his death were left sums of 6,000 and 3,000 livres according to their length of service.

The organisation of Richelieu's household is of importance for his biography because it reveals much of interest about the cardinal, as well as being of general interest for the social historian. The complexity of the cardinal's domestic arrangements is reflected in a necessary division of functions, so that Richelieu added to the post of *maître d'hotel*, primarily responsible for staff matters and normally of the same rank as the *écuyer* or stable manager and the chaplain, the posts of steward and financial administrator.

The *maître d'hôtel*, responsible for ordering provisions, and the steward, responsible for the prices at which they were purchased, inspected the provisions as they arrived each day, and rendered their accounts, with receipts, at least weekly to the financial administrator. Suppliers were subjected to formal contracts and, although Richelieu paid more for fifteen types of luxury goods than the duc de Nemours, whose accounts for 1639 we also happen to have, for twenty-nine ordinary every-day provisions Richelieu contracted to pay less. It was not unusual for contracts to specify 33 types of game, 22 types of fresh-water fish, and 36 types of sea-water fish, plus shell-fish which appear on the Condé Chantilly contracts, or for contracts to be renewed annually or biennally for a dozen years. It seems a pity that so much trouble was taken when all cooking was heavily enough spiced to disguise the flavour of the ingredients.

Richelieu's arrangements were remarkable only for the care he took to discourage prodigality and to make corrupt practices in the running of his household virtually impossible. Deloche has calculated from the quantity and cost of bread, and the entitlement to it of household members that the cardinal fed daily something between 171 and 177 mouths, a figure confirmed by the known size of the household, which he puts at 163. The horse guards ate separately and do not feature in the household accounts. There were two *tables d'honneur* in different rooms, seating respectively, according to Aubery, 30 and 14 persons.

Richelieu did not eat in the evening, but at dinner presided, when well enough, at the smaller of the two high tables, where only the very grand were invited to take their places, the cardinal de la Valette, the archbishop of Bordeaux, Séguier, the secretaries of state, and some named generals and dukes. There were four courses, and the wines were properly aged. Richelieu ate no more than two dishes and a salad, but insisted that everything should be spotlessly clean, the table laid with precision to the last detail and with exact respect for etiquette, and the linen, on which his expenditure was notably high, perfect, with napkins folded into patterns and a cloth reaching the floor. He disliked dining with the king, where traces of the preceding meal would still be discernible on the floor. When he dined alone with de Noyers, de Noyers dined again afterwards.

He does not appear to have employed long-term household musicians, although some itinerant ensembles of three or four players stayed for weeks or months. In February 1639, a few months after the birth of the heir to the throne and in spite of the recent death of Père Joseph, Richelieu must have hired musicians for his carnival *ballet de la Félicité,* danced for the king at Rueil on the 17th with a title recalling not only the recent birth, but also the 'palais de la félicité' erected in the Place Royale for the three-day celebration of the king's marriage in 1612. The *Gazette* of 29 February has left us an account.

The ballet was danced again on 6 March at Saint-Germain and on 8 March in the smaller theatre of the Palais-Cardinal, which had just been completed and, holding only 600 people, would later be kept for rehearsals. The king danced, and a magnificent collation was served to the invited guests. We know from the accounts that the three collations cost together 2,104 livres and that other expenses came to 908 livres. They must have included extra violins and the four lutes called for in the eighth of the 27 *entrées,* as well as the fees of twelve professional dancers and the hire of 19 crystal chandeliers at four livres each an evening. Richelieu was being correct, but not prodigal. The accusations of prodigality against him are simply malevolent.

The insistence on Richelieu's interest in silverware which appears in most of what has been written about him is worthy of remark, because the fashion for it came from Spain, the principal importer of silver to Europe from the new world, and was much boosted by the marriage of Anne of Austria to Louis XIII. In 1632 there were 425 gold and silversmiths in Paris, a number considered sufficiently excessive for the *parlement* to decree that only sons of masters should be taken into apprenticeship until the number was reduced to the 300 stipulated in a decree of 1612. As early as 1585 French inflation was being blamed on the influx of precious metals from the Americas.[30] On 6 June 1636 Richelieu signed a document donating the Palais-Cardinal, the superb chalice and paten, the great diamond and his silver plate to the crown, together with the Hôtel de Sillery, one and a half million livres in cash, and some of his furniture, although the gifts were not to take effect until his death, and have pride of place in the will. He was building, collecting and amassing money at least partly on behalf of France.

There is only one mention of Richelieu's niece, Mme de Combalet, from 1638 duchesse d'Aiguillon, in the 1639 accounts, but it makes clear that by that year she was in charge of the day-to-day running of Richelieu's personal affairs, that he consulted her on matters of taste and furnishings, and we know from the correspondence that she chose the scarlet satin material from which the great cloak was made for the standing portraits by Philippe de Champaigne.

Richelieu himself was fond of horses, and a good judge of them. He had two stables, the greater with between 30 and 40 animals, and the lesser with about 70 riding horses, 16 hired horses broken to harness and 16 hired mules. The stables cost together just over 20 per cent of the total household expenses. In 1639 the monthly stables bill, excluding horse purchases, was 6,500 livres out of a total for the household of 30,800. Here again, Richelieu's purchases were relatively modest. He paid between 500 and 600 livres for carriage horses and between 320 and 450 for riding horses, whose ordinary market value covered the spectrum from 30 livres to several thousand.

The pages, young boys from noble families placed in other noble households to be trained, were also in the charge of the *écuyer*, although the older pages, attached to the greater stables, had their own director, and formed an 'academy', while their younger contemporaries, attached to the lesser stables from the age of 11 or 12 for two or three years, constituted a 'college'. The services provided by pages varied greatly, but they always played some role in household pageantry, and had such ceremonial duties as serving at feasts. Richelieu's pages stood behind his chair at table and served drink, carried lights in front of him, stood guard by his bed, carried messages, acted as escorts and, when with the army, carried Richelieu's helmet and gauntlets. They could also be sent on sometimes dangerous military missions.

Richelieu was the author of three educational projects, one for an academy of 20 boys from noble families with entry at 14 and a two-year course, probably designed for, and perhaps also by, Pluvinel, one for an academy of 1,000 nobles, of whom 600 were destined for military careers and 400 for the church, and one for the academy at Richelieu itself. The education was almost exclusively devoted to physical exercise, horsemanship and fencing, with the mathematics and dancing skills required for military and social purposes. We know that Richelieu, like Descartes, favoured the introduction of philosophy in the vernacular, and, in this also like Descartes, that he thought the teaching of history and geography important, but there is little evidence that his pages had instruction in these subjects or in the humanities.

By 1639 Richelieu had two companies of guards, 100 mounted, and 100 musketeers with 50 recruits affected to his service. When he left the grounds of the Palais-Cardinal, unless he was to visit the king, he was normally accompanied by a hundred mounted guards. Such an accompaniment was also affected by several other heads of great families, but for Richelieu their presence was not otiose. In 1639 attempts to assassinate him were not yet over, and he was haunted by the sight of the crowd tearing Concini's corpse to bits and forcing out his eyes on 23 April 1617 when, had he been recognised as one of Concini's supporters, they might have done the same to him. Occasionally he would send his guards on other military duties, and he did once try to appease the angry Parisians after the loss of Corbie by going among them accompanied only by two noblemen, pages and valets.

Richelieu had moved into the Arsenal in 1633 to allow the construction of his new Palais in Paris. It was not really finished when he moved into it in 1639.[31] He was particularly attached to saving the trees in what he called his park, and it can be argued that his only real self-indulgence was his gardens, particularly that at Rueil. According to the duchesse d'Aiguillon, the gardens at Rueil cost more than 336,000 livres, while the buildings themselves cost no more than 410,000. It was the Rueil gardens that Louis XIV sent Le Nôtre to see as a model for what he wanted at Versailles.

It was because there was no water in the garden that Richelieu sold his château at Limours, south of Rueil, to Gaston d'Orléans, and he went to great lengths in filling the garden at Richelieu with water courses, lakes and fountains. It is characteristic of Richelieu's priorities that at Rueil, where so much money had been spent on the garden and which was Richelieu's favourite residence, there was no furniture of value, but that plate was kept at Richelieu, where he never went, and at the Palais-Cardinal, for grand entertainments. Richelieu bought in silver partly as an investment, partly as insurance, and partly because of the possible needs of the treasury.

The normal custom of grandees of this period was to keep houses unfurnished until they were to be used. Richelieu's arrangements for travel were as carefully organised as everything else he did, and involved a travelling party, excluding guards, of 180, some of whom went on ahead to prepare for his arrival, installing not only the beds (bought from Molière's uncle), but all the other bedroom and kitchen furnishings, including wall coverings. Whenever he did not need to resort to a *litière,* Richelieu travelled in a coach drawn by six horses, of which there were three more in the cortège. He liked to travel, in spite of the discomfort, and in 1639 made one long journey with the king, starting from Rueil on 25 May and going first to Hesdin, and then south to Lyons and Grenoble, returning to Rueil on 8 November. An account of that journey involves returning to the course of the war, and a narrative of Richelieu's last years.

11

The Final Danger

From early in 1638, the intensity of the Habsburg struggle to dominate Europe began to slacken. The Dutch had taken northern Brazil from Spain, much diminishing the quantity of precious metals imported by Spain from South America, and now controlled the main source of Europe's sugar supply. From 1631 to 1640 Spanish imports of precious metals were down to 60 per cent by weight on the preceding decade, while the proportion of silver to gold had doubled. Economic pressures elsewhere in Europe were also worrying. The commercial activities on which imperial prosperity had been based were anything but buoyant. Shipping in the Baltic was decreasing in volume, the price of rye and wheat had scarcely begun to recover from the low points of 1630, and the price of cloth on the Milan market had remained down since 1636.

Richelieu was forced to raise finance through a Jewish Spaniard called Lopez in Amsterdam, but even Lopez was so short of funds that he could not afford to buy up Rubens's tapestries which were to be auctioned at what were predicted to be bargain prices in Haarlem in 1640.[1] From early in 1638, Richelieu, although confident about France's military, and especially naval strength, was looking hard for a spectrum of alliances which would result in peace while respecting the integrity of France. A feeler about negotiations with Spain fell through on account of Richelieu's insistence on keeping Lorraine and Pinerolo, and Olivares's insistence on recovering Brazil from the Dutch.

France had 41 ships and six armies.[2] Unhappily, one of the generals, Châtillon in Flanders, stupidly overlooked a canal actually being used by the Spaniards and was forced to withdraw from besieging Saint-Omer, and another, Créqui, was killed in Italy. Cardinal la Valette, younger brother of the heir to the Epernon title, sent to succeed him, was defeated at Vercelli.[3] Richelieu needed to consider the position of Charles I of England, with whom an alliance would have secured mastery of the English Channel. An alliance with England and Bohemia looked particularly attractive since Charles, married to the sister of Louis XIII, was the brother of Elizabeth, the recently widowed queen of Bohemia, whose eldest son would have inherited the Palatine electorate had his father not been deprived of it by imperial ban. England, however, preferred to keep its continental options open.

There had been other important deaths as well as that of Père Joseph. The French duke of Mantua, formerly of Nevers, Charles de Gonzague, had died on 21 September 1637, and Victor Amedeus of Savoy on 7 October. The regent of Mantua, Maria the daughter-in-law of the dead duke, was Spanish by upbringing and inclination, and had immediately begun negotiations for peace with Spain, signing away Montferrat, including Casale, on 25 March 1638 to the Spanish governor of the Milan region. Richelieu had the governor of Casale, Montiglio, beheaded, although he had been promised immunity for co-operation with the enquiry into the loss of the fortress to France. The Grisons, too, deserted their French alliance, largely because French funding had dried up.

Charles of Lorraine had abandoned his wife Nicole in Paris and bigamously married his mistress, Beatrix Cosenza, princess of Cantecroix. After failing to raise the French siege of Arras in 1640, he broke with the Spaniards and sought peace terms from Richelieu, who did not trust him, but consented to receive him in February 1641. Eventually, he was restored to the duchies of Lorraine and Bar. For Bar he had to do homage to Louis. France would retain Nancy and Clermont until the end of the war. Before leaving Paris, Charles called on his wife, distantly addressing her as 'cousin'. Almost as soon as he got back to Lorraine, he began to conspire against France with Guise.

In Savoy, now a Spanish fief, the regent of the boy ruler was Christine, the sister of Louis XIII and therefore also the sister-in-law of Philip IV of Spain, but she confronted a strong pro-Spanish party headed by two brothers of Victor Amedeus, one of them, Maurice, an unordained cardinal, and the other Prince Thomas of Savoy. The Spanish devastation of Montferrat persuaded Christine to sign an anti-Spanish treaty with France on 3 June 1638, placing the Savoy forces under French command, but the young duke died, ending his mother's regency. Richelieu enlisted Mazarin's help in Rome, but failed to entice the Savoy cardinal to marry Condé's daughter. Eventually the French won a military victory over Prince Thomas at Turin in September 1640.

In the meanwhile Mazarin had come to Paris at Richelieu's invitation in 1639, had become a French national, and was to negotiate the 1640 Savoy settlement signed in Turin between Christine, France and the two brothers of Victor Amedeus. Prince Thomas's wife was the sister of Soissons, but she and the children were quasi-hostages in Madrid, and Savoy's strategic importance for France had much diminished since 1630.

In the south-west Spanish attempts to invade France on each side of the Pyrenees had been repulsed, but French efforts to take the war into Spain foundered at the refusal of the duc de la Valette, Epernon's son and heir, elder brother of the cardinal, and Richelieu's nephew by marriage, to cooperate in May with Sourdis, admiral and archbishop of Bordeaux, whose breviary Epernon, the duke's father, had once struck from his hands.[4] Sourdis had won a naval victory in the Atlantic in May 1638 against the returning Spanish fleet and landed troops on 22 August to join up with those of Condé and the duc de la Valette. Richelieu's correctly anticipated fury at the way in which this victory had been turned into defeat at Fuentarabia impelled la Valette, whose fault it was, to defect and seek refuge in England. Even after the town's walls had been breached, la Valette had failed to order his troops to enter it on 7 September, although there were twelve thousand of them, and the Spaniards had only seven or eight. Instead, the French were routed, leaving several hundred dead. Condé, called to account by Richelieu, accused la Valette of virtual desertion. Louis XIII held a *lit de justice* which condemned la Valette to be executed in effigy.

Two days before the catastrophe at Fuentarabia, the dauphin had been born. Richelieu was supervising the recapture of Le Catelet, and had to delay his return to court. He published an exuberant account of his no doubt authentic joy in the *Gazette*. There was now a male heir to the throne in the direct line and, although the dauphin still had to survive infancy, the chances of being faced with Gaston as king were already vastly more remote. It is perfectly possible that Richelieu really did see in the birth and survival of Anne's child a God-given sign of encouragement. Equally providential may have seemed the birth a few days later of an infanta in Madrid, Maria Teresa. It did not take Richelieu and Olivares more than moments to realise that in the later marriage of the two infants a solution to Europe's major political problem could be found. Renewed feelers for peace were immediately put out, although Richelieu was still prepared to hold out for favourable terms.

Richelieu was to discover just how unreliable his generals could be when his brother-in-law, Brézé, sought leave to absent himself from his command, apparently to enjoy the melons grown on his home estate and to get himself ready for the autumn hunting.[5] The assaults on Fuentarabia and Corunna came to nothing, but the fighting in the southwest had at least kept the Spanish forces from being active in Italy, and the war had provoked Catalonia to rise up in rebellion against Madrid, with a quarter of their nobles and 10,000 mostly Catalonian soldiers dead of disease or in battle defending Salses against Condé.

The repression in Catalonia by the Madrid authorities was bloody, and involved the unheard-of desecration of consecrated hosts, which brought excommunication on the perpetrators and turned popular resentment into a holy war. In the streets of Barcelona mobs burned the houses of government officials and murdered their occupants. Pont-Courlay with twenty-one ships met the Spanish fleet in the Mediterranean on 7 September, and sank two of the galleons, including the flagship. In spite of foreseeing the diplomatic disaster to which it would lead, Richelieu found himself forced to take Catalonia into French suzerainty and, although he needed peace more than ever, the Dutch were now prospering from the war. Richelieu was committed to not making peace without them, although both through the French ambassador, Estrées, in Rome, and Pujols, Richelieu's unofficial negotiator in Madrid, he was sounding out prospects for peace with the emperor and with Spain.

Richelieu also mistrusted the Swedes, with whom he renewed his alliance in March 1638 for a further three years at an annual subsidy of a million livres. He thought the emperor might have been able to buy peace with the Swedes by ceding Pomerania, which the Swedes were occupying. The last duke had just died and, if the Swedes made peace, so also might Bernard of Saxe-Weimar.

The annual subsidy of Bernard of Saxe-Weimar, ambitious to win the sovereignty of Alsace, was due in February 1638, but Bullion had raised only a quarter of it by April. Richelieu sent further promises of aid which remained unfulfilled, but Bernard nonetheless began a campaign at the end of January 1638, successfully attacking imperial garrisons in Alsace, and clearing the way to lay siege to Breisach, a Rhine town about fifty kilometres north of Basle and halfway between Colmar to the west and Freiburg to the east. Taking it would mean cutting all imperial communications between the Low Countries and the Alps. In December Richelieu heard that Breisach had fallen. The tide of war seemed to be turning in favour of France.[6]

Spanish inflation in 1638 was 80 per cent, and Richelieu also knew from his informers that Madrid was making overtures for peace with the Dutch. Olivares was unable to find the money he needed to finance the war, and, probably stirred by Richelieu's agents, an uprising against Spanish domination began in Portugal. Spain was imploding from east and west, and in 1642 Olivares finally fell from office.

In 1639, the French under Richelieu's cousin La Meilleraye had taken Hesdin in the north-east. The army was urged on by the king and Richelieu, who had come as far as Abbeville at the start of the journey mentioned in the last chapter.[7] It took Richelieu five days to travel with his suite from Rueil to Abbeville, where he stayed from 30 May to 7 July, filling overnight stops with precise instructions to dozens of people on scores of topics, while still putting the finishing touches to the *Traitté de la perfection du chrestien*. The eastern army was to take Arras in 1640 and Artois was reincorporated into France, with Richelieu insistent that the citizenry be won over by mildness, not repression. In 1639 Richelieu continued his journey with the king south to Savoy, with two and three-day stops, travelling by boat when they reached the Saône at Chalon on 4 September, and passing through Lyons both on the way to Grenoble and on the return, finally leaving Lyons on 24 October.

That French finances were impossibly over-stretched is clear. Further taxation could only fuel defensive price increases, as even Richelieu realised, in spite of the parade of economic ignorance he affected, and indeed sheltered behind. However widely differing the estimates for the income and expenditure of central government in France were from 1636, both France and Spain were unable not only to afford the war, but physically to find the money to finance it. Baroque concern for their respective *gloires* had reduced the populations of both countries, and of most of the rest of western Europe as well, to penury. Bullion sought to tax the church which, as Richelieu pointed out, had traditionally made *ex gratia* payments to the treasury in difficult times, and Richelieu encouraged the Dupuy brothers, Pierre and Jacques, at the centre of the capital's intellectual life, to defend the church's freedom from interference or taxation by the civil power.

Their book was condemned by 18 bishops at a private meeting in 1640, not because they wanted to be taxed but on account of its uncompromising Gallican principles. Richelieu, still steadfastly holding the separation of sacred and secular sovereignties and jurisdictions, needed to keep a foot in both camps, defending at the same time papal rights and Gallican freedoms in their respective spheres. He now supported a reply by Pierre Marca. Marca's position, arguing for the supremacy of the pope over a general council, was still gallican enough to maintain that, while the pope could make general laws and judge without appeal, secular sovereigns had no spiritual superiors in temporal matters. Rome objected, and the book was put on the index. Marca recanted in 1646, after Richelieu's death, but in the meanwhile Richelieu was supposed to have shared his views and was accused of preparing for a Gallican schism, no doubt on the original pre-Protestant sixteenth-century pattern of the Anglican church. Richelieu had Marca's book burnt, but was compromised by supporters of his own position, particularly by a Jesuit who invoked Gallican principles, justified the annulment of Gaston's marriage on the strength of the 'fundamental law' of France,[8] imposed on the king by the people in the late fourteenth century, allowed the taxation of the clergy, and argued that France did not need papal consent to turn itself into a patriarchate.

Richelieu resisted all pressure to be party to any move against Rome on behalf of the French clergy.[9] He was not helped when Urban VIII refused to hold a requiem mass at Rome for cardinal la Valette, who had died of pneumonia, a general of the French army, at the age of 47, during a truce which ended in the failure to save Turin for Christine of Savoy.

The squabbles at Rome between French and Spanish contingents intensified into a number of picturesque incidents, including asylum for Turkish slaves of the Spanish embassy in a French church, and the shooting of an equerry of the French ambassador whose Roman servant was condemned to the galleys for opening a gaming room. The dead equerry's head was exhibited with an identifying notice on a public scaffold before being thrown into a pit with the remains of common criminals.

The French ambassador, D'Estrées, reported to Richelieu that cardinal Barberini was thought to have paid the assassins, and was instructed to absent himself from papal audiences and Barberini receptions. Urban VIII now replaced his nuncio in Paris with the pro-Spanish Ranuccio Scotti, which was a tactless way of attempting to achieve the peace he was pursuing. Scotti duly became involved in a lengthy and to us doubtless laughable dispute about the protocol of shaking hands with Chavigny, who was not a prince, but only a secretary of state. When a meeting became unavoidable, it was arranged on neutral territory, and Chavigny was late. They argued about the Turkish slaves, the refusal of a requiem for la Valette, and the murder of the equerry.

Connoisseurs of the baroque will relish the incident which followed when the nuncio refused to accept a document demanding redress of grievances from the king to the pope. Chavigny tried in vain to read Scotti the document, and then had it delivered to the nuncio at his residence. When the nuncio turned out to be absent, the officials said they would wait. When the nuncio returned he refused to accept it. They attempted to read it to him, but he went into the next room, closing the door behind him and in the face of the French official deputed to deliver it, so the French official left it on a table. Someone threw it at him, but he would not pick it up. He had just got into his carriage when a servant from the nunciature ran after him and threw it into the coach. Even today, after three and a half centuries and in spite of the baroque values which made it all seem important then, it still shocks to find the representatives of France and Rome resolving issues of national autonomy by behaving like ill-behaved children playing silly games of protocol in a conflict in which the suffering was so hideous and the deaths so innumerable.

The bishops were then told to have nothing to do with the nuncio, and a guard was set to prevent all entries and departures at the nunciature between dusk and dawn. Richelieu stayed aloof and wrote a dignified but conciliatory letter to the cardinal secretary of state in Rome, although Scotti had much offended him by declaring that the French bishops were 'for the pope and against the king'. In February 1641 Richelieu was finally forced to allow an extraordinary meeting of the clergy assembly. After re-assembling at Mantes, it did vote Richelieu two thirds of the seven million livres for which he had asked. The pope issued a bull of condemnation because Richelieu, who had banned six bishops from intervening in the debates, had interfered with the rights of the church. Richelieu sent the bull to the *parlement* which, as Richelieu had intended, duly forbade its publication.

Louis XIII's affection for Claude, duc de Saint-Simon had waned from 1635, when Louis fell in love with Louise de la Fayette. Saint-Simon's lands were in January of that year erected into a *duché-pairie,* but he did himself no favour by suggesting to the king that he should make Louise his mistress. It was precisely her devout innocence which had attracted him. Finally, Saint-Simon was disgraced by Richelieu for warning his uncle, Saint-Léger, who had surrendered Le Catelet on 25 July 1636 after a defence of only two days, that the council had decided to try him, which meant certain execution. Saint-Simon was a member of the council, and thanks to his warning Saint-Léger was executed only in effigy, having escaped arrest by two hours. Saint-Simon obtained permission to retire to his lands.

Richelieu knew that the king needed another partner after Louise retired to her convent in May 1637 and Louis failed to find satisfaction in his relationship with Marie de Hautefort, with whom he never ceased to bicker. He did not allow her to marry, but denied her the status of mistress. Then, during the siege of Hesdin in 1639, he fell violently in love with the son of Richelieu's friend Antoine Coiffier de Ruzé, marquis d'Effiat and former *surintendant des finances*. D'Effiat's son, Henri, heir to the family *seigneurie* of Cinq-Mars, had already been made by Richelieu captain of one of the ten regiments of guards in 1635 when he was fifteen, and had been promoted grand master of the king's wardrobe on 27 March 1638.[10]

It has to be presumed that Richelieu knew exactly what he was doing, not only in furthering the career of the son of a deceased friend and supporter, whose family he used even occasionally to visit, but also in putting forward a handsome young man for the king's attention. Chavigny had no doubt that the new favourite was a *créature* of Richelieu, on whom Cinq-Mars was still entirely dependent, and Père Griffet suspected what was behind the appointment. Richelieu knew that the king 'needed a favourite with whom he could converse unreservedly' and 'on those familiar terms that give life its charm'.[11]

When Cinq-Mars was created *grand écuyer* of France by the king, and took the oath on 15 November 1639, the king told Mme de Hautefort in the same month that she could no longer retain his affections. He was, he said, entirely devoted to the young man. It had been very nearly two years since he had paid his last visit to Louise de la Fayette. Even at that date the post of *grand écuyer* was considered absurdly elevated for a nineteen-year-old. Cinq-Mars had virtually demanded it, although the duc de Bellegarde was currently still occupying it.[12] It entitled Cinq-Mars to be referred to officially as 'M. le Grand [Ecuyer]'. The king, we are told, 'had never before had such a violent infatuation'. Richelieu had certainly hoped to use Cinq-Mars to strengthen the king's faltering commitment to the war, shaken by the misgivings of conscience occasioned by Caussin's advice.

The ascendancy of Cinq-Mars over the king was complete by the end of 1638, and by that date had already led to unprecedented breaches of protocol, as when the king supported his favourite in a bout of cheekiness to the duc de Nemours. All contemporaries and all subsequent historians agree that Cinq-Mars was a boorish, bullying lout, arrogant, boastful, and with a grossly inflated ego. His wasteful extravagance mattered less, but angered Louis more, than his pugnacity and his profligate, disdainful libertinism. Cinq-Mars tried to dress the king expensively, but Louis, who never cared for his appearance, regarded the proposal as simply wasteful. The fifty-two expensive suits owned by Cinq-Mars are legendary, and the king refused to look at the prodigally extravagant carriage he had bought.

The king retired and rose early and looked for the company of his favourite in a day's hunting when Cinq-Mars was too exhausted from the preceding night's debauches with his young companions and the notoriously beautiful Marion Delorme to contemplate rising. His mother was as shocked as the king and came to the point of starting legal proceedings again Marion for seduction. Richelieu tried in vain to remonstrate with him and an open breach between Cinq-Mars and Richelieu followed. By 1640 the breach between the cardinal and M. le Grand was a matter of public comment.

When the French were besieging Arras in that year, Richelieu learned from captured Spanish despatches that a French convoy of six or seven thousand carts of mortars destined for the siege was to be intercepted by Spanish cavalry. Cinq-Mars heard of the plans to protect it and, wanting to distinguish himself, asked the king for command of the convoy. Louis, unknown to Richelieu, agreed. Richelieu was furious, not only to have the command taken away from him, but to have the captaincy of the convoy placed in such unreliable hands. He made representations to the king, who let it be clear that he regarded the matter as his personal concern, in which Richelieu had no right of hearing.

Richelieu did not give up, but negotiated with Cinq-Mars that he should not captain the convoy, but would instead command the 1,400 noble volunteers accompanying it. The band included princes of the blood, Enghien, son of Condé, and the sons of Vendôme, Mercœur and Beaufort, all of whom refused to take orders from Cinq-Mars. The king, too, quarrelled with him, and Cinq-Mars drew up a contract, just as squabbling lovers might, submitting their differences to Richelieu to arbitrate. Cinq-Mars mercilessly exploited the king's obsession with him, and the relationship had quickly become fraught with intense emotional struggles and reconciliations. The favourite plainly took pleasure in humiliating the king, who remained slavishly attached to him, and in affronting the proprieties of courtly etiquette. Louis was depressed by the favourite's impertinences, his sulks and his absences for days on end, but suffered them, abasing himself in constant complaints to Richelieu.

When at Arras Cinq-Mars's horse was shot, his companions jeered, intimating their view that Cinq-Mars was better at dancing than at fighting. The favourite tried to join in the action of another unit, but was ordered back to the firing line by the commander, Châtillon. Cinq-Mars was told that Richelieu had doctored the account of the engagement which appeared in the *Gazette* in order to spare the favourite embarrassment, while the *Mercure* attributed command of the band to Enghien. Cinq-Mars's opposition to Richelieu now became a matter of honour. Louis continued to report his lover's tiffs with the favourite to the cardinal, who could only hope that so tempestuous, destructive and risible an affair would burn itself out before it did too much damage.

It did, but not in a way of Richelieu's choosing. Firstly, Cinq-Mars increased his demands by requiring a royal bride, and then, when Richelieu vetoed a marriage to Marie de Gonzague, daughter of Nevers and sister-in-law of the Marie de Gonzague now duchesse de Rethel, which would incidentally have wrecked his Italian policy, Cinq-Mars joined in a treasonable plot which involved the murder of the cardinal. Richelieu meanwhile was early in 1641 organising the marriage of his ill-favoured twelve-year-old Brézé niece, Claire-Clémence, daughter of his sister Nicole, to the seventeen-year-old duc d'Enghien, later the grand Condé, but still heir to the first prince of the blood, and certainly the most eligible bachelor in France. His father, the current prince, had initiated the project, greedy for the grand Richelieu inheritance. However, Richelieu simply paid off the Condé debt by way of a 300,000-livre dowry, but announced his intention to leave Claire-Clémence out of his will. Condé hoped to overturn the will, not yet drawn up, and remained enthusiastic for the match, to which his son was not in the least drawn, although he was made to say he was.[13]

Like all the other grandees sufficiently hostile to Richelieu to wish to remove him, often enough by assassination if necessary, Cinq-Mars naturally turned first to the dissident faction surrounding the queen mother and Gaston d'Orléans, to whom the throne was no longer after 1638 destined automatically to fall on the king's death. The birth of a dauphin meant that Gaston's best remaining chance of becoming king lay in toppling his brother.

Hostility to Richelieu was also strong in the entourage of Jean-François-Paul de Gondi, from 1652 cardinal de Retz.[14] Retz alleges, in what are known as his *Mémoires,* that in 1638 he voluntarily offered to yield first place in the final exercises for the doctorate of theology to Richelieu's preferred candidate, a cousin called Henri de la Mothe-Houdancourt later to become bishop of Rennes and archbishop of Auch.[15] When Richelieu haughtily rejected the insulting offer, Gondi won the prize by a gratifyingly large majority. The *Mémoires* state that Richelieu threatened in consequence to pull down the new buildings which he was having put up for the Sorbonne.

Gondi's aunt, Mme du Fargis had been condemned to death while safely in Lorraine in 1631, and died in Brussels in 1639, but she was certainly implicated in the conspiracies and assassination plots against Louis XIII and Richelieu, and it is probable that Gondi was at least on their fringe. He may have been more actively implicated in the plot led by the comte de Soissons in 1641. Gondi's family had at any rate a long history of opposition to Richelieu ever since his brother had to vacate the generalship of the galleys to Pont-Courlay.

In 1641 all the elements of opposition came together for the first time since the day of dupes. Richelieu, having wrung money out of the clergy, had humiliated the *parlements.* The king held a *lit de justice* explicitly forbidding the sovereign courts which constituted the *parlements* to take cognisance of affairs of state, of administrative or financial matters, and of anything pertaining to government, so depriving them of any political role. They were henceforward limited to the dispensing of justice, while counsellors recalcitrant in accepting this limitation of their role found their posts abolished. The resentment that this absolutist measure caused, eliminating the last vestiges of participatory government, was naturally noticed in Spain, where Philip IV's brother, the cardinal-infante Ferdinand, saw that the best remaining hope for Spain and the imperial forces was to foment the trouble caused by Richelieu's policies within France itself.

In 1640 Vendôme, the elder of Henri IV's illegitimate sons by Gabrielle d'Estrées from whom little had been heard since he instigated the Chalais conspiracy, was reported to have incited two ancient hermits to assassinate Richelieu. Vendôme, invited to explain himself, got as far as the gates of Paris, changed his mind, and fled to England. Louis XIII instituted a trial, and an intercepted letter from Vendôme to Anne of Austria was produced in court. Vendôme had written that he might kill the cardinal in thought, but would never have taken part in any conspiracy to give effect to such whims.

In the king's eyes this proved Vendôme's guilt, but Richelieu prevailed on the king through Séguier to drop the matter. Then, in the spring of 1641, another intercepted letter from the duc de la Valette in England to his father, Epernon, showed that Soissons, a prince of the blood and Condé's cousin, with the ducs de Guise and de Bouillon,[16] were conspiring with Spanish backing to advance into France. Soissons would enter through Champagne while the Huguenots would rise up in the south and Soubise would attack the coast.

Soissons had taken a leading part in the anti-Richelieu conspiracy of 1626 which crystallised out of the objections to Gaston's marriage to Marie de Bourbon-Montpensier and aimed at the cardinal's assassination. His followers, Montrésor and Saint-Ibal, had planned with the son of Mme du Fargis, la Rochepot, to assassinate Richelieu at the baptism in the Tuileries of Gaston's daughter, but the cardinal was ill and did not come. They had also been the planners at Amiens in 1636 who had tried to enlist the support of Gaston and Soissons in their plot to assassinate Richelieu while he was planning what turned out to be the successful campaign against Corbie that November. Soissons, summoned by the king, had on that occasion fled to Bouillon's seat at Sedan, and had finally been promised a sufficient reward to return to France and remain loyal to the king in July 1637. By April 1641 Richelieu thought he had collected enough evidence to have Soissons deprived of the governorship of Champagne, to have Bouillon deprived of his French estates, and to have all trade with Sedan forbidden. Epernon was told to have no further contact with his son, the duke.

Bouillon and Soissons knew that they had either to declare their submission or to move to open rebellion. Although they wanted the overthrow of Richelieu, they sought peace and did not share the Spanish ambition to see France reduced to a subject nation.

It was Soissons who took the initiative in contacting Cinq-Mars through the embittered Louis d'Astarac, marquis de Fontrailles, who was ill-looking, but deeply resented Richelieu's careless but cruel reference to him as a 'monster'. Soissons wanted Cinq-Mars to persuade the king to remove Richelieu, and he also put himself in touch with Ferdinand the cardinal-infante, with Guise, with the baron du Bec, and naturally with Gaston d'Orléans. The messenger to Gaston was an infiltrated agent of Richelieu, who betrayed everything to the cardinal. Gaston, perhaps scenting danger, kept the king informed. Soissons, using Gondi, also set about organising the political prisoners in the Bastille, who included Bassompierre, Vitry, Concini's assassin there for the physical assault on Sourdis, du Fargis and Cramail, lover of Mme du Fargis.

In the end Soissons led into France along the Meuse an army based on Sedan, backed with Spanish money, and including a detachment of 7,000 imperial troops. The maréchal de Châtillon left Paris on 7 May leading an army of 8,000 against Soissons, and expecting help from Charles, duke of Lorraine, who had, however, defected again to the Spaniards, and on 28 July fled to Flanders. Châtillon's troops were routed by the invaders at La Marfée on 6 July 1641.

Soissons, however, was killed at the moment of victory, either because his habit of pushing up his visor with one of his pistols finally proved lethal when the pistol went off, which is how Bouillon and Tallemant relate his death, or because he was recognised or hunted by a soldier in Richelieu's employ who shot him, which is the official version. Châtillon says it happened at the beginning of the engagement. The comte de Roussillon says that one of Châtillon's soldiers, not recognising Soissons, shot the unknown commander he had at his mercy despite being offered a ransom of 60,000 livres to spare him. The abbé Arnauld suspected that it was an assassination.

The major French forces under La Meilleraye were besieging Aire-sur-la-Lys, while Louis XIII was advancing on Mézières and threatening Sedan. Bouillon immediately made an accommodation with the king, begged on his knees for pardon, and dined that evening with Richelieu. He later called on Cinq-Mars, and was horrified by the intensity of his hatred of Richelieu and by Cinq-Mars's suggestion that a conspiracy should be organised to replace Richelieu by Bouillon himself. Cinq-Mars had already approached Gaston, who had come to Amiens where the king had his encampment, to try to involve him in another attempt to have the cardinal dismissed, but Gaston was unwilling to be involved in the young man's conspiracy, however slighted he felt at being left out of the royal counsels in the conduct of the war.

The king wanted the corpse of Soissons made the object of posthumous proceedings, but was correctly advised by those who understood that such an action against a prince of the blood could only irritate a country still resentful of the new absolutisms, that a magnanimous gesture would be more appropriate for the warrior-king. The body was handed to the family for proper interment. The French rapidly re-occupied Lorraine, and duke Charles took up his career as an imperial general again. All Bouillon's followers were pardoned except for Guise and du Bec. Since they were not in the country, they would not come to physical harm by being decapitated in effigy. Not so lucky was Saint-Preuil, the governor of Arras. The French took a number of northern towns, Lens, La Bassée and Bapaume, whose Spanish garrison was promised a free passage. Saint-Preuil not knowing this, attacked them. He was decapitated at Amiens for causing the king's word to be broken.[17]

The failure of the Soissons revolt of 1641 by no means put an end to the fact that all France was smarting under the heavy taxation regime needed to pay for the war. Richelieu's policies, person and power were becoming increasingly unpopular. The king at 40 was prematurely senile in his tempestuous affair with a wastrel who, if he had had bravura bred into him, was nonetheless a braggart and a bully. However savage repression had been, further insurrection was a near certainty.

The intensely optimistic heroic cultural values increasingly explored in the literature of the century's first four decades had reached their apex, and by the early 1640s were clearly on the turn, no doubt as a result of the misery inflicted by the war.[18] The era of François de Sales, d'Urfé, Bérulle and the young Descartes was giving way to the gloomy religion of Jansenism, the ascendancy of the 'French school' of spirituality bereft of any confidence at all in human nature, and the socio-political upheaval which would climax in the Fronde. Pierre Corneille's heroic dramas were about to give way to the later political tragedies, and soon Pascal would be launching his satirical attack on the 'extravagance' of Jesuit baroque.

Cinq-Mars, now himself aspiring to marry Marie de Gonzague, the daughter of the duc de Nevers, finally installed as duke of Mantua, was not penalised for his role in the 1641 rebellion. Marie's father had died in 1637 and Marie had inherited the sovereign territory of Nevers. Born in 1612, she had never married, and refused to compromise her chastity with Cinq-Mars. But she did nothing to cool his hatred of Richelieu. When Marie de' Medici had taken Marie de Gonzague off and virtually imprisoned her at Vincennes in 1629 to prevent her from marrying Gaston, it had been another episode in the perennial feud between the Medici and Gonzaga families, but Marie de Gonzague blamed Richelieu, whom she fervently detested. One of the ways in which Cinq-Mars forced the king and Richelieu apart was by references he made to the king on the king's own emotional dependence on Richelieu. Cinq-Mars now decided to ask the king to make him a duke and peer in order to lessen the impropriety of his marriage to a princess. Richelieu bluntly, and in the circumstances rather richly, reminded Cinq-Mars of his comparatively lowly origins.

Early in 1642 Cinq-Mars began to articulate the widely-held view that Richelieu was subjecting the French people to the rigours of the war simply because its continuation was the condition for his retention of power. Cinq-Mars suggested to the king, still tortured by the scruples induced by Caussin, that Louis might open private negotiations with Rome and Madrid, perhaps using one of Cinq-Mars's friends, François-Auguste de Thou, son of the famous historian of the French religious wars, as intermediary.

The piquant but unreliable Montglat says that Cinq-Mars suggested to the king that Richelieu should be assassinated. The king was horrified more, it was said, by the consequent excommunication for conniving at the murder of a priest and a cardinal than at the act itself. The captain of his mounted musketeers, generally called Tréville, is said to have remarked that Rome would have no problem in absolving Louis XIII.[19] The whole story is difficult to believe, in spite of the king's sporadic but severe bouts of irritation with the cardinal at this time. What may well be true is that the king might, in a moment of irritation, have sounded less than resolute in his repudiation of that part of Cinq-Mars's plan. He certainly was not implicated in any plot to assassinate the cardinal, nor, as far as we know, did he ever actually conduct diplomatic negotiations behind Richelieu's back.

Richelieu offered to make Cinq-Mars governor of Touraine to move him out of the way. Cinq-Mars asked in vain for a seat on the royal council. He was in touch with Bouillon, now commanding the French army in Italy opposing Thomas of Savoy, and late in 1641 he told Gaston that Louis was planning to dismiss Richelieu. Could Cinq-Mars count on Gaston's support if he encouraged the king? Louis uncharacteristically unburdened his conscience to Gaston, who was convinced that Cinq-Mars had been right in suggesting that Louis wanted to be rid of Richelieu. More characteristically, he became yet again embroiled in a conspiracy against the cardinal.

Between Gaston and Cinq-Mars, the go-between was the embittered Fontrailles. Bouillon would support any uprising, but would need Spanish help to defend Sedan. A treaty was drawn up to be signed by Gaston and Philip IV of Spain guaranteeing rebel French support for an invading Spanish army. The document spoke of ruining, not killing the cardinal, although it seems certain that assassination was intended by Cinq-Mars and at least Fontrailles. At his trial, Fontrailles said that assassination had been the intention, while Cinq-Mars denied it. The plan was certainly treasonable, although Gaston put in an escape clause to say that he intended nothing against the king's will, presumably to cover himself if Louis did not move against Richelieu, and it was specified that, with Gaston as lieutenant-general, the rights of king, queen and dauphin would be respected.

The document appears to have been shown to the queen before it was taken to Olivares by Fontrailles, closely followed over the Pyrenees by one of Richelieu's agents. A letter from Gaston ensured the immediate reception of Fontrailles by Olivares, who was sceptical about any plan centering on Gaston, especially when principally supported by Bouillon and Cinq Mars, but thought it might offer a final chance to win the war in a situation in which he had little to lose. On 13 March Philip IV signed.

As the conspiracy was ripening, Louis announced his intention of being himself with his army in besieging Perpignan, the capital of Roussillon. Both Louis and Richelieu knew that they were both terminally ill. Richelieu was suffering badly from ulcers, and his right arm was virtually paralysed by abscesses. He would have preferred not to have had to accompany the king, and must have known that the king's loyalty to him was vacillating. He knew that the nuncio had reported as much to Rome.

Cinq-Mars tried to wean the king from his project, because planning would be easier if Richelieu remained in Paris. Louis, however, was adamant, and left Paris in February, with Richelieu following with his train a day or two behind. At Lyons, Louis joined an army of 15,000 foot and 14,000 horse under the command of La Meilleraye. Cinq-Mars had intended to act at Lyons, but would not do so without the presence of Bouillon, waiting in Auvergne to join the army in Italy. Bouillon wrote to Gaston that he felt that Guébriant's victory with Swedish troops at Kempen on 17 January, leading to the conquest of the duchy of Jülich in the upper Rhineland, made it uncertain that the Spaniards would any longer be able to support the intended uprising. Richelieu's brother celebrated Kempen with a solemn *Te Deum* in the presence of Richelieu and the king at Lyons.

The army moved on to Perpignan, and the king presented Mazarin with the cardinal's hat at Valence, on the way down the Rhône. Richelieu, taking great care of his safety, travelled two days behind the court, but was too ill to continue beyond Narbonne. He dictated a valedictory note to Chavigny telling him to say to the king that if he should die through the king's fault, the king himself would be lost. He then dictated his seventeen-page will, which he was unable to sign, and in which he stated that he had never failed in the obedience or the respect which he owed to the queen mother.

De Noyers and Chavigny kept him posted with information from the king's entourage at Perpignan, where Cinq-Mars appeared to have regained any power he might have lost over the king, although his impertinences were more outrageous than ever. Tallemant relates that the king complained of being kept waiting for hours while Cinq-Mars was off on his debauches, that Cinq-Mars was ruined by vice and lacking in desire to please, that a kingdom would not cover his expenses, and that he had three hundred pairs of boots.

Richelieu suspected that there was a plot against him, and

that Bouillon was involved. He wrote to Estrades, the French ambassador in The Hague, to obtain assurance of support from the Prince of Orange, saying that Cinq-Mars was plotting to take his place beside the king. The Prince said that he was horrified at the ingratitude of Cinq-Mars, and that it was only Richelieu's position in France that had prevented him from already coming to terms with Spain. Richelieu managed to move to Arles, where the Roman baths might relieve his pain, and en route received from the king a letter saying, 'I love you more than ever. We have been together for too long to be separated.' Dissimulation is possible, but it is more likely that the king realised that the tension between himself and Richelieu was getting out of hand, was detrimental to both their interests, and that he could give the necessary reassurance with complete honesty. It did not contain or imply a break with Cinq-Mars.

At Arles Richelieu received a copy of the treaty between Gaston and the king of Spain on or about 11 June. Louis, still anxious to make his wife feel her rejection, and disturbed by the affection shown by the dauphin and his young brother for their mother, the queen, had threatened to separate her infant children from her. It has been conjectured that it was she who leaked the treaty, in a desperate attempt to get the king to relent. She had been bombarding Richelieu with letters seeking his help since the end of April. Quite possibly it was Schomberg, whom Cinq-Mars had wished to enlist, and who was playing safe.[20] It might have been Pujols, Richelieu's private agent in Madrid. Although this conjecture has been heavily criticised, it still looks possible.

Fontrailles brought the signed copy back to Cinq-Mars, while the papal nuncio in Madrid informed Richelieu about the visit of Fontrailles to Madrid. Fontrailles rode to Toulouse to meet de Thou, who obtained a set of signed blank letters from Anne of Austria, intended for use as orders after the rebellion. On 20 May Fontrailles reported to Gaston that, in his opinion, the fall of Cinq-Mars was imminent. Marie de Gonzague had written to Cinq-Mars that the plot had been discovered, and Fontrailles had already advised Cinq-Mars to flee to Sedan. A little later Fontrailles saved his own life by travelling to England before the storm broke.

The day Richelieu received his firm evidence he sent Chavigny to Narbonne, where the king was, to confront him with it. Louis was still sleeping, and at first could not believe what he saw. Orders went out immediately to arrest Bouillon, who was negotiating with Thomas of Savoy at Casale, and that evening Louis signed the order to arrest Cinq-Mars, who had been warned, had tried to flee but, finding all the town gates locked against him, had gone into hiding. He was discovered next day. Bouillon attempted to flee from Casale, but was discovered and brought to Lyons. Gaston heard from the king, who referred to the insolence of Cinq-Mars but said nothing about Gaston himself. Gaston did not know that the treaty with Philip IV had been discovered, and was making his way to the Low Countries when the news of the arrest of Cinq-Mars reached him at Moulins.

Gaston reacted as Richelieu had learned to expect he would. He wrote to the king on 7 July disclosing all he knew. He denied having discussed with Cinq-Mars the assassination of Richelieu, and named his co-conspirators. Marie de Gonzague burnt her papers and successfully begged the duchesse d'Aiguillon to destroy all those in the cardinal's files in which she was mentioned. Cinq-Mars was imprisoned at Montpellier and de Thou at Tarascon. Richelieu, however ill, was completely in control of running France's affairs. He failed, nonetheless, to confront Gaston with Cinq-Mars and de Thou, as Gaston fled, this time to his sister Christine of Savoy at Annecy, where he heard of his mother's death at Cologne on 3 July. Richelieu persuaded him to come back to France in August, and Gaston certified at Villefranche on 29 August that the two unnamed conspirators in the treaty were Cinq-Mars and Bouillon.

On hearing of the death of Marie de' Medici, Richelieu wrote of his joy on hearing of her 'grande repentance' for her failings and of her dying pardon 'de bon cœur' of those she thought of as her enemies. A letter of Henri Arnauld written on 10 August 1642 tells us that, in spite of his debilitating ulcers, Richelieu continued to work from bed, although he could not get up. He worked and dictated from 7.00 to 8.00 a.m., was treated by his doctors from 8.00 to 9.00, saw those who needed to see him from 9.00 to 10.00, worked from 10.00 to 11.00, heard mass, dined, and talked to Mazarin 'et autres' until 2.00 p.m., when he worked again until 4.00, after which he again gave audiences. The surviving letters show his amazing energy and attention to detail. Even at this date he could give detailed directions for military activity both in and around Perpignan and in the north, make arrangements for the return of the queen mother's body to Paris, the settlement of her debts and the disposal of her effects, and settle details of the building work to be done at the Sorbonne, and precise measures to be taken against all those involved in the plot.

Perpignan fell after Brézé had defeated the Spanish fleet which was the last hope of relief, and the king returned northwards. In mid-August Richelieu decided to go up the Rhône to Valence. He took de Thou, leaving Cinq-Mars to be brought separately. Cinq-Mars reached Lyons on 3 March, de Thou, who had been sent by carriage from Valence, on the 4th, and Richelieu on the 5th. Gaston was as usual pardoned, but condemned to live as a private citizen.

Cinq-Mars and de Thou were tried in the first week of September, with Séguier presiding, and were tricked into implicating one another. Louis himself wrote that Cinq-Mars was an imposter and a calumniator, but de Thou, accused only of being an accessory, nearly escaped condemnation, since Cinq-Mars's evidence against him was not corroborated, and two judges voted for acquittal. Richelieu had left Lyons before sentence was pronounced. Cinq-Mars's mother was confined to Touraine, and the château of Cinq-Mars was destroyed. The regular executioner had broken a limb and his substitute botched the decapitations, which infuriated the crowd, who may actually have assassinated him. De Thou had been subdued, nervous and prayerful, but Cinq-Mars had strutted flamboyantly, demanding, and being refused, a platform for decapitation higher than that of de Thou, to reflect his higher rank, and at first refusing to remove his hat, which he finally tossed to the crowd, who appear to have been in sympathy with him.[21] Mazarin negotiated the surrender of Sedan in return for Bouillon's life, and Sedan was incorporated wholly into France.[22] Bouillon was allowed to retire to Rome, where he later became a Catholic and was put in command of the papal army.

The cardinal had travelled up the Rhône in great splendour, but lying down, and he was removed each night to prepared lodgings on his bed. On one occasion part of a wall had to be knocked down to get him through. At Nemours his bed was put in a carriage and he travelled by road to Fontainebleau. The king called on him, and de

Noyers and Chavigny helped him to rise. Then Richelieu and Louis spent three hours alone together. In October Richelieu was well enough to return to the Palais-Cardinal, where he drafted a long memorandum to the king on the Cinq-Mars affair and announced that he would tender his resignation yet again unless the king agreed to five undertakings, not to let his favourites be mixed up in politics, not to listen to accusations against his ministers, to uncover the truth of charges against them before acting, to punish those found guilty of calumny, and to keep private the proceedings of council meetings. He must have been rehearsing complaints occasioned by grievances incurred by him in the journey south, and while he was at Narbonne, Arles and Tarascon.

He went on to remind Louis of how he had himself been treated after Concini's death, banished on false suspicions. The king did not acknowledge receipt of the document, and Richelieu therefore again tendered his resignation on 5 November. Chavigny was with the king, who went hunting. Richelieu, not having heard, wrote again on 13 November, asking for a clear reply, and for the king to state on what conditions he would agree to peace with Spain. Finally the king made up his mind. He replied on 20 November that he had not believed the accusations made against Richelieu by Cinq-Mars, and that he wished Richelieu to act with greater power and liberty than ever before. He would not compromise over Lorraine, Arras, Hesdin, Bapaume, Perpignan, Breisach or Pinerolo. A week later he banished all the associates of Cinq-Mars from court.

There had clearly been mistrust in the king's mind about the continuation of Richelieu's policy, no doubt on account of the way Cinq-Mars had built during the journey south on the guilt aroused by Caussin, and Richelieu's lengthy memorandum must have been taking up points in the private conversation which had taken place at Fontainebleau. Richelieu was still admonishing the king in the firm, even authoritarian tone he might have used had he been the king's spiritual director, and which are to be found again in the *Testament politique,* where they contrast strangely with the almost obsequious formulae to which Richelieu adhered in his letters and memos to the king. The threat of resignation reads as if Richelieu were a doctor, defying the king to take his advice or find someone else.[23]

On 28 November pleurisy set in, and the cardinal's death agony began as he became increasingly feverish. By 2 December the doctors knew it was the end, although Richelieu had up to this point continued to give instruction to the secretaries of state who visited him. He recommended military commands for Bouillon's younger brother, Turenne, and Condé's son, Enghien, soon to distinguish himself at Rocroi. The duchesse d'Aiguillon looked after him and the king visited him, receiving Richelieu's final advice and himself serving the cardinal with his egg yolks. The king promised to retain the secretaries of state after Richelieu's death, although he had come to dislike Chavigny, and to appoint Mazarin to succeed Richelieu. He did not return to Saint-Germain, but waited at the Louvre for the cardinal's death.

Richelieu inquired of his doctors what his condition was, made his confession to the bishop of Chartres, heard mass and received communion at midnight, asked for the last sacraments from the parish priest of Saint-Eustache, the parish in which he had been born and whose parish priest at that date had baptised him, and died quietly with great composure late in the afternoon of 4 December, content that he had never wavered from his devotion to promoting the good of religion and the state. 'My master,' he said, 'my judge who will shortly judge me: I pray him with all my heart to condemn me if I have ever had any intention other than the good of religion and the state.' The king and his brother, Gaston, had come again at the very end. Richelieu had asked his niece to leave him, wishing to spare her the anguish of witnessing his death. The last words that history has recorded from him expressed Richelieu's wish that he had had a thousand lives to devote them all to the church.

Griffet notes that the cardinal was not beloved of the people. Bonfires were lit as the news of his death spread. The king must certainly have been relieved at the lifting of the constant constraints placed on his feelings and his judgement by Richelieu, particularly since the date when Caussin had worked on his genuine feelings of responsibility whose corruption into spiritually morbid scruples Cinq-Mars was ruthlessly to encourage. In January came news that Olivares had been disgraced, and in March 1643 Louis himself fell ill. He was to die on Ascension Day, Thursday 14 May.

He had kept Mazarin as chief minister, and it was Mazarin who persuaded him reluctantly to nominate the queen as regent, constrained, however, both by a council of which Condé was a member and the appointment of Gaston d'Orléans as lieutenant-general. On the king's death, with Mazarin behind her, Anne obtained from the *parlement* the annulment of her late husband's arrangements, and acquired for herself full powers as regent, to be exercised under Mazarin's guidance until the dauphin, Mazarin's godson, came of age. The constitutional proprieties were respected in the continuity of sovereignties, with a regent during the minority of Anne's elder son. More important for France was the real continuity between Richelieu and his appointed successor, Mazarin.

12

Postlude

Richelieu outlived his age. It is common enough for people to continue to adhere to the personal and social attitudes of their upbringing, even when their society has come to reject the hierarchy of values on which they were based. Richelieu, however, is unusual in that he himself powerfully contributed to the obsolescence of the value system which he helped to create, by which he continued to abide, and through which, in spite of its decline, he brought about the creation of a national identity for France.

The task he imposed on himself drained him of physical energy. The remarkable triple head painted by Philippe de Champaigne, now in London's National Gallery, shows a Richelieu exhausted by pain whose activity can have been sustained only by an intense concentration of nervous energy. It dates from 1642, the year of Richelieu's death, and was intended to enable Bernini in Rome to make a marble bust. It brilliantly catches the nervous, almost frightened eyes and and the drooping, lined cheeks mustering an impassive dignity to mask the suffering and the illness.[1]

He had presided over the government of France during a remarkable period. Its literate and articulate elite, its imaginative writers and its other creative artists universally reflect the need of a whole society to explore the intense confidence in human potential which had been generated during the Renaissance. Elsewhere in western Europe this fundamental characteristic of 'Renaissance' culture had continued in spite of regional setbacks more or less smoothly to expand and intensify through the eras of baroque and rococo towards the enlightenment era of belief in human perfectibility. Human nature was examined for its innate nobility. Outside France from the end of the sixteenth century, and within it from the end of the seventeenth, the possibility that the increasing optimism about human dignity and the perfectibility of the individual might be seriously misplaced was not a dominant theme of the creative imagination in western Europe before the romantic generation in the second quarter of the nineteenth century.

France was different. The blood-letting of the wars of religion between their eruption in 1562 and the date of 1594 conventionally assigned to their end split the country politically, and precipitated a cultural trauma which quite suddenly rendered any interest in the discussion of human perfectibility irrelevant, uninteresting and all but impossible during the last four decades of the sixteenth century.[2] The cultural trauma was reflected in the emergence at its core of the philosophical relativism popularly associated with Montaigne and Bodin and the moral stoicism associated with Justus Lipsius in the Low Countries and Guillaume du Vair in France. After the turn of the century, it was as if France's culture needed to catch up with Italy, Spain, England and the important cultural centres of German-speaking Europe. The pace of the change in France and the exaggeration of its value swing make clear what had been going on in the meanwhile at a more sedate pace in the cultural value systems of the rest of western Europe.

Quite suddenly in France François de Sales could base his whole spirituality on the 'natural desire' to love God, a concept, incidentally, cautiously accepted in Richelieu's spiritual works, but which had implications in the early seventeenth century not strictly compatible with orthodox Catholic theology.[3] A similar optimism underlies the early spirituality of Bérulle and the Catholic religious revival in France. It increases throughout the three chronologically staggered books of *Epîtres morales* by Honoré d'Urfé (1598, 1603 and 1608) the five-part *Astrée* (1607, 1610, 1619, 1627, and the conclusion by Baro of 1628), and is basic to the theology of the Jesuits, designed to allow to human beings the chance at least to accept the permanently available divine grace which justifies them before God, and to promote the confident spirituality to which that availability gave rise.

The imaginative explorations intensify with Corneille's fierce dramatic investigations of the 1630s and early 1640s into the heroic and the patriotic. The rehabilitation of the 'passions' is perceptible in Charron's *De la Sagesse* of 1601 and the early d'Urfé. It is brought to its apogee by Descartes, the purpose of whose philosophical achievement is still astonishingly misunderstood, and who spent a lifetime working out how philosophical principles, themselves absolutely certain, could lead us all simultaneously to the highest peaks of happiness and virtue which we are capable of attaining.[4]

We still do not understand very much about the mechanics of the process by which the hierarchy of ethical and other cultural values of any community constantly changes. It is clear, however, that western European societies since the Renaissance have constantly been creating new consensual conformities. They can for periods be suppressed, but eventually they force the modification of forms of administration and government. Historians generally fall back on hypotheses of discontinuity, to which we give classroom categories like 'renaissance', 'reformation' or 'enlightenment'. There is, however, inevitably no agreement about the nature of the cultural changes signified by such terms. We are a long way from understanding the many ways in which and reasons on account of which advanced societies modify their value systems and the personal and social attitudes which then flow from them.

Richelieu's society, however bitter its internal debates and hostilities, however physically violent the exercise and repression of protest, and however exciting the dreams which arose within it to explore possibilities of change, is still defined by a set of broadly agreed norms of social organisation and behaviour. Richelieu, the devoutly reforming bishop of a minor see from a recently ennobled family, was at first impelled by his desire to restore the family name and fortune, and then skilful and ambitious enough to work himself into the favour of, and then make himself indispensable to Marie de' Medici in exile at Blois. He worked in the belief that the king was God's anointed representative and that the king held correspondingly absolute sovereignty in the secular order. From 1624 Richelieu embraced, formulated and imposed a political system which created a politically and administratively unified France.

It was not entirely fair of Bremond, in spite of his still unsurpassed
understanding of the Catholic revival in early seventeenth-century
France, to say that, devout Catholic though he was, Richelieu's
kingdom was 'of this world'. Richelieu spent his career seeking
in the secular sphere to bring about what he sincerely believed to
be France's grandeur without ever trespassing against God's law.
He conceived of his activity as certainly in accordance with God's
transcendent sovereignty and, if we can trust the twelve sections
of the second chapter of the *Testament politique,* as virtually dictated
by it. The anti-papal attitudes and the Protestant alliances in no way
detracted from his religious commitment. His concern may have
been for the kingdom of France in this world, but his own spiritual
vision was not limited to wealth, power and political strategy.

Some form of political absolutism, imposing the exercise of a
single sovereign authority and the single sovereign jurisdiction
which is its corollary, was always going to be necessary to sustain
the larger territorial units which emerged in the late fifteenth
century. They were initially without single cultural identities,
but the French reliance on customary law and a miscellany of
heterogeneous legal systems, together with the religious wars of
the sixteenth century, allowed regional fiscal and administrative
autonomy to persist longer and become more entrenched in France
than it did either in Spain, after the fusion of Aragon and Castile,
or in England after the Tudor victory at Bosworth Field. Its final
reform was consequently more violent.

On the Italian peninsula the five great city-states of Milan,
Venice, Florence, Rome and Naples retained their individualities
and administrative systems, with Rome partly relying on its spiritual
authority. The fiercely independent political stance and administrative procedures of Venice were governed by its position linking
Greek and Moorish characteristics from the east with the banking
and mercantile culture of upper Bavaria to its north. Although
lip-service was paid to imperial authority in German-speaking
Europe, the large number of free cities and small states in the
empire ensured that no large integrated federation could emerge
there, particularly after the political power blocks were buttressed
by sectarian hostilities.[5] In spite of carefully nurtured appearances
of corporate government and some deference to popular sentiment,
nowhere in the Low Countries, the former Burgundian empire, or

in Italian or German-speaking Europe was there anything other than administrative absolutism, even though the units were smaller and the centrifugal forces less powerful than they were in France.

Richelieu's creation of an absolute monarchy throughout France has to be seen against the broad sweep of western Europe's political development, as variously assisted and held back by the unclear demarcation between sacred and secular sovereignties in both Catholic and schismatic territories. His anti-Huguenot campaign was justified by Richelieu not primarily, or even at all, on religious grounds, but because it threatened France's political integration. The inalienable sovereignty of the people was a political doctrine elaborated in a Calvinist milieu and enunciated by Althusius in his 1603 *Politica methodice digesta*. As a principle it lingered on in Geneva until Rousseau and the *Contrat social*. It turned out to be a blue-print not for democracy but for totalitarianism, differing in its principles but not in its effects from the theory of the divine right of kings embraced by the Stuart kings and defended by both Bossuet and Hobbes.

The temptation is to sympathise with the opponents of Richelieu's domestic policies in a way which involves misunderstanding the nature of the historical process. It looked for a moment as if Europe could have been totally unified under Habsburg control, whatever economic forces were driving its development. The outrage of the *grands,* former territorial suzerains, still feudally minded and chivalric in inspiration, is intelligible, but the process by which western Europe amalgamated into larger territorial groupings appears in retrospect to have been ineluctable. That ineluctability is a fact which requires understanding, and still awaits explanation. To welcome or deplore it merely bars the way to discovering why it happened.

The French religious wars had quickly become dominated by political considerations, and in particular by the overriding question of whether the great feudal families, headed by the *grands,* should be allowed to keep their own territorial sovereignties and their right to participate in the king's counsels, if necessary under the umbrella of Spanish government, or whether their rights needed to be extinguished in the interests of a French cultural identity and jurisdictional unification. When Richelieu set his heart on the creation of a unified France, he was pursuing the goal that

Henri IV had fitfully embraced during his fight for the throne, and which was carried on by his widow, Marie de' Medici, during her regency in the years following his assassination. In pursuit of this goal, Richelieu was indeed never unfaithful to her.

The political Catholicism of the revival is less likely to engage modern sympathies, if only because it was based on radical misconceptions about the spectrum of relationships between sacred and secular sovereignties potentially viable in the Europe of 1600. Hostility to Richelieu's Protestant alliances anchored itself in the notion that papal spiritual sovereignty, deriving from God and exercised through the bishop of Rome, was superior to temporal sovereignty. The papacy was by now sure of its teaching authority among Catholics, but was still fighting for the supremacy of jurisdiction recently enough challenged by the conciliar movement, which drew on serious theological considerations to affirm the superiority of a general council over the pope in matters of teaching and jurisdiction.

The church's authority was often used as a cloak for worldly ambitions, as Richelieu points out in the *Testament politique*. It is here that the neglected but all-important difference between spirituality and theology needs to be remembered. The connection between credal statements of confessional belief and the spirituality of religious devotion can be tenuous, and the distinction between statements of belief and the implications of devotional practice is vital. Religious rites and devotional practices came to achieve a spiritually elevating and morally comforting effect related only obliquely to dogmatic affirmations.

For technical reasons, the theology of grace was still in the early seventeenth century completely intractable. It had become impossible within the parameters of the seventeenth-century concept of 'nature' to reconcile the gratuity of justifying grace with the autonomous power of spiritual self-determination in man, although it was heretical to deny either.[6] But not to allow the individual any power to determine the soul's ultimate fate, heaven or hell for endless time, was to remove the Christian religion's major hold over European culture. By the late middle ages superstition was already filling in the spiritual needs which the spiritualities based on orthodox theology were unable to satisfy. Traditional Christian spiritualities, rites and devotion were necessarily threatened by the view that the individual's eternal fate might arbitrarily be determined by a God who might have created souls whose damnation was predetermined. Such a god might have come from the Greek pantheon.[7]

Whatever the clashes or accords of dogmatic debate, what motivated religious behaviour in the early seventeenth century was a series of spiritualities claiming Christian parentage, whether or not schismatically at odds with a parent community of different credal affiliation, which implied that the conduct of life on earth could modify the soul's experience after death.[8] Both François de Sales and Fénelon underwent serious spiritual crises, involving in each case around six weeks of interior anguish, supposing that they might have been predestined to damnation. They both emerged to embrace the Jesuit doctrine of grace.

Jansenism was a spirituality, gestated by Bérulle's Oratorian reliance on the neoplatonist spirituality of Denis the Areopagite, before ever it became a theology. It was as a spirituality that it was embraced in the 1630s by Saint-Cyran, who was to find too little unctuousness in the 1640 *Augustinus*. The theology deprived the individual, even Christian, of any power of self-determination, but Saint-Cyran never quite drew for Christians the devotional consequences of that view. After Richelieu's death, there was a considerable debate about how Christian moral principles might be reconciled with Jansen's theology of grace. Pascal's *Pensées* show him grappling with the problem but failing to solve it. Richelieu's hostility to Jansenism was the product not only of an acute theological perception of the spiritual implications of Jansen's theology, but also of a serious Christian reaction to Saint-Cyran's incipient but infectious religious paranoia, according to which nature was sinful and all human beings born worthy of damnation. Richelieu sensed that this rejection of the values in which he had been educated was threatening to take hold in a society suddenly losing the immense confidence by which it had previously been buoyed up.

The priority which Richelieu gave to France's territorial integrity and cultural integration over the physical needs of its population is more difficult for us to understand. It must have contributed not only to the king's scruples and finally his doubts, but also to the clear and widespread diminution in cultural optimism discernible almost from the date of France's formal entry into the Thirty Years War, and certainly from 1640. From the liberal modern point of view, humanitarian considerations should have outweighed the political and cultural advantages in pursuing the war to what turned out to be the compromise to be reached at Westphalia in 1648. The cost in fiscal extortion and human suffering was simply too great for the advantages for which Richelieu demanded that France should pay, and in consequence he died probably the most hated of all France's great statesmen.

But it is inappropriate to judge Richelieu whether from a modern liberal or any other point of view. The historian's real tasks are simply to observe and understand. Richelieu's piety was as sincere as his values were baroque from the beginning of his career to the end. In 1630 the attempt to topple him was still only the culmination of France's interior power struggle, in which Richelieu urged the king to achieve heroic stature by exercising a personal sovereignty against those who thought they had some right, or who merely wished to share in its exercise. Circumstances gave Richelieu a narrow victory, to be consolidated notably with the executions of Marillac and Montmorency.

Richelieu could not foresee the size of harvests, and he did not willingly impose greater hardship than he felt the cause of France's grandeur warranted. But by 1635 his own baroque values were in danger of being swept away as the cultural optimism began to recede. It is quite usual for cultural movements, as reflected in the imaginative explorations of their values in writers and artists, to reach their apex after their foundations have already been undermined, and the social consensus on which the continuation of the war ultimately depended was rapidly eroding.

In 1635 the heroic merit of Rodrigue in Pierre Corneille's *Le Cid* of January 1637 was still to create its tidal wave of enthusiasm, and Descartes had yet to announce his discovery that the certainty of all non-empirical knowledge as well as virtue and happiness were within our power in the 1637 *Discours de la méthode*. But by 1635 the work linking Oratorian theology with Jansenism, Gibieuf's *De libertate dei et creaturae,* had already been written, and it was based on a concept of freedom which denied the individual any self-determining role in personal salvation. In the same year Saint-Cyran became director of Zamet's new Institut du Saint-Sacrement, and began by simply reversing Zamet's own eucharistic spirituality. He made the nuns abstain from receiving the sacrament for a month.

Richelieu was successful in creating a unified France with its own independent cultural identity, extending throughout its territory and separating it from any other, whatever may be felt about the horrific cost. He achieved his aim by sticking with apparently unwavering conviction to the principles towards which he had reasoned and prayed his way. He was an ascetic, unswerving in his dedication, a diplomat capable both of immense charm and of a high degree of calculated severity, and he was as meticulous in carrying out the tasks he set himself as he was fastidious in his personal habits. His energy, grasp of complex detail and assiduity were all prodigious. His ability to acquire the information he needed was at times sinister.

He was brave, not only in the field, but also in not infrequently confronting the probability that his life's work would be destroyed with the succession of Gaston d'Orléans to the throne, or that the enemies of his policies would persuade the king to remove him from office. He was clever, whether dealing with his own intricate financial enrichment or with finding means to pay and provision armies in the field. Finally, he was entirely loyal to the king, not as a human being whom at times he scarcely even liked, but as anointed by God to carry supreme authority in secular matters.

What we do not know is whether he knew his own tragedy, which was to have been guided throughout his life by a hierarchy of values which had become obsolete before he died. It may have been worse if, as seems in the end probable, he found himself condemned to carry on acting as if he did not have the doubts by which he was too intelligent, too sensitive and too religious not to have been assailed.

Notes

1 Churchman and Statesman: Aims and Ambitions

1 French society was officially regarded as comprising three 'orders' or 'estates', the clergy, the nobility, and the commoners, although the situation was, of course, very much more complex than this division suggests. From occasional provincial assemblies during the late middle ages, in which each of the three 'estates' was represented, emerged the 'Estates-General', in which each of the three orders from each province was represented at a national gathering. The Estates-General of 1614–15 was the last to be held before that of 1789, immediately preceding the revolution.

2 Clement V had settled at Avignon in March 1309 because it belonged to his vassals, the Angevin kings of Naples, and Clement VI had bought the town and the state outright in 1348. Richelieu was to be exiled there.

3 The tax on the sale or inheritance of offices known as the *paulette* was called after its inventor Charles Paulet, secretary of the *chambre des comptes*, whose daughter was a well-known red-headed court beauty. The *paulette* was intended by Sully (1560–1641), Henri IV's financial adviser, to break the power of the Guise faction, the king's ambitious rivals who bestowed on their supporters revenue-producing legal offices which could not automatically be passed to their heirs. The *paulette* was an annual tax of one sixtieth of the value of an office, but it gave its holder full rights of possession, so that it could normally be inherited or sold. Office-holders had mostly acquired a law degree, intended also to serve administrators. 'Arts' was the undergraduate course, which could be completed by the age of about sixteen. There were only four graduate degrees, law, canon law, theology and medicine, and

Paris did not teach civil law. There is an extensive literature on the legal
and administrative background of Richelieu's France, to parts of which
reference will later be made. See for the general background Roland E.
Mousnier, *The Institutions of France under the Absolute Monarchy 1598–1789*,
(Paris 1974) tr. Brian Pearce, Chicago and London 1979 and Richard
Bonney, *Political Change in France under Richelieu and Mazarin 1624–1661*,
Oxford 1978.

4 In spite of the large numbers of often excellent books and articles
devoted to aspects or periods of Richelieu's career, we are not well
served with reliable biographies. The standard six-volume biography
by Gabriel Hanotaux and the duc de la Force, *Histoire du Cardinal
de Richelieu*, Paris 1893–1947, can no longer be regarded as entirely
reliable. There are two modern full general biographies in English, D.P.
O'Connell's *Richelieu*, London 1968, and G.R.R. Treasure's *Cardinal
Richelieu and the Development of Absolutism*, London 1972, to which
must be added the more professionally researched works of Joseph
Bergin, especially *Cardinal Richelieu. Power and the Pursuit of Wealth*, New
Haven and London 1985 and *The Rise of Richelieu*, Manchester 1991. For
a general introduction in English to France's political situation during
Richelieu's lifetime, see the 1974 translation by D. McN. Lockie of the
second (1967) edition of Victor-L. Tapié's *France in the Age of Louis XIII
and Richelieu*, London 1974.

5 On the recent revival of interest in the *école française*, see Yves
Krumenacker, *L'Ecole française de spiritualité*, Paris 1998.

6 On the exploration of heroic values in early seventeenth-century France,
especially in such authors as François le Métel de Boisrobert, Jean-Pierre
Camus, Jean Desmarets de Saint-Sorlin, Marin le Roy de Gomberville,
La Calprenède and Honoré d'Urfé, see Gustave Reynier, *Le Roman
sentimental avant 'L'Astrée'*, Paris 1908; *Héroïsme et création littéraire sous
les règnes d'Henri IV et de Louis XIII*, ed. Noémi Hepp and Georges
Livet, Paris 1974; John Costa, *Le Conflit moral dans l'œuvre romanesque
de Jean-Pierre Camus (1584–1652)*, New York 1974; Mark Bannister,
Privileged Mortals, The French Heroic Novel 1630–1660, Oxford 1983;
Eric Caldicott, 'Richelieu and the Arts' in *Richelieu and his Age*, ed.
Joseph Bergin and Laurence Brockliss, Oxford 1992, pp. 203–235;
and the relevant essays in Anthony Levi, *Guide to French Literature,
Beginnings to 1789*, Detroit and London 1994. Among the major
visual artists exploring similarly heroic values or the innocence of that
which is natural and instinctive are the early Philippe de Champaigne,
Gaspar Dughet, Claude Gellée (Le Lorrain), Laurent de la Hyre,
Charles Lebrun, Nicolas Poussin and Simon Vouet, on whom see,
for instance, Anthony Blunt's volume in 'The Pelican History of Art',
Art and Architecture in France: 1500–1700, Harmondsworth 1953, and the
historical and critical essay by Pierre Rosenberg in his catalogue of the

1982 exhibition (Paris, New York, and Chicago), *La peinture française du XVIIe siècle dans les collections américaines*, Paris 1982. Discussions about freeing women from male tyranny and about the whole social role of women, which began to assume a quite new urgency very shortly after the turn of the century, played an important part in this cultural movement.

7 The painting is now in the Louvre.

8 François de Sales, his doctrine endorsed by the status of 'doctor of the church', elaborated advice to a penitent, Louise de Charmoisy, in the 1609 *Introduction à la vie dévote* in which he allowed the legitimacy of both make-up and dancing. He also included a chapter 'De l'honnêteté du lit nuptial' which was dropped by prudish editors from most of the nineteenth-century editions. The later *Traité de l'amour de Dieu*, which he wrote partly with Jeanne-Françoise de Chantal in mind, co-founder with him of the Visitation order, breaks radically with established theological usage in erecting a whole spirituality on the human heart's 'natural' inclination to love God, an achievement supported in his first four books with seventy quotations from Augustine himself. At this date those religious writers most anxious to emphasise the sinfulness of human nature, like the later Jansenists, normally appealed primarily to Augustine (see Anthony Levi, *French Moralists*, Oxford 1964, pp. 113–26).

9 The father of Louis XIII was Henri IV, whose uncle was the first prince of Condé and the founder of the junior branch of the Bourbon family, next in line to the throne if neither Louis XIII nor any of his siblings had male offspring. By 1626 there was no male heir in the direct line.

10 Richelieu was concerned to adjust the image of himself which he left to posterity, and meticulously destroyed huge quantities of private documents. The eight large quarto volumes of *Lettres, instructions diplomatiques et papiers d'Etat du cardinal de Richelieu* (Paris 1853–77, ed. D.L.M. Avenel), are only a selection from those generally concerned with official business, and often need de-coding. Some letters to the king reveal real emotional warmth, but other letters expressing emotion are simply conventional, or were intended to have a different effect from that suggested by their surface message. The *Mémoires* are reliable overall, but not in detail, and the *Testament politique*, being a private document for the posthumous attention of the king, is a reliable guide to the advice Richelieu wished to leave to Louis XIII, but to nothing else. How to discount the prejudices of the authors of memoirs, pamphlets, and chronicles varies from one document to another. The only documents we can really trust are formal and legal, but, like Richelieu's own final will, they, too, often conceal complexities of intention.

11 See Honor Levi, 'Richelieu collectionneur' in *Richelieu et la culture*, ed. Roland Mousnier, Paris 1987, pp. 175–184.

2 Family Background and Family Bishop

1 French peerages were conferred by erecting the peer's estate into a duchy which carried the title, constituting it a *duché-pairie*.

2 Richelieu's genealogy and the social status of his family are subjects about which the cardinal was notoriously sensitive. As early as 1631 André Duchesne, supervised by Richelieu himself, included an approved account of the cardinal's ascendancy in his *Histoire de la maison royale de Dreux et de quelques autres familles*. Modern accounts derive from L.A. Bossebœuf, *Histoire de Richelieu et des environs au point de vue civil, religieux et artistique*, Tours 1880. See also Auguste Bailly, *Richelieu*, Paris 1934, Jean-Claude Aubineau, *Richelieu 'Par ordre du Cardinal . . .'*, Paris 1980, and J. Bergin, *Cardinal Richelieu. Power and the Pursuit of Wealth*, New Haven/London 1985, and, with genealogical tables, *The Rise of Richelieu*, Manchester 1991. The fatal brawl is mentioned by Pierre de l'Estoile in his famous *Journal pour le règne de Henri III (1574–89)* (ed. L.-R. Lefèvre, Paris 1943, p. 105). L'Estoile describes Antoine as 'mal famé et renommé pour ses voleries, larcins et blasphèmes, étant resté grand ruffian et gruier de tous les bourdeaux . . .'

3 The 'wars of religion' lasted from 1562 to 1594. Although more or less continuous, with peaks and troughs, they are normally divided into eight distinct wars, of which the first was ended by the peace of Amboise in March 1563.

4 See Natalie Zemon Davis, *Fiction in the Archives*, Oxford 1988.

5 On the other hand Montglat, in his *Mémoires* (Amsterdam 1727, vol. i, p.22), recalls that François de la Porte, Suzanne's father, whose clients included the order of Malta, was also lawyer to Richelieu's father ('un gentilhomme de Poitou nommé Richelieu'), whose father 'avoit mangé tout son bien et avoit laissé sa maison fort incommodée. Et comme il étoit son voisin . . . il lui donna sa fille en mariage'. Montglat has mixed up the generations, as it was Richelieu's father, not his grandfather, who left the family relatively impoverished, but he presents the marriage as a *mésalliance* for the La Porte family, not the Rochechouarts. That view is probably wrong. In his edition of Tallemant's *Historiettes*, Antoine Adam quotes a number of mid-seventeenth century quips about the plebeian origins of Suzanne's family, including one from cardinal de Retz, a scurrillous verse, and a pamphlet referring to François de La Porte as a 'misérable notaire de village' (vol.1, Paris 1967, p. 1003).

6 See J. Bergin, *The Rise of Richelieu*, Manchester 1977, p. 21.

7 The *conseil d'état* (*privé* or *des parties*) was the royal supreme court of

appeal which under Louis XIV took over the appellate function of the *parlements*. In 1578 the term refers to the royal *grand conseil* or council of state, comprising the half dozen or so members of the king's advisory body containing *ex officio* princes of blood and the queen, together with those who acted as ministers by royal appointment. The king in his council was the supreme governing body in France. The *grand prévôt de France* was a judge with jurisdiction over all cases arising within the royal household and, in the case of François de Richelieu, also within the court and its followers.

8   Antoine Aubery, *Histoire du cardinal-duc de Richelieu*, Paris 1660.

9   The sources for the sixteenth-century history of the du Plessis family include Hanotaux and la Force, *Histoire du Cardinal de Richelieu* and Maximin Deloche, *Les Richelieu. Le Père du Cardinal*, Paris 1923. Professor Bergin's researches have led him to modify his view about Richelieu's family history, and I have here followed his later view, presented in *The Rise of Richelieu*, Manchester 1991 (second edition 1997).

10 See David Potter and P.R. Roberts, 'An Englishman's view of the court of Henri III, 1584–1585: Richard Cooke's "Description of the Court of France"', in *French History*, ii, 1988 (pp. 343–4).

11 On the catastrophic state of the royal finances in the last years of Henri III and the early years of Henri IV, see Richard Bonney, *The King's Debts*, Oxford 1981, pp. 25–53.

12 On the loans of the *grand prévôt*, see Mlle H. Michaud, 'L'Ordonnance-ment des dépenses et le budget de la monarchie, 1587–89' in *Annuaire-Bulletin de la Société de l'Histoire de France*, (1970–71), Paris 1972, pp. 87–150. On the issue of corruption, the general standards of the period must be kept in mind. When in 1632 Louis de Marillac, a marshal of France, was condemned and executed for the embezzlement of funds allocated for building at Verdun much earlier in his life, all French officialdom knew that the charge was a transparent pretext which allowed the king to remove someone who might make dangerous use of the French troops under his command and by which he could make an example of someone whose loyalty to him had become suspect. Even the special court could only muster a majority of thirteen judges for to ten against for execution.

13 The three brothers were Henri, the third duke, who instigated the mur-der of the Huguenot leader Coligny on the feast of Saint Bartholomew 1572, Louis de Lorraine, the second cardinal de Guise, and the duc de Mayenne, duke and peer from 1573, who had served Henri III before leading the resistance to Henri de Navarre.

14 Henri de Navarre became heir presumptive on 10 June 1584, on the death of François d'Anjou, fourth son of Catherine de' Medici and brother of François II, Charles IX and Henri III. François had been elevated from the duchy of Alençon to that of Anjou when he had

himself become heir presumptive on the death of Charles IX in 1574 and his brother Henri, duc d'Anjou and king of Poland, had become king of France. Navarre and Condé had been declared incapable of succeeding to the French throne by the pope, Sixtus V, who in 1585 released all their vassals from allegiance to them. Although many historians still write as if Navarre's claim to succeed to the French throne by right of birth in 1589 was a matter of constitutional propriety, it was at best only marginally better than that of the Spanish infanta, granddaughter of Henri II and niece of Henri III, and not better at all without the *ad hoc* application of an extended version of the medieval Frankish codes known as Salic law, which from the fifteenth century were revived in France to exclude the inheritance of land (but not thrones) through the female line, and were not applied in either Spain or Navarre.

15 On Isabelle, see Maximin Deloche and Pidoux de la Maduère, 'Une sœur ignorée de Richelieu', *Revue des Deux Mondes*, 8th series, 36, Paris 1936, pp. 162–179. Joseph Bergin tentatively accepted the existence of this third daughter in *Cardinal Richelieu. Power and the pursuit of wealth*, New Haven and London 1985. However, in *The Rise of Richelieu*, Manchester 1997, Professor Bergin prefers to leave open the question of Isabelle's existence.

16 Tallemant des Réaux, the historian, moralist and gossip-monger, the full text of whose *Historiettes* was published for the first time only in 1961, was studiously well informed, if also libellously amusing. He is particularly scurrilous about Gabriel Beauvau, whom Richelieu appointed his *maistre de chambre* and had made bishop of Nantes in 1636, 'C'est un terrible evesque que ce sire là. Quoy que grand jureur, grand desbauché, grand batteur et plus meschant voisin du monde, le cardinal de Richelieu l'a faiut evesque, parce qu'il est son parent . . .'

17 Few accounts of the Catholic religious revival are reliable, and the best are still in Henri Bremond, *Histoire littéraire du sentiment religieux en France depuis la fin des guerres de religion jusqu'à nos jours*, 12 vols., Paris 1921–36, and Jean Dagens, *Bérulle et les origines de la restauration catholique 1575–1611*, Paris 1952. It is necessary to distinguish between those central figures of the revival who were mystics in the strict sense, those who were founders of the new religious congregations or reformers of established monasteries, those motivated by missionary goals, those who devoted themselves primarily to education or to the care of the sick or the poor, and those who allied a credal Catholicism inherited from the League with a strongly pro-Spanish political orientation. The groups are by no means mutually exclusive but their very different spiritualities diverged, often to become incompatible with one another. Bérulle has often been regarded as the most important figure of the revival, although his legacy is at best controversial. He established

the Oratorian congregation, brought the discalced Carmelites into France, and based his christocentric spirituality on the renunciation of natural human powers, as Christ's incarnation had renounced the use of divine privileges. Bérulle's insistence on the 'annihilation' of all in the individual which derives from natural instinct and his promotion of adherence to the divine by means of the eucharist sharply distinguish his spirituality from that of other wings of the revival represented on the one hand by François de Sales, Jeanne-Françoise de Chantal, the Visitation order which they founded together, and by Richelieu, and on the other by the spirituality of 'Jansenism' developed from Bérulle's own doctrine. His true spiritual legacy is the spirituality of what has become known as the *école française*.

18 See Joseph Bergin, *Cardinal Richelieu. Power and the pursuit of wealth*, New Haven and London 1985, p. 33.

19 Amador de la Porte was the son of Suzanne de la Porte's father's second wife. See Gabriel Hanotaux and La Force, *Histoire du Cardinal de Richelieu*, 6 vols., Paris 1893–1947, vol. i, p. 68.

20 On the maréchal de la Meilleraye, see Tallemant's unusually hostile portrait (*Historiettes*, vol.1, Paris 1967, pp. 324–33) and Antoine Adam's notes. Tallemant implausibly recounts the gossip that Richelieu was emotionally obsessed by La Meilleraye's second wife, Marie Cossé de Brissac. It was one of the many pieces of tittle-tattle about Richelieu which flourished in Paris. Richelieu's opponent, cardinal de Retz, lover of Mme de la Meilleraye, also has it in his '*Mémoires*'.

21 An *écuyer* was a noble, often for a time placed as a member of some grander or older noble's household, although any noble could assume the title, unlike the restricted *chevalier*.

22 See Joseph Bergin, *Cardinal Richelieu. Power and the pursuit of wealth*, New Haven and London 1985, p. 30, quoting from the *Minutier central des notaires de Paris* (viii, 423 of 1 October 1601) and Auguste Bailly, *Richelieu*, Paris 1934, p. 14.

23 See Aimé Martineau, *Le Cardinal de Richelieu*, Paris 1866, pp. 381–85. Silence is not evidence, but it is possible that Suzanne de la Porte's children were never closely linked to her emotionally. Auguste Bailly (*Richelieu*, Paris 1934, p. 108) draws attention to the fact that Richelieu did not attend his mother's funeral.

24 As early as 1598, he acquired one of the mortgages on the seized property of La Vervolière, and in 1606 he completed the purchase, paying only 1,780 livres in cash. The rest, 15,340 livres, was waived by the *grand conseil* on the grounds that it was the unpaid dowry of his grandmother, Françoise de Rochechouart, whose principal heir he remained. By 1605 he had became one of the two directors of the syndicate of his father's creditors, a position which means that his position as creditor had become regarded as preferential, and from

1602 Henri was invariably the highest bidder at the auctions at which what had been the family lands, or rights to income from them, had come up for sale. When once he was beaten into second place, he successfully invoked his family right of *retrait lignager*. On Henri's financial activities, which occasion his whole character to be viewed in a quite new light, as the saviour of his family's finances rather than a selfish spendthrift, see the impressive documentation given by Joseph Bergin, *Cardinal Richelieu. Power and the pursuit of wealth*, New Haven and London 1985, pp. 25–32.

25 See Louis Battifol, *Richelieu et les femmes*, Paris 1931.

26 See Hugh Trevor-Roper, 'The Sieur de la Rivière' in *Renaissance Essays*, London 1985 and J.H. Elliott, 'Richelieu l'homme' in *Richelieu et la culture*, ed. R. Mousnier, Paris 1987.

27 There were four Bouthillier brothers, sons of a lawyer, Claude, who had worked for the Richelieu family. The eldest of the four sons, also called Claude and born in 1581, was successively a councillor of the Paris *parlement*, secretary of Marie de' Medici on Richelieu's recommendation, and from 1628 a secretary of state, before becoming in 1632 joint *surintendant des finances* with Bullion. On his appointment to the royal council, see Orest Ranum, *Richelieu and the Councillors of Louis XIII*, Oxford 1963, p.34. One brother, Sébastien was canon, then dean of the Luçon chapter. Richelieu procured for him the see of Aire. A third brother, Victor, was successively bishop of Boulogne and archbishop of Tours, first chaplain to the king's brother, Gaston d'Orléans. Denis, also under Richelieu's patronage, became another *secrétaire des commandements* of Marie de' Medici and then a councillor of state. The son of the eldest brother, Claude, was Léon le Bouthillier, known as the comte de Chavigny, a minister and, like his father, secretary of state for foreign affairs. Born in 1608, he was implausibly rumoured to be Richelieu's son. Later on, Richelieu worked closely with him, using him to screen visitors and virtually to act as his agent at court, one of his functions being to report back daily to Richelieu what was the king's disposition towards him. He called his son Armand after the cardinal, but was disgraced after Richelieu's death for choosing the party of Gaston d'Orléans rather than that of Mazarin. He was brilliant, jealous and arrogant.

28 On Le Masle, see Maximin Deloche, *La Maison de Richelieu*, Paris 1912, especially pp. 103–114. Richelieu's loyalty to his household, and theirs to him, are worthy of remark in view of much that has been said about the cardinal's imperiousness, and the impossibility of working for him.

29 We shall meet this situation again. Episcopacy is the highest of the three grades of the sacrament of order inseparable, for instance, from the power of validly ordaining priests. Whether episcopacy also confers

ecclesiastical jurisdiction automatically and, if it does, how much, was (and is) disputed. Episcopal jurisdiction was normally thought of as delegated papal jurisdiction, conferred by papal bulls which specified them, and without which a bishop's diocesan powers were not enabled. Bishops in any country, like France, which had a concordat or similar financial arrangement with the pope, also needed a royal mandate to enjoy the temporalities of their benefice.

30 Henri Carré recounts Richelieu's decision to accept the Luçon see, 'J'accepterai tout pour le bien de l'Eglise et la gloire de notre nom' (*La Jeunesse et la marche au pouvoir de Richelieu, 1585–1624*, Paris 1944, p. 19).

31 The Latin biographer of Armand-Jean's brother Alphonse (1653) and of Armand-Jean himself (1656), historiographer, and author of a partly satirical novel *La Prétieuse*.

32 Du Val is of serious interest as a theologian. It was he who identified the 'apex mentis' with the heart, creating the religious vocabulary which Pascal was later to adopt by way of Saint-Cyran's devotional *Le cœur nouveau*. For François de Sales and Bérulle the 'apex mentis', the 'scintilla synteresis' of the Rhineland mystics, had been the 'fine pointe' of the soul in which the highest mystical experiences took place. In du Val's new anthropology the heart had become the seat of both knowledge and love. On Du Val, see especially Jean Dagens, *Bérulle et les origines de la restauration catholique 1575–1611*, Paris 1952, and the fourth volume of P. Féret, *La Faculté de théologie de Paris et ses docteurs les plus célèbres*, 7 vols., Paris 1900–1907.

33 Montaigne scoffs at Ficino's doctrine of love in *Les Essais* III, v, 'Sur des vers de Virgile'. The clearest intellectual associations between stocism and scepticism were forged a little later than Montaigne in Charron's (1601) *De la sagesse*, and, with greater rigour, in a series of works by Justus Lipsius and Guillaume du Vair, a certain source for the methodic doubt which is the point of departure for the philosophy of Descartes. See A.H.T. Levi, *The Theory of the Passions: 1585–1649*, Oxford 1964. When the religious wars ended, the rehabilitation of optimistic neoplatonism was very swift. Of the three volumes of Honoré d'Urfé's *Epîtres morales*, the first, written in prison in 1595, is conventionally neostoic; the second, largely written by 1597, discreetly shows the influence of Ficino; the third, first published in 1608, is openly neoplatonist. The link established by d'Urfé between instinctive emotion and the merit of its object relies on Ficino, quoted verbatim in d'Urfé's magnificent pastoral novel, *L'Astrée*, where the definition of love is also taken verbatim from Ficino.

34 But see the third volume of Bremond's *Histoire littéraire du sentiment religieux*, Paris 1921–36; E. Gilson, *La Doctrine cartésienne de la liberté et la Théologie*, Paris 1913; L. Cognet, *Les Origines de la spiritualité française au*

XVIIe siècle, Paris 1949; Jean Orcibal, 'Néo-platonisme et Jansénisme du *De libertate* du P. Gibieuf à l'*Augustinus*' in *Nuove Ricerche storiche sul Giansenismo*, Rome 1954, pp. 333–57, and R. Bellemare, *Le Sens de la créature dans la doctrine de Bérulle*, n.p. 1959.

35 At this date 'Richelieu' still refers to Henri.

36 Du Plessis was allowed to keep his priories. Henri IV's letters had been quite insistent, 'I write in such a way that this request should not be refused.' There is documentary evidence in the letters of the French ambassador, d'Halincourt, to Henri IV's secretary of state, Villeroy, about the high opinions du Plessis gained in Rome. He did have charm, but he was also very anxious to please.

37 See, for instance, Auguste Bailly, *Richelieu*, Paris 1934, quoting the pope, 'It is only right that someone above his age in wisdom should be ordained below it' (p.29). Everyone, from Tallemant on, quotes the pope's quip about Armand-Jean's deceit that, 'if this young man lived long enough, he would become a great cheat ("furbo")'. Paul V confided his doubts about Henri IV to du Plessis, who firmly defended the king, already true to his later principle 'n'être éloigné ni de Dieu ni du roi'. Aubery (*L'Histoire du Cardinal duc de Richelieu*, Paris 1660, p. 8) tells us that the decisive factor was the excellence of du Plessis's Latin presentation of his case, but he clearly got on well with Paul V.

3 The Rise and Fall of the Young Bishop

1 Richelieu's position, in some ways linked to that of the *politiques* during the religious wars, known by Richelieu's time as *bons catholiques*, is often contrasted with that of the *dévots*, linked to the old Catholic league and transformed into a pro-Spanish political party associated with Bérulle, the Marillac half-brothers, Michel and Louis, and, later, Marie de' Medici. The Catholic revival in early seventeenth-century France, however linked with political Catholicism, was never exhausted by it, and it encompassed both strong gallicanism, minimalising papal juridical interference with the French church, and papalist anti-gallicanism, the 'ultramontane' tendency. It is, however, seriously misleading to suppose that gallicanism, like other forms of anti-papal sentiment, was incompatible with being authentically *dévot*.

2 La Rocheposay, who was also to make Duvergier his vicar-general, illustrates the general situation. While it was no doubt idiosyncratic and controversial, it was not yet regarded as intolerable even for prelates with active pastoral responsibilities to take up arms. The pamphlet shows that Duvergier, not yet devoured by the consciousness of guilt which he would form into Jansenist spirituality, started off with much more relaxed moral views than those for which he later became famous. There

is a two-volume biography by Jean Orcibal, *Jean Duvergier de Hauranne, abbé de Saint-Cyran, et son temps*, Louvain and Paris 1947–48 (vols. 2 and 3 of *Les Origines du jansénisme*). For an assessment of Saint-Cyran's career and the development of his doctrine, see Anthony Levi, *Guide to French Literature*, Detroit 1994, vol. 1, pp. 769–779.

3 Now the Palais-Royal. On Richelieu's liking for privacy, perspectives and long formal avenues which he could walk up and down with companions facing him and at his side, see especially Claude Mignot, 'Richelieu et l'architecture' (pp. 54–60) and Françoise Bercé, 'Le Palais-Cardinal' (pp. 61–66) in *Richelieu et le monde de l'esprit*, Paris 1985.

4 In the contract of June 1609 the bishop agreed to pay a third of what was needed to repair the cathedral buildings, without further responsibility for maintenance.

5 Clement VIII had also granted an annulment of Henri's marriage with Marguerite de Valois on account of her inability to conceive, although the technical grounds were undispensed consanguinity and coercion by Marguerite's mother, Catherine de' Medici, and brother, Charles IX. The powerlessness of Julius II to grant a dispensation from consanguinity to the future Henry VIII because it was an impediment by divine law had been at the centre of the legal argument in favour of the annulment of Henry VIII's marriage to Catherine of Aragon, his brother's widow. At that time the papacy had taken a different view of the law.

6 Condé had married Charlotte de Montmorency, daughter of the *connétable*, France's chief military officer, at Chantilly on 17 May 1609, but immediately removed her from Paris to escape the predatory attentions of Henri IV, who had conceived a passion for her. By March 1610 the poet Malherbe was writing love verses to her on the king's behalf.

7 This is disputed. Elizabeth Marvick (*The Young Richelieu. A Psychoanalytical Study in Leadership*, Chicago 1983, and *Louis XIII. The Making of a King*, New Haven and London 1986) has from a generally Freudian point of view explained the adult behaviour of both Louis XIII and Richelieu in terms of excessively compensatory psychological mechanisms, whereas Louis Battifol in his numerous books and articles has supposed the childhood of Louis XIII to have been reasonably happy. A. Lloyd Moote (*Louis XIII, the Just*, Los Angeles and London 1989) has attempted to find truth in both interpretations of Louis's psychology in what he proclaims to be an attempt to rehabilitate Louis XIII. For a brief historiography of Louis XIII, see Georges Mongrédien, *La Journée des dupes*, Paris 1961.

8 On the continuities and discontinuities in policy and administration immediately after the assassination of Henri IV, see Richard Bonney, *The King's Debts*, Oxford 1981, pp. 73 ff. Sully, detested by the great nobles, was adamantly opposed to the regent's profligacy with the public purse, especially to her attempts to buy off the princes. He paid

Henri IV's gambling debts, financially looked after his mistresses, and cherished a grand plan against the Habsburgs, but after eight months finally resigned on 26 January 1611. Du Plessis's relations with him were never to be cordial, although Henri knew him well.

9 Richard Bonney, *The King's Debts*, quotes an expenditure on the magnates of at least ten million livres between 1610 and 1614. Condé received 3.4 million, Mayenne 1.7, Conti 1.3, Nevers 1.2, with further significant sums to Soissons, Longueville, Guise, Vendôme, Epernon and Bouillon.

10 Léonora Galigaï was given powers over royal patronage and had to approve all gifts and pensions. She awarded herself 60,000 livres and, from 1613, an annual 30,000 livres. She was accused, no doubt rightly, of arranging to receive very much more. For the evidence, see Richard Bonney, *The King's Debts*, pp. 80–81.

11 See Joseph Bergin, *The Rise of Richelieu*, Manchester 1997, from whose account of du Plessis's activity many details in this and the immediately following paragraphs have been taken. They correct or supplement more general treatments such as those of Bailly's *Richelieu*, Paris 1934, and Victor-L. Tapié, *France in the Age of Louis XIII and Richelieu*, tr. D. McN. Lockie, London 1974.

12 The council of Trent (1545–63) was the long-awaited council called to review the church's disciplinary arrangements, but best remembered for its succinct and reactionary dogmatic definitions, chiefly aimed against the reformed communities which had broken with Rome. The ordinary adjective used of the council and its decrees is 'Tridentine'.

13 Hanotaux dates from 1609 a memoir discovered by Armand Baschet and published in 1880, *Instructions et maximes que je me suis données pour me conduire à la Cour*, which suggests that du Plessis was certainly by the date of its composition looking on Luçon as a stepping stone. The memoir, accepted by Hanotaux as authentic but subsequently thought not to be by Richelieu, gives interesting advice for getting on with Henri IV, who liked to be answered back, but only with respect. He needed to be watched carefully when he was drinking. This memoir is the document in which occurs the explicit admonition to burn dangerous letters, and to keep quiet, which was certainly to be Richelieu's practice. See Auguste Bailly, *Richelieu*, Paris 1934, pp.51ff.

14 The exemption from episcopal jurisdiction was confined to the religious 'orders', of which technically the last to be founded was the Society of Jesus, the 'Jesuits', in 1540. Later groups were known as congregations, and their houses were not exempt from episcopal jurisdiction and supervision. The Visitation, originally conceived as a half-way house between Carmel and lay devotion, was instituted, wrote François de Sales, 'so that no great harshness should prevent the weak and the sick from entering it to cultivate there the perfection of the love of

God'. Intended to pursue charitable work among the poor and the sick, it was soon forced to abandon the statutes written by François de Sales, who died in 1622, and to become contemplative, with cloister and enclosure.

15 See Joseph Bergin, *The Rise of Richelieu*, Manchester 1997, pp. 86–88. Père Joseph's great ambition was to mount a new crusade to wrest the holy places from the Turks. He was a considerable administrator and ecclesiastical politician. Tallement has a *Historiette* (ed. Adam, vol. 1, p. 295–96) on him. Son of the ambassador to Venice and a graduate of Pluvinel's academy, he joined the Capuchins in 1599 and had already attracted attention at court when du Plessis met him. See G. Fagniez, *Le Père Joseph et Richelieu*, 2 vols., Paris 1894, and L. Dedouvres, *Politique et apôtre – le Père Joseph de Paris*, Paris 1932.

16 This view is based on the Jesuit theory of grace, known (not entirely accurately) as 'Molinism'. God foresees what you would do, if your nature had the unfettered power to accept or reject grace, and gives you or witholds from you a determining grace according to this *scientia media*. Molina's theory avoids Pelagianism, although that of his disciple, Lessius, did not. Jansen's theory emphasises that God creates you in the state of original sin which condemns you to eternal damnation, although through his mercy God saves a few from the 'massa damnata'. Individuals can do nothing to obtain or to reject God's justifying grace. Much in Jansen derives from Oratorian theology. François de Sales was prominent among the upholders of the Jesuit view of grace, which he adopted after undergoing a terrifying six-week personal crisis during which he was convinced that he was predestined to be eternally damned. Fénelon was to undergo an exactly similar crisis, similarly concluding to a belief in the autonomous human power of spiritual self-determination to good, leading to eternal heaven, or to evil, leading to eternal hell.

17 The famous society of prominent laymen founded in 1627 and dedicated to the public furtherance of the Catholic cause and the imposition by civil law of Catholic moral norms, as well as to works of charity, the *Compagnie du Saint-Sacrement*, was also dedicated to the Blessed Sacrament. See Raoul Allier, *La Cabale des dévots 1627–1666*, Paris 1902, and the series of articles in the *Revue des deux mondes* in 1903.

18 Zamet (1588–1655), bishop of Langres, had wished to become an Oratorian and remained a friend of the Oratory. He made himself effectively the superior of Port-Royal until that position was usurped by Saint-Cyran.

19 The name changes are sufficiently confusing to warrant a reminder that Gaston was known as Anjou until 1626, when he was elevated to the duchy of Orléans. As the king's younger brother, he was also known as 'Monsieur'. The Condé here referred to is Henri II de Bourbon-Condé

(1588–1646), son of Henri IV's eldest first cousin and known as 'Monsieur le Prince'. He married the sister of the Montmorency to be executed for treason after the battle of Castelnaudary in 1632, and was father of 'le grand Condé', himself known until he succeeded to the Condé title in 1646 as the duc d'Enghien. The Soissons mentioned here is count Charles (1566–1612), whose son Louis, comte de Soissons, lived from 1604 to 1641.

20 In addition to the Estates General, there were regional estates in Auvergne, Brittany, Burgundy, Languedoc, Normandy and Provence, which were known as the *pays d'états* and had more autonomous administrations than the others (known as *pays d'élus*). Most of them also had their own *parlements*, of which a number had been established and dissolved in the sixteenth century.

21 Although the ordinary age of majority by Parisian custom was 25, feudal law considered males adult at 20 and females at 15. By the 1374 law of Charles V, kings of France 'commonly enriched while still young with many virtues and fine qualities which are not to be found in others of baser condition', came of age on their thirteenth birthday. See Roland E. Mousnier, *The Institutions of France under the Absolute Monarchy 1598–1789*, tr. Brian Pearce, Chicago and London 1979, pp. 651–52.

22 The most prominent preacher to the estates was Jean-Pierre Camus, bishop of Belley, author of some two hundred volumes and equally weak as a devotional writer, a novelist, a controversialist and an interpreter of François de Sales, whose *Esprit* he published in six volumes (1639–41). According to Nicéron, *Mémoires pour servir à l'histoire des hommes illustres dans la république des lettres*, 43 vols., Paris 1727–45, Richelieu later reproached Camus with his detestation of monks, without which Richelieu would canonise him. Nicéron records Camus's reply, 'Would to God . . . that that could happen, we would both have what we wanted; you would be the pope and I would be a saint' (vol. 36, Paris 1736, p.93). Jean Descrains has published Camus's sermons to the estates, *Homélies des Etats Généraux (1614–1615)* (Geneva 1970). See also Peter Bayley, *French Pulpit Oratory (1598–1650)*, Cambridge 1980. In Paris, du Plessis stayed in the new and highly fashionable Place Royale (now Place des Vosges). This is where at Easter 1612 some 50,000 people watched the spectacular three-day celebrations to celebrate the marriages arranged between the French and Spanish royal houses.

23 For the text of the speech, see Richelieu, *Mémoires*, 10 vols., Paris 1907–31, vol. 1, pp. 340–65. The *Mémoires*, partly dictated or revised by Richelieu, were compiled from his papers after his death. On Du Plessis's speech, see Pierre Blet, *Le Clergé de France et la monarchie*, 2 vols., Rome 1959. The 'petitions' put forward to the administration the reforms desired by the representatives of the three constituencies.

24 The third estate had made the radically gallican proposal that 'no power on earth, whatever it be, can deprive the the king's sacred person of his realm'. The clergy was not prepared to go so far in denying the subordination of temporal to spiritual authority. See Pierre Blet, 'L'Article du Tiers aux Etats Généraux de 1614' in *Revue d'histoire moderne et contemporaine*, 1955, pp. 81–606.

25 On the situation in France immediately after the end of the estates, see J.M. Hayden, *France and the Estates General of 1614*, Cambridge 1974.

26 See Joseph Bergin, *Cardinal Richelieu. Power and the Pursuit of Wealth*, New Haven and London 1985, p. 72.

27 See Richard Bonney, *The King's Debts*, Oxford 1981, p. 89. At the time it was thought, perhaps correctly, that it was Sully's advice on a visit to court that persuaded Marie de' Medici to imprison Condé. For a different, but neglected tradition of the circumstances surrounding the arrest, see A. Arnould and Alboize de Pujol, *Histoire de la Bastille*, 7 vols., Paris 1844, vol. 4. The Paris mob sacked Concini's residence in the Faubourg Saint-Germain, doing damage for which he received in August 1617 a compensatory payment of 450,000 livres.

28 The second volume of Richelieu's *Mémoires*, Paris 1907–31, contains an account of his role as intermediary with Condé. In his appointment to the Concini administration, his speech to the estates counted for very little, if anything at all. In October 1616 a second diplomatic negotiation with Nevers was a failure.

29 See for the figures E. Griselle, ed. *Etat de la maison du roi Louis XIII, de celle de sa mère, Maries de Medicis; de ses sœurs etc.*, Paris 1912, p. 60; Gabriel Hanotaux and the duc le la Force, *Histoire du cardinal Richelieu*, 6 vols., Paris 1893–1947, vol. ii, pp. 121 and 133; and Joseph Bergin, *Cardinal Richelieu. Power and the pursuit of wealth*, New Haven and London 1985, pp. 72 and 73.

30 Louis Battifol, 'Le Coup d'état du 24 avril 1617' in *Revue historique* 95 (1907), pp. 292–308, and 97, (1908), pp. 27–77 and 264–86, quotes this information (pp. 43–44) from the contemporary *Relation exacte de tout ce qui s'est passé à la mort du maréchal d'Ancre*, first published in 1659 and probably written by Luynes's brother.

31 The marquis de Vitry, Nicolas de l'Hospital, was clearly impetuous. His elevation continued until, as governor of Provence, he lost his temper and struck the archbishop of Bordeaux, for which Richelieu had him sent to the Bastille in 1637. He was released only after the cardinal's death, when Louis XIII elevated his lands to a duchy, carrying a peerage. The *Relation exacte* (see previous note) names those who fired at Concini, or into his corpse, as Vitry's brother, Du Hallier, and four other named officers.

32 *Lèse-majesté*, deriving from the 'majestas (laesa)' of Roman law, originally the 'majestas laesa populi Romani' before it became the 'majestas

imperatoris', was used for any crime against the state or its ruler, and was subject to the worst punishment known to Roman law in the infamous *Lex quisquis*. The punishment included death, posthumous disgrace, expropriation, disinheritance and disabilities inflicted on heirs. It was used in the ancient world to punish counterfeiters, exploiting the emperor's image on coins, and in the high middle ages to justify the death penalty for heresy.

33 On the trial, see Georges Mongrédien, *Léonora Galigaï. Un procès de sorcellerie sous Louis XIII*, Paris 1968. It was Léonora Galigaï's wealth, coveted by Luynes, which cost her her life. Richelieu's *Mémoires* recount that the death sentence was obtained on absurdly flimsy evidence only on Luynes's assurance to the advocate general that the king would commute any death sentence. Without her execution, her son might eventually have inherited her wealth.

34 See Fernand Hayem, *Le maréchal d'Ancre et Léonora Galigaï*, Paris 1910.

35 The *Mémoires* give a very different account of the exchange with the king standing on the billiard table, not mentioning any dismissal, but substituting protests of affection. The style of the *Mémoires* account betrays cosmeticisation, but may well be nearer the truth than the more dramatic traditional account. See A. Bailly, *Richelieu*, Paris 1934, pp.126–27.

36 For a Catholic to dedicate to the king a refutation of a Huguenot work also dedicated to the king was not a new device. Duplessis-Mornay's *Traité de l'Eglise* of 1578 was dedicated to Henri de Navarre, but its refutation by Pierre Charron, best known as a disciple of Montaigne, in his *Trois Vérités*, was also dedicated to Navarre in 1593, on the eve of his confirmation as Henri IV.

37 Especially at this point in his career, Du Plessis's attitudes have wrongly seemed to justify Bremond's definitive judgement (*Histoire littéraire du sentiment religieux en France*, vol. 2, Paris 1923, p. 168), 'Il a peur de l'enfer, il aime la théologie; il ne se désintéresse pas tout à fait des choses de Dieu, mais enfin son royaume est de ce monde'. For Bremond, Richelieu fell short as a mystical theologian, because he was not interested in promoting or classifying ecstatic states of soul.

4 Rehabilitation and Red Hat

1 On these negotiations, see the *Négociation commencée au mois de mars de l'année 1619 avec la reine mère Marie de' Medicis par M le comte de Béthune et continuée conjointement avec M. le cardinal de La Rochefoucauld*, Paris 1673, and Pontchartrain's *Mémoires*, ed. C.B. Petitot, Paris 1822. Accounts of

these incidents are to be found in the *Histoire de la vie du duc d'Epernon* (Paris 1655) by Guillaume Girard, who entered Epernon's service in 1619, and was an eye-witness to some of them.

2 See the account in Girard (note 1), who witnessed the incident. The swords were of different types, with different lengths. Lauzières was wounded but managed to get his shorter blade under Henri's guard to inflict the lethal wound.

3 The term 'political Catholic' is used to replace the usual *dévot*, which has been so much abused as to have lost any useful function. *Dévot* has been used as if it had a purely religious significance, covering a very wide diversity of incompatible spiritualities, but has also been used, often pejoratively, to denote adherence to a form of political Catholicism, generally, but not always, papalist ('ultramontane') as opposed to 'gallican', a term of which the meaning changed according to the degree in which it denoted the upholding of the autonomy of the French church in matters of financial consequence. Richelieu was a *dévot* in the purely religious sense, but politically he was certainly not a member of either *dévot* or gallican groups. Bérulle increasingly extended his religious views to embrace political positions, and ended up firmly in the pro-Spanish political camp. On his contribution to the development of the spirituality of the *école française*, normally associated with Jean-Jacques Olier, see Yves Krumenacker, *La Spiritualité de l'école française*, Paris 1998, which not uncontroversially seeks to modify the conclusions of earlier analyses.

4 See E. Griselle, 'Louis XIII et sa mère' in *Revue historique*, 105 (1910), pp. 302–31 and 106 (1911), pp. 82–100 and 295–308.

5 On Luynes's public position in detail in 1619–20, see Joseph Bergin, *The Rise of Richelieu*, Manchester 1997, pp. 198–213.

6 For a summary, see Richelieu's *Mémoires*, Paris 1907–31, vol. 3, p. 39–44.

7 The council of Trent had laid down that the college of cardinals should contain national representatives. The most senior curial officials, together with ex-nuncios supported by the sovereigns to whom they had been attributed, were also customarily elevated to the purple. On the creations of cardinals, generally in groups, see Ludwig Freiherr von Pastor, *The History of the Popes from the Close of the Middle Ages*, tr. Dom Ernst Graf, 40 vols., London 1891–1953. For the reigns of Gregory XV (1621–23) and Urban VIII (1623–44), see vol. 29, London 1938. Urban VIII, a Barberini, made cardinals of his nephew and brother, but papal nepotism had not yet ceased to be the norm in a Europe in which the city-states were founded on dynastic principles. Some Renaissance popes genuinely believed that the church needed a territorial basis with military and diplomatic strength, magnificent buildings and exquisite artefacts to fulfil its spiritual mission. Several attempted to establish

what amounted to a papal dynasty, analogous to those ruling in Rome, Milan, Naples and even Florence, but with the succession going to nephews.

8 See G.R.R. Treasure, *Cardinal Richelieu and the Development of Absolutism*, London 1972, p. 28, for the figures, which must have been counted out from the daily diary entries of Louis's doctor, Jean Hédouard.

9 *Testament politique*, I, vi (ed. Louis André, Paris 1947, p. 266). This work, addressed to the king, 'V[otre] M[ajesté]', refers to him in the third person, 'His mind so absolutely dominates his body that the least emotion captures his heart and disturbs his physical equilibrium . . . I have never seen him ill for any other reason'. A little later Richelieu aptly sums up the king's character as 'of a delicate disposition, weak health, and a nervous and impatient temperament' (p. 269). Religious 'scruples' in the formal sense, have little to do with the sense of guilt with which most of the human race has to some degree to live. They are symptoms of a seriously incapacitating psychological aberration which are not only painful to endure, but which can preclude the mature adult's capacity for moral choice.

10 Tallemant's editor, Antoine Adam, is certainly right in tracing Tallemant here to a manuscript source now in the Bibliothèque Nationale (fonds français 10210) which uses the word 'love' to describe Louis's relationship with the coachman, whom Tallemant confuses with his father. Louis is said in the manuscript to have sent one of the Saint-Amours to Madrid to report on the physical features of Anne of Austria, and the manuscript supplies details of the relationship with Haran. Vendôme was the illegitimate son of Henri IV and Gabrielle d'Estrées who has already been mentioned.

11 Professor Moote (*Louis XIII, the Just*, Los Angeles and London 1989), whose biography of Louis XIII is almost hagiographic, not only admits that on the wedding night the marriage was not consummated, which is common ground among historians, but draws attention to the fact that 'Marie de' Medici was sufficiently legal and crude to display the bedsheets the next morning' (p.85), holding that Louis retired with a 'glande rouge' and 'Anne accepted a painful, unconsummated entry' (p.85). Such was the political importance of the matter, that Marie de' Medici was perfectly prepared to deceive. Professor Moote also speaks of 'the king's subsequent shrinking from any physical contact with the queen' (p.142), although he assumes without any evidence that could be regarded as convincing that the repugnance in respect of the queen was later from time to time to be overcome.

12 For Héroard, see the *Journal de Jean Hérouard sur l'enfance et la jeunesse de Louis XIII (1601–28)*, ed. Soulié and Barthélemy, vol. 2, Paris 1868, p. 186, entry for Wednesday 25 November. Politically, so much turned on the consummation of the marriage, that at least one account of the

wedding night was published, *Détail singulier de ce qui se passa le jour de la consommation du mariage de Louis XIII* (reprinted in *Revue rétrospective ou bibliothèque historique*, 1st series, vol. 2, Paris 1834, pp. 250–52). The date on the document is wrong. It tells of the corralling of a passing cleric by Marie de' Medici to bless the special curtained bed into which Anne had been put, of Louis being roused by his mother at around 8.0 pm, of the call for fur slippers and dressing gown, of the procession (queen mother, two nurses, the king's governor, his doctor, members of wardrobe, preceded by Béringham with a candle), of what the queen mother said, and of Anne's assent, which she gave in Spanish. All except two nurses withdrew, and they confirmed that the king performed his duty twice. The king then slept, returned to his room accompanied by the same procession, and went to bed 'showing great satisfaction at the perfection of his marriage'. The doctor, Héroard, among those waiting outside, is briefer in his diary and reports the twofold consummation, but only 'according to what he [the king] told us'. This account reads as if it was produced for Spanish consumption. For Tallemant see the *Historiettes*, ed. Antoine Adam, vol. 1, Paris 1967, pp.333 ff. The *historiette* on Louis XIII starts with a paragraph about the wedding night, which goes on to the anecdote about Louis leaving his bath with an erection and meeting the master of the wardrobe.

13 Arnauld d'Andilly's diary says that Luynes carried the king in his arms. Only the first lady-in-waiting remained in the room. See also the *Mémoires* of Pontchartrain and Armand Baschet, *Le Roi chez la Reine ou histoire secrète du mariage de Louis XIII et d'Anne d'Autriche*, Paris 1866. It was not unusual, particularly where property, inheritance and *a fortiori* thrones were at stake, to have a witness to the consummation of marriage, and there was even a set of rules prescribed for attesting in front of up to a dozen officials that a husband was or was not capable of consummating his marriage. All Paris laughed about the humiliating failure of M. de Langey in this regard in 1660. Mme de Sévigné was tittering in a coach two doors up while the *congrès* was taking place.

14 'Most Christian' was a formal way of referring to the king of France. The king of Spain was 'the Catholic king'.

15 For Richelieu and Marie de' Medici, see for instance the anonymous pamphlet *Amours secrètes du cardinal de Richelieu avec Marie de Médicis*, Paris, year XI (1803–1804). For a resumé of the evidence of Richelieu's alleged love for, and rejection by Anne of Austria, see Tallemant, relying on the *Mémoires* of Montglat and La Rochefoucauld, and Antoine Adam's notes to his edition of the *Historiettes*, vol.1, Paris 1967, pp. 905–907. Tallemant himself certainly does not believe in an affair between Richelieu and Marie de' Medici: 'There was a lot of gossip about the cardinal de Richelieu, who was handsome, and the queen mother. During this *galanterie*, she decided to take up the lute again . . . She

calls in Gaultier: now everyone is playing the lute. The cardinal learnt, too, and it was the most absurd thing you could imagine, to see him taking lessons from Gaultier.'

16 For details, see Joseph Bergin, *Cardinal Richelieu. Power and the pursuit of wealth*, New haven and London 1985.

17 On the unexpected and intricate financial complications, lawsuits and settlements, see Joseph Bergin, *Cardinal Richelieu. Power and the Pursuit of wealth*, New Haven and London 1985, p. 34–40.

18 On Richelieu and the Sorbonne, see Marc Venard, *La Sorbonne et Richelieu*, Paris 1973, and especially, René Pillorget, 'Richelieu, renovateur de la Sorbonne', in *Richelieu et la culture*, ed. Roland Mousnier, Paris 1987, pp. 43–54. The position of *proviseur* implied some mixture of patron and protector, with authority but without jurisdiction. The Sorbonne in the sense of being not a college but the seat of the theology faculty was jealous of its privileges, and hostile to the danger of seeing them usurped by the Jesuits, regulated directly from their Roman curia. Richelieu favoured a Jesuit and an independent college in all large towns, but himself financed the physical rebuilding of the Sorbonne *qua* college of the university.

19 The theology faculty had no civil jurisdiction, although it could at some periods count on the *parlement* to impose civil penalties at its request, and it had historically become adept in presenting the canonical *crimen* of heresy as the civil crime of blasphemy in pursuit of suppression by the civil authorities. It is still controverted whether it had acquired by delegation or prescription power to pronounce in the name of the *magisterium* on what was and what was not orthodox doctrine.

20 On the Richer affair, see Pierre Blet, *Le Clergé de France et la monarchie, 1615–1666*, 2 vols., Rome/Paris 1959.

21 Henri de Gondi, bishop of Paris, became in 1618 the first cardinal de Retz. He was the uncle of the more famous memorialist, archbishop of Paris and also cardinal de Retz. In 1622 Paris became ecclesiastically independent of the archdiocese of Sens and was erected into an archdiocese in its own right.

22 Fancan, a canon of Saint-Germain-l'Auxerrois, truculently anti-clerical as well as pro-Huguenot, was the sharpest-penned of the pamphleteers seeking a political figure to establish royal authority. He only slowly adopted Richelieu as the likeliest candidate to succeed in the mission, probably entering into a formal relationship with him as an *écrivain à gages* in about 1618. Fancan's most damaging attack on Luynes, the *Chronique des favoris*, did not appear until 1622, as he began to take the side of Marie de' Medici. Fancan turned his attacks against Condé and La Vieuville, Richelieu's predecessor as chief minister, but was himself the victim of attack and was sent to the Bastille in June 1627 for the rest of his life. Matthieu de Morgues alleges that his downfall was partly the

work of Père Joseph. Fancan spoke on behalf of the nobility deprived
by La Vieuville of pensions and military appointments. Their bitterness
is confirmed by the memorialist Fontenay-Mareuil, who was himself a
military member of the nobility. Fancan also attacked the financiers for
charging 16.66 per cent interest on their loans to the state instead of
the prescribed 5–6 per cent.

23 See A.D. Lublinskaya, *French Absolutism in the Crucial Phase, 1620–1629*,
tr. Brian Pearce, Cambridge 1968, pp. 264–66, and A.F. Allison
'Richard Smith, Richelieu and the French Marriage' in *Recusant History*,
7 (1964) pp. 148–211. See also Maximin Deloche, *Autour de la plume de
Richelieu*, Paris 1920 and Léon Geley, *Fancan et la politique de Richelieu
de 1617 à 1627*, Paris 1884.

24 The title of principal minister later conferred on Richelieu was customarily given to all members of the inner council.

5 First Minister: Strategies 1624 –9

1 '. . . pour servir après ma mort à la police et à la conduite de votre
Royaume' (ed. Louis André, Paris 1947, pp.90–91). On the nature of
the *Testament*, see Roland Mousnier, '*Le Testament politique* de Richelieu'
in *Richelieu et le monde de l'esprit*, Paris 1985, pp. 297–304. The book
derived its title from its intention to be useful to the king after its
author's death for the polity and governance of the kingdom. It is a
private work, intended for the king alone, a testament to be seen only
after Richelieu's death, and it goes as far as to warn the king against
the defects in his character and the dangers of his temperament.

The authoritative tone, trenchantly critical of its addressee, has
puzzled commentators by its difference from the ostentatiously flowery
way in which, earlier, Richelieu had in his correspondance habitually
professed his willingness to serve only the king's interests. The explanation lies in the *Testament*'s literary register, which is very close to that of
the letter of spiritual direction, as exemplified, for instance, in the letters
written at the same period by François de Sales to Jeanne-Françoise de
Chantal, co-founder with him of the Visitation order, or to Angélique
Arnauld, who considered applying to join it, or by the Jesuit Jean-Joseph
Surin to the Ursuline Jeanne des Anges at Loudun, generally thought
to be diabolically possessed, or later by the abbé de Rancé to a variety
of different penitents. In the early seventeenth century, it was a very
well known genre.

The content is different. Instead of spiritual direction concerned
with the path of progress towards that spiritual perfection to which all
those under religious vows had a formal obligation to strive, Richelieu
instructs the king with almost brutal psychological perceptivity in the

means by which Louis can overcome his weaknesses to augment his royal stature and to obtain greatness for France. While Machiavelli was gloomily aware of how a prince had to behave in order to achieve political ends, Richelieu is optimistically clear-headed about the paths and pitfalls on the way to the achievement of heroic grandeur for Louis and of European pre-eminence for France.

The *Testament* seems largely to have been written in collaboration with Père Joseph, who died on 18 December 1638, and it had been begun by 1635. Parts were dictated by Richelieu, who from 1634 suffered from an abscess on his right arm which made the physical process of writing often painful, but parts were emended or polished by him in his own hand. Even at that late stage in his career, Richelieu could not formulate clear tactics by which to achieve his overall political strategy, since he had had continuously to respond to pressing immediate constraints. The *Testament* is more concerned with general principles than with appropriate specific actions. Ten years after beginning to play his leading role as royal adviser, Richelieu was still learning, reacting pragmatically to situations as they arose, analysing his reactions, and in the *Testament* writing down for the king the lessons to be drawn.

The ethic underlying the *Testament* is that developed from the neostoicism prevalent during the religious wars and transformed by such authors as Guillaume du Vair, twice keeper of the seals, in his 1585 *La Philosophie morale des stoïques*, where virtue is defined as 'the firm disposition of our will to follow what is upright and good'. Descartes, who relies heavily on du Vair, from whom he takes his methodic doubt, also defines the principal virtue 'générosité' as 'a firm and constant resolution to use well the free disposition of our wills, that is to say never to lack the will to undertake and exercise all the things which are judged to be best'. In a letter of 18 August 1645 Descartes unifies the twin goals of virtue and true happiness, for which 'we must follow virtue, that is to say have a firm and constant will to execute everything we judge to be the best, and to employ the whole strength of our understanding to judge well'. It is a characteristic of this ethic that there are no objective ethical norms. Virtue consists essentially in the vigour with which the will strives to achieve the perceived good, but in a context in which moral grandeur is divorced from strictly ethical values. Corneille, like Richelieu, regards virtue as necessarily 'mâle', without connotations of gender, and creates morally heroic ('mâle') characters like Cléopâtre in *Rodogune*, who are ethically evil.

2 *Testament politique*, ed. Louis André, Paris 1947, pp. 93–95.

3 Mathieu de Morgues (1582–1670), turned bitter anti-Richelieu pamphleteer and defender of the queen mother from 1631, includes some biting jibes at Richelieu's infirmities in his 1631 *Charitable Remonstrance de Caton Chrestien à Monseigneur l'éminentissime Cardinal de Richelieu.*

4 On the lively debate at this date about whether the personal quality of *gloire* could be merely internal or whether it required external recognition, see notably F.E. Sutcliffe, *Guez de Balzac et son temps. Littérature et politique*, Paris 1959.

5 Boisrobert was a convert who emerged from the entourage of Marie de' Medici, becoming a canon of Rouen. He was exiled to his abbacy in Burgundy on 23 January 1641. Jean Chapelain, critic, author, and influential man of letters, gives a slightly different account of the same incident, but says there were two women involved, not just the otherwise unknown 'mignonne', 'la petite Saint-Amour Frerelot' named by Tallemant.

6 See for these details Jules Jacquin and Joseph Duesburg, *Rueil, le château de Richelieu, la Malmaison*, Paris 1845, and J. Bergin, *Cardinal Richelieu: Power and the Pursuit of Wealth*, New Haven and London 1985. The inventory of Rueil made after Richelieu's death includes a number of garden tools, some in silver, on which Richelieu's arms were engraved (*Inventaire*, ed. Honor Levi, items 1750 and 1751, *Archives de l'Art français*, nouvelle période, vol. 27, Nogent-le-Roi 1985, p.75). Were they for his personal use? Prints from the period show the huge scale of Richelieu's building operations at Rueil, as in Paris and at Richelieu. Particularly impressive is the prodigality of the expenditure on the series of fountains and cascades.

7 Among the more unbelievable allegations are those contained, for instance, in such anonymous pamphlets as the 1693 *Les Amours d'Anne d'Autriche . . . avec Monsieur le C[ardinal] D[e] R[ichelieu], le véritable Père de Louis XIV*, carrying Cologne as the no doubt fictitious place of publication, and that containing the accusation of incest with his niece, then Mme de Combalet, *Histoire secrète du cardinal de Richelieu, ou ses amours avec Marie de Médicis et Mme de Combalet, depuis duchesse d'Aiguillon*, ed. Chardon de la Rochette, Paris 1808.

8 Michel de Marillac, born in 1563, became keeper of the seals in 1626, and Louis, born in 1573, was made a marshal in 1629.

9 La Vieuville had been 'principal ministre', a title not again formally used as such until the king began to use it again of Richelieu in 1629. In August 1624 Richelieu became 'premier ministre' only in the sense that, together with the other cardinal, the elderly François de la Rochefoucauld, he ranked above the other members by virtue of his cardinalate. The *chef du conseil* continued to be La Rochefoucauld.

10 On these matters, see Louis Battifol, *Richelieu et le roi Louis XIII*, Paris 1934, pp. 10–20. Richelieu remained 'principal ministre' in official documents even when his estates were erected into a *duché-pairie* in 1631, although by then the title 'premier ministre' was in common usage.

11 The Swiss cantons formed a virtually independent confederation from

the end of the fifteenth century, although in was only in 1648 that they were formally released from allegiance to the Empire and formed their *Eidgenossenschaft*.

12 They are now in the Louvre.

13 Strictly, Marie de Rohan-Montbazon, widow of Luynes, was not yet Mme de Chevreuse. She married her lover, Claude de Lorraine, third son of Henri de Guise, prince de Joinville, and later duc de Chevreuse, on 20 April 1622. Among her lovers in 1625 was Buckingham, by whom she had a child. Mlle de Verneuil, illegitimate daughter of Henri IV, married Epernon's son, Bernard de la Valette, on 12 December 1622.

14 One at least of Richelieu's biographers goes as far as to sympathise with Anne's plight in face of the king's 'éloignement, . . . timidité, . . . prodigieuse froideur physique, qui ressemblait à de la répulsion' (Auguste Bailly, *Richelieu*, Paris 1936, p. 167).

15 Roughly co-terminous with Rheinland-Pfalz.

16 Like Richelieu, Olivares discreetly exercised plenary governmental power before he was appointed to the position which entitled him to do so. From 1623, the year in which Olivares became thirty-six and Philip IV eighteen, Olivares was effectively Philip IV's principal minister. On the relationship between *Richelieu and Olivares*, and on their astonishingly parallel careers, see Auguste Leman, *Richelieu et Olivarès*, Lille 1938, and J.H. Elliott, *Richelieu and Olivares*, Cambridge 1984.

17 On the negotiations for the treaty of Monzón, see A.D. Lublinskaya, *French Absolutism: the Crucial Phase 1620–1629*, tr. Brian Pearce, Cambridge 1968, pp. 277–81, drawing on hitherto unpublished letters which radically alter earlier accounts of the negotiations.

18 Among the pamphlets of late 1625 attacking Richelieu were the *Mysteria politica* and the *Admonitio ad regem Ludovicum*. Among those to enter the lists on Richelieu's side were Fancan, Père Joseph and the Jesuit Père Sirmond. The anonymous *Le Catholique d'Etat* argued for the legitimacy of political alliances which crossed religious boundaries, a view already made very clear in the *Instructions de M. de Schomberg*, intended for Schomberg's German embassy and dated 29 December 1616. They were drawn up by Richelieu and signed by Louis XIII (Avenel, *Lettres*, Paris 1853, pp. 208–35) and strongly affirm that religious differences do not affect political allegiances.

19 In the 1626 edict issued at Saint-Germain, Richelieu was styled *grand maître, chef et surintendant général de la navigation et du commerce de France*. The post of admiral of France was abolished in January 1627 together with that of *connétable*, its last occupant, the converted Huguenot Lesdiguières, having died the previous September. Richelieu himself argued that it would save the treasury money if the financial jurisdictions attached to these offices could be brought under central

control (*Mémoires*, vol. 6, p.297; see Richard Bonney, *The King's Debts*, Oxford 1981, pp. 132–33). Montmorency, who had inherited or purchased the jurisdictions on the northern and western coasts, was compensated by 1.2 million livres, payable by the royal treasury in annual *rentes* of 96,000 livres. Guise kept his office until 1629 and gave help to a revolt at Aix in 1630. He had to leave France the following year. In 1635 Richelieu was to purchase the office of *général des galères*, which he bestowed for some years on his nephew Pont-Courlay. On the complex modalities of Richelieu's enrichment from the commercial and marine offices, themselves unremunerated, see J. Bergin, *Richelieu. Power and the Pursuit of Wealth*, New Haven and London 1985, pp. 94–118. Abolishing the posts of *connétable* and admiral of France naturally strengthened Richelieu's centralist control. During his early years in office, Richelieu was also assiduously collecting governorships (Bergin, *op.cit.*, pp. 80–94). The more lucrative of Richelieu's ecclesiastical benefices dated only from after 1628. On the concentration of power into Richelieu's hands, see A.J. Lublinskaya, *French Absolutism: the Crucial Phase 1620–29*, Cambridge 1968, pp. 287–89. Richelieu also created eight posts of *inspecteurs-généraux des affaires de la marine*, to which he appointed persons whom he could trust. Some were office-holders in the provincial courts, appointed to mollify the *parlements*.

20 See J. Petit, *L'Assemblée des notables de 1626–1627*, Paris 1936.

21 On d'Effiat, who was a firm supporter of Richelieu, was created a marshal of France on 6 January 1631, and held the *surintendance* until his death in 1632, and on the interpretation of the proceedings of the Assemblée, see especially the concluding chapter of A.D. Lublinskaya, *French Absolutism: the Crucial Phase 1620–1629*, Cambridge 1968.

22 Louis Batiffol, *Richelieu et le roi Louis XIII*, Paris 1934, gives Marie de Bourbon's wealth as nearly a million livres in gold, and a million livres of revenues as well as innumerable estates carrying the titles of marquis, count or viscount.

23 Tallemant (*Historiettes*, ed. Adam, vol. 1, Paris 1967, p. 535) says that Chalais's rival was arriving back from the country in 1626, and was forced to duel wearing his country boots. The *Mercure français* for 1626 reports the duel, but the abbé de Marolles reports the duel as an assassination.

24 Mme de Rambouillet's *salon* known as the *chambre bleue* becomes important in the context of Richelieu's literary patronage.

25 See Victor-L. Tapié, *France in Age of Louis XIII and Richelieu*, tr. D.McN. Lockie, London 1974, p. 158 and A. Lloyd Moote, *Louis XIII, the Just*, Los Angeles 1989, p.191. Chalais was certainly guilty of connivance in Gaston's escape, which could be construed as *lèse-majesté*.

26 Brevet of 26 May 1626. On Richelieu's guards, see Louis Batiffol, *Autour de Richelieu*, Paris 1937, pp. 51–94.

27 Avenel, *Lettres*, vol. 2, p. 260.

28 The sacrament is conferred by the partners on each other when the marriage is consummated, but the wedding is nonetheless invalid unless the ceremony, with the exchange of vows, is formally witnessed by a representative of the church with appropriate jurisdiction, which is ordinarily territorial. Richelieu, no longer a bishop, possessed no ecclesiastical jurisdiction anywhere, and it is for this reason that he did not preside over the ceremony. Fontenay-Mareuil explains that the cardinal presided over the betrothal (*fiançailles*) but, for the marriage 'it was the curé himself who did it so that all the formalities would be observed, and no opening would be left to challenge it' (*Nouvelle collection des Mémoires pour servir à l'histoire de France*, ed. Michaud et Poujoulat, vol. 5, Paris 1837, p.181, col. 2).

29 According to Mme de Motteville, the queen, defending herself, said she would not have profited enough by the exchange. The king had summoned her to the council on 10 September to answer accusations of complicity in the plotting.

6 La Rochelle, Mantua and the Crisis of Confidence

1 Secular sovereignties extended to the Italian city-states as well as to German cities and provinces. The term admits of degrees, both in the nature of sovereignty and in its legitimacy. In the end, sovereignty can be measured only in the ability to enforce jurisdiction.

2 It is now the Place des Vosges, and still has an equestrian statue of Louis XIII in the middle.

3 Avenel prints a famous letter of 29 March 1636 (*Lettres*, vol.v, pp. 435–36) from Richelieu to his confessor, noting where Richelieu had emended the dictated version in his own hand, in which Richelieu asks in what circumstances duelling can still be justified. His tone shows him not to have been wholly unsympathetic to the practice of resolving disputes through duels, while realising that the number of duels still in 1636 needed to be diminished.

4 The five were Bouteville's mother, the princesse de Condé, and the duchesses de Montmorency, d'Angoulême and de Vendôme. There is no reason to doubt Richelieu's distress and desire to recommend clemency as recorded in the *Testament politique*, (ed. Louis André, Paris 1947, pp. 102–103), but it did not outweigh the reasons for refusing pardon. The executions, as he put it to the king, would be a suitable, but not infallible, means of procuring the end of duelling; clemency would be a certain way of ending the authority of royal edicts. Louis XIII became ill at the emotional strain of refusing clemency. Richelieu wrote letters of condolence on 24 June to the duc d'Angoulême, Charlotte de

Montmorency's husband, and to Henri de Montmorency himself, 'The king was more grieved than I can say to find himself reduced to this extremity in his regard, but the frequency of the deliberately committed relapses in a matter which directly challenged his authority meant that, to sever the root of an evil so deeply embedded in his kingdom, he believed himself obliged in conscience before God and before men, to let justice takes its unimpeded course on this occasion . . .' (*Lettres*, ed. Avenel, vol. ii, letter cccclxxix, p. 480). See on this whole episode Louis Battifol, *Richelieu et le roi Louis XIII*, Paris 1934, pp. 159–68.

5 Richelieu despised Buckingham, instantly recognising the narcissism behind the good looks and the oscillation between common sense and near-mad megalomania. He also realised that so powerful an untrustworthy adventurer was dangerous.

6 See J.H. Eliott, *Richelieu and Olivares*, Cambridge 1984, pp.88–90 and David Parker, *La Rochelle and the French Monarchy*, London 1980.

7 The generalship of armies and navies is important here primarily because it repeatedly shows the rivalry to have social ambition recognised in military rank, and in particular how aggravated the king's brother was at being deprived three times of important generalships when Louis himself took over. His sinecure appointment on this occasion is a minor event in the stormy story of his relationship with the king.

8 On the chivalresque side to the Ile de Ré campaign, see G.R.R. Treasure, *Cardinal Richelieu and the Development of Absolutism*, London 1972, p.102 and Victor-L. Tapié, *France in the Age of Louis XIII and Richelieu*, tr. D. McN. Mackie, London 1974, pp. 181–85. Richelieu penned to Toiras the message dictated by Louis XIII calling on him and his troops 'to endure . . . all the extremes of hardship and discomfort that men of valour devoted to [the king's] service can and should bear'.

9 Speculation about the result of failure at this juncture is not entirely fruitless, since it allows a more refined assessment of Richelieu's actual situation in 1628. Failure to reduce La Rochelle would have meant disgrace within France, and either banishment to the still small *seigneurie* at Richelieu or, to avoid the embarrassment, some sort of curial appointment in Rome. It is difficult to think that any pope could now have used Richelieu's immense diplomatic abilities for ambassadorial purposes within Europe, most of whose monarchs distrusted or hated him. Richelieu was, of course, no longer territorially (as distinct from sacramentally) a bishop.

10 'Inexplicably' is a euphemism. There has been a rich variety of explanations, from pressure put by Richelieu on Anne of Austria to exploit Buckingham's passion for her (court rumours reported by Voltaire: unlikely), to the Dutch view that Buckingham had simply been bribed (unlikely), or Bossuet's that Henrietta-Maria had used

her influence on Charles I (next to impossible). Charles I appears to have been genuinely upset to learn of his fleet's performance. Bailly (*Richelieu*, Paris 1934, pp.196–97), suspects some chicanery on Richelieu's part (not improbable), but we do not know what, or how, or at what price.

11 See A.D. Lublinskaya, *French Absolutism: the Crucial Phase 1620–1629*, Cambridge 1968, pp. 218–19. The mole was eventually to be washed away by a storm.

12 There are even, perhaps not surprisingly, letters ending 'Votre Majesté bruslera, s'il luy plaist, ceste lettre' (*Lettres*, ed. Avenel, vol. 2, letter dxv of 24 December 1627, p. 769). Richelieu used the future tense in the sense neither of a prediction nor an order, but to mingle suggestion with request.

13 There are two people called Marie de Gonzague. One is the daughter of the duc de Nevers, whom Gaston wanted to marry, and was later the object of Cinq-Mars's passion, and the other is the niece of Vincenzo of Mantua, who married the son of Nevers, the duc de Rethel, and eventually became regent of Mantua.

14 The accusations of irreligion against Richelieu in neglecting the political aims of the Catholic party were doing him more damage than he appears to have realised. When Bérulle suddenly died, it was popularly believed that Richelieu had had him poisoned. Richelieu asked the Oratorian Père Bertin to quash the rumour in Rome and, at the same time, to obtain for him the previously mentioned commutation of his obligation to recite the divine office daily.

15 Avenel, *Lettres*, vol. iii, p. 151.

16 Avenel, *Lettres*, vol. iii, p. 180.

17 Gaston had been widowed since 4 June 1627. In spite of great protestations of grief, his entourage were discussing possible candidates for his remarriage four days later. Three names were being mentioned, the emperor's daughter, the daughter of the duke of Nevers and Mantua, Marie de Gonzague, and a Medici sister of the grand duke of Florence, preferred by Marie de' Medici and the pope.

For much of the complex relationship between the Gonzaga/Gonzague and the Nevers families, see Tallemant's *historiette*, 'La Reyne de Pologne et ses sœurs' (ed. Antoine Adam, vol.1, Paris 1967, p. 584–92, and the editor's notes, p. 1191–1200). The Marie de Gonzague with whom Gaston fell in love, born probably in 1612, was later courted by Cinq-Mars, but did finally marry Ladislaus IV of Poland in 1646, and subsequently his brother John II Casimir. She died in Warsaw in 1667, and was known as Louise-Marie, because in Poland the name 'Marie' standing alone was reserved to the Blessed Virgin. Gaston seemed likely to try to remove Marie from the home in France provided for her by Mme de Longueville, born Catherine de Gonzague, and married to Henri I de Longueville, who died in 1629.

18 There are two accounts of Richelieu's triumphant return on 14 September 1629, accompanied by the court, which had gone as far as Nemours to meet and accompany him. One recounts that the king was still hunting, and Richelieu tells us that he was received by the two queens, and that Marie de Medici's frigid attitude puzzled and caused consternation to everyone present. Mathieu de Morgues, on the other hand, accuses Richelieu of impertinence at the interview and of attacking Bérulle and others of the queen mother's entourage with 'effrontery'. On the return of Louis XIII, Richelieu tells us that he asked to speak to him, was treated with great affection, but said that he had no option but to seek permission to withdraw from his ministry. He also wrote to the queen mother, resigning from his responsibilities in her household, while expressing his eternal devotion to her. The king, bewildered, realised that matters had to be patched up, and Bassompiere tells us that they were. The court on the whole sided with Richelieu.

19 See Louis Batiffol, *Richelieu et le roi Louis XIII*, Paris 1934, pp. 216–22. Zorzi, the Venetian ambassador, wrote on 6 November, after Bérulle's death, that Bérulle had been the author of the growing hostility of Marie de' Medici towards Richelieu.

20 Richelieu had relied on Bérulle for help in reforming his diocese, but by 1629 a note of obsequiousness had crept into Bérulle's gratitude, and it was only after Bérulle's sudden death on 2 October 1629, when he was fifty-three, that Richelieu discovered the extent of Bérulle's inner hostility, due at least in part to Bérulle's conviction that his attitudes were being directly inspired in him by God.

21 La Valette, Epernon's third son whose ugliness was a popular joke in Mme de Rambouillet's *chambre bleue*, was born in 1593 and died in 1639. As youngest son, he was constrained by the family to take orders, became archbishop of Toulouse and cardinal in 1621, and was to offer Richelieu firm support during the crisis he underwent in 1630.

22 In a memorandum of 13 April 1630, Richelieu realised that the choice was between success in Italy, securing respect for France's *grandeur*, and domestic reform 'repos, épargne et règlement du dedans du royaume' (see Victor-L. Tapié, *France in the Age of Louis XIII and Richelieu*, London 1974, pp. 205–209).

23 Georges Mongrédien gives a list which is certainly not exhaustive of a dozen such uprisings for the years 1624–1630 (*La Journée des Dupes*, Paris 1961, p. 38). See also Roland Mousnier, *Fureurs paysannes*, Paris 1967.

24 We have at least seven first-hand accounts of what happened by Richelieu, Gaston d'Orléans, Bassompierre, Fontenay-Mareuil, Montglat, Brienne and Mme de Motteville. There is also an account by Saint-Simon,

almost certainly based on a written eye-witness account handed down to the memorialist by his father, the king's favourite and gentleman of the chamber, to which Georges Mongrédien gives much weight (*La Journée des dupes*, Paris 1961).

25 The three accounts were those of Bassompierre, Fontenay-Mareuil and Marie de' Medici. Richelieu confirms in a letter that appears to have been overlooked by historians that it was the unlocked door that allowed him entry, 'Dieu s'est servi de l'occasion d'une poirte non barrée qui me donna lieu de me deffendre lorsqu'on taschoit de faire conclure l'exécution de ma ruine' (letter from Richelieu to Chavigny and de Noyers, about 25 May 1642, in *Lettres*, ed. Avenel, vol. vi, letter cccclxx).

26 'Avis donné au roy . . .', Avenel, Lettres, vol.iv, pp. 269–73. On the legal improprieties, see Georges Mongrédien, *La Journée des dupes*, Paris 1961, pp. 104–28. Brienne notes that Richelieu strongly opposed clemency.

27 Georges Mongrédien gives a detailed account of Marillac's trial and the political need for condemnation and execution in *La Journée des dupes*, Paris 1961, pp. 104–28.

7 The Defence of Victory

1 In the 'Succincte narration' preceding the *Testament politique*, we read Richelieu's words to the king 'Votre procédé fut si sage que vous n'accordâtes rien à la Reine qui fût contraire à votre Etat et ne lui refusâtes aucune chose que ce que vous n'eussiez pu lui accorder sans blesser votre conscience et agir autant contre elle que contre vous-même' (ed. Louis André, Paris 1947, p. 114).

2 Le Coigneux was made a *président à mortier*, or senior judge, in the Paris *parlement*, while Puylaurens received a gift of 150,000 livres and was promised, but not given, a dukedom. Le Coigneux was involved at the time in a paternity case with a woman claiming to be his wife. Both now began inciting Gaston to leave the court.

3 See Victor-L. Tapié, *France in the Age of Louis XIII and Richelieu*, London 1974, pp. 239–40.

4 In the fourteenth and fifteenth centuries, the king had each year and in each province convoked meetings of the deputies of the three estates, clergy, nobility and citizenry. These 'provincial estates' voted taxes, raised troops and sent deputies to the estates-general, but were gradually replaced by territorial *élections*, in which taxes were levied directly by royal commissioners. In spite of being called *élus*, they were by the seventeenth century centrally appointed. By 1620, France was divided into the five *pays d'états* (Burgundy, Languedoc, Brittany,

Provence and Dauphiné, plus some small counties), which themselves distributed within their borders the burden of taxation, based not on income but on non-manorial land, and took responsibility for public works, and the *pays d'élection*, where taxation was centrally administered and based on land. Richelieu attempted to centralise the administration, partly by abolishing the considerable privileges of the *pays d'états*, generally in favour of intendants established by Richelieu himself and responsible to him. See, on the intendants, Richard Bonney, *Political Change in France under Richelieu and Mazarin 1624–1661*, Oxford 1978, and on the provincial estates, particularly Languedoc, Roland E. Mousnier, *The Institutions of France under the Absolute Monarchy 1598–1789*, tr. Brian Pearce, Chicago 1979, pp. 606–42 and Julian Dent, *Crisis in Finance: Crown, Financiers and Society in Seventeenth-Century France*, Newton Abbot 1973.

5 See Simon du Cros, *Histoire de la vie de Henry, dernier duc de Montmorency*, Paris 1643.

6 We know from the *Mémoires* that Richelieu believed that Montmorency, 'le premier des grands du royaume', had seriously divided the kingdom and weakened the royal authority. He pointed out the consequences of all three possible courses, pardoning Montmorency, holding him hostage for Gaston's good behaviour, and of executing him, leaving the king in no doubt about which course was the safest. There appears even to have been discussion of a summary execution which did not involve the Toulouse *parlement*.

7 Vignier (*Le chasteau de Richelieu ou l'histoire des dieux et des héros de l'Antiquité avec des réflexions morales*, Saumur 1676), who was governor of Richelieu from 1662 to 1684, says the painting left by Montmorency to Richelieu was a Saint Francis.

8 Most of the information about Richelieu's health has to be gleaned from sparse references in the letters, but see the chapter devoted to the subject in Maximin Deloche, *La Maison du cardinal de Richelieu*, Paris 1912, pp. 197–227. Richelieu had in his household the 'trinité invariable de la santé' (Deloche), a doctor, an apothecary and a surgeon. Surgeons had not yet risen in medical status. They ranked just below the nobles, mostly military personnel or pages, but above the highest household domestic officers.

9 Henri de Sourdis succeeded his brother, the cardinal, to the archbishopric of Bordeaux in 1629, having already succeeded his uncle, also Henri, to the bishopric of Maillezais.

10 Versailles, it should be remembered, was still just a small hunting lodge.

11 But see J. Schloder, 'Un artiste oublié, Nicolas Prévost, peintre de Richelieu' in the *Bulletin de la Société de l'histoire de l'art français*, 1980, pp. 64–65.

12 On the reconstruction of the château and the building of the town at Richelieu, see Claude Mignot, 'Le Château et la ville de Richelieu en Poitou' in *Richelieu et le monde de l'esprit*, Paris 1985, pp. 67–74, and Louis Batiffol, *Autour de Richelieu*, Paris 1937.

13 Avenel, *Lettres*, vol.iv, p.643.

14 On the complicated entails by which Richelieu attempted to ensure the glory of his family name in perpetuity, see J. Bergin, *Cardinal Richelieu. Power and the pursuit of wealth*, New Haven and London 1985, pp. 256–263.

15 The greatest of all the *surintendants des finances*, Nicolas Foucquet (1615–80), who still belonged spiritually to Richelieu's generation, tried to make the same sort of statement at the magnificent mansion he constructed at Vaux-le-Vicomte, but was toppled by Colbert within three weeks of the opening celebration on 17 August 1661. Convicted of peculation, he was to die in prison. Four thousand other financiers fell with him. On the development of the value system of Richelieu's society, see A.H.T. Levi, *French Moralists: the Theory of the Passions: 1585–1649*, Oxford 1964 and F.E. Sutcliffe, *Guez de Balzac. Littérature et politique*, Paris 1959.

16 On Rueil, see Jean-Pierre Babelon, 'Le château de Rueil et les autres demeures du cardinal', in *Richelieu et le monde de l'esprit*, Paris 1985, pp. 75–82.

17 On the Palais-Royal the literature is considerable. See Françoise Bercé, 'Le Palais-Cardinal' in *Richelieu et le monde de l'esprit*, Paris 1985, pp.61–66.

18 For an account of the circumstances, expenditure, or receipts of Richelieu's acquisitions and disposals of the many properties which passed through his hands, together with his other sources of income, see J. Bergin, *Cardinal Richelieu. Power and the pursuit of wealth*, New Haven and London 1985.

19 On this subject, see Claude Mignot, 'Richelieu et l'architecture' in *Richelieu et le monde de l'esprit*, Paris 1985, pp. 54–60.

20 On Richelieu and the Sorbonne, see Louis Batiffol, *Autour de Richelieu*, Paris 1937, pp. 95–141. There is also a short illustrated survey by Marc Venard, *La Sorbonne et Richelieu*, issued by the Chancellerie des universités de Paris in 1973, which prints Le Mercier's plan of the chapel, and a photograph of Richelieu's tomb. The duchesse d'Aiguillon had rejected a design for the tomb by Bernini, largely on account of the position in which he wanted it placed, and herself decreed in a contract of 12 April 1675, exactly how the king's sculptor and rector of the academy of painting and sculpture, François Girardon, should execute the work. The features of Richelieu's nieces were given to the figures of Piety and Doctrine. Twenty-seven members of Richelieu's family are buried in the crypt alongside him, together with some Sorbonne

doctors. Venard narrates the posthumous fate of the body, from which at one point the head was removed.

8 Religious and Cultural Background

1 Avenel quotes Richelieu promise's to appoint a chaplain with an annual revenue of 36 livres to say mass at Richelieu in thanksgiving every Sunday 's'il plaist à la divine bonté, par l'intercession du bienheureux apostre et bien aimé S. Jehan, me renvoier ma santé et me délivrer dans huict jours d'un mal de teste extraordinaire qui me tourmente' (*Lettres*, vol. I, p. xcix). Deloche (*La Maison du Cardinal de Richelieu*, Paris 1912, p.17) quotes this promise as a characteristic manifestation of Richelieu's obsession with numerical detail even in the smallest matters and even, Deloche might have added, in his dealings with God, as if Richelieu expected God to barter over the time limit for the relief of pain or the sum offered for the chaplain.

2 This assertion is made by Auguste Bailly (*Mazarin*, Paris 1935, p.43).

3 Surprisingly, there appear to have been no French musicians of note working in France between 1620 and 1640. The *New Oxford History of Music*, vol.4, 'The Age of Humanism, 1540–1630', Oxford 1968, p. 591 devotes only half a page to French musicians, and most of them had been associated with Baïf's academy under Henri III.

4 D'Urfé was the author of three volumes of *Epistres morales*, published in 1598, 1603 and 1608, and of the five volumes of the *L'Astrée*, published in 1607, 1610, 1619, 1627 and 1628, of which the fourth volume was finished and the fifth written by his secretary. Du Vair published *La sainte philosophie* before the 1585 *La Philosophie morale des stoiques*, and in 1594 *De la Constance et consolation ès calamitéz publiques*.

5 See the sixth part of the *Discours de la méthode* (ed. Etienne Gilson, Paris 1947, pp. 61–62).

6 Descartes regarded ethics as the final fruit and purpose of philosophy. He abandoned his early intention to write an ethic, but in some sense substituted for it the posthumous *Les Passions de l'âme*. The kernel of Descartes's ethical thinking is clearest in his lengthy series of letters to Elisabeth of Bohemia. Both du Vair and Descartes emphasise that virtue is proportional to strength of purpose in pursuing the perceived good.

7 For a summary biography of Descartes and analysis of the development of his thought, see Anthony Levi, *Guide to French Literature: Beginnings to 1789*, Detroit and London 1994, pp.200–207.

8 Richelieu regarded nobility of birth as a qualification for government and, in the *Testament politique* (ed. André, Paris 1947, p. 153) goes as far as to say that the virtuous noble often has 'a special aspiration to

honour and gloire producing the same effects as the zeal caused by the pure love of God'.

9 Bérulle still divides historians of spirituality. The most perceptive analysis of the spirituality is still Bremond's in the third volume of the twelve-volume *Histoire littéraire du sentiment religieux en France*, vols. 3 (1921) and 7 (1928). But see also Paul Cochois, *Bérulle et l'école française*, Paris 1963, and Yves Krumenacker, *La Spiritualité de l'école française*, Paris 1998. For Bérulle's activities, which included the founding of forty-one houses of the Oratory and helping to oversee the foundation of forty-three Carmelite houses, see above all Jean Dagens, *Bérulle et les origines de la restauration catholique (1575–1611)*, Paris1952. Bérulle's religious inspiration was drawn overwhelmingly from neoplatonist sources, the Rheinland mystics and Denis the (pseudo-)Areopagite, still widely believed to be at once the first convert of saint Paul at Athens, the first martyr and patron saint of France, and the author of the *Celestial Hierarchy*.

10 Among the best-documented cases of corporate hysteria interpreted as diabolic possession is that of the community of Ursuline nuns at Loudun, quite near to Richelieu, which led to the burning of Urbain Grandier. The ill-named Père Tranquille was replaced as exorcist by Jean-Joseph Surin whose letters have been edited by Michel de Certeau (Paris 1966). See also M. de Certeau, *La Possession de Loudun*, Paris, 2nd ed. 1980.

11 Two formal approbations were required. Bérulle printed twenty-three.

12 Although Saint-Cyran and Jansen knew one another, had lived together, and continued to correspond, their concerns were different. Saint-Cyran developed his guilt-ridden spirituality and insistence on abstinence from the eucharist without protracted penitential preparation on the basis of the spiritual teaching of Bérulle and other early Oratorians. His spirituality was haunted by the sense of sin, the impossibility of salvation for ancient pagans and unbaptised babies, and the strictness of the spiritual discipline which even the elect had to impose on themselves. Jansen's theology was more academically concerned to attack as heretical the view that human beings had a natural power to accept or refuse grace. It is true that Jansen's theology, published posthumously in the 1640 *Augustinus*, did provide support for Saint-Cyran's spirituality, but the two phenomena developed almost in independence of one another. Saint-Cyran had however sent Jansen notes for a panegyric on saint Augustine in 1623 which Jansen used for the *prooemium* to the second volume of his *Augustinus*, a vast three-volume tome which seemed to Saint-Cyran too drily theological. The irreconcilability between Bérulle's political ideal, a supranational but political European Catholicism, and that of Richelieu became apparent after Bérulle's

contribution to the 1626 treaty of Monzón. Richelieu did not think Bérulle deserved the cardinalate of August 1627, which required a papal dispensation from Bérulle's vow not to accept a benefice, and Bérulle was in fact disgraced on 15 September 1629, a fortnight before his death. Had he lived he would have been exiled, no doubt to Rome.

13 On the history of Saint-Cyran's relations with Richelieu, Jansen, Zamet, Angélique Arnauld, and the convents, see the essays on Saint-Cyran, Jansenism, Port-Royal, and Pascal, much influenced by Saint-Cyran, in Anthony Levi, *Guide to French Literature, Beginnings to 1789*, Detroit and London 1994.

14 In 1635 Easter was on 8 April.

15 The 'écoles de Port Royal' were never separate establishments. 'Ecoles' in this context means 'classes'.

16 Given the level of humour of the French troupes, it is unlikely that the Italians, relying on mostly unscripted plots, improvisation, clowning and acrobatics, were banned simply on account of their frequent bawdiness. The Italians could certainly be indecent, but they specialised in parody, often parodying a French scripted drama within twenty-four hours of a first performance. Their satirical wit could be subversive of officialdom and they were regarded, as they regarded themselves, as superior to the 'talking apes' of the French troupes who did not even have to declaim verse, let alone improvise, sing, or develop circus acrobatics into a sophisticated stage art, ingeniously using intricate mechanical devices for the generation of spectacle. Their box-office prices had been double those of the French troupes, and on their return were reduced only because of the high level of subsidy, 15,000 livres a year from 1663. It was largely from their mechanical devices, music, dancing, singing and stage effects that French opera and ballet were eventually to develop when in 1672 Lulli acquired the *privilège* which accorded him the quasi-monopoly of all dramatic entertainment involving music in Paris. See Georges Couton, *Richelieu et le théâtre*, Lyon 1986, and 'Richelieu et le théâtre' in *Richelieu et la culture*, Paris 1987, pp. 79–101.

17 They were the Comédiens du roi under the actor Bellerose, Montdory's troupe, that under Estienne de Ruffin, and the Comédiens du Prince d'Orange managed by Charles Lenoir. Bellerose became director of the Comédiens du roi soon after1630. His troupe took over the Hôtel de Bourgogne. Montdory, who created the lead role in Corneille's *Le Cid* when his declamatory style was already obsolescent, directed the Marais troupe when Richelieu moved Lenoir, Jodelet and other members of Montdory's Marais company to the Hôtel de Bourgogne in 1634. The Marais troupe had had the comte de Belin, lover of Lenoir's wife, as patron, and Mairet, another Belin protégé, wrote roles for her.

Belin, like Montmorency and the Condé family, was generally hostile to Richelieu.

18 See Margaret McGowan, *L'Art du ballet de cour en France (1581–1643)*, 1963.

19 This was presumably the same Marais called by Tallemant in his *historiette* of Louis XIII the 'bouffon du roi'. On Desmarets, see H. Gaston Hall, *Richelieu's Desmarets and the Century of Louis XIV*, Oxford 1990. Dr Hall may have conflated two different persons called Desmarets.

20 Durand was put to death eleven days after Léonora Galigaï, his patron.

21 After Anne of Austria's two sons, then Gaston d'Orléans, then the duc de Condé. Marriage to Claire-Clémence was fiercely resisted by Enghien, and turned out to be very unhappy. There was a ball after *Mirame*, and some weeks later, after signature of the contract, the most magnificent ballet anyone had seen, the *Ballet de la Prospérité des armes de la France*, devised by Desmarets with thirty-six *entrées* divided into five acts.

22 The estimate, by Henri Arnauld on 18 November 1640 may well be an exaggeration, although the low value put on the furnishings of the theatre in the inventory made after Richelieu's death cannot be used as an argument. The inventory omits fixtures, presumably part of the bequest to the king, and diminishes all values in the interests of the duchesse d'Aiguillon, the residuary legatee. The roof of the larger theatre, to cost 300,000 livres and later to collapse under the weight of what was built on top of it, was made of oak beams two feet in diameter and nineteen and a half metres long, giving an interior width of some eighteen metres.

23 The convincing evidence for the cardinal's authorship, both direct and circumstantial, is assessed by Georges Couton, *Richelieu et le théâtre, Lyons 1986*, pp.40–55.

24 The five authors were the dramatists Jean Rotrou (1609–1650) and Pierre Corneille (1606–1684), the librettists Claude de l'Estoille (1597–1652), François le Métel de Boisrobert (1589–1662), and the poet Guillaume Colletet (1598–1659), although their names were not revealed before Pelisson's 1653 *Relation* on the foundation of Richelieu's *Academy*. No one knows why Corneille left the group, still known as 'the five', or whether he was forced to resign.

25 The ambiguous sexuality of Mme du Vigean was a matter of common gossip about which Tallemant was, as usual, well informed. See Tallemant's *historiette* of Mme d'Aiguillon, and Adam's notes, in vol. 1 of the *Historiettes*, Paris 1967. Tallemant in this case derived his information from the *chambre bleue* of Mme de Rambouillet.

26 The first edition of the text (1628) was dedicated to Montmorency, and we know of a total of fourteen editions between 1628 and 1635, with eight more later in the century.

27 Richelieu had just succeeded in getting Gaston to leave Brussels (8 October) and make peace with the French court. Aiguillon was immediately
erected into a *duché-pairie* under the name of Puylaurens, who married
Marguerite de Pontchâteau, Richelieu's cousin, the youngest child of
his father's youngest sister. On the same day Marguerite's elder sister,
Marie, married Epernon's son, the duc de la Valette, brother of the
cardinal archbishop of Toulouse, who was at once military commander,
friend of Richelieu, lover of Condé's wife, and assiduous frequenter
of the Hôtel de Rambouillet. Also on the same day Antoine II de
Grammont, still comte de Guiche, married Françoise-Marguerite de
Chivré, daughter of Hector du Plessis, another of Richelieu's cousins.
Puylaurens, who regarded himself as rehabilitated, was arrested only
two months later, on 14 February 1635, and committed to the
Vincennes dungeon, where he died on 30 June 1635. Tallemant
tells us that he died 'à cause de l'humidité d'une chambre voustée
et qui a si peu d'air que le salpestre s'y forme' (*Historiettes*, ed. Adam,
vol.1, p.245).

28 The other two plays were the *Grande Pastorale* of January 1637 and the
Aveugle de Smyrne of 22 February of the same year. We know from
Chapelain's correspondence with Boisrobert that Richelieu's authors
would read to him work he had commissioned, and received the texts
back with Richelieu's annotations, most often dictated, but occasionally
in his own hand. Repeated drafts were submitted in this way before
a text was found acceptable. Georges Couton (*Richelieu et le théâtre*,
Lyons 1986, pp. 21–25), draws attention to the possible plurality of
authors of a theatrical entertainment, of which the principal was the
proposer of the play's dramatic construction, author of the 'invention'
or 'disposition', not the proposer of the subject or the versifier(s).
Molière, under royal pressure to complete *Psyché*, enlisted the help of
Corneille for the versification of all but the prologue, the first act and
two other scenes. Corneille used no less than fifteen other versifiers to
help get the piece ready on time. Racine, too, considered his principal
task completed when he had produced his prose sketch of the drama's
development.

29 D'Aubignac's sharp attack on the tragicomedy *Roxane* of Desmarets, certainly admired, and perhaps partially conceived by Richelieu, together
with his quarrel in 1639 with the independent-minded Ménage, scholar,
lawyer, much-beneficed ecclesiastic and important literary figure, were
to ensure his exclusion from the Academy. His *Pratique du théâtre* was not
to be published until 1657, well after Richedelieu's death, but reflects
the public attitudes and dramatic norms of 1640. It is strongly critical
of Pierre Corneille.

30 The marquise and Cospeau were walking in the fields one day in 1627
when they came across a tableau of young nymphs, led by the daughter

of the marquise, Julie d'Angennes, dressed as Diana, with bow and arrow. The marquise insisted to Cospeau that he must be suffering from a hallucination.

31 We know of Richelieu's ambitions for the Academy shortly before his death from his doctor, La Mesnardière who, in his own 1655 *Discours de réception*, published in 1656, gave an account of the 'longues et glorieuses' audiences he had with the cardinal shortly before his death. This account was known to Tallemant des Réaux, who draws on it for his 'historiette' of Richelieu, written between 1657 and 1659 (Tallemant de Réaux, *Historiettes*, ed. Antoine Adam, vol. 1, Paris 1967, p. 274). The most important account of the foundation of the academy is in Pellisson and d'Olivet, *Relation contenant l'histoire de l'Académie française*, ed. C. Livet, Paris 1858. Pellisson's account was originally published in 1653, when many of the original members were still alive. See also Marc Fumaroli, 'Les Intentions du Cardinal de Richelieu, fondateur de l'Académie française' in *Richelieu et la culture*, Paris 1987, pp. 69–78.

32 On the constitution of this group, the nucleus of the future Academy, see Antoine Adam, *Histoire de la littérature française du XVIIe siècle*, 5 vols., Paris 1962, vol. 1, pp. 220–32. Pellisson dates the gatherings to 'four or five' years earlier than 1635.

33 Séguier succeeded Châteauneuf as keeper of the seals and became chancellor in 1635. On Faret, see Maurice Magendie, *La Politesse mondaine et les théories de l'honnêteté en France au XVIIe siècle*, 2 vols., Paris 1925.

34 Georges Couton ('Richelieu et le théâtre' in *Richelieu et la culture*, Paris 1987, pp. 79–101) refers to d'Aubignac's *Projet de rétablissement du théâtre français*, written in 1640, as 'un acte de candidature à la fonction d'Intendant des théâtres'.

35 The lines (1832–33) run

'Sire, quelle apparence à ce triste Hymenée
Qu'un mesme jour commence et finisse mon deuil'.

36 On Scudéry's theoretical writings, see Evelyn Dutertre, *Scudéry dramaturge*, Paris 1988, and *Scudéry théoricien du classicisme*, Paris 1991.

37 For cultural activities outside teaching, Colbert was to move much further in the direction projected by Richelieu. He was to endow practising artisans with professional status and security, but only by forming them into 'academies' subject to central control. Colbert was also to erect the monarch into the earthly embodiment of a quasi-divine power, and for the decade of his real ascendancy to remove Louis XIV from all important monarchical activities other than the formality of the day-to-day exercise of administrative sovereignty, like appending signatures and chairing committees.

9 The Thirty Years War

1 Tallemant tells us that the *Milliade* contained fire but nothing else, that a number of persons were sent to the Bastille, but that the author was never discovered. Tallemant conjectures that it originated in the household of the Gondi/Retz family, hostile to Richelieu, as later to Mazarin. The accusations in the *Milliade* are fierce, but turn chiefly on the literary preoccupations of Richelieu when he should more actively have been fighting the Spaniards, who had taken Corbie in the autumn of 1636:

> Lorsqu'il doit penser aux combats
> Il prend ses comiques ébats . . .
> Il décrit de fausses douleurs
> Quand l'Etat sent de vrais malheurs . . .
> Et consulte encore Boisrobert
> Quand une province se perd.

2 Sweden wanted the restoration of Frederick V in the Palatinate while Richelieu wanted the electorate to go to Maximilian of Bavaria, and Sweden needed to protect its trade in timber and minerals with Spain. Richelieu knew that Gustavus needed French money, and a treaty which left major disputed issues unresolved was eventually signed at Bärwalde on 23 January 1631. Political historians have held that Richelieu did more harm to France by disturbing the equilibrium of power in German-speaking Europe than he achieved good with the Mantuan campaign.

3 The Spanish economy was in an even worse state than the French. Between 1600 and 1630 the tonnage of Spanish shipping to the New World had slipped by 75 per cent, the number of sheep by 60 per cent, and the number of textile manufacturers by 75 per cent. Spanish support for the rebellions of Gaston d'Orléans was a substitute for the direct confrontation with France which Olivares would have liked to have been able to afford. See H. Lonchay, *La Rivalité de la France et de l'Espagne aux Pays-Bas 1635–1700. Etude d'histoire diplomatique et militaire*, Brussels 1896.

4 See A. Leman, *Urbain VIII et la rivalité de la France et de la maison d'Autriche de 1631 à 1635*, Lille 1920.

5 See H. Lonchay, *La Rivalité de la France et de l'Espagne* and D.P. O'Connell, *Richelieu*, pp. 280ff.

6 It is possible to exaggerate the extent and efficiency of Richelieu's network of informants. Here, as at La Rochelle and on other important occasions to be mentioned, Richelieu, whose thirst for sensitive information was widely known, was considerably helped in receiving vital information by luck.

7 On the ordinance, and the meaning of 'abduction', see Roland E. Mousnier, *The Institutions of France under the Absolute Monarchy, 1598–1789*, tr. Brian Pearce, Chicago 1979.

8 As with well-known cases in the sixteenth century, like that involving the dispensation on which the validity of the first marriage of Henry VIII depended, it is simply senseless to question whether the marriage of Gaston and Marguerite was or was not valid. It depended which side you were on, and therefore which legal principles you considered to outweigh the others.

9 Grotius (1583–1645) was Dutch ambassador to London before his arrest in 1618 with his patron Jan Barneveldt (1547–1619), who was executed. After twenty months he escaped to France, and wrote his great work of legal philosophy *De iure belli ac pacis* (1625), dedicated to Louis XIII, and chiefly notable for being the first full natural law theory not to invoke a divine law-giver. It became the foundation of international law. In 1631 Grotius returned to the Low Countries, but was forced to leave again for siding with the Arminians against the stricter Calvinists. In 1634 he entered the Swedish diplomatic service. The practice of paying pensions to distinguished foreign men of letters, alongside French writers willing to sing the royal praises, had already been inaugurated, and was further to be systematised after Richelieu's death.

10 It is difficult to know how daring the king was being. Homosexual acts were in theory (and sometimes in practice), punishable by death, even if the accused was the victim of rape. They were also considered mortally sinful wherever consent was involved.

11 On Louis XIII's profligate use of the *lit de justice* twenty times, see Sarah Hanley, *The Lit de Justice of the Kings of France: Constitutional Ideology in Legend, Ritual, and Discourse*, Princeton 1983.

12 Four horses pulled apart a doll substituted for the absent du Bec, governor of La Capelle, condemned for high treason, in the Place de Grève in Paris.

13 Richelieu argued i) that the diet had been convoked to discuss peace and not to elect a king of the Romans, for which notice was required, ii) that elections had to be held at Frankfurt, iii) that the Elector of Bavaria had usurped the Palatinate vote, and iv) that the Elector of Trier was a Spanish prisoner, all of which invalidated the election under the Golden Bull which regulated it.

14 See D.P. O'Connell, *Richelieu*, London 1968, p. 365. The figure for the duration of the pregnancy should be treated with caution.

15 See Tallemant's *historiette* of Montmorency (ed. Adam, vol. 1, Paris 1967, pp. 1032–33). The offending lines had been written for Montmorency by Théophile de Viau:

> Plust au Ciel qu'un jour seulement
> Jupiter m'eust donné sa face,
> Et qu'il voulust pour un moment
> Me laisser régner en sa place.

At a ballet danced before the king, there could be only one Jupiter.

16 The other was to be the execution of Marillac in 1633. Whatever arguments Richelieu put to the King (see p.76 above), he needed the executions of Montmorency and Marillac in order to impose his polices.

17 For instance:

> Je me sens criminelle, aimant un étranger
> Qui met pour mon amour cet Etat en danger

See the notes of Antoine Adam to the *historiette* of Richelieu (vol. 1, Paris 1960, pp. 906–907).

18 Once again it is worth noting how meticulously the legal niceties were observed, however high-handed the judgement might have been. The chancellor had civil jurisdiction allowing him to search the property and the archbishop ecclesiastical jurisdiction to remove the abbess.

19 Tallemant is quite clear about the physical indecencies involved in this relationship, quoting the saying that, since buggery, held to be 'the Italian vice' had crossed the Alps, there was no reason why the decrees of Trent should not do so, too. Of Louis XIII, Tallemant wrote 'Il aima Barradas violemment; on l'accusoit de faire cent ordures avec luy; il estoit bien fait. Les Italians disoient: "La bugerra ha passato i monti, passera ancora il concilio"'.

20 Marie de Hautefort by virtue of her duties at court is correctly referred to as 'Madame' (and not 'Mademoiselle') even before her marriage in 1646.

21 On the important dispute between Jean-Pierre Camus, bishop of Belley, and the Jesuits on the subject of 'disinterested' love of God, see G. Joppin, *Une querelle autour de l'amour pur. Jean-Pierre Camus, Évêque de Belley*, Paris 1938. The matter was also at the heart of Fénelon's dispute with Bossuet. 'Eliciting an act', as of contrition, is normal devotional language, drawing on an ancient vocabulary in which human 'faculties' (intellect, will) were specified by their 'acts', and acts by their objects. In practice devotional 'acts' normally took the form of prayerful expressions of sorrow, love, adoration, intercession, and so on.

22 Séguenot was disavowed by the Oratory, his book condemned by the faculty, and he was not released from the Bastille until after Richelieu's death.

23 On Caussin, see Camille de Rochemonteix, *Nicolas Caussin, Confesseur de Louis XIII, et le Cardinal de Richelieu, documents inédits*, Paris 1911. Caussin is the author of a much-translated baroque work of piety, covering all aspects of the Christian life, the 1624–25 *La Cour sainte*.

24 The *approbation* of the *Traitté*, is dated 26 May 1646, and it will have been published shortly afterwards. The work forms a logical conclusion to the *Instruction du chrestien*, finished at Avignon in 1618.

25 Paris 1756, published as vols. 13–15 of the *Histoire de France, depuis l'établissement de la monarchie française dans les Gaules*, by Gabriel Daniel S.J., 17 vols., Paris 1755–57.

26 Saint-Maur-des-Fossés, near Charenton, which was about nine kilometres from Paris, and where there was a sixteenth-century château.

27 G.R.R. Treasure (*Richelieu*, London 1972) regards the story of the storm as based on 'gossip'. A. Lloyd Moote, *Louis XIII, the Just*, Berkeley and Los Angeles 1989, accepts the congruence of the king's last visit to Louise de La Fayette, 5 December, and the storm, but draws attention to the king's expectation that Anne would give birth in August. D.P. O'Connell, *Richelieu*, London 1968, writes simply 'The storm continued and he [the king] was forced to share her [the queen's] bed. The result was the birth of Louis XIV, ten months and two days later, on 5 September 1638'. Victor-L. Tapié (*France in the Age of Louis XIII and Richelieu*, London 1974) grants that 'we cannot be sure that the evening of 5 December 1637 did bring about an exceptional reconciliation between king and queen' after commenting on Griffet's narrative, 'his story has so much charm that it would be sad indeed if it were not true. But is it true? – for there can be no impeachable authority for an episode like this.'

28 Mazarin was impressed by Richelieu, praising to Barberini 'sa parfaite bonne grâce, jointe à tant de prudence et à un génie si élevé'. See on Mazarin, Auguste Bailly, *Mazarin*, Paris 1935 and Georges Dethan, *Mazarin et ses amis*, Paris 1968.

29 The solemn vow of chastity is taken with the sub-diaconate. The three degrees of the sacrament of order are diaconate, priesthood and episcopacy, all conferring different sacramental powers, and the last two minor forms of jurisdiction. The cardinalate is not sacramental, confers no power, and implies neither a vow of chastity nor any jurisdiction.

30 Mme de Motteville uses similar understatement when she writes of Anne's surprise at finding herself alone 'et apparemment importunée par quelque sentiment trop passionné du duc de Buckingham'.

31 The original has been lost.

10 Domestic Affairs: Public and Private

1 William of Ockham (c1285–1349) was a Franciscan theologian who emphasised the transcendance of God against the 'naturalism' of Aquinas (1225–74) for whom man shared in divine rationality and for whom, therefore, divine law had to correspond with human moral aspirations.

For Ockham this implied the concept of a God who did not fully transcend his creation.

2 See on these matters Pierre Blet, *Le Clergé de France et la monarchie. Etude sur les assemblées générales du clergé de 1615 à 1666*, Rome 1959, and Roland Mousnier, *Fureurs paysannes. Les paysans dans les révoltes du XVIIe siècle*, Paris 1967.

3 The gold coins held by Euzenat, Richelieu's treasurer, in 1639 had a nominal value of 8,875 livres, but were by weight worth only 6,558 livres, having been debased, filed or clipped away to the extent of over 26 per cent.

4 The Forty Hours devotion was fairly common. Urban VIII ordered the Forty Hours exposition of the Blessed Sacrament in Santa Maria de la Victoria when Munich fell to Gustavus Adolphus in 1632. He also said a mass of thanksgiving on the death of Gustavus Adolphus.

5 The best account of these uprisings and their causes is in Mousnier, *Fureurs paysannes*, mentioned in note 2.

6 Among the points of contention were the tariffs charged for transporting wine on the Charente, more than double those applied to the transport of wines worth five times as much on the Garonne.

7 The term *créature* as conventionally used in the context of Richelieu's appointees is not derogatory, and implies only dependance, not sycophancy.

8 From 1630 the *conseil d'en haut*, or *conseil des affaires*, delegated judicial, administrative and ecclesiastical affairs not important enough to engage its detailed attention to a *conseil des dépêches*, leaving to the *conseil des finances* its own specialised business. Underneath these councils was a series of ten *commissions*. Richelieu entrusted with power those on whom he knew he could rely. These were chiefly Léon Bouthillier, comte de Chavigny and son of Claude Bouthillier, for foreign affairs; his father, a joint *surintendant des finances* with Bullion from 1632; Sublet de Noyers who succeeded Servien as secretary for war in 1636; Bullion himself, and Séguier. Chavigny was also Gaston's chancellor, and served as go-between in negotiation with the king's brother. His father, Claude Bouthillier, was also Richelieu's representative at court and on his personal business, as in the negotiations for the marriage of his niece, Claire-Clémence de Maillé, to the future grand Condé.

9 On the erosion of the power of the sovereign courts, see Richard Bonney, *Political Change in France under Richelieu and Mazarin*, Oxford 1978, ch. xi, p. 238–258.

10 See Richard Bonney, *The King's Debts, Finance and Politics in France, 1589–1661*, Oxford 1981, pp. 132–34 and D. P. O'Connell, *Richelieu*, London 1968, pp. 372–73. Richelieu had in 1626–27 advocated the repurchase of alienated crown lands. They had been sold with the reservation that the crown could repurchase them at the sale price,

however much their value had increased in the meantime. They were therefore a potential source of crown income, although inadequate for the circumstances of 1637.

11 *Testament politique*, ed. André, Paris 1947, part 1, section 4, ch. 5, pp. 253–55.

12 On the evolving attitude to *gloire* in the late sixteenth and early seventeenth centuries, see A.H.T. Levi, *French Moralists: the theory of the passions: 1585–1649*, Oxford 1964, pp. 177–201. The ethical values centred on *gloire* have been analysed by F.E. Sutcliffe in *Guez de Balzac et son temps. Littérature et politique*, Paris 1959. Guez de Balzac, like Nicolas Faret, had regarded the desire for *gloire* as a 'belle passion . . . [qui] s'accorde avec la plus haute Sainteté; avec celle qui est la plus proche de la divine' (Balzac, *De la gloire*, written about 1640). The relationship between the interior virtue and the external recognition of merit was not yet firmly established. *Gloire* remained essentially what was implied in the line from Corneille's *Attila*, 'La gloire de répondre à ce que je me doi' (act II, sc. 6). The most memorable line from Corneille's *Le Cid* must be Chimène's 'Il y va de ma gloire. Il faut que je me venge'.

13 At the end of his meticulous research into Richelieu's wealth, *Cardinal Richelieu, power and the pursuit of wealth*, (Oxford 1985), Joseph Bergin suggests that Richelieu's estate on death was worth about 20,000,000 livres without the Palais-Cardinal. Of this sum over 1,000,000 livres was owed by the crown, and the sum included payments to close relatives which were effectively wholly or partly irrecoverable loans or advances on inheritances paid as dowries to secure status-enhancing marriages, but which in French customary law still in 1642 belonged to the estate. The most realistic view of Richelieu's wealth has to be founded on the possession of his two *duché-pairies*, his lands, residences and collections. The *inventaire après décès* reflects the duchesse d'Aiguillon's interest in exaggeratedly diminishing the valuation of the furniture and collections which had not been left to the king.

14 Avenel, *Lettres, instructions diplomatiques et papiers d'état du cardinal de Richelieu*, vol. vi, pp. 173–74 and vol. viii, p. 165.

15 Security was a serious problem in the seventeenth century. Even when Louis XIV had taken the court to Versailles, it was possible for the unentitled to wander in and out, unchallenged and unidentified. The deaths of Henri III, Henri IV and Concini together with the series of planned attempts on the life of Richelieu show how difficult was protection against assassination. The terrible punishment of Ravaillac is an example of the way in which deterrence was substituted for unattainable security.

16 Bergin, *Cardinal Richelieu, power and the pursuit of wealth*, pp. 254–55.

17 See Montglat, *Mémoires*, Amsterdam 1727, vol. 1, p. 372. Richelieu had

d'Effiat replaced by Claude Bullion and Claude le Bouthillier as joint *surintendants de finance* on 4 August 1632.

18 The document has been analysed by Maximin Deloche, *La Maison du Cardinal de Richelieu*, Paris 1912. Deloche reminds his readers that Richelieu was quite capable of conducting through his personal representatives diplomatic negotiations of which ambassadors were unaware. He also relates the well-known anecdote concerning Bautru's request to the bookseller Bertier to publish his memoirs of his embassy to Olivares. Bertier counselled against publication, revealing that, while Bautru represented the king in Madrid, he, Bertier, was negotiating on behalf of Richelieu something quite contrary to what Bautru was instructed to achieve.

19 Morgues, who had been in the service of Marie de' Medici since 1620, had in about 1627 replied in the *Advis d'un Théologien sans passion* on Richelieu's behalf to the score of pamphlets directed against him in 1625 and 1626. Richelieu personally revised the text. Morgues was still writing on Richelieu's behalf in 1630, before Richelieu's rupture with the queen mother.

20 In part 1, ch. 7 of the *Testament politique* Richelieu reiterates his intention to offer posthumous advice to the king and goes as far as to expostulate, 'Comme . . . il n'y a jamais eu Roi, qui ait porté plus haut la dignité de son État que V[otre] M[ajesté], aussi . . . il n'y en a jamais eu qui ait laissé ravaler si bas le lustre de sa maison'. Richelieu goes on to say that the king's principal household officers would not have dared to aspire even to subordinate positions under his predecessors. The king's table, at which the crown officers and the great should have eaten, was now shared by valets and simple gendarmes. Even some of those were fastidious enough to disdain what should have been a sought-after privilege. Richelieu adds an exhortation to cleanliness and, with much else, remarks on the importance of 'l'opulence des meubles' because 'les étrangers ne conçoivent pas la grandeur des princes que par ce qui en paraît à l'extérieur'.

21 Deloche narrates a series of anecdotes illustrating the relationship between the heads of great households and their servants. In *La Maison réglée* (Paris 1700) Audiger lists the size of households appropriate to the status of the head, and provides a guide to the functions of each member. By his standards half a century later, Richelieu's household expenditure was reasonable and in some ways even modest.

22 See Deloche, *La Maison du Cardinal de Richelieu*, pp. 61–62.

23 We have several accounts of life in the Bastille, and a semi-official eight-volume *Histoire de la Bastille*, ed. A. Arnould and Alboize du Pujol (Paris 1844) whose tenor is exaggeratedly hostile to Richelieu. It regales us with a description of him relaxing, 'homme aimable et galant', trying to forget that he was an ecclesiastic and a minister. Richelieu is depicted

as jealous of Chalais for the affections of Mme de Chevreuse. The work is more reliable on the mildness of the prison regime.

24 Avenel prints a minute written by Charpentier of a letter of 29 March 1636 from Richelieu to Lescot on the delicate subject of duels, already referred to. Richelieu asks if there are any circumstances in which kings may permit duels and, if there are not, how such permissions given in the past and authorised by the church can be justified. Richelieu speculates that the occasional permission might reduce the great number of illicit duels. In three places the minute has fairly insignificant additions in Richelieu's own hand.

25 Late in 1638 and again in 1640 Richelieu offered Bullion the use of his silver to raise loans for the treasury. He had already lent his valuables, mostly rings, for this purpose in 1627. One of his Huguenot opponents joked that he pawned so many he scarcely had any left with which to give episcopal blessings.

26 Surgeons had not yet risen in the medical ranks from barber-surgeons. Richelieu paid his doctor 900 livres, but the apothecary and surgeon only 150 livres each. They ranked just below the nobles, mostly military personnel or pages, but above the highest household domestic officers. Only the chief Paris gardener, Boutticourt, paid 400 livres, came between the doctor and the other two medical officers. The architect of the garden at Rueil rather than just the chief gardener, Maignan, was paid no less than 1,000 livres in salary.

27 The source for this account of Richelieu's sleeping arrangements is Aubery, *Histoire du Cardinal de Richelieu*, but it is confirmed by the cardinal himself in a pamphlet of 1627 known as the *Lettre déchiffrée* and published in the 1639 *Recueil de diverses pièces pour servir à l'histoire*, p.30.

28 *Mémoires*, Geneva 1756, p.43.

29 They prevented him from from sleeping and from urinating for six days at Bordeaux in November 1632, and there were recurrences in May 1634 and during the same month in 1635.

30 See Du Haillan, *Discours sur les causes de l'extresme cherté qui est aujourd'huy en France*, 1586, and the other sources mentioned by Deloche, *La Maison du Cardinal Richelieu*, p. 436.

31 Richelieu had acquired the old Hôtel de Rambouillet only in 1624, adding the Maison de l'Hermine in 1627, the Hôtel des Trois-Pucelles and the Maison du Chapeau-Rouge in 1639.

11 The Final Danger

1 See D.P. O'Connell, Richelieu, London 1968, pp. 392–96, and Victor-L. Tapié, *France in the Age of Louis XIII and Richelieu*, London 1974, ch.10.

2 There were armies in Flanders under Châtillon, in Picardy and Champagne under La Force, in Alsace under Bernard of Saxe-Weimar, in Franche-Comté under Longueville, in Guyenne under Condé, and in Italy under Créqui.

3 The cardinal, Louis de Nogaret, also a general, lived from 1593 until 1639, when he died of pneumonia, having become archbishop of Toulouse and cardinal in 1621. Notoriously ugly, he was popular in the *chambre bleue*, and it was he who persuaded Richelieu to confront the king on the *journée des dupes*. Tallemant quotes a scurrilous verse in which he is accurately alluded to as lover of Charlotte de Montmorency, and Richelieu inaccurately as lover of his niece, Mme de Combalet.

4 Henry d'Escoubleau de Sourdis was born in 1594. His elder brother Charles was a marshal, and had serious intellectual interests. His own godparents were Henri IV and Gabrielle d'Estrées. In 1623 Henry became bishop of Maillezais, then in 1629 he succeeded his brother, the cardinal François, as archbishop of Bordeaux. It was Henry who was struck in 1633 by Epernon. In 1636 Richelieu sent Vitry to the Bastille for a much more serious fight with Henry. On the Vitry episode, Chavigny indecorously wrote to cardinal de la Valette on 6 December 1636 'M. l'archevêque de Bordeaux . . . a reçu quelque vingt coups de canne ou de bâton, comme il vous plaira. Je crois qu'il a dessein de se faire battre de tout le monde, afin de remplir France d'excommuniés.' Excommunication was ordinarily incured by striking a prelate. Tallemant says of Sourdis in the *historiette* devoted to him that he could boast of being the world's most beaten prelate (*Historiettes*, vol.1, p. 377).

5 It is difficult to take this anecdote at its face value. Tapié relates it seriously, but without a reference (*France in the Age of Louis XIII and Richelieu*, London 1974, p.383).

6 Père Joseph suddenly became violently ill in December. On the 13th he made a general confession, his mind still full of the crusade for which he had never ceased to hope. He was brought to Rueil where he appeared in no imminent danger, and Richelieu was attending a play in his theatre there when news was brought to him of Père Joseph's final stroke. After a coma lasting three days, he died on 18 December. On the day of his funeral oration, two days after the requiem mass, Richelieu heard the news from Breisach.

7 On the route, the suite of guards, secretaries and household officers, the mode of transport, and the immense range of written instructions, given by Richelieu on this journey, see Maximin Deloche, *La Maison de Richelieu*, Paris 1912, pp. 452–59.

8 On this statute of the French state, see Roland E. Mousnier, *The Institutions of France under the Absolute Monarchy 1598–1789*, tr. Brian Pearce, Chicago 1979, pp. 649–53.

9   On Franco-papal relations at ths date see Pierre Blet, *Le Clergé de France et la monarchie 1615–1666*, 2 vols., Rome and Paris 1959, the same author's introduction to the *Correspondance du nonce en France Ranuccio Scotti 1639–14*, Rome 1965, and Joseph Bergin, *Cardinal de la Rochefoucauld, Leadership and Reform in the French Church*, New Haven and London 1987.

10 From this point on Henri d'Effiat is referred to simply as Cinq-Mars or 'the marquis' unless there is any risk of confusing him with the abbé who was Richelieu's *maître de chambre* until he was made bishop of Auxerre. Cinq-Mars was also officially known as 'Monsieur le Grand'.

11 See Tapié, *France in the Age of Louis XIII and Richelieu*, London 1974, p. 391–92.

12 Bellegarde had been a favourite of Henri III and lover of Gabrielle d'Estrées. He had refused to sell his appointment to Brézé, and bargained hard before yielding to the king's insistence when Cinq-Mars wanted it.

13 On the testamentary dispositions and the intricate double entail on the two *duchés-pairies*, see Joseph Bergin, *Cardinal Richelieu. Power and the pursuit of wealth*, New Haven and London 1985, pp. 256–63. Condé was in vain to challenge the will on the grounds that the entails by-passed French customary law, which still kept inheritances intact by neglecting the claims of younger children.

14 Retz's aunt, Mme du Fargis, after being a devout Carmelite, had married Charles d'Angennes, comte du Fargis, a member of Gaston's retinue, and led a scandalous life after appointment in 1624 as lady-in-waiting to Marie de' Medici.

15 Retz's *Mémoires*, as they are now called, although he never published them, nor referred to them as memoirs, were an attempt made by Retz in old age to justify his youthful behaviour to Mme de Sévigné. Unfortunately, much of the first part is missing. On the identity of the person to whom the document was addressed, see the relevant entry in A.H.T. Levi, *Guide to French Literaure. Beginnings to 1789*, Detroit and London 1994.

16 Bouillon was the brother of Turenne and prince of Sedan, which lay on the French frontier, and is today just inside France, near the Belgian border with Luxembourg.

17 This is what the official record shows, but for this penalty to have been inflicted it is virtually certain that Richelieu, or possibly the king, also had other grounds for severity.

18 There is an analogy in the sixteenth century. The highly optimistic values of the Renaissance in France, building on the view that human nature was not only perfectible, but was itself a guide to virtue and happiness, was still clear in late Rabelais and in lesser-known figures who came later. Their optimism turned with astonishing

abruptness in the moral writing of 1562–63, at the outbreak of the religious wars.

19 The captain's name was Armand-Jean de Peyre, comte de Troisvilles, but spelling and pronunciation had corrupted into Tréville. Richelieu was certainly convinced that the king had, or might, order his assassination, and suspected that the execution would be undertaken by Tréville and three other captains, Tilladet, des Essarts and La Sale. See Antoine Adam's notes to his edition of Tallemant's *Historiettes*, Paris 1967, vol.1, p.957.

20 On 21 May Henri Arnauld wrote of the 'intelligence qui paroist entière' between Schomberg and Cinq-Mars, adding that the brightest members of the court were waiting to see what the result would be.

21 It may have been on account of the sympathy for the victims among the French people that Richelieu arranged to absent himself. The executions took place on 12 September. Richelieu wrote to Chavigny and de Noyers on the 15th: 'M le Grand est mort avec constance et quelque affectation de mespriser la mort; il a porté son humeur hautaine jusques à l'eschafaut, ayant désiré d'en avoir un séparé de celuy auquel seroit exécuté M de Thou et qui eust plus de dignité, ce qui n'a pas esté, comme vous pouvés croire. Jusques à la pronociation de son arrest il avoit apparemment peu pensé à Dieu. Son confesseur tesmoigne estre fort content de sa repentance et de l'estat auquel il est mort. Il a parlé sur la selete, de son propre mouvement, fort avantageusement de moy.' The last statement was not quite true, as what Cinq-Mars said about Richelieu was no more than courteous. See Avenel, *Lettres*, vol. 7, p. 125.

22 Richelieu wrote to Chavigny and de Noyers that Bouillon was so frightened by the executions of Cinq-Mars and de Thou that, if he had had three Sedans, he would have given them all up to save his life.

23 The memorandum, dictated by Richelieu to be presented to the king by Chavigny and already referred to, put into Chavigny's mouth the statement to the king, 'If God had called the cardinal to himself, Your Majesty would have realised what he had lost; it would have been much worse if you lost him yourself since, by losing him in this way, Your Majesty would lose all the confidence placed in him.'

12 Postlude

1 Champaigne's triple portrait of Richelieu is inspired by van Dyck's similar triple portrait of Charles I dating from 1635, from which Bernini made a marble bust of which only plaster casts now exist. The three heads of Charles I show him, unlike Richelieu, wearing different clothing, and the idea of supplying Bernini with a head from

three angles must have been inspired by Lorenzo Lotto's *Portrait of a Goldsmith in Three Positions*, in 1635 in Charles's collection and now in the Vienna Kunsthistorisches Museum. See on both the van Dyck and the Champaigne the entry by Judy Egerton in the catalogue of the exhibition *Van Dyck 1599–1641*, London and Antwerp 1999, pp. 292–94.

2 Montaigne, in his chapter 'Des cannibales', argues that his contemporaries were no better than cannibals. In the eighteenth century, Voltaire, in spite of his derision at what was only a caricature of Leibnizian optimism and his desire to imitate Racine, interestingly never investigated even in his stage tragedies the real potential for emotional, as distinct from political human tragedy. Even in Racine, during a period in which reaction struggled to dominate French culture, it is difficult to argue that love is portrayed as intrinsically tragic, any more than it is in Shakespeare. In so far as the eighteenth century in France was concerned with tragedy at all, it was primarily interested in a *drame bourgeois*, which extended it to persons not of elevated birth or position.

3 The natural desire to love God is explicit and fundamental in the major work of François de Sales, the 1616 *Traité de l'amour de Dieu*, but it is already implicit in the 1609 *Introduction à la vie dévote*. It means that human beings can contribute to their own salvation by virtue of their own nature, a view regarded as heterodox because it meant allowing justifying grace to the 'pagans'.

4 Descartes never wrote the ethics which was the purpose of his whole endeavour but, as mentioned earlier, its most important elements appear in his letters to Elisabeth of Bohemia, daughter of Frederick V, the exiled elector Palatine.

5 Already by the late sixteenth century political realities took precedence over religious ideologies. The dictum 'cujus regio, ejus religio' enjoining conformity to the sovereign's religious creed had already taken hold. Its strength was to be felt until Rousseau and beyond.

6 The dilemma, as it applied to the Jansenism of seventeenth-century France, is analysed in detail in the entries on Saint-Cyran, Pascal, Jansenism and Port-Royal in Anthony Levi, *Guide to French Literature, Beginnings to 1789*, Detroit and London 1994.

7 Calvin was reluctantly forced into theological acceptance of the doctrine of predestination on the dogmatic level, but Calvinist piety was never devotionally centred round it, and even as a dogma it was notoriously soon controverted and abandoned by Calvin's 'Arminian' followers in seventeenth-century France.

8 Even in the eighteenth century Voltaire thought that society would break down without the retributive justice of the Christian God after death, however much Voltaire disliked the rites which he thought led to superstition and the credal affirmations which he thought led to

intolerance. Not until very late in the seventeenth century, and even then not in France, could Pierre Bayle openly discuss the possibility that there could be such a thing as an atheistic society.

Index